What others are saying about this book:

"Poynter is at his best when discussing such specifics as starting one's own publishing house; dealing with printers; establishing discount, credit and return policies; promoting, advertising and selling a book; and order fulfillment."

—Publishers Weekly

"A deeply researched how-to book on writing, printing, publishing, promotion, marketing and distribution of books."

—The College Store Journal

"Poynter covers the production basics but his emphasis is on the business of books."

— Booklist

"The strength of this book is the detailed discussion of various marketing methods."

— Choice

"The book is a must for those considering publishing as a business, for writers who want to investigate self-publishing, and is eminently useful for its new and old ideas to those who have already begun to do it. A fine and handy guide by a fine and successful publisher."

— Small Press Review

"A handy, concise and informative sourcebook.... Expertly organized and chock full of hard facts, helpful hints and pertinent illustrations.... Recommended for all libraries."

—The Southeastern Librarian

"All the information is here, and various aspects of small publishing are discussed in a complete and comprehensive manner. A publisher who follows Poynter's advice can hardly go wrong."

—The Independent Publisher

"This is by far the best book of its kind."

—Writing & Publishing

"This is the best self-publishing manual on the market."

—Judith Appelbaum, *How to Get Happily Published*

The Self-Publishing Manual
The guide that has launched thousands of books

The
SELF-PUBLISHING
MANUAL

How to Write, Print and Sell Your Own Book

Dan Poynter

Fourteenth Edition
Revised

 Para Publishing • Santa Barbara, California

The Self-Publishing Manual
How to Write, Print and Sell Your Own Book
by Dan Poynter

Published by:
Para Publishing
Post Office Box 8206
Santa Barbara, CA 93118-8206 U.S.A.
Orders@ParaPublishing.com
http://ParaPublishing.com

Unattributed quotations are by Dan Poynter

ISBN, print ed.   1-56860-073-9
ISBN, PDF ed.   1-56860-074-7
ISBN, LIT ed.   1-56860-075-5
First Printing 1979
Second Printing 1980, revised
Third Printing 1984, completely revised
Fourth Printing 1986, revised
Fifth Printing 1989, completely revised
Sixth Printing 1991, revised
Seventh Printing 1993, revised
Eighth Printing 1995, completely revised
Ninth Printing 1996, revised
Tenth Printing 1997, completely revised
Eleventh Printing 1999, revised
Twelfth Printing 2000, completely revised
Thirteenth Printing 2002, Completely revised
Fourteenth Printing 2003, revised
Printed in the United States of America

Library of Congress Cataloging-in-Publication Data
Poynter, Dan.
The self-publishing manual : how to write, print and sell your own book/ Dan Poynter.
— 13th ed., completely rev.
P.cm.
Includes bibliographical references (p.) and index.
ISBN 1-56860-073-9
1. Self-publishing—United States. I. Title.
2. Desktop Publishing—Computer publishing, etc.
3. Publishers and Publishing—Handbooks, manuals, etc.
4. Printing, Practical—Handbooks, manuals, etc.
5. Authorship—Handbooks, manuals, etc.
Z285.5.P69 2002
070.5'93'0973—dc21   99-057841 CIP

Contents

About the Author
Preface—Note to the Reader
Acknowledgments
Warning—Disclaimer

A common observation by those who use a highlighter to indicate the important parts of The Self-Publishing Manual is that their copy winds up completely yellow.

About the Author

Dan Poynter fell into publishing. He spent eight years researching a labor of love. Realizing that no publisher would be interested in a technical treatise on the parachute, he went directly to a printer. The orders poured in, and the author was suddenly a publisher.

In 1973, he became interested in a new aviation sport but couldn't find a book on the subject, so the skydiver and pilot sat down and wrote one. So far, *Hang Gliding* has sold over 130,000 copies—a best-seller!

Continuing to write, Dan has produced over 80 books and revisions, some of which have been translated into Spanish, Japanese, British English, Russian and German. His books are loaded with facts and figures and detailed inside information. They are always up to date because he revises them before going back to press.

Dan is an early adopter. He believes in buying machinery and has always been on the leading edge of technology. He published the first laser-typeset book in 1981. He was the first to send a galley to *Publishers Weekly* electronically in 1983. He embraced the fax in the mid-1980s and pioneered fax-on-demand to sell reports. He has been selling downloadable reports from his Web site since 1996.

Dan has always accurately predicted the future of publishing. Now the required technologies he describes have converged. Dan is about to open your eyes to the "New Book Publishing Model."

Dan was prompted to write this book because so many authors and publishers wanted to know his secret to selling so many books. Now he is revealing to you the secrets of writing, producing and promoting *your* book—the good life of self-publishing.

Preface—Note to the Reader

This is an exciting time to be in the book business. Book writing, publishing and promoting are changing—for the better. You may wish to read Chapters 1 and 11 first and then to continue on from Chapter 2.

You will encounter stories of my own experiences and those of people like you who wanted to write and perhaps play a part in influencing what others think and do, to possibly even change the course of a reader's life. They accepted the challenge of self-publishing and shared their experiences with me. I hope you enjoy their stories. I have also included quotations from experts in the field of writing or publishing and some of my own thoughts (they are the unattributed quotations).

There is not enough room in one manual to include everything that you should know about self-publishing. Consequently, Para Publishing has prepared many supplemental reports (called documents, special reports or instant reports) that are referenced in relevant places throughout this manual. You may not want or need these supplements right now, but when you do, you can find them on our Web site (by typing in the document number in the search box) or by contacting us by email, telephone or fax. Appendix 2 gives a comprehensive listing of these resources.

Dan Poynter, Santa Barbara

Acknowledgments

I have not attempted to cite in the text all the authorities and sources consulted in the preparation of this manual. To do so would require more space than is available. The list would include departments of the federal government, libraries, industrial institutions, periodicals and many individuals.

Scores of people contributed to the earlier editions of this manual. Information and illustrations have been contributed to this edition by Jay Abraham, Bill Alarid, David Amkraut, Judy Appelbaum, Walter Becker, James Scott Bell, Susan Bodendorfer, Jerry Buchanan, Dan Buckley, Gordon Burgett, Judy Byers, Jack Canfield, Jack Dennon, Dave Dunn, Robbie Fanning, Elizabeth Felicetti, Alan Gadney, Bud Gardner, Barbara Gaughen-Müller, Eric Gelb, Peggy Glenn, Scott Gross, Bill Harrison, Don Hausrath, Ken Hoffmann, LeeAnn Knutson, John Kremer, Paul Krupin, Andrew Linick, Terri Lonier, Ted Maass, Tess Marcin, Maggie Mitchell, John McHugh, Susan Monbaron, Jan Nathan, Christine Nolt, Terry Paulson, Raleigh Pinskey, Tag Powell, Ed Rigsbee, Joel Roberts, Joe Sabah, Ellen Searby, Dan Snow, Ted Thomas, Doug Thorburn, George Thornally, Jan Venolia, Dottie Walters, Mary Westheimer, Liz Zelandais and Irwin Zucker.

Special thanks go to Carolyn Porter of One-On-One Book Production for book design, typography and copyediting; Alan Gadney of One-On-One Book Marketing for technical editing; Nancy Gadney for fact checking and Robert Howard for cover design.

I sincerely thank all these fine people. I know they are as proud of the part they have played in the development of entrepreneurial publishing as they are of their contribution to this work.

Warning—Disclaimer

This book is designed to provide information on writing, publishing, marketing, promoting and distributing books. It is sold with the understanding that the publisher and author are not engaged in rendering legal, accounting or other professional services. If legal or other expert assistance is required, the services of a competent professional should be sought.

It is not the purpose of this manual to reprint all the information that is otherwise available to authors and/or publishers, but instead to complement, amplify and supplement other texts. You are urged to read all the available material, learn as much as possible about self-publishing, and tailor the information to your individual needs. For more information, see the many resources in Appendix 2.

Self-publishing is not a get-rich-quick scheme. Anyone who decides to write and publish a book must expect to invest a lot of time and effort into it. For many people, self-publishing is more lucrative than selling manuscripts to another publisher, and many have built solid, growing, rewarding businesses.

Every effort has been made to make this manual as complete and as accurate as possible. However, there *may be mistakes*, both typographical and in content. Therefore, this text should be used only as a general guide and not as the ultimate source of writing and publishing information. Furthermore, this manual contains information on writing and publishing that is current only up to the printing date.

The purpose of this manual is to educate and entertain. The author and Para Publishing shall have neither liability nor responsibility to any person or entity with respect to any loss or damage caused, or alleged to have been caused, directly or indirectly, by the information contained in this book.

If you do not wish to be bound by the above, you may return this book to the publisher for a full refund.

1
YOUR PUBLISHING OPTIONS

Why You Should Consider Self-Publishing

Books are the main source of our knowledge, our reservoir of first faith, memory, wisdom, morality, poetry, philosophy, history and science.
—Daniel J. Boorstin, Librarian of Congress Emeritus

Nearly everyone wants to write a book. Most people have the ability, some have the drive, but few have the organization.

Therefore, the greatest need is for a simple system, a road map. The basic plan in this book will not only provide you with direction, it will promote the needed drive and expose abilities you never thought existed.

Magazines devoted to businesspeople, sales reps and opportunity seekers are littered with full-page advertisements featuring people with fabulous offers. Usually, these people discovered a successful system of business in sales, real estate or mail order, and for a price, they are willing to let the reader in on their "secret." To distribute this information, they have written a book. Upon close inspection, one often finds that the author is making more money from the *book* than from the original enterprise. The irony is that purchasers get the wrong information; what they need is a book on how to write, produce and sell a *book*.

Writing a book is probably easier than you think! If you can voice an opinion and think logically, you can write a book. If you can *say it,* you can *write it.* Most people have to work for a living and therefore can spend only a few minutes of each day on their book. Consequently, they can't keep the whole manuscript in their head. They become overwhelmed and confused, and find it easy to quit the project. The solution is to break up the manuscript into many small, easy-to-attack chunks (and never start at page 1, where the hill looks steepest). Then concentrate on one section at a time and do a thorough job on each one.

People want to know "how to" and "where to," and they will pay well to find it. **The information industry**—the production and distribution of ideas and knowledge as opposed to goods and services—now amounts to over one-half of the gross national product. There is money in information. To see how books are tapping this market, check the best-seller lists in the back of *Publishers Weekly, USA Today,* the *Wall Street Journal* or the *New York Times*.

Your best sources for this salable information are your own experiences, plus research. Write what you know. Whether you already have a completed manuscript, have a great idea for one, or need help in locating a suitable subject, this book will point the way.

Since poetry and fiction are very difficult to sell and, even when sold, have a short sales life, we will concern ourselves with nonfiction. Writing nonfiction doesn't require any great literary style; it is simply a matter of producing well-researched, reorganized, updated and, most important, repackaged information. Some of the recommendations here can be applied to fiction, just as the chapters on publishing, promotion and the mail order business can be taken separately and used for other products and businesses. However, all the recommendations are written toward, and for, the reader who wishes to become an author or an author-publisher of useful information.

Writing ranks among the top 10 percent of professions in terms of prestige.
> **—Jean Strouse,** *Newsweek*

BECOMING A CELEBRITY AUTHOR

The prestige enjoyed by the published author is unparalleled in our society. A book can bring recognition, wealth and acceleration in one's career. People have always held books in high regard, possibly because in past centuries books were expensive and were, therefore, purchased only by the rich. Just 250 years ago, many people could not read or write. To be an author then was to be an educated person.

Many enterprising people are using books to establish themselves in the ultimate business of being a celebrity information provider. Usually starting with a series of nonpaying magazine articles, they develop a name and make themselves visible. Then they expand the series of articles into a book. Now with their credibility established, they operate seminars in their field of expertise, command high speaking fees and issue a high-priced business advice newsletter. From there, they teach a course in the local college and become a consultant, advising large corporations and commenting on legal briefs for lawyers. They find they are in great demand. People want their information or simply want them around. Clubs and corporations fly them in to consult, because it is more economical than sending all their people to the expert.

This dream product is the packaging and marketing of information. Starting with a field you know, then researching it further and putting it on paper, will establish you as an expert. Then your expert standing can be pyramided with interviews, articles, TV appearances, talks at local clubs, etc. Of course, most of this activity will promote your book sales.

Books through the ages have earned humanity's high regard as semi-sacred objects.
—Richard Kluger, author and editor

In turn, all this publicity not only sells books, but it opens more doors and produces more invitations, leading to more opportunities to prove your expert status and make even more money for yourself. People seek experts whose opinions, advice and ideas are quoted in the media. Becoming an expert does not require a great education or a college degree. You can become an expert in one small area if you are willing to search the Internet, read up on it and write down the important information.

I am a parachute expert who advises attorneys, judges and juries about what happened or what should have happened in skydiving accidents. I am not a lawyer or even an engineer but I have written seven books on the subject. My technical books on parachutes and my popular books on skydiving give me the expertise to be hired and the credibility to be believed.

A BOOK LASTS FOREVER

A book is similar to a new product design or an invention, but is usually much, much better. A patent on a device or process runs only 17 years, whereas a copyright runs for the author's life plus 70 years. Patents cost thousands of dollars to secure and normally require a lot of legal help. By contrast, the author with a simple two-page form and $30 can file a copyright and there is no waiting period. Once you write a book, it is yours. You have a monopoly on your book and there is usually little direct competition.

Many people work hard at a job for 40 years and have nothing to show for it but memories and pay stubs. Some take their knowledge and write a book; the result is a tangible product for all to see. A book lasts forever, like a painting or a sculpture, however, there are many copies of the book, not just one. While a sculpture can only be admired by a limited number of persons at any one time in the place where it is displayed, books come in multiple copies for all the world to use and admire simultaneously.

Another success secret is to cut out the *intermediaries* who are the commercial publishers and produce and sell the book yourself. You can take the author's royalty and the publisher's profit. You get all the rewards because you are both of them. Now, in addition to achieving the wealth and prestige of a published author, you have propelled yourself into your own lucrative business: a publishing house. This shortcut not only makes you more money (why share it?), it saves you the frustration, trouble and time required to sell your manuscript to a publisher. You know the subject and market better than some distant corporation anyway.

It circulated for five years, through the halls of 15 publishers, and finally ended up with Vanguard Press, which you can see is rather deep in the alphabet.
—Patrick Dennis

Publishing doesn't mean purchasing a printing press and actually putting the ink on the paper yourself. Nearly all publishers leave the production to an experienced book printer.

MAIL ORDER

In addition to the writing and publishing of your book, you will want to investigate its distribution. Today, more books are sold through the mail than through bookstores. In fact, books are the leading mail order product. One-third of all these books are in the how-to category.

Mail order is considered one of the best ways for the beginner with no previous business experience to start a venture of his or her own. Selling books by mail is a good, solid day-to-day business opportunity. Your book will be sold in bookstores, but you will sell even more books through the mail directly to your readers.

Mail order is an ideal way to build a second income or a new life. You don't have to give up your job, there is little overhead, there are tax breaks, you work for yourself and the business can be operated anywhere; you only need to be near a post office. No one knows about your age, education, race or sex; your opportunities are indeed equal.

Direct mail marketing is like fishing. You throw out a line by promoting your products and you find out almost immediately if you have made a sale. Every day is like Christmas; opening envelopes and finding cheques is great fun.

Initially, you will warehouse your books in a closet or your garage, and will slip them into padded bags for mailing. It is quite easy, and starting out is not expensive or time-consuming.

YOUR OWN PUBLISHING BUSINESS

Your "writing/publishing/mail order" company is actually combining three profitable fields and concentrating on only the best parts of each. A business of your own is the great American dream, and it is still attainable. In your own business, you make the decisions to meet only those challenges you find interesting. This is not goofing off; it is making more effective use of your time by working smarter, not harder. After all, there are only 24 hours in a day and only one day at a time. You have to concentrate on what will bring in the most return if you are to prosper.

Running your own enterprise will provide you with many satisfying advantages. You should earn more money because you are working for yourself rather than splitting your efforts with someone else. You have job security and never have to worry about a surprise pink slip. If you keep your regular job and moonlight your own enterprise as recreation, it will always be there to fall back on should you need it. You start at the top, not the bottom, in your own company, and you work at your own pace and schedule. You will meet interesting people, because as an author and publishing executive, you will be sought out by them.

In your own small business, you may work when and where you wish; you do not have to go where the job is. You can work till dawn, sleep till noon, rush off to Hawaii without asking permission. This is flexibility not available to the time clock punchers.

Before you charge into literary battle to attack your keyboard, review Chapter 12. It describes how your life will change once you become a published author. You should know what you are getting into.

Being an author-publisher sounds like a good life, and it can be. Working for yourself requires organization and discipline, but work doesn't seem so hard when you are counting your own money.

THE BOOK PUBLISHING INDUSTRY

To help you understand what is ahead, here are some definitions and some background on the book publishing industry:

- **To Publish** means to prepare and issue material for public distribution or sale or "to place before the public." The book doesn't have to be beautiful, it doesn't even have to *sell*; it needs only to be *issued*. Salability will depend upon the content and the packaging.

- **A Publisher** is the one who puts up the *money*, the one who takes the risk. He or she has the book assembled for the printer, printed and then markets it, hoping to make back more money than has been spent to produce it. The publisher might be a big New York firm or a first-time author, but he or she is always the investor.

A Book by International Standards is a publication with at least 49 pages, not counting the covers. The U.S. Postal Service will accept publications with eight or more pages for book rate postage. Books should not be confused with "pamphlets," which have less than 49 pages, or "periodicals," such as magazines and newspapers. They are published regularly and usually carry advertising.

THE BOOK PUBLISHING INDUSTRY in the U.S. consists of some 55,000 firms (up from 3,000 in 1970), according to the R.R. Bowker Co., but there are many more thousands of publishers who do not bother to apply for a listing. Altogether, they publish over 100,000 titles every year. The large publishers, based in New York, are consolidating, downsizing and going out of business; there are just five left. There are perhaps 300 medium-sized publishers and over 54,000 small ones. Some 8,000 new publishing companies are established each year. Sales amount to over $25 billion per year for the over 1.4 million active titles listed in *Books in Print*.

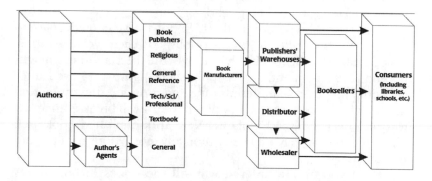

How books get from writer to reader

Authors do detailed research on the subject matter but seldom do any on which publishing house is appropriate for their work.
—**Walter W. Powell,** *Getting Into Print*

YOUR PUBLISHING CHOICES

An author who wishes to get into print has many choices. You can approach a large New York general publisher or a medium-sized niche publisher. You can work with an agent, deal with a vanity press (bad choice) or publish yourself.

As you expand your list of titles and publish other authors, you can graduate to the ranks of the medium-sized publisher. You could one day even become a large general publisher. Here are the choices.

1. BIG PUBLISHING FIRMS are like department stores: they have something for everyone. They publish in many different fields and concentrate on books that anticipate audiences in the millions. A look at the numbers in big publishing will help us to better understand their challenges.

It has been estimated that 2 million book-length manuscripts are circulating to publishers each year, and many of the large publishers receive 3,000-5,000 unsolicited manuscripts each week. Reading all these manuscripts takes an enormous amount of time, and a high percentage of the submissions do not even fit the publisher's line; they are a waste of editorial time. Consequently, many of the publishers refuse delivery of unsolicited manuscripts by rubber-stamping the packages "Return to Sender"; writers are being rejected without being read.

The 12,000 bookstores in the U.S. don't have enough space to display all the 100,000 titles published each year, so they concentrate on the books that move the best in their neighborhoods. Consequently, most publishers figure that even after selecting the best manuscripts and pouring in the promotion money, only 3 books out of 10 will sell well, 4 will break even and 3 will be losers. Only 10% of the New York-published books sell enough copies to pay off the author advance before royalties are paid.

Have you ever wondered why all the books in bookstores have very recent copyright dates? They are seldom more than a year old because the store replaces them very quickly. Shelf space is expensive and in short supply. The books either sell in a couple of months or they go back. If one title doesn't move, another replaces it.

Large publishers have three selling seasons per year. They keep books in bookstores for four months and then replace them.

Most initial print runs are for 5,000 books. Then the title remains in print (available for sale) for about a year. If the book sells out quickly, it is reprinted and the publisher dumps in more promotion money. If the book does not catch on, it is pulled off the market and remaindered (sold off very cheaply) to make room for new titles.

The financial demands cause publishers to be terribly objective about the bottom line. To many publishers, in fact, a book is just a "product." If they already cover a subject, they won't be interested in a new manuscript on the same topic. They already serve that interest and do not care that your version might be better. Many big publishers are not interested in whether it is a good book; all they want to know is whether it will sell. Therefore, they concentrate on well-known authors with good track records or Hollywood and political personalities who can move a book with their name. Only occasionally will they accept a well-written manuscript by an unknown, and then it must be on a topic with a ready and massive audience. A published writer has a much better chance of selling than an unpublished one, regardless of the quality of the work.

Few of the major trade publishers will take a chance on a manuscript from someone whose name is not known.
—Walter W. Powell, *Getting Into Print*

Publishers, like most business people, seem to follow the 80/20 principle: they spend 80% of their effort on the top 20% of their books. The remaining 20% of their effort goes to the bottom 80% of their line. Most books have to sell themselves to induce the publisher to allocate more promotion money.

Many publishers today suggest that their authors hire their own PR firm (at the author's expense) to promote the book.

There is a story about one author who sent her relatives around to bookstores to buy up every copy of her new book. The sudden spurt in sales excited the publisher, who increased the ad budget. The increase in promotion produced greater sales and her book became a success.

Royalties: The author will get a royalty from the large publisher of 6% to 10% of the net receipts (what the publisher receives), usually on a sliding scale, and the economics here are not encouraging. For example, a print run of 5,000 copies of a book selling for $20 could gross $100,000 if all were sold by the publisher at the full retail list price, but an 8% royalty on the net (most books are sold at a discount) may come to just $4,000. That isn't enough money to pay for all the time you spent at the computer. The chances of selling more than 5,000 copies are highly remote, because after a few months, the publisher takes the book out of print. In fact, the publisher will probably sell less than the number of copies printed, because some books will be used for promotion and unsold books will be returned by bookstores.

Your publisher will put up the money, have the book produced and use sales reps to get it into bookstores, but they will not extensively promote the book, contrary to what most first-time authors think. Authors must do it. Once authors figure out that very little promotion is being done, it is too late; the book is no longer new (it has a quickly ticking copyright date in it) and is about to be remaindered. They also discover, to their dismay, that their contract dictates that they must submit their next two manuscripts to this same publisher.

Big publishing houses provide a needed service, but for many first-time authors, they are unapproachable. Once in, the author doesn't get the best deal, and getting out may be difficult. To begin with, the publisher may sit on the manuscript for many months before rejecting it. Or, once accepted, they often chop it up editorially, change the title, and take a year and a half to publish it. Consequently, authors lose artistic control of their delayed book.

All these changes might be acceptable if the big commercial publishers were great financial successes. They aren't, or at least they haven't been so far. One publishing house even admits it would have made more money last year if it had vacated its New York office and rented out the floor space.

> *Recognition is everything you write for: it's much more than money. You want your books to be valued. It's the basic aspiration of a serious writer.*
> **—William Kennedy**

The publishing industry attracts lovely, creative people who find their rewards in its nonmaterialistic aspects. They often come from tax-supported academic or library communities; they have never been marketing oriented. In fact, the *editorial* division in most publishing houses jealously guards its independence so it won't be "corrupted" by the *marketing* department. This leads editors into the greatest trap in publishing: producing titles that should be published but do not sell. When a book fails to earn back its investment, the publishing house calls it a *prestige* book and justifies its production as a public service.

Many of the people working in the big firms know the "editorial versus marketing" approach is wrong (or that losing money is not what business is all about), and they are frustrated by it. But no matter how many seminars they attend or books they read, they can't pull their companies out of their rut.

In the big firms, salaries are too low to attract highly motivated marketing people. Without better marketing, the companies can't afford to pay more. It is a vicious circle, and there has been little effort to reverse it. The answer might be for the marketing department to select the manuscripts they feel they can sell and to confine the editors' work to editing.

But there is a brighter side for the small publisher who understands who his or her readers are and where they can be found. Since the old-line, *big department store-like* publishers only know how to sell through bookstores, there is a lot of room left for the smaller *boutique-like* publishing house and self- publisher.

Be careful if you hang around with people from the traditional book industry. Learn, but don't let their ways rub off. Study the big New York publishing firms, but don't copy them. You can do a lot better.

To the smaller publisher, there is no front list or back list; it is an only list.

2. MEDIUM-SIZED NICHE (SPECIALIZED) PUBLISHERS are the smaller and newer firms that serve specific technical fields, geographic regions, categories of people or other special- ized markets (business, hiking, boating, etc.). Some of these publishers are very small, some are fairly large, but the most successful ones concentrate on a single subject area.

The owners and staff are usually *participants* in their books' subject matter. For example, those who publish parachute books do it with a sense of mission—because they like to jump out of airplanes. Participants know their subject matter and where to find their reader/buyer because they join the same associations, read the same magazines and attend the same conventions.

The secret to effective book distribution is to make the title available in places with a high concentration of your potential buyers. When a niche publisher takes on your book, they can plug it right into their distribution system. For example, while some parachute books are sold in bookstores, over 90% are sold through parachute stores, skydiving catalogs, jump schools and through the U.S. Parachute Association for resale to its members. Usually three or four calls to major dealers can sell enough books to pay the printing bill—before the book is even printed!

Some writers may think a large New York publisher is more prestigious (good for impressing people at cocktail parties), but a small- to medium-sized publisher will usually sell more books because they sell to non-book trade accounts as well as to bookstores. Remember, most book buyers are interested in the subject matter of the book and want to know if the author is credible. No one ever asks who the publisher is.

Professionals sell then write while amateurs write then try to sell.
—Gordon Burgett

Contacting a niche publisher: If you decide you want your book published by someone else, the secret is to match the manuscript to the publisher. To find the right publisher, check your own bookshelf or go to your nearby bookstore and consult the shelves where your book will be. Check the listings at an online bookstore such as amazon.com. Look for smaller publishers who do good work. When you contact a niche publisher, you will often get through to the top person. They know and like the subject, and they are usually very helpful. They will be able to tell you instantly whether the proposed book will fit into their line.

Book publishers tend to be helpful and friendly. No two books are alike; it is rare if two books on the same niche subject are published in the same year. Consequently, publishers do not feel threatened by other publishers. In fact, publishers often promote other books and each other. This is why when you contact a publisher and they decide that your manuscript is not for them, they are eager to recommend another publisher. They know of lots of other publishing companies, and most relish being able to help you and the other publisher get together.

A manuscript not submitted is a book not published.

3. **VANITY OR SUBSIDY PUBLISHERS** produce around 6,000 titles each year; roughly 20 firms produce about 70% of all the subsidized books. Subsidy publishers offer regular publishing services, but the author invests all the money. Under a typical arrangement, the author pays the full publishing costs (more than just the printing bill) and receives 40% of the retail price of the books sold and 80% of the subsidiary rights, if sold. (See a fuller explanation of subsidiary rights in Chapter 8.) Many vanity publishers charge $10,000 to $30,000 to publish a book, depending on its length.

Vanity publishers claim they will furnish all the regular publishing services including promotion and distribution. All this might not be so bad if they had a good track record for delivery. But according to *Writer's Digest*, vanity publishers usually do not deliver the promotion they promise, and the books rarely return one-quarter of the author's investment.

> Soma Vira, Ph.D., paid $44,000 to have three of her books produced by a well-known subsidy publisher. She received 250 books but could not verify how many were printed and suspects they made very few for stock. The books were not properly edited, typeset, proofed or manufactured. Distributors, bookstores and reviewers refused to consider books from this and other vanity presses. The books she received cost her $176 each and she had to start over. (http://www.SpaceLinkBooks.com)

The ads reading, "To the author…" or "Manuscripts wanted by…" easily catch the eye of the writer with a book-length manuscript. Vanity presses almost always accept a manuscript for publication and usually do so with a glowing review letter. They don't make any promises regarding sales, and usually the book sells fewer than 100 copies. Vanity publishers don't have to sell any books because the author has already paid them for their work. Therefore, subsidy publishers are interested in manufacturing the book (as few copies as possible), not in editing, high quality cover design and typesetting, promotion, sales or distribution. Since they are paid to publish, they are really selling printing contracts, not books. They are simply taking a large fee to print unedited and poorly reproduced manuscripts.

Legitimate publishers don't have to look for manuscripts.
—L.M. Hasselstrom

Since binding is expensive, the subsidy publisher often binds just a few hundred copies; the rest of the printed sheets remain unbound unless needed. The "advertising" promised in the contract normally turns out to be only a tombstone ad that lists many titles in the *New York Times*. Sales from this feeble promotion are extremely rare.

Review copies of the book sent to columnists by a subsidy publisher usually go straight into the circular file. The reviewer's time is valuable, and they do not like vanity presses because they know that very little editing has been done to the book. They also realize there will be little promotional effort and that the book has not been distributed to bookstores and will not be available to their readers. The name of a vanity publisher on the spine of the book is a kiss of death.

One major vanity press lost a large class-action suit a few years ago, but they are still advertising in the yellow pages. Before considering a subsidy or vanity publisher, get a copy of *Should You Pay to Have it Published* from *Writer's Digest*. See their Web site at http://www.writersdigest.com.

4. LITERARY AGENTS match manuscripts with the right publisher and negotiate the contract; 80% of the new material comes to big publishers through them. The agent has to serve the publisher well, for if he or she submits an inappropriate or poor manuscript, the publisher will be reluctant to consider anything more from that agent in the future. Therefore, agents like sure bets too, and many are disinclined to even consider an unpublished writer. Their normal commission is 15%.

Agents are 85% hope and 15% commission.

The agent makes manuscript suggestions, negotiates the contract and tries to sell the book to one of his or her many contacts, exploiting all possible avenues. If your manuscript is a bookstore-type book with a wide audience, it is wise to have professional management.

According to *Literary Agent's Marketplace*, about 40% of the book agents will not read manuscripts by unpublished authors, and a good 15% will not even answer query letters from them. Of those agents who will read the manuscript of an unpublished author, 80% will charge for the service. Eighty percent of the agents will not represent professional books; 93% will not touch reference works; 99% will not handle technical books; 98% will not represent regional books, satire, musicals and other specialized manuscripts. Although most agents will handle novel-length fiction, only 20% are willing to take on either novelettes or short stories, and only 2% have a special interest in literature or quality fiction.

It's harder for a new writer to get an agent than a publisher.
—**Roger Straus, president,
Farrar, Straus & Giroux**

On the fringe, there are people who call themselves agents who charge a reading fee and then pay students to read and critique the manuscript. They make their money on these fees, not from placing the manuscripts. For a list of literary agents, see *Writer's Market, Literary Agents of North America* and *Literary Market Place*. Also see the directory of agents on the Writers Net Web site at http://www.writers.net and the Association of Author's Representatives, Inc., an organization of independent literary and dramatic agents, at http://www. publishersweekly.com.

5. SELF-PUBLISHING is where the author bypasses all the intermediaries, deals directly with the editor, cover artist, book designer and printer, and then handles the marketing and distribution. If you publish yourself, you will make more money, get to press sooner and keep control of your book. You will invest your time as well as your money, but the reward is greater. You will get it all.

Self-publishing is not new. In fact, it has solid early American roots; it is almost a tradition. Well-known self -publishers include Mark Twain, Zane Grey, Upton Sinclair, Carl Sandburg, James Joyce, D.H. Lawrence, Ezra Pound, Edgar Rice Burroughs, Stephen Crane, Mary Baker Eddy, George Bernard Shaw, Edgar Allen Poe, Rudyard Kipling, Henry David Thoreau, Walt Whitman, Robert Ringer, Spencer Johnson, Richard Bolles, Richard Nixon and many, many more. These people were self-publishers, though today the vanity presses claim their books were "subsidy" published.

Years ago, some authors elected to go their own way and self-publish after being turned down by regular publishers, but today most self-publishers make an educated decision to take control of their book—usually after reading this book.

Do self-publishers ever sell many books? Here are some numbers (at last count): *What Color is Your Parachute*, 22 revised editions and 5 million copies; *Fifty Simple Things You Can Do to Save the Earth*, 4.5 million copies; *How to Keep Your Volkswagen Alive*, 2.2 million copies; *Leadership Secrets of Attila the Hun*, over 0.5 million copies, and *Final Exit*, over 0.5 million copies. These authors took control and made it big. For an expanded self-publishing success list, see Document 155 at http:// ParaPublishing.com.

Self-publishing is not difficult. In fact, it may even be easier than dealing with a publisher. The job of the publishing manager, or a self-publisher, is not to perform every task but to see that every task gets done. Self-publishers deal directly with the printer and handle as many of the editing, proofing, cover and page production, promotion and distribution jobs as they can. What they can't do, they farm out. Therefore, self-publishing may take on many forms, depending on the author-publisher's interests, assets and abilities. It allows them to concentrate on those areas they find most challenging and use outside services for the rest.

Properly planned, there is little monetary risk in self-publishing. If you follow the plan, the only variable is the subject of the book. Unlike poetry and fiction, most nonfiction topics sell relatively easily, especially to their target markets.

Because the big publisher only tries a book for a few months and then lets sales dictate its fate (reprint or remainder), the first year is most important. The self-publisher, on the other hand, uses the first year to build a solid market base for a future of sustained sales. While a big publisher may sell only 5,000 copies total, the self-publisher can often count on 5,000 or more each year, year after year.

Para Publishing's *Is There a Book Inside You?* has a self-paced quiz to help you decide between a large publisher, a medium-sized niche publisher, an agent, a book producer, a vanity press and self-publishing.

Do you realize what would happen if Moses were alive today? He'd go up to Mount Sinai, come back with the Ten Commandments and spend the next eight years trying to get them published.

—Robert Orben, humorist

EIGHT GOOD REASONS TO SELF-PUBLISH

1. **To make more money.** Why accept 6% to 10% in royalties from a publisher when you can have 35% from your bookstore distributor (or 100% if you sell direct to the reader)? You know your subject and you know the people in your field. Certainly you know more than some distant publisher who might buy your book. Although trade publishers may have some good contacts, they don't know the market as well as you do, and they aren't going to expend as much focused promotional effort. Ask yourself this question: Will the trade publisher be able to sell four times as many books as I can?

2. **Speed.** Most publishers work on an 18-month production cycle. Can you wait that long to get into print? Will you miss your market? The 18 months don't even begin until after the contract negotiations and contract signing. Publication could be three years away! Why waste time shipping your manuscript around to see if there is an agent or publisher out there who likes it? Richard Nixon self-published *Real Peace* in 1983 because he felt his message was urgent; he couldn't wait for a publisher's slow machinery to grind out the book.

    Typically, bookstores buy the first book published on a popular subject. Later books may be better, but the store buyer will pass on them since the store already has the subject covered.

3. **To keep control of your book.** According to *Writer's Digest*, 60% of the big publishers do not give the author final approval on copyediting; 23% never give the author the right to select the title; 20% do not consult the author on the jacket design; and 36% rarely involve the author in the book's promotion.

    The big New York trade publishers may have more promotional connections than you, but with a huge stable of books to push, your book will most likely get lost in the shuffle. The big publishers are good at getting books into bookstores, but they fail miserably at approaching other outlets or doing specialized promotion. Give the book to someone who has a personal interest in it—the author.

4. **No one will read your manuscript.** Many publishers receive hundreds of unsolicited manuscripts for consideration each day. They do not have time to unwrap, review, rewrap and ship all those submissions, so they return them unopened. Unless you are a movie star, noted politician or have a recognizable name, it is nearly impossible to attract a publisher. Many publishers work with their existing stable of authors and accept new authors only through agents.

5. **Self-publishing is good business.** There are many more tax advantages for an author-publisher than there are for just authors. Self-publishers can deduct their lifestyle.

6. **Self-publishing will help you think like a publisher.** You will learn the industry and have a better understanding of the big picture. A book is a product of yourself, somewhat like your own child. You are very protective about your book (you would not tell a mother or father their child is ugly), and you naturally feel that your book is terrific and that it would sell better if only the publisher would pump in more promotion money. Publishers respond that they are not anxious to dump more money into a book that isn't selling. So if you self-publish, you gain a better understanding of the arguments on both sides. It is your money and your choice.

7. **You will gain self-confidence and self-esteem.** You will be proud to be the author of a published book. Compare this to pleading with people to read your manuscript.

8. **Finally, you may have no other choice.** There are more manuscripts than can be read. Most publishers don't have time to even look at your manuscript.

The greatest challenge facing the smaller and newer publisher today is finding a system for *managing the excitement*. Nonfiction book publishers in their how-to books provide valuable information that readers willingly buy because it is going to save them time and money. We send out review copies, make direct mail solicitations and circulate news releases on our books—and customers respond. That is exciting! Publishing is an easy business, a profitable business and a fun business. The publishing business is truly *excitement driven*.

SHOULD YOU SELF-PUBLISH?

Would-be author-publishers should be cautioned that self-publashing is not for everyone. Writing is an *art*, whereas publishing is a *business*, and some people are unable to do both well. If you are a lovely, creative flower who is repelled by the crass commercialism of selling your own product, you should stick to the creative side and let someone else handle the business end.

On the other hand, some people are terribly independent. They will not be happy with the performance of any publisher, no matter how much time and effort is spent creating and promoting the book. These people should save the publisher from all this grief by becoming their own publisher and making their own decisions. You must understand all the alternatives so you can make an intelligent, educated choice.

SELLING OUT: Many self-publishers find that once they have proven their books with good sales, they are approached by big publishing houses with offers to print a new edition. If you decide to sell out to a large publisher, see "Selling Out" in Chapter 8.

> Richard Paul Evans took six weeks to write the 87-page *Christmas Box*. He did so well selling it for two holiday seasons that Simon & Schuster paid him $4.2 million for it. Now it is in 13 languages. Many authors begin as self-publishers, get attention and sell out.

THE FUTURE OF PUBLISHING

Packaged information is becoming increasingly specialized. More and more books are being printed in smaller quantities. The information in books is going out of date faster. Books are being produced more rapidly. Computerized equipment is now used to write, edit, lay out, print and deliver books. The customer wants more condensed and targeted information, faster

The chapters that follow describe in detail an alternative route to traditional publishing. This self-publishing route will enable you to get your book into print at minimum cost. This book could be your second chance. It will show you the way to publication, fame and extra income—a new life.

Obviously, your success cannot be guaranteed, but many people are doing very well in the writing/publishing business. This isn't a get-rich-quick scheme; there is work involved. Even though you are working for yourself, at your own pace, it is still *work*. You won't get rich overnight. Building a sound business venture takes several years.

Make effective use of your most valuable asset: your time.

The secret is to invest your labor. Your time is precious. Like gold, there is a finite quantity. You have only 24 hours of time each day. You can use your time in several ways: you can throw it away, sell it or invest it. You can waste your valuable time in front of the television set; time is easy to lose. Most people punch a clock, go to work and get a cheque. They trade their labor for money on a one-to-one basis. If you don't punch in, you don't get paid. But isn't it better to invest your time in a book that will sell and generate income while you are away doing something else? Your labor becomes an investment that pays dividends for years while you are playing or working on another investment. Don't throw away your time; invest it. It is up to you.

You have all the ingredients to be a successful published author. This book is your recipe.

I have never met an author who is sorry he or she wrote their book. They are only sorry they did not write it sooner.
—Sam Horn, *Tongue Fu*

2
Writing Your Book

Generating Salable Material

Write on a subject you love. Your profit center should also be your passion center.

What are your talents and what do you want to do? Do you enjoy writing, or do you want to be a published author but find writing painful? Analyze your abilities, motivations and overall agenda. Do you want to write, publish or sell books, any combination of these activities, or even all three?

In this chapter I will cover all three areas to help you make an educated, personal choice. First, I will discuss how to get your thoughts on paper. Then I will look at both sides of publishing: as seen by the author and as seen by the publisher.

I love being a writer. What I can't stand is the paperwork.
— **Peter de Vries**

PICKING A SUBJECT

This is the first step. Consider the elements necessary for selling nonfiction:

- **The subject is interesting to you.** What subject do you want to be talking about three years from now?

- **You have the expertise** (education) **or experience** (you have been there, done that).

➽ **The subject interests others; it must be salable.** If you build it, will they come?

➽ **The subject matter is tightly focused.** Readers want specific, narrowly-targeted information today.

➽ **The market is easy to reach.** You know *who* your potential customers are and *where* your customers are. You know what stores they visit, what associations they join, what magazines they read and what events they attend.

➽ **The market of potential buyers is large enough.**

There are three rules to successful writing: (1) Have something to say, (2) Know how to say it, and (3) Be able to sell it.
— **David Hellyer**

The book should be on a subject you are interested in and on which you are an expert or on which you would like to become an expert. You have spent years working at, specializing in and learning something, and there are thousands of people out there willing to pay good money to get the inside information from you. Write what you know! If you select your hobby, there are a number of advantages: you know what has been written in the past, you have the contacts for gathering more information and your further participation in that hobby will become tax deductible.

If you need help evaluating your project, contact author-publisher Gordon Burgett at Gordon@sops.com. He will read your manuscript and make recommendations on market targeting, manuscript rework (if necessary), publishing and marketing.

FICTION VS. NONFICTION

There is a difference between entertainment (fiction) and information (nonfiction). Every nonfiction book is unique. The buyer interested in raising llamas is not necessarily a good prospect for a book on skydiving or wastewater treatment.

Fiction, on the other hand, is related to all other fiction in its category. A reader who buys one mystery is a prime candidate for another mystery. Consequently, as entertainment, fiction must compete for a person's leisure time. They must choose not only between reading this book of fiction and reading other books but between reading this book and engaging in other forms of entertainment, such as going to a movie, renting a video or walking on the beach.

Nonfiction does not compete for time. Nonfiction is information that people buy because it will save them time or money. It is much easier to convince people to buy nonfiction than fiction. Consequently, the unknown poet or fiction writer is at the same point as the unknown painter or musician.

Fiction writers can't be trusted—they make things up.

Poetry is even more difficult to sell. Since we receive so many requests for information, we have assembled an Instant Report 606, *Publishing Fiction and Poetry,* at http://ParaPub lishing.com.

At Para Publishing, we specialize in coaching nonfiction book publishers to sell more books. We do not claim to have any expertise in magazine or newsletter publishing, fiction or poetry. There are many kinds of publishing. Some of our programs, ideas, leads and resources will work for creative literature, but that is not our specialty.

The how-to article is to writing as McDonald's is to restaurants; it enjoys no epicurean status. Nevertheless, McDonald's advertises "billions and billions sold," a point the writer might keep in mind.

— Leonard Bernstein

Nonfiction. The subject of a book, not the name of the publisher or the comments of a reviewer, is what sells it. Every new national craze requires how-to books. According to *Newsweek,* there are over 1,300 books on fitness and health currently in print. Do not be discouraged if your subject has already been covered. That just proves someone else thought it was important. Using your own experience and the latest information, you can do it better. The subjects with the best sales potential are how-to's, money, health, self-improvement, hobbies, sex and psychological well-being. Find a need and fill it.

One specialized book that sold for years was my *Hang Gliding.* It went through the press 10 times for 130,000 copies in print.

There may be more money in publishing your information in short monographs than in longer books. Timely monographs usually command a higher price, can be published in shorter runs and take less time to produce. You can even sell them on the Web as downloadable information. Do not overlook well-researched short reports.

OBTAINING A MANUSCRIPT

You have the choice of buying written material from others or writing it yourself (are you an author or a writer?). In this chapter, I will discuss the many possibilities—only one has to be right for you. If one possibility clicks, you are on your way. First, I will cover how to write material yourself, and then I will show you how to obtain some or all of the material from others.

WRITING IT YOURSELF

Creating your own material is easy if you have a system; all it takes is organization and discipline. Following our system, creating copy becomes challenging fun and allows you to see the progress you are making, which is encouraging.

Although writing a book is not difficult, it is not for the lazy. Like Alcoholics Anonymous or a diet, you will have to change your lifestyle. This means waking up one morning and making a decision to do it now. Getting into the system and developing good habits will provide you with a sense of purpose and a feeling of accomplishment. Once you have selected a topic, only the decision to start stands between you and the finished book.

For detailed, step-by-step instructions on how to write your book, see *Writing Nonfiction: Turning Thoughts into Books* at http://ParaPublishing.com.

> *Writing has to come first.*
> **—Sue Grafton**

Time, or lack of it, is the most frequently heard excuse. But somehow we always find time for those things that are important to us. We just put them first. Often we can fit in an hour of writing time each day by completing our other chores faster. Another way is to get up one hour earlier each day. This is perfect scheduling, because the house is quiet, the telephone does not ring, and you are refreshed; and most writers find the early morning to be their most creative and productive time. But you must put this hour first and not let anything interfere with it. Once you gather momentum in your project, you will find that rising early will be easy; you won't even miss that hour of sleep.

Set up a writing area in a spare room or a corner of the living room. Keep your computer and research tools there. Your creative writing time is precious; do not waste it trying to get started.

CHOOSING A TITLE: Spend some time on your title. A good title is half your sales package. If you have a poor title, your potential customer may never recognize the book as being valuable to him or her.

Start with a short, catchy and descriptive title and add a longer, explanatory subtitle. The first word of the title should be the same as the subject to make the book easy to find in the book directories.

Brainstorm the title and come up with a good one-liner that tells a complete and compelling story. Write down all your ideas. Your title will evolve and change as you write the book. The title is perhaps the single most important piece of promotional copy you will draft for the book.

See Document 630, *Selecting a Book Title that Sells*, at http://ParaPublishing.com.

- **Front cover:** Select a title and subtitle. Keep the title short and make the subtitle descriptive. List the most important person in your field (association or industry) for the foreword (and please note the spelling of *Foreword*.) You will try to get him or her to pen the foreword later.

- **Spine:** Stack the title on the spine so it will read more easily on the shelf. Use a bold, san-serif, vertical-legged typeface such as Arial Black Bold. See the spine on this book.

- **Back cover:** Write your back cover copy before you write your book. This exercise will help you focus on the audience for your book and what you plan to give them. You have to draft the back cover copy eventually, so you might as well do it before you write the book.

No one reads a book in the bookstore before they buy it. Sales reps only carry book covers and jackets to show store buyers, and wholesalers and distributors ask only for the cover copy. All buying decisions are based on the illustration/design and the sales copy on the outside of the book. Yes, packaging is everything.

Stores have tens of thousands of books displayed with their spines out. With all this congestion, it is hard to get attention. Initially, all that buyers see is the book's spine. If they take it down, they will gaze at the cover about four seconds and the flip it over to read the back cover. On average, they will spend just seven seconds here, so the trick is to keep them reading longer. Your copy has to be punchy and laden with benefits; it has to speak to the potential buyer.

Category:
HEADLINE

Description:

Promises & Benefits...

You will discover...
- **(1)**
- **(2)**
- **(3)**
- **(4)**
- **(5)**
- **(6)**

Testimonials:
(1)

(2)

(3)

Author Bio:

Sales closer:

ISBN
Bar code
Price

Back cover layout

Your book-cover designer will lay out the package and incorporate the illustration, put it all on disk and send it to your printer, but you must draft the sales copy. The back cover layout shown on the previous page will take you step-by-step through the sales copy draft process. Use your computer so you will be able to move the copy around once it has been entered.

Here are explanations for each area of the worksheet.

●❖ *Category*: Visit a bookstore and check the shelf where your book will be displayed. Note the categories on the books and the shelves. Listing the proper category on the back cover of your book will ensure your book will be easy to find, because the bookshop personnel will place it on the right shelf.

●❖ *Headline*: Now you need an arresting headline addressed to potential buyers. You want them to relate to the book and find themselves in it. Do not simply repeat the title here; do not bore the potential buyer. You have already printed the title on the front. Use an alternate approach. For example, *The Self-Publishing Manual's* back cover headline is "Why Not Publish Yourself?"

●❖ *Description*: Concisely (two to four sentences) state what the book is about. What will the reader gain by reading this book? Get to the point: many times this is all the potential buyer will read before skimming the rest to make a buying decision.

●❖ *Promises and benefits*: Promise to make readers better at what they do. Pledge health, wealth, entertainment or a better life. Focus on who your audience is and what they want. Think: Who are you talking to and what are they going to get from the book?
    Say, **"You will discover:"** and then list the benefits:
    ● "[benefit]
    ● [benefit]
    ● [benefit]
    ● [benefit]"

●❖ *Testimonials and endorsements*: Dream up three different endorsements from people you would *like* to quote. If

"This book changed my battlefield strategy." — **Colin Powell** would look good, try it. Use *names* or *titles* recognizable in your field, sources that might impress potential buyers. This is just a draft; dress it up. You will secure some of these quotations later.

- *Author*: Show that you, the author, are the ultimate authority on the subject. Just two or three sentences will do.

- *Sales closer*: End with a sales closer in bold type. Ask the browser to buy the book. Use something like "This book has enabled thousands to... and it will show you the way too."

- *Price*: Bookstores like a price on the book. The price is a turn-off, so place it at the end of the sales copy. Never locate the price at the top of the back cover. If this is a hardcover book, place the price at the top of the front flap.

- *Bar code* with International Standard Book Number (ISBN) and price. The bar code on a book identifies the ISBN, which in turn identifies the publisher, title, author and edition (hardcover, etc.). Make room for, but do not worry about, the bar code and ISBN just now.

Your *title*, *subtitle*, back cover *headline* and *benefits* may be swapped. Once you have written them, you may wish to move some of them around. For example, one of your benefits might actually be a better subtitle.

Back cover copy on most of the books you see in bookstores is weak and uninspiring. The title is repeated and then is followed by several quotations and a bar code and that's it! Haphazard copy is the sign of a lazy (or maybe inexperienced) copywriter. This lack of effective competition on the shelf will give you the upper hand.

If you need help with drafting mouth-watering, action-producing, customer-stampeding, riot-provoking wallet-grabbing sales copy, contact Joe "Mr. Fire" Vitale, tomorrow's copywriter, at his Web site: http://www.mrfire.com.

Years ago I said, "Write your ad before you write your book." This was to help you focus on your audience and what you were going to give them. Then I realized that the most important "ad" you will ever write is your back cover copy. Now I say, "Write your cover copy before you write your book."

Unfortunately, many nonfiction books are written without a specific market in mind, and since the book does not provide what the potential buyers want, it does not sell. The book cover worksheet will help you focus on who your customer really is.

For more information on covers, see Document 631, *Covers That Sell Books*, at http://ParaPublishing.com.

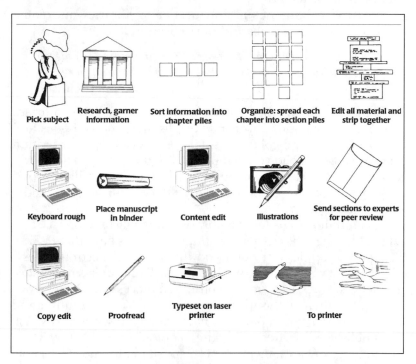

The flow of the manuscript

Faulty research is like a faulty septic tank. Sooner or later the evidence will surface and become embarrassing.

— Rex Alan Smith

RESEARCH is simply reading, making notes, condensing and rearranging the gathered pertinent information. There is no need to leave home—just turn on your computer and click to the Internet. All research should begin with the Web because you will pick up more current information there than at any library or bookstore. Almost everything you need for your research will be found there. Register your information needs with Excite and they will send you clippings from several sources. See http://www.excite.com/info/newstracker/quickstart.

Start with an online bookstore such as amazon.com. Research what has been written in your field. Use the search engines to find more information.

Next, visit both public and academic libraries and some bookstores for both books and periodicals.

The greatest part of a writer's time is spent in reading in order to write; a man will turn over half a library to make one book.
— **Samuel Johnson**

Be a detective. When you run out of leads, ask the librarian. Libraries carry hundreds of indexes, listings, source books and extensive periodical collections. Gather everything ever written on your subject. Load yourself up with so much material you will have to decide what to leave out. Overdo it, and you will be proud of the result, secure in the knowledge that you have covered the subject completely.

Get a roll of coins for the library's copy machine or ask for a renewable magnetic charge card (many libraries have them). Take a couple of floppies with you to download useful electronic files.

You want your readers to know about all the books, magazines, newsletters, tapes, software and other references available on your subject. List them in the appendix of your book. As an author and opinion molder, you should not have to buy these resources. Ask the publishers for free "checking copies." Now that you are researching, you are a member of the print media and will be able to attend a lot of related events free. Use your new business card to get a press pass, media packet and preferential treatment.

COPYRIGHT is the subject that most interests potential authors. They want to know how to protect their precious material from others and also how much they themselves can borrow.

Copyright does not cover facts or ideas. Copyright covers only the *expression* of ideas or a sequence of words. Copying ideas is research, copying words is plagiarism. So copy ideas, copy facts, but do not copy words. Make it a rule never to repeat any three words in a row.

Writing from notes is not plagiarism but solid, thorough research and an efficient system made possible by Xerox. There is nothing new in the universe. Practically every nonfiction book is simply a repackaging of existing and new material.

If you find material that you wish to use as is, contact the author for permission. Your letter might go like this:

Permission to reprint material

Dear:_____

I am writing a book tentatively titled *The Skydiver's Handbook*. I would like your permission to include the excerpts as outlined in any and all editions of the book, as well as in advertisements and promotion, nonexclusively, throughout the world.

In exchange for your permission, you will be listed in the acknowledgments and will be sent a copy of the book. I hope you will agree to our giving your book greater exposure.

For your covenience, enclosed are a self-addressed, stamped envelope and a copy of this letter for your records.

Sincerely,
(Your name)

Material to be reprinted:

Title & Author:

Copyright date and holder:_____

Page:_____, Line:_____. To page: _____,Line:_____.

Permission letter

The 1987 Copyright Act was amended by the Sonny Bono Copyright Term Extension Act in 1998. Now, anything printed prior to 1922 is safe. See the Copyright Office Web site for details at http://www.unc.edu/~unclng/public-d.htm.

Many documents are not copyrighted. If you want to find out whether some material is protected under either the current or pre-1978 law, the U.S. Copyright Office at the Library of Congress will conduct a search for you. Send them as much information as possible, such as the author, title, publisher and publication date. The easiest way is to photocopy the title page and copyright page of the book. They charge for the time spent, and they should be able to make two searches per hour. Get a copy of Copyright Office Circular 22, *How to Investigate the Copyright Status of a Work,* by calling the Copyright Office at 202-707-3000 or the forms hotline at 202-707-9100 or print out the circular from the Copyright Office Web site at http://www.loc.gov /copyright/forms.

Government and military publications are in the public domain. Even if they were not, the Freedom of Information Act would probably cover them. If you really need a piece of material, military or civilian, ask for permission. It is safer and cheaper than hiring a lawyer later to prove you had a right to use it.

Your copyrighted material is valuable property, or it may become so one day. File copyright forms on all those magazine articles you write but don't get paid for. You may need an article for inclusion in a book someday, and the expenditure on fees for your copyright application will justify to the IRS that you really are in the word business.

If, on the other hand, you are asked for permission to reprint some of your work, you might consider limiting the permission to a section or two and stipulating that an editor's note must indicate that the material was used with your permission and came from your book. This will show, once again, that you are an expert; it is also good publicity for the original work. A copyright on your book is not only for protection—it carries prestige because it shows you are a professional. Copyright is discussed in several other places in this book. See the Index. For more information on copyrights, see the Copyright Office Web site at http://www. loc.gov/copyright.

ORGANIZE YOUR MATERIAL WITH THE "PILOT SYSTEM"

Start by drawing up a preliminary Table of Contents; just divide your notes into 10 or 12 chapters. Then sort all your research material and "pile it" as required.

SORT, SHUFFLE AND MARK: Decide on your chapter titles and, using scissors, tape and staples, sort all this photocopied material into the applicable chapter piles. During your research, you must have written down a number of interesting observations and many of your own experiences. Add those notes to the piles.

Now spread out the individual chapters. They will probably completely fill your living room. Pick an interesting pile—any one, not necessarily the first—and go through it, underlining important points and writing in your additional comments. Write out longer thoughts on a tablet and place those sheets of paper in the pile in the order you plan to write that chapter.

This floor spread will enable you to see the whole interrelated project, lending excitement and encouragement—a great incentive. Move the piles around to ensure a good, logical flow of thought and to avoid duplication of copy. Condense the material by discarding unnecessary and duplicate material.

This use of information from other sources is not "plagiarizing," it is "research." Your notes ensure that you will not leave out any important points. And, you will be entertained as you compare what other authors say about the same item. The similarities are often remarkably coincidental, sometimes to the point of including the same words and phraseology (which is why you should explain the information differently). This experience also emphasizes the importance of being accurate. Others will research and refer to your work in the future.

As you read what others say on a particular point, your memory will be jogged. You will have additional points, a clearer explanation or an illustrative story. Where you disagree with another author, you can always say, "Some people believe . . .," and then tell it your way. You have the advantage of the most recent information, since you came last.

MAKE NOTES: Carry paper and pen with you at all times, especially when driving, running or engaging in any solo activity. This is a time to think, create, compose; this is when there is no one around to break your train of thought. Some authors keep a writing tablet in their car and compose while commuting. I know of a detective-writer who outlines his stories while on stake-outs. When you are confined, captive, isolated, you have nothing else to do but create. Make use of any available time. A lot of good material develops while attending dull meetings.

Some people like to work with a small pocket tape recorder, but remember that someone must transcribe your dictation into a computer and onto paper. It all depends on what you are used to, how you perform best. If you regularly dictate letters and have a secretary transcribe your tapes, this may be the most comfortable and most efficient method for you.

When a particularly original thought or creative approach hits you, write it down or you will lose it. Keep on thinking and keep on taking notes. Add your thoughts and major pieces to the piles. As you go along, draw up a list of questions as they come to mind, so that you will remember to follow up on them for answers.

Strip your notes by cutting, sorting and taping. Paste the strips together with Magic transparent tape so you can write on the tape as well as the paper when adding more notes.

There is nothing to writing. All you have to do is to sit down at the keyboard and open up a vein.
— **Red Smith**

INPUT: Keyboard (or dictate with speech recognition software) from the pasted strips of notes. With practice, you will learn to think, create and compose at the computer. Write as you speak; relax and be clear. Do not worry about punctuation, grammar or style. You will edit the work later, and it is always easier to edit than it is to create. Right now, all you want to do is get your thoughts and research material onto the hard disk. Make notes where you are considering illustrations.

Read the whole section of pasted-together notes to grasp the overall theme. Then boil it down and use your own words. Think about the section and how you might explain the basic message better. Can you say it more clearly with fewer words? Do not just write from the paper strips sentence by sentence; that method approaches plagiarism and diminishes your own creative thoughts. For organization, list the main points and rearrange the pieces. If you are having trouble with a section, skip ahead and come back to it later.

NON-LINEAR WRITING: Do not start writing chapter one–to do so makes book writing look like an impossibly steep climb, and it is hard to get started. Select the chapter pile that looks the smallest, easiest or most fun. It may simply be the most interesting, but it is sure to go the fastest. Once you have drafted it, take the next most interesting chapter and so on. Skip around. Soon you will be past the halfway mark and the going will be downhill. You will be encouraged and will gather momentum. Using this approach, you will probably find you are writing the first chapter last. This is as it should be, because the first chapter is usually introductory in nature to the overall book, and you cannot know where you are truly going until you have reached the end. Many authors wind up rewriting and reslanting the first chapter because they wrote it first.

The last thing one discovers in writing a book is what to put first.
—Blaise Pascal

Do not be concerned with what goes into the computer the first time around. The important thing is to get it down. Often these first impressions are the best; they are complete, natural and believable. Later you will go through the draft making corrections, additions and deletions.

As you keyboard the rough first draft, and later as you review it, you will decide that whole paragraphs are misplaced and belong elsewhere. With your computer, it is an easy matter to move and modify material. Writing on a computer with all the capabilities of word processing software allows you to create in a non-linear (random) fashion. You can easily move around, add, delete, change words and thoughts—much like the "mind" works.

If you lack a certain piece of information, a number or a fact, leave a blank space, put a note in the text to remind yourself and move on. Do not lose momentum. Some authors use three asterisks (***), because asterisks are easy to see (or find with a computer search). Similarly, if you find yourself repeating material, make a note with three asterisks so you can compare it with the other material later. Keep on writing.

CONCENTRATED WRITING: If possible, keyboard one whole section at a time. One whole chapter at a time is better, and the entire book straight through is the best way to go. Most beginning authors are working at other jobs and can devote only a short period each day to their writing. But the more time you can put into each piece of the book, the better, because there will be greater continuity, less duplication and clearer organization. If you can do only a small section at a time, try arranging the pieces in the evening, reviewing them in the early morning, thinking about them while commuting, etc., and then after you have formulated the section in your mind, come home to keyboard it.

On the other hand, if you can, take two weeks off from work, shut out all distractions and become totally involved in the manuscript. Do not pick up the mail or answer the telephone. Eat when hungry, sleep when tired and forget the clock except as a gauge of your pace. Keep up the pressure and keep on keyboarding. Pace yourself at, say, one chapter per day. You should not have to force yourself to write, but you will need organization and discipline. After a couple of books, you will find yourself making very few major changes in your original draft.

Writing from notes is much easier than composing from thin air. Thin air produces writer's block. Incidentally, many writers say the hum of a computer—knowing the electricity is on— prompts them to work.

Do not throw out your materials and notes once your draft is typed. Put them in a cardboard carton. Someone may ask where you found a particular piece of information and you may need to trace it. Traceability is especially important with photographs and artwork.

LAY OUT THE BINDER

Now that you are generating copy, you need a place to store it. Find a three-inch, three-ring binder and add divider cards corresponding to the chapters you have selected. Punch and insert the rough draft pages as you complete them. As the piles come off the floor, across the desk and flow through the computer into the binder, you will gain a great feeling of accomplishment.

Inserting the front matter of the book into this binder will further encourage you. As you encounter resources, add them to the appendix in the back. Soon you will have a partial manuscript, the book will be taking shape and you will have something tangible to carry around. The binder will make you feel proud and will give you the flexibility to proofread and improve your manuscript when you are away from home.

Write your name and address in the front of the binder with a note that it is a valuable manuscript. You do not want to misplace and lose your future book. With your binder in one place and your hard disk in another (and your book also back-up copied on a CD), you will not have to worry about the financial and emotional disaster of losing your work in a fire, theft or computer crash.

Carry that binder with you everywhere you go. Busy people often have trouble finding the time to return to their desk and their book. With the binder system, the book is always with you. As you go through the day and find a minute here and there, open the binder—to any section—and write in your changes, notes and comments. Periodically enter your changes into the computer and print out new pages. The binder is an anti-procrastination crutch, and it works. With the binder under your arm, the book will be continually in your thoughts. Your work and your manuscript will improve.

> Ed Rigsbee agreed the binder was helping him stay on his project, but he also found an added benefit: His wife became much more supportive of the project once she saw the tangible evidence.

ORDER BLANK: The last page of your book should contain an order blank; place it on a left-hand page—facing out. Some readers will want to purchase a copy for a friend, and others may want a copy for themselves after seeing your book at a friend's home or in the library. Make ordering easy for them by listing the full price of the book, including sales tax (if applicable) and shipping. This order blank system works. Several orders on the coupon are received for *The Self-Publishing Manual* each week.

> My first book on parachutes took eight years to produce. I worked on this labor of love without guidance or direction. The huge, steady-selling manual became the foundation upon which I built my publishing company. My second book was a study guide for an obscure parachuting rating; it sold better than expected.

In 1973, I became interested in the new sport of hang gliding. Unable to find any information at the library, I wrote the first book on the subject. I foresaw a trend and cashed in on it; the book sold 130,000 copies over 10 years, allowed me to move back to California and buy a home in Santa Barbara. Total writing time: two months.

By this time, I had developed a writing system. My fourth book took less than 30 days from idea and decision until I delivered the boards to the printer. And most of this time was used in waiting for answers to my many letters requesting information. The first draft took only five days.

From there I concentrated on several high-priced, low-cost course pamphlets, turning out most of them within a week. My ninth book took all of two weeks to first draft, and it was typed clean. Very few editing changes had to be made to the original copy.

Using a word processor, I took 31 days to write, edit and typeset a book on computer. The actual time spent working on the book was just 18 days. Lately, my books have been longer and have required more time, but I still produce manuscripts efficiently. Writing a book is easy if you know the formula.

WRITING STYLE

Before writing an article for a magazine, always read one or more editions of the periodical thoroughly to absorb the style and subconsciously adapt to that magazine's way of writing. The same technique can be used in writing a book by reading a couple of chapters of a book by a writer you admire.

I just sat down and started all by myself. It never occurred to me that I couldn't do it as well as anyone else.
— Barbara Tuchman

Writing is a communication art. You should not try to impress anyone. Write as you speak, avoiding big words where small ones will do. Most people regularly use only 800 to 1,000 of the approximately 26,000 English words available to them. Use simple sentences and be precise with words. Vary sentence and paragraph length, and favor the shorter ones. Try to leave yourself out of the copy; avoid the word "I." Read Strunk & White's *The Elements of Style*, which revolutionized writing in the 20th century.

Relax, talk on paper, be yourself. Explain each section in your own words as you would to help a friend who is new to the subject. Keep your writing short. You are paying for the words, so edit out the junk.

If a reader doesn't understand a paragraph, don't blame the reader.

Like a speech, every paragraph of your book should have a beginning, a middle and an end. The first sentence of the paragraph either suggests the topic of the sentence or it helps the transition from the preceding paragraph. Stay with one subject per paragraph. Each paragraph should tie in with both the preceding and following paragraphs (good transitions).

The writer does the most who gives his reader the most knowledge and takes from him the least time.
— Charles Caleb Colton

Be a professional and give the readers their money's worth. Your material will be used by others in coming years and you will be quoted. If you are accurate and correct now, you won't be embarrassed later by the written legend you have created. As a published author, you have the responsibility of being a recognized expert. Use proper terms; don't start a new language. Steer away from jargon (words that are unique to a certain audience), coinages (words that aren't in the dictionary) and buzzwords (words that move in and out of vogue); you will only turn off your reader.

In the early 1970s, hang gliding was a hot new subject. It was the rebirth of aviation, using a wing made in the sail industry, whose participants were kids off the streets. The terms for flying and parts of the glider could have come from the aviation community, the sail industry or popular (new) jargon could have been used. Obviously, aviation terms were in order. This was impressed upon the early book and magazine writers; aviation terms were used almost exclusively, and this usage aided the introduction of hang gliding into the community of sport aviation.

One technique for educating your readers in the correct terms is to use the proper term and then follow it with the more popular word or explanation in parentheses. Educating the reader as you progress through the book is preferable to making readers wade through a glossary.

You are finished when the manuscript is 99% complete and 100% accurate. Do not wait for one more photo, one more statistic, one more piece of information. Get your book to press and to your buying public. Hopefully, you will sell out in a few months, make corrections, add some updated material and return to the press with a revised edition.

OTHER WAYS TO A MANUSCRIPT

Help is available to those who still cannot write even after learning the tricks mentioned previously.

1. HIRE A WRITER (Work-for-Hire): If you cannot get your thoughts on paper, try the team approach. There are a lot of writers out there—people who love to put good thoughts into words. Look for a moonlighting newspaper reporter. They are trained to listen and put your thoughts down accurately. Once they have your material written out, you may edit the work for rewriting. The reporter might even wind up doing a feature story on you, and his or her media contacts are invaluable.

If you use a contract, make sure it has a **work-for-hire** clause, or you may wind up not owning what you have hired the person to write. For more information on collaborating, responsibility charts, an explanation of work-for-hire and a sample contract, see *Is There a Book Inside You?* in Appendix 2 under Para Publishing Books & Reports or at http://ParaPublishing.com.

> Joe Karbo sold millions of dollars-worth of *The Lazy Man's Way to Riche$*, and although he "authored" the book, he did not write it. He gathered his original thoughts and materials and hired a writer to put it all on paper.

2. HIRE AN EDITOR: Perhaps you can get your thoughts down on paper, but all that good information does not read very well. What you need is an editor, someone who can take your information, restructure, rewrite and put energy into it.

> Dr. Rick Hartbrodt wrote a medical book about a common disease. The manuscript contained a lot of solid, helpful information but was hard to read. He contacted writers' groups, editorial services and secretarial services through the yellow pages and located four people who were willing to help. He gave each a copy of the first chapter and asked them to edit a couple of sample pages and to quote their fee. Some editors only wanted to dot the i's and cross

the t's, whereas others wanted to do complete rewrites. Using this method, he was able to compare their work and select the type of work he wanted, the editor he liked most and the best per-page price.

Many recognized authors cannot type or spell, so they hire people who can. The big winner is the reader/book buyer who receives good information expressed well. See the list of editors and copyeditors in the Suppliers section of our Web site at http://ParaPublishing.com.

The best book collaboration is between the author and the reader.
— **Barbara Tuchman**

Many people who are not professional writers get into print. If they cannot pick up the skills, they ask for help. You can too.

3. **COMMISSIONED WRITING:** Some of the more successful book houses approach publishing from a hard-nosed marketing position. They know what they have been able to sell in the past, and they often stay in their field of expertise by hiring writers to produce more of these types of books. Once you decide on an area of concentration, you too can approach others to write for you by paying cash outright or using modest advances and royalties as an inducement. But the accounting is easier and the arrangement is often more cost effective when you pay outright for material rather than paying royalties (a share of the proceeds). Flat fees for shorter books are often $5,000 to $10,000, half on assignment and half on acceptance. Moonlighting advertising copywriters might wrap up these books in less than 60 days.

4. **AUTHOR SUBMISSIONS:** Another source of material is the traditional one of unsolicited author submissions. If you are concentrating on a certain genre or interest area and selling books to a select market, you are also in contact with those people best qualified to generate new material for you. Once you publish something they like, they will come to you. Many people have always cherished the dream of becoming an author, and they will seek you out once they recognize your publishing success.

Publishing is an active life while writing is a quiet life.
— **Linda Meyer**

You can always wait for manuscripts in your interest area to come to you, but you will save time and a lot of useless manuscript reading by soliciting manuscripts yourself. Prepare one-paragraph outlines of books you need to round out your catalog of books and send them to writing magazines such as *Writer's Digest*. (See http://writersdigest.com) Also fill out a form for a publisher-listing in *Writer's Market*. Make it easy for qualified writers to find you.

5. COAUTHORSHIP (Multiple authors): If you have a book you want to write yourself, but recognize that you lack the required technical expertise, consider coauthorship. Find an expert in the field to write part of it while you write the other part, and then each of you can edit the other's material. This approach has many advantages, including the endorsement of an expert, more credibility for the book and another body to send on the promotional tour. The disadvantages are smaller royalties, extra accounting and author hand-holding, which requires a lot of time (you have to teach them the business and explain what you are doing and why).

> I shared the responsibilities for the *Frisbee Players' Handbook* with disk expert Mark Danna. Danna wrote the throwing and catching chapters, and I wrote on history, record attempts and competition, and assembled the appendix. I came up with the unique package and marketing idea (a circular book packaged in a Frisbee) but did not have enough expertise or credibility as a Frisbee player. Mark Danna rounded out the team well.

Spouses may choose to coauthor a book if one is an expert in the field and the other is a better wordsmith. A project like this gets both of them published, provides them with a common project (which may do great things for the marriage) and elevates their job stature.

6. GHOST WRITERS: Lee Iacocca did not write those two best-sellers by himself. Iacocca is the author (it is his material), but he is not the writer. He does not have time to write. If you do not have the time or inclination to write, but you do have material recorded in articles, on tape, collected in files, etc., you can hire a ghostwriter to put it all on paper. See *Is There a Book Inside You?* at http://ParaPublishing.com for details.

7. **REPUBLISHING ARTICLES:** Many author-publishers have gone the easy route by simply editing the material of others after they had researched a subject they were interested in and found that many fine experts had already written about it. The collection of these articles, one per chapter, can form a book called an anthology. To pursue this course, contact each author for permission to use his or her material, send a copy of the article and ask each to update it with any new information or changed views. This makes your chapter better than the original article. If the chapter must be shortened, ask the author to do it. This is faster and easier than doing it yourself and then negotiating your changes with the author.

If, for example, you are deeply involved in the sport of skydiving, you might contact the national association and its magazine about gathering articles on skydiving that have appeared over the years and republishing them in a series of booklets. Booklet number one might consist of all the best articles on student training. Your primary market would be the members of the association. You would sell them through the organization's store and via mail order. Thus, the association is providing both the material and the customers. As an editor, you simply repackage the information.

8. **OUT-OF-PRINT BOOKS:** Sometimes you can find good books that large publishers have let go out of print. Normally, the copyright has reverted to the author. These authors are usually thrilled to have a new publisher put their books back into print. See the R. R. Bowker directory called *Books Out of Print* available at your library.

> Bill Kaysing discovered an out-of-copyright book called *Thermal Springs of the World*. He abstracted just the data on hot springs in the western U.S., added some original comments and reprinted it as *Great Hot Springs of the West*. Review copies sent to several major magazines resulted in an entire column of flattering coverage in *Sunset*. Some 3,000 copies were sold in a little over a year.

9. **TRANSLATIONS:** These offer another source of material and are a royalty consideration. Look for foreign language or English language titles at U.S. and overseas book fairs that you can acquire, have translated and then publish. If the book is already in British English, all you have to do is convert to

"American Style" English and U.S. conventions. Contact publishers in other countries that specialize in books that interest you. See *International Literary Market Place* and the PMA Foreign Rights Virtual Book Fair Web site at http://pma-online.org.

A good translator is a highly skilled artist whose writing does not read like a word-for-word translation. He or she will spend hours searching for the single right word or phrase to convey the original meaning. Translators must be bilingual, English (the destination language) must be their first language and they must be good writers. To find translators, see the American Translators Association Web site at http://www.atanet.org.

The English language rights to foreign language books are rarely expensive, so this is another interesting source of material.

NEGOTIATING AND CONTRACTING WITH AUTHORS

The object of an author-publisher contract is to clarify thinking and positions by laying out all the details on the table and arriving at a mutually beneficial agreement. There will never be a second book if one side takes unfair advantage of the other; it pays to keep the future in mind. Small publishers should not offer less than the industry norm unless they will be satisfied with just one book per author, and there is no need to offer more.

Each contract will be somewhat different, but you can start with a standard one. For sample contracts with explanations, see *Publishing Agreements* by Charles Clark. For sample contracts ready to load into your computer, see Para Publishing's *Publishing Contracts* on disk in Appendix 2 under Para Publishing Special Reports and our Web site at http://ParaPublishing.com. It is easier to edit form-contracts than to create them from scratch.

First-time authors will be eager to become published and may not be terribly concerned about the contract initially. Many creative people are not business- or commercially-oriented. It is imperative that contract negotiation and signing be taken care of first to avoid misunderstanding later. Print out the contract and ask the author whether it is generally acceptable. If he or she has made any other commitments, such as for some subsidiary rights, this information must be added to the contract. Include a work schedule and a clause allowing you to cancel if he or she fails to meet deadlines; always keep the pressure on writers to perform. (See *Is There a Book Inside You?* at http://Para Publishing.com.)

Unless you have a narrow field of interest or the writer has very strong feelings about a particular aspect of the contract, you want a contract that includes all possible rights and territories. Once you have published the basic book, you want to entertain the possibilities of translations into other languages. Then there are book club adoptions, film rights, magazine excerpts, newspaper serializations and mass-market paperback rights. You will also want to sell through bookstores, other types of stores, through the mail, to associations, over the Internet, etc. Your promotion will rub off on all areas, so take advantage of it by taking control of the complete project. Remember that people who write contracts slant them their way. Take control. Use *Publishing Contracts on Disk* (at http://ParaPublishing.com) to provide your own contract.

Many first-time authors are not concerned about the advance or royalties; they seek the notoriety. They get smarter on their second book and look for the money.

ADVANCES, ROYALTIES AND FEES

ADVANCES (money paid "in advance" by the publisher) depend on the proposed retail selling price, projected print run and sales potential of the book. The advance seals the deal, which is an important legal consideration and puts pressure on both the author and the publisher to perform. The advance makes the author feel accepted and has great psychological value; it does not have to be large to work as an incentive.

Advances generally range from $100 to $5,000, and small publishers often keep them low as that is all they can afford. A good rule of thumb is to offer an advance equal to the projected first-year royalties (the author's share of the book's proceeds). One way to create an incentive, or at least make the author feel morally obligated, is to make progress payments. One-third can be paid on signing the contract, one-third when the writer submits the first draft and one-third when he or she completes the proofreading.

Advances are paid against royalties, that is, potential royalty payments are first deducted from any advances issued to the author before royalties are actually paid out. Advance payments are not in addition to the royalty percentage. Ordinarily, advances are nonrefundable; the author keeps them even if he or she fails to deliver the manuscript or the book is never published. This is another good reason for publishers to protect the investment with progress payments.

Advances work both ways. Authors demand high advances from publishers in order to commit the publisher to push the book. The publisher, with a lot already invested in a book, has to bring it to market quickly and promote it well. The advance is the publisher's gamble.

FLAT FEES OR ROYALTIES: Should contributors get a percentage of the book or be paid a flat fee? Obviously, flat fees are simpler, and they are occasionally cheaper (you avoid extensive accounting). An illustrator creating a major portion of the book should get royalties, whereas someone doing basic research, keyboarding or contributing a drawing should be paid a set fee. Everyone must understand clearly what is in it for him or her. If you require a few drawings, go to a graphic artist to have them drawn to order. Then pay the bill and be done with it. The artist deserves no more a piece of the action than the person who painted your car before you sold it. One exception is a children's book, where the illustrations are considered to be equally as important as the text.

THE ROYALTY FORMULA traditionally has been to pay the author 10% of the *list* (cover) price for each *hardcover* book sold through regular channels, such as book wholesalers, bookstores and to libraries. Remember that after discounting the book to dealers, this 10% royalty will amount to 15% to 20% of the "wholesale" selling price. Graduated royalties for the *hardcover* edition might be 10% of the list price on the first 5,000 books sold, 12.5% on the next 5,000 and 15% on sales over 10,000. Often *softcover* authors command 7% for the first 12,000 sold and 9% above that number.

In the late 1980s, most publishers changed their terms by offering authors 6% to 10% of the *net* on books. They amended their contracts with some generous-sounding wording such as "We will pay you 6% of the net receipts." The challenge is that many of the books are sold at varying wholesale discounts of 50% or more, so authors receive half of what they used to receive.

Further, the accounting required is a heavy burden, and this is another expense to be considered. A percentage of the list price is preferable to both author and publisher because it is much easier to calculate.

Royalties for college texts range from 10% to 18%, and those for heavily illustrated elementary and secondary school texts run from 4% to 10%. Royalties for children's books range between 10% and 15%, to be split between the author and illustrator. Mass-market paperback publishers usually pay 4% to 7.5%, but they print in much greater quantities. So potentially high sales make up for the lower discounts.

Most contracts call for the author and publisher to split the subsidiary rights (films, book clubs, etc.) 50/50. Many of the big publishers barely break even on the book itself and hope to make their money on the subsidiary rights.

Before going on to Chapter 3, turn to Appendix 1, "Your Book's Calendar." You might also like to skim Chapter 12. Before you start, it is nice to know where you are going. For more information on publishing choices and self-evaluated quizzes to help you make a decision, see *Is There a Book Inside You?* at http://ParaPublishing.com.

My hobby is writing. Fortunately, I have found a way to turn my avocation into my vocation.

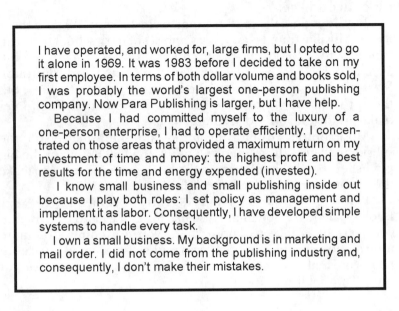

I have operated, and worked for, large firms, but I opted to go it alone in 1969. It was 1983 before I decided to take on my first employee. In terms of both dollar volume and books sold, I was probably the world's largest one-person publishing company. Now Para Publishing is larger, but I have help.

Because I had committed myself to the luxury of a one-person enterprise, I had to operate efficiently. I concentrated on those areas that provided a maximum return on my investment of time and money: the highest profit and best results for the time and energy expended (invested).

I know small business and small publishing inside out because I play both roles: I set policy as management and implement it as labor. Consequently, I have developed simple systems to handle every task.

I own a small business. My background is in marketing and mail order. I did not come from the publishing industry and, consequently, I don't make their mistakes.

If the big publishers are doing so well, why do they require authors to send return postage with their manuscripts?

3
Starting Your Own
Publishing Company

Forming your own publishing company is not difficult, and many of the requirements can be postponed until you are ready to send your manuscript off to the printer. But you do need a system and must get into the habit of using it. Publishing your book is, after all, a business.

Writing a book is a creative act. Selling a book is a business. A finished book is a product.

Having a business is just good business. Tax laws favor businesses because they can deduct goods and services that the wage earner must pay for with after-tax dollars. If you don't have a business, you don't get to deduct very much.

Gross ——▸Taxes ——▸Net
Job

Gross ——▸ Expenditures ——▸Net ——▸Taxes
Business

If you own a business, a lot of what you are already buying becomes deductible because it is part of maintaining your business (car washes, membership dues, magazine subscriptions, travel, taking people out to dinner, the business portion of your home, etc.). Your own business will improve your lifestyle.

My take-home pay won't take me home anymore.

BUSINESS STRUCTURES

There are three forms of business: **sole proprietorship, partnership** and **corporation,** and each has advantages and disadvantages. You do not have to make the choice right now. If you do not file for corporation status, you will be operating as a sole proprietorship anyway. All you have to do is say, "I am a business," and file a Schedule C (Profit or Loss from Business) with your tax return. Schedule C is where you list your deductions.

Here are a few things to keep in mind while you are focusing on your most important concern: *your manuscript.*

•◆ As a **sole proprietor,** what the business earns is yours to keep; what the business borrows is money you owe. The business is you. In a book publishing sole proprietorship, you have the choice of keeping your financial records on a modified *cash basis* or an *accrual basis.* The cash system is easier to understand, allows you to defer more income and requires less bookkeeping, which makes more sense for a small business. You can always switch to accrual when you grow larger; however, you must get IRS permission to make the change. And once you use the accrual system, you cannot switch back to cash. Most accounting software programs such as QuickBooks operate only in the accrual system.

•◆ Many business consultants discourage the formation of **partnerships** because their success rate is not much better than that of marriages—for a lot of the same reasons. It is a rare pair who complement each other well enough to divide the work so that both are happy. If two or more people want to form a company, they should consider a corporation.

•◆ In a **corporation,** you are an employee of the corporation, not the company itself. This means more accounting, payroll deposits, taxes, paperwork, annual meetings with published minutes, corporate taxes and possible annual registration fees. Incorporation may lend an air of permanence, but it can also be expensive to form, and saddle you with unwanted paperwork, meetings and legal bills.

Incorporation limits liability. Although the corporation can be sued, the individual stockholders, employees and officers are normally protected. However, the attorney for the plaintiff will name both the publishing company and the author as defendants, so incorporation may not protect all of those with interests in the book.

There is a recently popular business structure that also limits your liability—a **Limited Liability Company (LLC).** This may be less expensive to form, less complex to manage and offer better tax aspects than a corporation, yet provide many of the same benefits.

There is also a corporate structure called a **Sub-S Corporation (S-Corp)** that allows corporate income and deductions to pass directly to the individual shareholders who then pay only their individual taxes rather than also being taxed at the corporate level.

All these business structures offer benefits and drawbacks and should be discussed with your lawyer and accountant.

WHERE TO LOOK FOR HELP

The Small Business Administration (SBA) provides a toll-free answer desk at 800-827-5722 to provide information on free counseling, prebusiness workshops and many other SBA services. The national office is in Washington, D.C., and can be reached at 202-205-6665. You may find your local office more helpful, however. Look for its number in the U.S. Government section of the white pages of your telephone directory under Small Business Administration. Its Web site is also helpful: http://www.sba.gov. They have numerous educational, business development and loan guarantee programs.

SCORE (Service Corps of Retired Executives) is the Small Business Administration's volunteer network of experienced men and women whom you can call or email to counsel you. There is no charge for this service except for occasional out-of-pocket traveling expenses. There are several hundred SCORE chapters around the country. Call the SBA office nearest you to see if there is a local SCORE chapter. Look in the U.S. Government section of the white pages under Small Business Administration. Tell them what you need, and they will find someone tailored to you and your business. Naturally, it is always best to get this advice before you get into trouble; do it sooner, not later. SCORE's Web site is http://www.score.org.

PUBLICATIONS: *Publishers Weekly* magazine will teach you about the publishing trade, provide many stimulating ideas and generate enthusiasm. Purchase a copy of *Literary Market Place*; it is *the* resource of the book industry. Due to its price, I used to recommend using a library copy whenever it was needed, but it has become too important for just occasional use. You can also subscribe to it online at the LMP Web site, http://www. literarymarketplace.com. Some areas of the site are free. Get accounting and business books, such as Bernard Kamoroff's *Small Time Operator* (see Para Publishing Books & Reports: *The Business of Publishing* in Appendix 2). Also get *Working Solo* by Terri Lonier, http://www.WorkingSolo.com. Writing references, such as dictionaries, thesauri and writing style and usage manuals, can be purchased inexpensively in used book stores.

SETTING UP YOUR BUSINESS

YOUR COMPANY NAME will have to be selected before you go to press, so keep thinking about it. You could name it after yourself, such as Fran Halpern Enterprises or Bud Gardner Publishing Company, but these choices do not make your company look as "big" as if you used a fictitious name. The use of the word "enterprises" is often the sign of a rank beginner and may give the impression that you don't know yet what your company is going to do. If the business succeeds and one day you decide to sell out, the name will be sold with it. After all, what is the value of Bud Gardner Publishing without Bud Gardner? A good name will have more value. For instance, toward the end of the 20th century, any company name with a dot com in it got a lot more attention and a lot more value. A year later, that changed. Looking big may be important when applying for credit from your vendors (suppliers) or asking a paper mill for samples. A fictitious company name will create the impression that you have a going business.

Starting your company name with an A will place your company high in alphabetic listings. Peggy Glenn changed her PiGi Publishing to Aames-Allen to ensure top billing in directories.

Non-English names can pose cataloging problems. Would you list La Cumbre Publishing under L or C? If people do not know where to catalog you or where to look for you, you may not be found, and you could lose business.

Geographical names can be limiting. Which makes you sound larger, East Weedpatch Press or North American Publishing? Which company would you rather run? What happens if you move to West Weedpatch?

To find a new name, one that isn't being used in the publishing industry, go to the library and look through *Books in Print, International Directory of Little Magazines and Small Presses, Literary Market Place,* and your local telephone directory. Also, *The Publishers Directory* from the Gale Group offers an exhaustive list of existing publishing companies. Then ask the reference librarian for more directories. This search is fun, and you will find that the newer publishing companies have some pretty interesting names. As a new, small outfit, it does not hurt to have a handle that attracts attention. You might also consider a name that specifies the type of books you publish.

Pick a name that isn't being used by anyone else. If you select a name that has already been taken (or is even close), you will receive some of their mail, some of their returns and calls from confused customers. No name is worth that hassle.

After you select a name for your new publishing company, you will probably be required to file it as a fictitious business name with your city or county and run a notice in a local newspaper. This Doing-Business-As (DBA) notice is your way of letting the public know that you and the publishing company are the same person.

YOUR LOGO is a graphic image, an easily recognizable symbol; it may consist of a drawing or just the company name in a distinctive style of type. If you can dream up something clever and easily recognizable, start putting it on all your letterhead, labels, business cards and brochures. If you look carefully at the Para Publishing logo on the following page, you will see a parachute canopy.

▚▚▚ *Para Publishing*

YOUR PLACE OF BUSINESS will be your residence for a while. Initially, you will not need a lot of space to write, store or ship books. When you have several titles, need more space and have employees, you may need to move out. But for now, home has many advantages. Working in your home (your house, apartment, mobile home, camper, etc.) can save on gasoline, clothes, additional rent, utilities and the headaches of a second property. And, as we will discuss later in this chapter, you can write off part of the household rent, mortgage and expenses on your tax return. Working at home requires some organization and discipline, but for many it is very comfortable working in an atmosphere with less stress.

Almost 40 million people in the U.S. work out of 35 million households; they can measure their commute with a yardstick. According to the *Wall Street Journal*, many states are now realizing that home-based businesses are more stable than large companies.

Before you begin sorting, shipping and selling books in your living room, quietly check the zoning ordinances. Local regulations may allow only certain types of business to be run from your home. Your business will be small at first, and as long as you don't have employees and large trucks aren't pulling into the drive every few minutes, no one is likely to complain. Avoid walk-in traffic and refer to yourself as an "author" or "writer" rather than a "publisher," and you shouldn't encounter any difficulty.

Working from your home should not be confused with an "office" in the home. The IRS has cracked down on offices that are *in addition* to one's place of business outside the home. If you use 50% of your home for your business activities and do not have another office, you may deduct 50% of most of the house expenses, for example, mortgage or rent payments, electricity, gas, water, insurance and cleaning. If you use more of the home for business, you may deduct proportionately more.

If you are worried that a visiting vendor or client might not be favorably impressed with your home setup, make a lunch appointment in a restaurant. Actually, the visitor will probably envy you. Working out of your home is more comfortable, more efficient, cheaper and safer—you don't have to commute at night.

I never said starting your own publishing company would be easy. I just said it would be worth it.

PO BOX OR STREET ADDRESS: There are many good arguments for each. Some people feel quite strongly that a street address is more effective in a mail order ad or sales brochure because the location reflects more substance and stability. But today, even the big firms are using boxes. This is probably the result of the high incidence of urban crime. There was a time when the mail was sacred and no crook would dare to touch it, but not anymore.

If you rent a box from a private company such as Mail Boxes Etc., you must write "PMB" (Private Mail Box) in the address. Make sure the private box company is stable. If it goes out of business or loses its lease, you will have to change a lot of stationery and you will lose a lot of mail order business. Incidentally, you may not call a your private mail box a "suite" in Pennsylvania. In 1991, Attorney General Ernest D. Preate Jr. said it is misleading to call a 5" x 3" cubbyhole an "office" or "suite."

Depending on your address, ("1234 Northwest Whispering Valley Parkway, Suite 1701" vs. "Box 3") could cost you more in classified ads where you are charged by the word.

You will have to go to the post office or private mail box company regularly to ship books, so you might as well pick up your mail there. Box mail is available earlier in the day than home-delivered mail. Another advantage of a box is that you can maintain the same address even if you move a few blocks. Perhaps the most important reason to maintain a box is to keep your excited, loyal readers from dropping in at all hours to meet their author.

Apply for a box now, and consider getting a large one. In some areas, boxes are in short supply, and there is quite a waiting list. It may take you months to get one. Write your name, your company name and the title of your book on the box registration card, so you will get your mail from the post office no matter how it is addressed. Remember, all your stationery and business references need an address, so get a box soon.

The greatest challenge to a self-publisher is managing the day-to-day excitement.

STATIONERY AND DESK SUPPLIES: You will not need much letterhead stationery, since 99% of your outside contact will be by email and telephone. Use your computer and laser printer to lay out letterhead and print out several sheets on 20# bond (copier) paper.

Window envelopes save time, because you only have to type the name and address once. Also order business cards and a rubber stamp or labels with your company name and address. Shipping labels and supplies are covered in Chapter 10.

Your mail order clients rarely meet you; they only see your written materials. Put your best face forward. Make your cards and letters look good.

TELEPHONE: You will need more telephone lines. Fortunately, telephone service is becoming less expensive. Retain your present line for the family and get a new one for your company. Get a third line for your fax and modem. When business picks up, get a fourth line just for outgoing calls so you will not block incoming orders.

Do not fool with fax/phone switches or call waiting. Without dedicated lines, you will not appear to be running a real business.

YOUR COMPUTER is your most important piece of machinery; spend the money and get a good one. You are a wordsmith now and require the best and fastest word processing equipment you can afford.

Your computer will speed up your writing, and it can be used for correspondence, mailing list maintenance, typesetting, order entry and bookkeeping. In fact, you will save enough on typesetting just one or two books to pay for the whole system. See Document 621, *Computers for Publishers*, at http://Para Publishing.com.

LICENSES AND TAXES

The legal requirements of operating a business are covered in many parts of this book, just as you will encounter them in every facet of your daily publishing life. The following is what you need to run your business, but remember that most of this can be postponed until you are ready to go to press, move out of the house or hire employees. These tips, of course, are food for thought, not a substitute for legal counsel or accounting help.

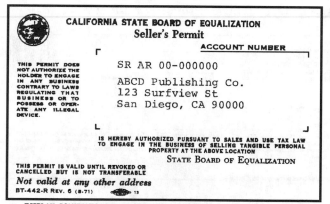

THE CITY OF SAN DIEGO
MUNICIPAL BUSINESS LICENSE

PURSUANT TO CITY ORDINANCE AND CONDITIONED UPON PAYMENT OF THE
REQUIRED FEE OR TAX AT THE TIME OR TIMES DUE. LICENSE IS HEREBY
GRANTED FOR THE TERM AND PURPOSE STATED. PENALTY FOR DELINQUENT
PAYMENT IS 10%. THIS LICENSE VALID ONLY AT THE LOCATION SHOWN.
IT MAY BE TRANSFERRED TO ANOTHER LOCATION AFTER REQUEST IS MADE
TO THE CITY TREASURER'S OFFICE. THIS LICENSE IS **NOT** TRANSFERABLE
TO ANY NEW OWNER WHO MAY ACQUIRE BUSINESS LICENSED.

ISSUED BY:

CITY TREASURER

SEP-6'77

ABCD Publishing Co
123 Surfview Street
San Diego, CA 90000

BUSINESS LOCATION
123 Surfview Street

ZIP CODE / ROOM NO. / BUSINESS TYPE
90000 / sole proprietor

POST IN CONSPICUOUS PLACE AT LOCATION LICENSED

LICENSE NO.	DATE ISSUED	EXPIRATION DATE	CODES	A/T	ASSESSMENT FEE	LICENSE FEE	TOTAL FEE OR TAX
4							

Business License

CALIFORNIA STATE BOARD OF EQUALIZATION
Seller's Permit

ACCOUNT NUMBER

THIS PERMIT DOES
NOT AUTHORIZE THE
HOLDER TO ENGAGE
IN ANY BUSINESS
CONTRARY TO LAWS
REGULATING THAT
BUSINESS OR TO
POSSESS OR OPER-
ATE ANY ILLEGAL
DEVICE.

SR AR 00-000000

ABCD Publishing Co.
123 Surfview St
San Diego, CA 90000

IS HEREBY AUTHORIZED PURSUANT TO SALES AND USE TAX LAW
TO ENGAGE IN THE BUSINESS OF SELLING TANGIBLE PERSONAL
PROPERTY AT THE ABOVE LOCATION
STATE BOARD OF EQUALIZATION

THIS PERMIT IS VALID UNTIL REVOKED OR
CANCELLED BUT IS NOT TRANSFERABLE
Not valid at any other address
BT-442-R REV. 6 (8-71) ⬤ 13

DISPLAY CONSPICUOUSLY AT THE PLACE OF BUSINESS FOR WHICH ISSUED

Resale Permit

Interview a friend or acquaintance who has recently set up a small business in your community. He or she will be happy to tell you what happened to them and whom you must deal with on city, county, state and federal levels. In some areas, you must register your business with local authorities, but not in all. Do not volunteer. Most registrations come with a fee or tax.

As a sole proprietorship, your business will not need a separate bank account, and until you hire employees, you will avoid Employer Identification Numbers (EIN) and special accounts.

We do not charge sales tax here, we just collect it for the state.

SALES TAX: Most states have a sales tax. If your state does, you are required to collect it only on those books sold and shipped to end-users at destinations within the state. The sales tax is collected only once at the retail level from the ultimate purchaser. It is not collected from dealers such as bookstores or wholesalers within your state who will in turn "resell" the book to an end-user. (Instead, the reseller will collect the sales tax from the end-user purchaser.)

As a commercial firm, you must either collect the sales tax from a sale within your state, show by the shipping address on the invoice that the goods are going out of state, or claim to be selling the books to another dealer in your state, "for resale." Many states require you to maintain a file of customer resale numbers. Some dealers list their resale number on purchase orders, but usually you have to send a standard resale number request card with the invoice. Type "for resale" on the invoice.

```
FIRM NAME _____

I HEREBY CERTIFY,                                       0  72782 41128   2
That I hold valid seller's permit No. _____
issued pursuant to the Sales and Use Tax Law; that I am engaged in the business of selling


that the tangible personal property described herein which I shall purchase from:


will be resold by me in the form of tangible personal property; PROVIDED, however, that in the event any of such property is used for
any purpose other than retention, demonstration, or display while holding it for sale in the regular course of business, it is
understood that I am required by the Sales and Use Tax Law to report and pay for the tax, measured by the purchase price of such
property.

Description of property to be purchased: _____


Dated: _____ 19 _____     Signature _____

at _____     By and Title _____

Phone _____     Address _____
      AVERY FORM NO. 25-098              AVERY                    PRINTED IN USA
```

California resale number request card

In some states, shipping supplies, such as cartons and tape, are not subject to the sales tax. Be careful what taxes you pay. Other states exempt certain nonprofit or public institutions, such as libraries and schools, from paying sales tax. Be careful what you collect.

Before you go to press, obtain your resale permit. Then if your books are printed in your state, you won't have to pay sales tax when you pay the printing bill. Many of the larger book printers require a copy of your resale permit no matter what state you live in, because they have sales offices in numerous states.

Find the retailers' sales tax office in the telephone directory. In California, it is called the State Board of Equalization; in Massachusetts, it is the Sales and Use Tax Bureau of the Department of Corporations and Taxation. Check the posted resale permit at a nearby store; the name of the controlling agency will be on it.

When you apply for your sales tax license or resale permit, tell them you are just starting out as an author and hope to sell a few of your books. Tell them that most sales will be wholesale to bookstores or shipped out of state. This way you may be able to avoid giving the tax agency a deposit, and you may be allowed to report sales tax collections annually instead of quarterly, thus saving both money and paperwork. For example, in California, if you say the taxes you might collect on sales (retail and within the state) might amount to more than $300 per month, you must place at least $100 on deposit with the Board of Equalization before you start. If you say you might be collecting over $12.50 per month in sales taxes, they will want you to fill out the forms and remit the taxes quarterly instead of annually. As your business grows and you collect more sales taxes, the taxing authorities will require you to report more often. When you apply, the tax office will supply you with an explanatory sheet detailing your responsibilities for sales tax collection in your state.

THE LAWS YOU MUST KNOW

As an author-publisher your legal concerns are copyright, defamation (libel), right of privacy, illegal reproduction and negligence.

> ●◆ **Copyright** works both ways: It protects your work from others and their work from you. Take pride, do your own original work and make your book better than the others. For a detailed explanation of the copyright, see Chapters 2 and 5.

●◆ **Defamation** is "libel" in the printed word and "slander" when spoken. *Black's Law Dictionary* defines defamation as "the offense of injuring a person's character, fame or reputation by false and malicious statements." Libel may take the form of either words or pictures. The offense is in the "publication" of the matter, so you are not excused just because you read it somewhere else first. You are safe if the statement is true; this is the perfect defense, but check the source. The best advice is never to say anything nasty about anyone. You will need all the support you can get to sell your book. If you disagree with another authority, leave his or her name out and write, "Some people will argue…" or "Many authorities believe…," and then tear up their position with your view. If you don't like someone, the worst thing you can do to them is to leave them out of your book altogether. Cover yourself and stay out of court; the legal game is expensive.

●◆ **Right of privacy** is another area of law you may face. Unless a person is part of a news event, they have a right to keep their photo out of publications. Most people love to see their photo in a book and in fact are prime customers for the finished product, but if you suspect there may be a problem, have them sign a written release.

●◆ **Illegal reproduction** covers the promoting of lotteries, financial schemes, fraudulent activities, printing of securities, reproducing postage stamps, etc. In other words, don't print money. If you are writing about these subjects, you probably already know about the challenges and the postal and other laws relating to them. If not, seek legal advice.

●◆ **Negligence.** A reader could sue you, claiming your book misled them, to their great damage.

> Warner Books recalled 115,000 copies of *First Love* when Dr. Ruth Westheimer and Dr. Nathan Kravetz mixed up the "safe" days for the rhythm method of birth control. Suits have been brought against the publishers of a diet book and a cookbook, but so far the courts have sided with the publishers.

In most cases, the courts have not found books to be "products," so publishers are not strictly liable for their content. It must be proven that the publisher knew or should have known of the inaccuracies. Books are not the reader's only source of information.

See Document 636, *Insurance for Publishers*, at http:// ParaPub lishing.com.

Today, many books contain **disclaimers** warning readers not to exclusively rely on the text. See the disclaimer in the front of this book and paraphrase it.

RECORDS AND PAYING TAXES

TAXES are one place an author-publisher gets a big break. Not only are the costs of printing your book deductible, so are all the direct expenses incurred while writing, producing and promoting it. If you are writing about your favorite hobby, you may deduct the expenses of pursuing that too. For example, if you are writing on aviation, you can probably deduct flying lessons and trips to the national convention since you are also conducting research as you pursue your avocation. With detailed records, the IRS will have a hard time declaring your business a "hobby."

Then there are publicity and sales tours, and if your office is in your home, you can even write off a portion of your rent or mortgage, utilities, cleaning, etc.

Assuming you are already employed and Uncle Sam is withholding 30% or more from your weekly cheque, that amounts to thousands of dollars a year. The game is to see how much you can get back. How much did you pay to the IRS last year? Would you like to get a full refund? Getting money back is fun and rewarding. Of course, if your book is a great success, you will make more money and have to pay taxes on it. For complete details, get a copy of publication 334, *Tax Guide for Small Business*, from your nearest IRS office or from your Enrolled Agent or other tax professional. See "What You May Deduct" below for possible deductions.

"Profit" is not a dirty word.

RECORD KEEPING must be done from the beginning of your writing, because it is difficult to justify deductions you have not recorded. In starting a new business, many people are so involved with their great idea and the process of pursuing it, that at year-end they find they have not kept good records (or any at all). The best thing to do from the beginning is to write cheques for or charge every possible deductible expense and keep receipts, so that you have a paper trail.

Open a separate business chequing account (the bank will require that you have filed a fictitious business name statement). Select one charge card to use exclusively for business, using only that card for authoring and publishing expenses. Always record the category of expense on the cheque and in your chequebook register or on your charge card slip (for example, office supplies, rent, printing, advertising, etc.). That way, at year-end you have already done most of the work, leaving you with simple entries into the computer or creating columns for the categories you've selected. Then, all you have to do is record and add. This makes tax time a breeze.

Be sure to report all your income. If you're audited, the IRS will probably ask about all your bank deposits. If $50,000 went through your bank account yet you reported only $35,000 in income, you'll have some explaining to do. If the extra cash flow is from gifts or loans, be prepared to prove this.

No one takes better care of your money than you do.
—Cliff Leonard, *License to Steal*

While most business failures are due to poor marketing and pricing decisions, some occur because of poor record keeping. If you don't know your costs, you won't know the prices you must charge to make money. If you don't know you are spending more for something than you should, you won't realize that changes in operations, procedures or suppliers should be made. You also need past information about income and expenses to serve as a guide to future projections and business planning.

Start right now by ordering an accounting program. For example, Quicken has invoicing, accounts payable and general ledger. This is all you need to start. QuickBooks has these features plus inventory and accounts receivable; it is a full accounting program. These and other programs are listed under Order-Entry Software in Appendix 2.

You can't prove the deduction if you don't record it.

WHAT YOU MAY DEDUCT: Label the columns in the expense ledger as follows: meals (ME), travel (TR, with sub-headings if you like for lodging—TL, airfares—TA and other incidentals—TI), car expenses (CE, with sub-heading recommended for car lease—CL, gas—CG, repairs and maintenance—CR and car insurance—CI), office supplies (OS), equipment (EQ, which you also need to itemize individually to depreciate or take an "expense deduction" on your return), equipment repairs (ER), shipping and postage (SP), advertising and marketing (AD), cost of goods sold (GS, with sub-categories for cost of printing—GP and other such costs which can be written off only as the books are sold), dues and licenses (DL), subscriptions and books (SB), telephone (TL), refunds and allowances (RE) and office supplies (OS). Minimize use of the category called "miscellaneous," since the IRS likes to inquire about such expenditures. If there are other categories or expenses you regularly incur, add those to your list.

The best way to get into the habit and to learn what is deductible is to list EVERY cent you spend the first year. Get receipts whenever possible: at the post office, for parking, tolls, meals, motels, etc.

You have already decided to carry pen and paper at all times to record your thoughts for your manuscript, so carry one more sheet for recording expenditures. Any money spent in the pursuit of income is deductible, so write down every cent. As you learn what is deductible, you will find that you become generous where an expenditure can be written off and stingy where it can't. This is good discipline and good business.

Keep an envelope in the car. Each day, as you get in and start the car, let the engine warm up a moment as you record the date, odometer reading and places you intend to go. Use the envelope to hold the receipts you acquire during the day. Start a new envelope every month.

At the end of each month, use your accounting program to post the petty cash expenses from your pocket notes and car envelope.

At the end of the year, total up the columns and take the printout with totaled figures to your accountant. The accountant will do the rest, and the charge will be reasonable. You will be amazed at the size of your refund, and the accountant will compliment you on your work. Record keeping is so easy, and yet many people think there is some great mystery to accounting.

You don't even have to make money to claim deductions. You can claim a loss for at least three years in a row before the IRS questions whether you are a hobbyist rather than an author-publisher. Chrysler lost money for years and still took deductions. Keep good records, and you will be able to prove you are in business.

High cash flow often means taking in lots of money but being unable to find much of it.

FINANCING YOUR BUSINESS

Raising the money you need to pay for the production and promotion of your book will take you into the world of finance, unless you have a lot of loose, ready cash lying about. Insufficient capitalization is one of the greatest challenges facing most new businesses. Money won't come looking for you. You have to find it by selling yourself and your book. But the money is there; it is available.

According to the *Wall Street Journal*, most entrepreneurs spend their own money to start their business. Roughly 48% rely on savings, 29% borrow from banks, 13% shake down their friends, 4% look for individual investors, less than 1% strike deals with venture capital firms or government agencies and 5% are successful with other sources.

Do not expect the large national book printers to be interested in postponing the printing bill. They are printers, not publishers.

FINANCIAL PARTNERS: Do not take in partners on your book. Partners are rarely "silent." They want to know why the book is not selling better, why it is not in the airport bookstore, why you are spending money to attend a book fair, etc. You will spend more time explaining the publishing business to your partner(s) than you will spend promoting the book. If you go to family and friends for financing, they may simply loan you the money rather than requiring you to establish a formal investment structure, which can be expensive.

Only two people make money on a book: the printer and the investor.

SELF FINANCING: In the beginning, you won't run up bills by hiring help or renting space, and you will even save some leisure time money by staying home to write, so you will not have any immediate needs for large sums of cash. Many people have more money than they need for necessities and throw away their disposable income on frivolous purchases. As you will need to find time to work on your book, the elimination of some movies, dining out, amusement parks and extended trips will give you new blocks of time for writing that you thought you didn't have and gain you lots of money in the process.

Some people advise the use of OPM (other people's money) rather than your own. Then if your business goes bust and you lose all the borrowed funds, you still have your own money in reserve. But as you tuck your prized manuscript under your arm and venture off, you are going to find that locating OPM takes some searching.

> Bernard Kamoroff found seven friends to participate in the first and second printings of his *Small Time Operator*. He reasoned: Why be selfish; why not let your friends share in the project? His best-selling accounting book has been through more than 20 revised printings in the past 25 years.

THE SMALL BUSINESS ADMINISTRATION used to prohibit financial assistance to book publishers, bookstores, movie theaters, news operations, filmmakers and other "opinion molders." This was to avoid financing radicals who might promote seditious activities and then file for bankruptcy, which would then leave the taxpayers with a social problem and the bill for starting it. The "opinion molder" rule was overturned in mid-1994. Contact your local SBA (in the U.S. Government section of the white pages under "Small Business Administration") or visit the national Web site at http://www.sba.gov. They have numerous educational and loan guarantee programs available.

BANKS don't seek loan applicants in the start-up publishing industry. They like successful firms with upbeat balance sheets; like everyone else, they are in business to stay in business. Banks look on manuscripts and books as speculative. Even armed with a detailed market research report on your product, you may find that you can't even get an appointment with the loan officer. A stack of books is not considered good collateral to a bank; if you defaulted, they would not know how to turn the books back into money to pay the debt. If you ask for money to go into the publishing business, the bank probably won't be interested.

You know you have arrived when you don't have to check the balance before writing a cheque.

Basically, there are two ways to borrow money from a bank. The first is the term loan, which is normally used to finance purchases such as a car. Term loans are paid back monthly and are usually limited to 36 months. The second is an ordinary signature loan with interest at the prime rate plus about 5%. A signature loan runs for a period of months and you pay it off at the due date. But although the loan is written for a stated period, it is common to pay just the interest and renew it. Many authors have been successful in acquiring money by leaving the manuscript at home and asking for a vacation loan instead.

You may need collateral, perhaps a second mortgage. If you have enough real and personal property, you will be able to get the money on your signature alone. Don't think small; large amounts are often easier to borrow. An SBA loan guarantee can substitute for some of your collateral requirements.

All banks are not the same; shop around not only for loans, but for chequing account charges. Banks are not doing you any favors; you are doing them a favor by storing your money with them and paying interest on the loan. Stop by several banks and pick up pamphlets on their chequing account and loan policies. Take the brochures home—compare them. Do they charge for each cheque deposited? You will be receiving a lot of small cheques, and any cheque charges will add up fast. Do they pay interest on personal or business chequing accounts, and if so, what is the minimum required balance? Will they let you bank by mail, and will they pay the postage? Don't just think of your present needs; think of the future.

Do not pay interest rates comparable to credit card interest. Shop for mortgage-level rates.

Incidentally, you may be better off working at your new publishing company part time initially. Then if it fails, at least you are not out of a job too.

CHANGING YOUR W-4 FORM by decreasing the amount of your income tax "withholding"is advocated by some people as a way to have the IRS lend your withholding back to you. If you have a regular job, and a lot of money is being withheld from each paycheck, you can claim a zero exemption from withholding by making out a new W-4 form with your employer early in the year. If you are in the 30% tax bracket, this is like getting a 50% raise. Of course, you must be serious about starting your business, keep good records and take full deductions. Done correctly, you should be able to spend and deduct as a business expense the formerly withheld money and zero out at tax time. Once you are working for yourself full time, you will file estimated tax forms rather than W-4s.

PREPUBLICATION SPECIALS are often used to raise money. As the book goes to press, send out a brochure to all who might be interested in the book and offer to pay the postage for a prepublication order and/or autograph the copies, (but never offer to discount a brand new book). Emphasize that the manuscript is complete and that the book is on the press. Tell them you won't cash their cheque until the book is shipped. Mention a shipping date, but give yourself an extra month or two. Make another special offer to dealers. Prepublication sales sometimes bring in enough money to pay the printing bill.

> Alan Gadney and Carolyn Porter made far more in advance than just their printing costs. They started promoting their first book, a unique reference directory, a year before it was printed. They offered free shipping on advance orders, periodically notified all purchasers of the book's progress, and by the time it came off the press, they had collected over $10,000 in advance orders. And nobody ever asked for their check back...they all wanted the book hot-off-the-press.

GRANTS are available from many foundations for worthwhile publishing projects. Check your state arts agency, the National Endowment for the Arts at http://arts.gov/guide, and see the listings in *Grants and Awards Available to American Writers*, edited by John Morrone. Additional listings may be found in *Literary Market Place*. There are several magazines for fund raisers. Ask your reference librarian. Make a search for *grants and awards* on the Web. Many large cities and educational institutions have grant centers (such as the Grantmanship Center in Los Angeles and The Foundation Center in New York and elsewhere), all stocked with excellent information.

Most grants and fellowships are for fiction and poetry. If your book qualifies, it can mean a large amount of money, but there will be a lot of paperwork to go along with it. If your book project deals with a special subject, you might look for grants available in your subject area, rather than general writing grants open to all. You might also bundle your book with related product(s) and apply for a grant covering both.

WRITERS' COLONIES often supply free room and board to support budding authors. Some have rigid rules limiting the length and number of stays. For a list, see *Writer's Market*, *Writer's Digest*, and *The Writer* magazine.

FAMILY AND FRIENDS will often lend on a book. They have faith in you and want to see your name on a book as much as you do. But if you do borrow from friends or relatives, make the same presentation to them that you would to a bank. Talk figures and do not get emotional. Then write a loan contract and pay them the 10% to 15% interest that you would pay the bank. Put the loan on a business basis and keep the friendship, or things may get testy when you attend the annual family gathering.

> *Fortune assists the bold.*
> **—Virgil (70-19 B.C.E.), Roman poet**

OTHER POSSIBILITIES include credit unions, retirement plans, the Veterans Administration (if appropriate) and the Farm Home Loan Association, which is said to be very liberal in its definition of a "farm community."

See Document 626, *Raising Money to Publish Books,* at http://ParaPublishing.com. All these suggestions for funding assume you have a good salable book to begin with.

HOW MUCH DOES IT COST TO PUBLISH?

That is like asking how much a car costs. All books are different. If you are planning to print 3,000 copies of a 192-page, 5.5" x 8.5" softcover book with a few photographs, black ink on white paper with a four-color cover, the printing will cost less than $2 per book, so your printing bill will run around $6,000. Then there is typesetting ($1,100-$1,300), book cover design ($1,800 for softcover, a hardcover dust jacket will be more because of the larger size), other prepress expenses and trucking from the printer. Printing a hardcover book of the same dimensions with a dust jacket might cost about $3 each.

After the book is printed, it has to be promoted with book reviews, news releases, flyer mailings, co-op marketing and some direct-mail advertising. Money will not be coming in right away. There is a lot of lead-time for writing, printing and promotion, and bookstores are notorious for paying slowly. For a book like the one described here, you should budget about $15,000 to get started (cover and page production, printing and initial marketing and promotion). If you print 500 according to the new book model, you should budget about $10,000 for production, printing and initial marketing. (See Chapter 11.)

A book with fewer photos, fewer pages and a one-color cover could run much less, but without a good-looking book and some promotion money, the book is not likely sell. For details, see Chapters 6 and 7 on pricing and promotion.

On your first venture, the printer will probably want payment in installments: one-third to start, one-third when the plates are made and one-third on the completion of the printing. After a book or two, they will no doubt give you normal 30-day terms and want their money a month after they deliver the books to you. If they want installments, agree, but request a 2% discount for cash (2% of $6,000 is $120).

LEAN AND MEAN: Run a streamlined, efficient operation. Do everything yourself and buy only those services you cannot perform. Avoid employees initially; they cost you time (management), money and paperwork. Print in small quantities to keep the inventory low. Once you have learned the business by doing every part of it yourself, farm out the repetitive and least enjoyable tasks. When contracting for services, remember that although most businesses are ethical, everyone is in business for himself or herself first; you come second. Some of the subcontractors you hire may try to sell you more than you need. They don't care about your business as much as you do, because they have less to lose. Be careful taking advice from someone who is trying to sell you something. If this is your first business, check out the Working Solo Inc. Web site: http://www.workingsolo.com.

Keep on top of costs. If you can save $1,000 per year by streamlining procedures and your net profit is normally 3%, the effect is the same as if you increased sales by $30,000.

Don't waste anything. For example, save the stamps from the incoming mail. Stamp collecting is big business, and years from now you may be able to sell them to stamp companies. Check the Yellow Pages and call several local stamp dealers for prices. Recycle your shipping supplies, sell used printer cartridges to re-fillers (you can get $10 or more for some models), reuse scrap paper and cardboard, and price-shop the Web.

MACHINERY: As your publishing company grows, look for labor-saving machinery to multiply your efforts. Personal computers, photocopy machines, color printers, cordless telephones and package scales will save you time. They are much better buys than an employee, and you will find that with depreciation, machines are not very expensive. As machinery accumulates, you will begin to understand the advantages of owning your own business.

See Document 624, *How to Set Up & Run a Successful Book Publishing Business*, at http://ParaPublishing.com.

Do you get more done on the weekends? Then quit your job and become a writer/publisher and every day will be a weekend.

4
Producing Your Book

Designing Books
Typesetting
Layout
Book Printing Materials
The Printing Process

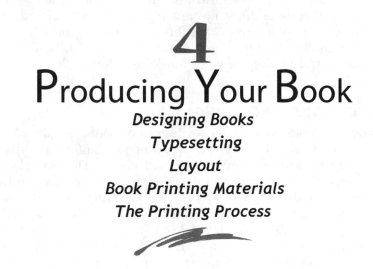

Now we'll go into what you can expect when your book enters the production stage. This explanation of the design, typesetting, layout, materials and the printing process is meant to be brief and yet provide you with enough information to turn your words into an attractive product. Also see *Writing Nonfiction* (on prepress: composition, layout, editing and design) and *Buying Book Printing* the Appendix or at http://ParaPub lishing.com.

Book production is entering its third evolutionary change in modern times. The first was the migration from hot lead type to offset printing in the late 1960s. The second was computer typesetting in the late 1980s. Both saved a great deal of money and both speeded the process. The computer also gave the author more control over the output.

In the early part of the third millennium, the new publishing model is the "electronic book" that the Web makes possible. Since producing an electronic book involves much more than typesetting, layout and reproduction, more coverage will be found in Chapter 11. In addition to the production of the *eBook*, we will discuss *ePromotion* and *eCommerce*.

Books as we know them will be around a long time, so the chapter you are reading is not just historical padding. You will still have your book printed, but the electronic edition will be in addition to the "dead tree" version, not instead of it. Besides, to understand new ways, we need the knowledge of the old as a foundation.

INFORMATION PACKAGING

Do not think of yourself as a book author or book publisher. You are an *information provider*. People want your information but may not have the time or desire to read a book. They will gladly pay more to get the same information presented in a form convenient to them. That's why you see the exact same information sold as a $20 book, a $60 audio series, a $100 noncredit course, a $150 video set, a $200/year newsletter, a $200/hour consultation or a $500 seminar. Each client learns best in different ways. Some need to read, some prefer to listen, some require a classroom setting and so on.

The information in each edition is the same; only the format is different. You will provide your core information in any form your customer wants and needs. Wring maximum value out of your information. Let's start with books.

This book will concern itself with square-backed softcover and hardcover books, those you normally see in a bookstore. If you have a book-length manuscript, one that will fill a book of 100 pages or more, it will sell best as a clean, sharp, professional-appearing product. You want a book you can be proud of, and you want it to be acceptable to the stores and the customer.

PRODUCTION AND PRINTING TIME

For a 100-page book, the typesetting and layout should take less than a week if you do it yourself on a computer, and about three to five weeks (depending on the complexity of the book's design) if you give the work to a typesetter. Copyediting may take a week and proofreading will take a few days.

> *Proofread. It is less expensive to put ink on paper than to take it off.*

You can figure on about five weeks to print, bind and deliver softcover books to you (slightly longer for hardcover books, because of the binding process), but the work may take longer if your printer can't do all the work in-house and has to farm some of it out. For example, many book printers have to send books out for hard bindings, or duplicating a CD and affixing it to the inside cover. Subcontracting can add a couple of weeks to the schedule. Softcover reprints usually take about three weeks. Trucking may take two to six days depending on the destination. Overseas color printing and shipping to the U.S. can take up to 10 weeks.

BOOK DESIGN

Go to a bookstore to search for a book you can use as a *model*. Look for books in your subject area. If you can't find a book in your subject area that you like, try other subject areas that would appeal to your intended audience.

You will find that most books in each category have their own look and feel. Give your customers what they want, expect and deserve. If this is a business book, it should be in hardcover with a dust jacket; if it is a professional reference book for doctors, lawyers or accountants, it should be in hardcover without a dust jacket; if it is a children's book, it should be oversize, in four-color, hardcover and have a dust jacket.

Consider paper, binding, layout, everything. Buy that book design you liked and place it above your desk; it is your model. You will use it as a guide for typesetting, layout, printing and binding.

A book should not be just something to read, it should be something to possess.

—Lee Collins

Book printers can produce an acceptable book, but that book design will be boring unless you provide some direction. What usually happens is that the author-publisher spends a great deal of time on the text, and the manufacturing becomes an afterthought. The package design is left up to the printer. What we see today are many 5.5" x 8.5" softcover books that look the same. Printers can supply foldout pages, gold foil on the cover, die-cut jackets, embossed covers and many other things. All you have to do is ask, so find a book you like and use it as a model. Do not just leave book design to the printer.

BOOK DESIGNERS will plan, typeset and lay out your book and cover if you do not have the time, desire or skill. Since they use computerized equipment, they do not charge much. For a list of book designers, see Book Designers & Cover Artists Appendix 2.

BOOK FORMAT

Note that the first chapter of a book ordinarily begins on a right-hand page, and subsequent chapters usually start on a right-hand page. If this leaves you with a blank on the left, fill the space with a photograph, chart or quotation. Never leave a blank page; fill it with something, even if it is just a page number. Buyers sometimes return books with blank pages (thinking there is a manufacturing defect).

Type can be set to *run around* illustrations, but it is simpler and cheaper to make a break in the text and insert the photo or drawing full width, from margin to margin. The width of the text in this book is 4.108 inches, and most illustrations run margin to margin.

RUNNING HEADS are lines of type that appear across the top of the book page. Usually the title of the book appears on the left-hand page, and the chapter title is on the right.

FOLIOS are page numbers. Folios may be placed in the top outside corner, bottom middle or even on the side of the page. The folio is usually part of the running head. Traditionally, pages received Roman numerals in the front matter and Arabic numbers in the text, because the text was set separately, and then the front matter was expanded or contracted to use up left over pages in the printing signatures. Today, many publishers take a tip from the magazine companies and start the count (though not the printed numbering) from the initial page. This makes the final page count higher and makes the reader feel he or she is getting more for their money, and the same goes for the publisher. The argument goes, "I paid [the printer] for those pages, so I'm going to count them." See this book, for example.

STANDARDIZE AND SAVE MONEY: If you move away from the norm, your creativity may cost you sales. Occasionally, variations can be justified and the book will still be successful. For example, the following photograph is of a die-cut, circular book on Frisbee play that comes nestled and shrink-wrapped in a custom 119 Frisbee disk. The unusual design feature contributed to the sales of the book. Remember, too, that libraries and bookstores have standardized shelving. You want your book to fit. Most short-run books are 5.5" x 8.5", perfect bound (glued spine) paperbacks, with or without photos and drawings, on a 50- or 60-pound paper stock. The cover is four-color on a 10-point C1S (coated one side) cover stock. Beyond this basic specification, a number of variations are possible.

If all publishers thought alike, all books might look alike

TRIM SIZE: There are many standard book page trim sizes, and you want to give your customer what they expect. If it is a cookbook or computer book that is usually in a wide format so it will open and lie flat, you must provide the same.

The conventional 5.5" x 8.5" size is suitable for both hard-cover and softcover. It is one of the most economical, fits a library shelf well and is by far the most popular. A book with 144 pages (5.5" x 8.5") has a much nicer feel than 77 pages (8.5" x 11"). The only good reason to go oversize is if you have too much material or if your subject area demands a larger size (children's, art, and coffee-table books). If you have a few large illustrations such as charts, consider foldout pages. The printer can insert them between signatures; specify where you want the foldouts.

Some digital and web presses will not yield a full measurement. Instead of 5.5" x 8.5", the finished trim will be 5.375" x 8.375". If you require a full trim size, specify it in your Request For Quotation (RFQ).

Whatever size you select, make all your books measure the same to standardize your shipping bags and cartons. Even though some books are 5.5" x 8.5" and others are 8.5" x 11", they will still stack well together. If some are 6" x 9", you will have packaging challenges.

NUMBER OF PAGES: You need 8 pages to qualify for the U.S. Postal Service's Media Mail (book rate), 50 to get a Library of Congress catalog card number, 50 for a listing in R. R. Bowker's *Books in Print*, and 50 pages to qualify for a listing in H. W. Wilson's *Cumulative Book Index*. Over 100 is psychologically good and will help to justify your price, so if you have just 90 pages, set the book in larger type, widen the margins, put more leading (space) between the lines, expand the appendix or add some illustrations.

Your book will be printed on several very large sheets of paper that will be folded down into *signatures*. (Originally, the person who sewed the pages together *signed* their work.) The number of book pages in each signature will depend on the size of your printer's press. The sheet-fed press usually works in multiples of 32; 16 pages are printed on the top side of the sheet (16 up) and 16 are put on the underside. Web presses usually work in multiples of 48.

To visualize a signature, take a sheet of paper and fold it in half four times. The folding results in 16 panels on each side of the sheet (16 up and 16 down), for a grand total of 32 pages in the signature.

You will save money using the faster web press with 48-page signatures. Aim for 144 to 288 total interior pages to be economical. A book of just 96 pages (2 x 48) will not command the price you want. A book of 720 pages (15 x 48) will be very expensive to produce because of the cost of paper.

Aim for even signatures or even signatures with a single half signature of 24. The last signature will be shot twice and run side by side, but the press will be stopped at half the count.

In order to finally "page out" your book, you will need to select a printer and know if the book will be printed on a press using 32- or 48-page signatures or some other page combination. You can, then, construct your final page count in full-, half-, and quarter-signatures (groups of 32, 16 and 8 pages or groups of 48, 24 and 12 pages.)

Include all pages in your total count and move any left over blank pages elsewhere in the book so they do not gang together at the end. Leaving blank pages at the back is bad book design. Instead move them to the front matter, or fill them with a chart or illustration, turn them into section dividers or "note pages." You can also expand or condense the back matter and index to compensate for a couple too many or too few extra pages.

If you want your book to sell like a book, it has to look like a book.

TYPESETTING can be done with your word processing program and laser printer.

LAYOUT can be done with your word processing program, or it can be automated somewhat by pouring the file into a page layout program such as Microsoft Publisher, PageMaker, InDesign, QuarkXpress or Ventura Publisher.

The file can be sent to the printer as camera-ready hard copy, electronically on disk or as an attachment to an email file. Hard copy is produced with your 600 dpi or better laser printer. The electronic version will be in PostScript or Adobe Acrobat PDF format.

MANUSCRIPT FORMAT: Many authors like to write their books in book layout format rather than with double-spaced Courier typeface like a traditional manuscript. The advantages to a book format are the text looks like a book, you always know approximately how many pages you have, and the book is nearly typeset.

To make your manuscript look like a book page, set your margins so that the text block will be about 4.2" wide and about 7" tall.

To set your margins in Microsoft Word, click on *File\Page Setup* and change *top* to 1.8", *bottom* to 2.3", *left* to 2.5", *right* to 1.9" and *header* to 1.3".

To make a header with the book title and page number at the top of the page, click on *View\Header and Footer*. Type in the tentative title for your book, then click on the *insert page number* icon, which is in the header and footer box. Underline both your header and your page number. Then set them in Helvetica or Arial, bold, 12-point type.

For your text, select a nice type font such as Bookman or New Century Schoolbook. Click on *Format\Paragraph* and set the line spacing for *Single*.

With your manuscript laid out as it will look in the book, you will know how many pages you have. Now you can adjust the margins, type size and leading and add or subtract resources in the appendix to achieve the desired number of pages. You have control and your design will be economical.

TYPE FONTS: Here are some examples of various type fonts, (that is, typefaces and their various styles, such as regular, bold, italic) their characteristics and how they can radically change the inside look of your book.

BOOKMAN Regular	Univers Regular
BOOKMAN Italic	*Univers* Italic
BOOKMAN Bold	Univers Bold
BOOKMAN Bold Italic	*Univers* Bold Italic

A *type style* can be regular, italic, bold or bold italic

TYPE FONTS are many and varied. Your word processing or page layout program will have a selection. Pick a *serif* type font such as Bookman or New Century Schoolbook for the body copy and a *sans serif* font such as Arial for headlines. Serif type fonts have little "feet" on the vertical parts and are easier to read than sans serif fonts.

Arial

Four type factors affect legibility: *font type* such as serif or sans serif, *type size* (make it large enough), *leading* (rhymes with "heading" and is the space between the lines), and the *column width* (the human eye has been trained to read narrow newspaper columns).

Garamond

To give your book some type style variation, you can use *italics,* **boldface,** ***bold italic,*** SMALL CAPS and larger sizes for chapter heads, captions, subheads and for lending emphasis.

Times New Roman

Here are some more type terms to make you sound as though you know what you are talking about: *Point size* is the height of a capital letter (and its mount), as in 10-point type. There are 72 points to the inch. A *pica* is the printer s standard measurement for the length of a line and the depth of a page. There are 12 points to a pica and six picas to the inch. Therefore, 24 picas means a 4"-wide column. *Leading* or *slug* is the space between the lines. Printers used to use a strip of lead, hence the name. If you have nine points of type plus two points of leading, the specification would be written out as 9/11.

Bookman

Nine on eleven leading is about as small as you should go
for a legible book. Ten on twelve is very common, though
children and older people with failing eyesight prefer 12
on 14. Most page layout programs will set your leading
automatically at single space unless you specify what you
want.

New Century Schoolbook

Some type fonts, such as Goudy, are condensed. They allow you to
get more words on a page. On the other hand, if you want to fill up
more pages, use an expanded font such as Bookman. (See above.)

Goudy

Some computer programs put more type on a page than
others, using the identical type font, size, spacing and
leading. It all depends on how the machine is
programmed. Try to use the same machine for revisions.

AvantGarde

Do not venture too far from the common type
fonts, such as Times Roman, Palatino,
Baskerville, Caldonia, Bookman and New
Century Schoolbook.

Courier

Read the above and compare the various type fonts.

---

6 Arial

8 Arial

10 Arial

12 Arial

14 Arial

16 Arial

18 Arial

20 Arial

22 Arial

24 Arial

Character heights are measured in points.
There are 72 points to the inch.

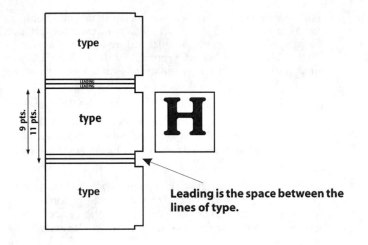

Leading is the space between the lines of type.

HEADLINES, such as chapter titles, are usually set in larger type, often in a sans serif typeface.

ILLUSTRATIONS will augment the text, enhance the appearance of the book and foster the salability of your words. Don't be cheap with illustrations. Each one is very inexpensive when the cost is spread out over the entire print run of the book. If a photo or drawing will make the book more attractive, readable or useful to the buyer, include it. Also consider charts, graphs, tables and sample forms to make your book as user-friendly as possible.

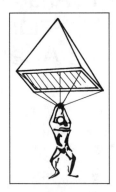

Line Drawing

Extra lines were crowded into this line drawing to give it the appearance of shading.

LINE ART may consist of type, charts or sketches. Drawings may be created on your computer or drawn separately and scanned in.

Art can be taken from old magazines and books. If the copyright has expired, the art is in the public domain and may be used by anyone.

HALFTONES must be made of any artwork, such as a photograph, which is not solid black and white as in the illustrations on the previous page, but instead has "grey scale" (shades of grey), as seen below. To make a halftone, the original photo is rephotographed through a screen. The resulting print is composed of minute dots, and the eye blends the dots together into a continuous tone. Making a halftone of a photo, pencil drawing, watercolor, etc., costs $8 to $15 each. The cost is very little per book manufactured.

Photo printed unscreened

Same photo screened. Study with a magnifying glass or loupe to see the dots.

Screens come in several values and are measured in dots per linear inch (dpi). The more dots, the crisper the printed halftone. Newspapers commonly use a 65- or 85-line screen (85 dots per inch), and books are commonly printed with 120-, 133- or even 150-line screens. Black-and-white photographs screen best. Color prints reproduced in black and white tend to become muddy.

Photos taken from other magazines and books have already been screened. Reshooting or rescreening usually makes them muddier, or they will pick up moiré patterns that look like wallpaper.

With both photos and drawings, reductions are preferable to enlargements. Reductions become sharper, but enlargements only magnify flaws, losing clarity. Start with larger photographs. Reduce and scan them into your manuscript so you can size and crop them to fit.

Use a digital camera and import the 300 dpi image into your manuscript. Images can be imported into the word processing file or linked. If linked, it will be easier to extract the photo for making adjustments such as to the light/dark level. The printer will screen the photo when going to film or plate. Using digital photo files will make the whole process faster, easier and cheaper.

You can't tell—but you can sell—a book by its cover.
—Wall Street Journal

COLOR PRINTING

Four-color printing should be used on covers but is normally too expensive for inside pages. To reproduce a color photo or slide, it is rephotographed (or laser scanned) four times, each time with a different colored filter over the lens. This produces four negatives consisting of the three primary colors (red, blue and yellow) plus black. The result is called a four-color separation negative (sep-neg). Then the paper is run through the press four times, each time with one of the colors, and the color photo is recreated. Naturally, four-color printing is more expensive because of the additional camera work and press time.

Transparencies usually produce the best covers. If you are taking photographs for the cover and have a choice, use slide film, not color print film.

With very few exceptions, covers today must be four-color. We live in a four-color world. Our magazines, television and newspapers are in color. Buyers for both chain and independent bookstores are looking for books with good package design that will inspire a purchase. Everyone buys a book by its cover. The ultimate purchaser reads the outside cover, but they do not read the inside prior to purchase. Sales reps take only covers (books are too heavy) when they visit the bookstores and book-chain buyers. Even the wholesalers only want to see the covers.

Some publishers have found considerable savings on color processes outside the U.S. They have color separations made in Singapore, printing done in Hong Kong, etc. If you have a lot of inside color work for a children's book or coffee table book, get prices from the Far East (Hong Kong, Korea, Japan, and Singapore) and Italy, where color printing prices can be half those found in the U.S. For more information on foreign printing, see *Buying Book Printing* in Para Publishing Special Reports in Appendix 2 or at http://ParaPublishing.com.

Anyone who says you can't judge a book by its cover has never met the buyer from Barnes & Noble.
                          —Terri Lonier, *Working Solo*

PRINTING MATERIALS

PAPER is even more confusing than type fonts, and although you should know what to look for, you will need the guidance of your printer to make a final choice. Book printers stock 6 to 10 types of paper. They can provide these papers at a good price because they purchase them in huge quantities. If you want a paper they do not stock, they have to make a special small order and the cost will be considerably higher.

Basically, you have four general paper choices:

- **Newsprint:** inexpensive, but it looks cheap, it yellows quickly and the photo reproduction is poor.
- **Uncoated book stock:** looks good, photos OK. Most common.
- **Coated book stock** (matte or gloss): looks great, photos great, more expensive.
- **Fancy textured papers:** may be hard to print, especially photos. Expensive.

Unless you are doing an art book, an uncoated book stock is what you need. Your printer will probably suggest a 50-pound or 60-pound "white offset book."

Paper comes by the sheet (for the sheet-fed press) or the roll (cut into sheets after printing on the web press). You must consider many criteria when selecting paper:

- **Weight** is expressed in pounds per 500 sheets, but the measurements of the sheet vary according to the category to which the paper belongs. Sixty-pound cover stock and 60-pound book papers are not the same. For example: 16-lb. bond office paper = 40-lb. Book paper;

D DELTA LITHOGRAPH COMPANY

TEXT PAPER COMPARATIVE COST FINDER

Many of our customers are interested in cost comparisons of the various weights and shades of text papers. The reasons for this are varied; weight savings, bulking, shade preferences and others. The cost trade-offs involved are often significant in reaching a decision. This Text Paper Comparative Cost Finder will help in these decisions.

The use of this chart is very easy. Using 50# Delta White offset book rolled stock as the base, or 100%, compare the other shades and stocking to calculate the comparative prices.

For example, if you have an estimate based on 10,000 copies of a book printed on 60# White sheets and want to calculate the approximate savings if printed on 50# White rolls, compare the 50# rolls listed below to the 60# sheets, or 100 vs. 130. Paper savings on the job would be 30%.

Text paper costs run between 28% and 50% of the total printing costs, depending on total pages in the book and the quantity of books produced. Therefore, in the example given, the overall cost savings would probably be about 15% (50% of 30%).

These figures cannot be used to calculate exact figures. They are only intended to give you a guide in figuring the comparative costs and specifications for your book.

STOCK	AVAILABLE IN	COMPARABLE PERCENT
50# Delta	Rolls	100
50# Delta	Sheets	112
60# Delta	Rolls	115
60# Delta	Sheets	130
45# Delta	Rolls	92
45# Delta	Sheets	105
70# Delta	Sheets	185
30# Omega Book	Rolls	78
35# Alpha Workbook	Rolls	65
50# Theta Natural Text	Rolls	115
50# Theta Natural Text	Sheets	130
50# Litecoat Beta Book	Rolls	110
60# Pica Matte	Sheets	215
60# Kappa Coated Book	Sheets	195

Delta is the difference

Paper comparison chart
(#= weight in pounds)

20-lb. bond (common photocopy paper) = 50-lb. book; 24-lb. bond = 60 lb. book; and 28-lb. bond = 70-lb. book. Cover stock is rated in point sizes, with 10 point (10/1000" thick—similar to the thickness of a business card) being very common. Although 12-point cover stock will provide a slightly more substantial cover. Dust jackets for hardbound books are usually 80- or 100-pound gloss enamel.

Most books are printed on 50-, 55- or 60-pound stock. Generally, heavier paper is more expensive, although some of the newer lightweight papers (developed to combat postal rates) are even higher in price. If the paper is too thin, the book will look and feel cheap; if it is too heavy, the pages may be too stiff as you turn them. In either case, you have wasted your money. In the metric system used by overseas printers, the weighing technique is easier; paper is simply weighed in grams per square meter (gsm) of paper. There are no categories.

Texture: Some highly textured porous paper does not accept ink well; it diffuses into the paper. This spreading of the ink lowers the quality of halftones. Use a smooth paper such as 50-lb. white offset book.

Color or shade: Most informational books are printed on white stock. However, if you want a warm feel to your book, you might consider an off-white stock (called cream, antique or natural). Some of these are higher bulk and will add thickness to your book.

Opacity: You don't want the type on the other side of the page to show through. Lightweight paper can be very opaque, especially when coated. You can test opacity by placing a printed sheet under the sample sheet to see how much type shows through.

Bulking factor is expressed in pages per inch (ppi). A 45-pound paper may have a bulking factor of 640 pages per inch, while a 55-pound higher-bulk stock might be 370 ppi, and a firm 60-pound stock might bulk at 444 ppi. Thus, heavier weight does not always mean thicker paper. Bulking depends on the fiber content of the paper and the milling process used. Whipping air into the paper during manufacture, which produces a thicker paper without increasing weight, can also produce a high bulk. However, this fluffed-up paper allows ink to diffuse more, so halftones are not as crisp. PPI is measured by the even inch. Once you know the bulking factor of the paper you plan to use, you can calculate the width of the spine for your finished cover.

FORMULA FOR DETERMINING SPINE WIDTHS

To determine the spine width, you must know the final page count and the pages per inch (PPI), or thickness, of the text stock being used. Paper is a fluctuating commodity constantly changing. PPIs used are averages for house brands currently used.

The formula for figuring your spine width is as follows:
Divide the page count by the PPI, and then add .03 (1/32 of an inch) to allow for the cover stock and the glue and air between the signatures.
Example: 176 (page count) ÷ 400 (PPI) = .44 + .03 = .47

You can use a ruler that measures in 100ths or use a ruler that measures in fractions and use a "Decimal Equivalents of Fractions Chart," which will convert the decimal reading from your calculator to fractions.

DECIMAL EQUIVALENTS OF FRACTIONS

1/32	.03125	17/32	.53125
1/6	.0625	9/16	.5625
3/32	.09375	19/32	.59375
1/8	**.125**	**5/8**	**.625**
5/32	.15625	21/32	.65625
3/16	.1875	11/16	.6875
7/32	.21875	23/32	.71875
1/4	**.25**	**3/4**	**.75**
9/32	.28125	25/32	.78125
5/16	.3125	13/16	.8125
11/32	.34375	27/32	.84375
3/8	**.375**	**7/8**	**.875**
13/32	.40625	29/32	.90625
7/16	.4375	15/13	.9375
15/32	.46875	31/32	.96875
1/2	**.5**	**1**	**1.0**

Courtesy of Central Plains Book Manufacturing

Spine width calculator

❖ Grain in paper is similar to the grain in wood—it has a direction. Grain affects the way the text and cover lie. If the grain of the text is not parallel to the spine, the book will want to snap shut. Grain is also important if you plan to fold the paper for a foldout page, since it will fold better in one direction than another. Printing presses are grain specific. The press used for 5.5" x 8.5" books cannot be used for 8.5" x 11" books because the grain will run the wrong way.

If the cover grain is perpendicular to the spine, the cover will tend to curl or pop open. Sometimes the cover will even crack on the folds. The challenge is that some automated book machinery trims the books cleaner when the grain is perpendicular to the spine than when it is parallel. When the grain is parallel, the trimmer may make small tears in the cover stock where it curves around the spine of the book. With such machinery, the choice is between cover curl and cover tear. See the discussion of cover coatings and lay-flat film later in this chapter.

❖ Grade refers to type of paper, be it writing grade, book, cover stock, envelope, gummed, blotting, chipboard, etc.

❖ Coating is done with a clay-like material and produces a smooth, shiny finish. On clay-coated stock, the ink dries on the clay surface, rather than down in the fibers of the paper, so the printed pages look crisper and cleaner. Coated stock, while more expensive, makes halftones look much better. It is essential for art books. Smooth finishes can also be produced by drawing the paper over a blade edge, or through calendering (a heat and pressure roller process). The result will be a duller finish that is easier on the eyes.

❖ Acid-free paper lasts longer and should be used for books of long-term interest. Some printed products, such as newspapers and magazines, are made to be read and discarded. There is no need to save them. Sixty percent of the university presses (which sell primarily to libraries) and 21% of other publishers produce their hardcover books on acid-free paper. You may wish to specify acid-free paper.

●◆ **Recycled paper** is becoming increasingly popular, but the price is still higher than for new paper. The price is expected to drop as more publishers use it. If you want to extend the life of the landfills, specify recycled paper.

PURCHASING PAPER: If you attend one of the many publishing seminars, you will probably be advised to purchase your own paper and "save about 15%." This makes about as much sense as taking your own oil to the gas station when you want it changed. Printers aren't happy about losing their markup and sometimes charge you a handling fee if you bring your own paper. Or they may raise your price later, claiming the job was "hard to print."

If you buy your own paper, you will have to pay for it sooner, will be faced with storage and transportation charges and might lose it all if the printer botches a press run. It is far safer to obtain several quotations on the finished product and let the printer worry about the materials. After all, what you want is the least hassle and best price. Incidentally, printers and paper sales-people continually use the same pressure tactic, claiming there will soon be a paper shortage. Expect it. For more information on paper, see *Pocket Pal* in Appendix 2 under Para Publishing Books & Reports: *Printing*.

INK comes in a lot of colors and types, but both you and your printer will probably want black. If you are doing something special, ask to see the printer's ink color sample books and run some tests. Remember that inks are transparent. If you print a drawing in blue and then overprint part in red, that part will become purple. Similarly, if you print blue ink on yellow paper, the print will be green. Unless you are doing a special art-type book, you should stick to the traditional black ink on white paper. Using more than one color of ink inside your book can increase the printing cost considerably. The different colors have to be separated in the negatives, the job has to be run through the press separately for each color, and there may be additional wash-up (press cleaning) costs.

HARDCOVER OR SOFTCOVER

Traditionally, publishers printed in *hardcover* at a higher price and waited until sales dropped to come out with a cheaper *softcover* version. They might also publish a *library edition* with a supposedly reinforced hard cover or maybe an extra-fancy *deluxe edition* on special paper with gold-stamped leather covers, numbered and autographed. Then there might be a *large-type edition* for both the elderly and visually impaired and, finally, an inexpensive *mass-market paperback* edition. But what has emerged more recently is the very popular *oversize paperback*, also known as quality, trade, large format, large size, special or higher priced paperbacks. These softcover books fill the gap between the mass-market pocket size book and the hardcover version. Today, more and more books are being published in a softcover edition only. Softcover books are printed on the same quality paper as the hardcover version. The differences are that the softcover edition is not normally sewn, has a thinner cover and usually does not have a jacket. Now your choice of covers is narrowed to the hardcover and the softcover.

Catalog copy [is] designed for the people who will sell the book and the flap copy for those who will buy it.

—**Hugh Rawson**

HARDCOVER BOOKS are somewhat more expensive to produce and must carry a higher cover (list) price—libraries used to prefer them. Today, however, libraries know how many times books can be lent out (about 18 for softcover) before they fall apart. If the price difference between the two is too great, it becomes less expensive to purchase copies of the softcover edition and replace them more often.

A few reviewers still do not take softcover books seriously; they do not consider a title to be a real book unless it is published in hardcover. Some also assume a softcover book is not new and that the reviewer just missed the hardcover version.

It is usually less expensive to publish all the books in either hardcover or softcover than to split the run. Hardcover will cost about $1 more per book to print than softcover, and you can usually charge $5 or more for the book. Give your customers what they expect. If this is a business book, they expect hardcover with a jacket. Most people still think hardcover books are fresher, newer and more important. If your major mission is to use your book as a "calling card," an introduction to your consulting, speaking or other work, consider hardcover. Hardcovers do make a nicer presentation than a softcover edition, which can be especially important if you are trying to impress a large corporation to hire you as a high-paid consultant. You will also be prouder of a hardcover book.

COATING SOFTCOVER BOOKS: The covers of softcover books must be coated. Traditionally, this was done with varnish. The cover made another pass through the press filled with varnish instead of ink. Today, ultraviolet-set plastics and plastic laminates are more popular. The extra treatment on the cover protects it against scuffing during shipment and provides a shiny *glossy finish* or wet look. An alternative is the same plastic film with a duller *matte finish*. The slight additional cost is easily justified, because fewer books are returned damaged.

The plastic laminate used to be polyester or polypropylene, which was moisture proof. Since humidity could not enter the plastic-coated side, the cover would curl as the other side expanded. Now there is a *lay-flat laminate* made of nylon film that has very tiny holes for admitting humidity. Always specify lay-flat laminate.

The cover outside should reflect the text inside.

THE BOOK COVER

The cover of your book has two purposes: to protect the contents and to be a selling tool. Book covers sell books. In the U.S., companies spend over $50 billion on product design and packaging. That huge sum is not for the products themselves or for the wrapper but just for the *design* of the wrapper. Good packaging sells soap, breakfast food, computer games—and books. A good spine, front cover and title say, "Pick me up." Good back cover sales copy says, "Buy this book." Unfortunately, most authors put all their effort into the text; the cover becomes an afterthought. Meanwhile, most large publishers slap some type onto a plain background and call it a cover design.

According to the *Wall Street Journal*, the average bookstore browser who picks up a book spends 8 seconds looking at the front cover and 15 seconds reading the back. And this assumes the spine stood out enough to catch their attention, enticing them to pick up the book in the first place. Every word on the outside of your book must be used to sell what is inside. In mass-market (small size, high volume) paperbacks, this hype consists of about 12 words on the front cover and 75 on the back. The blurbs use words like "stunning," "dazzling," "moving" and "tumultuous."

> Alan Gadney commissioned covers for three computer books he planned to write. He had the covers printed in four colors and made into dummy books for display at the ABA Book Fair in Dallas. His books were the talk of the show and he took a number of large orders. Covers must be important—he had not yet written one word on the subject.

FRONT COVER: The front cover should include the title, subtitle (helps to identify the subject), name of the author and a related photograph or drawing with impact. The print shouldn't be so fancy that it is hard to read at a glance. It is said that red attracts and sells best, and many cover designers like to use it. Visit a bookstore and check the section where your book will be shelved. Consider what colors are there and pick something contrasting and bright that will stick out. For an action sport, an eye-catching color photo will sell more books than straight lines of type.

A book cover should stop a browser cold in their tracks at 10 feet and suck them in like a magnet.

The colors must contrast with each other. Your color photographs of the book will be sent to some black-and-white magazines. Darker colors side by side may run together and look muddy when reproduced in black and white. If the intensity of the background is too similar to the intensity of foreground objects, you may also have a problem distinguishing them in black and white.

Your front cover is the "sales poster" for your book. It must be bold, distinctive and intriguing enough to catch the eye and sell; it must stand out from the thousands of books around it. Important new information, such as a quotation from a prestigious book review, can be printed on a cover sticker. Make the sticker a contrasting color, and apply it at an angle so it doesn't look printed on. A gold stick-on medallion with black and white type announcing that the book won an award, has been known to boost sales exponentially.

The design and production of a good softbound book cover will cost about $1,800 for the complete mechanical (front, spine and back) ready for the printer. That may sound like a major portion of your book production budget, but it is worth it, because book packaging is extremely important to the sale of the book. A good cover designer will read through the text to get the feeling into the cover. For a list of book cover designers, see Consultants and Book Designers & Cover Artists in Appendix 2. Also see the Suppliers listing at http://ParaPublishing.com.

SPINE: The spine usually has the title, the name of the author and an eye-catching symbol. If it is a dog book, include the outline of a dog. The symbol may attract the buyer more readily than the printed word. Traditionally, the name of the publisher was included on the spine, but since you are the publisher and no one has heard of your company yet, don't include it. Besides, people buy books by content or author, not by publisher.

Stack the title on the spine (see this book) so that it will be legible on the shelf from a distance. You want your book to stand out.

Beware of too much spine clutter, such as trying to include a lengthy subtitle. Your book will probably end up on the bookstore shelf with only the spine showing. Make the spine an eye-grabber.

BACK COVER layout is covered in Chapter 2. Many back covers have a photo and biographical sketch of the author. If you are a well-known celebrity, put your photograph there; if you are not immediately recognizable, do not waste valuable selling space on an ego trip (put your photo inside on the "About the Author" page instead). Sometimes the back cover is used to promote other books by the author, but this valuable space shouldn't be wasted this way either; mention your other titles inside. Use whatever words that will sell the book in that valuable back cover territory. Make every word count on the front cover, spine and back cover.

COVER OVERRUNS: Ask your printer to send you 200 extra covers (trimmed to proper size), plus the *overrun*, which will come off the print line before they are scored, folded and installed on the texts. These covers are beautiful and look very nice framed. You might like to send a flat cover to those who provided you with a lot of help, such as the cover designer.

Commissioned sales representatives carry covers to the book-stores and wholesalers rather than heavy books, so your book trade distributor and library distributor may each need 20 to 30 covers.

THE BINDING

Binding is your book packaging, the final touch. There are many binding choices; here are the most common types:

Saddle stitched   **Side stitched**   **Perfect-bound**

Plastic comb   **Spiral wire**

- **Perfect binding** is the standard glued-on cover you see on most softcover books. The pages are folded into signa-tures, often of 48 pages each, stacked and roughened on the edge, and then the cover is wrapped around and glued on the spine. The greatest advantage, besides cost, is that perfect binding presents a squared-off spine on which the book title and name of the author can be printed. A text of more than 50 pages is required for a square spine, so you might have to use a high-bulk paper to achieve a sufficient thickness.

- **Lay-flat binding:** If it is important that your perfect-bound book open to lie flat, such as a cookbook or exercise manual, specify Otabind or a similar lay-flat binding. This system leaves the cover stock free of the spine as it goes around to the back of the book, so the book flexes better when opened and will easily lie flat. Multiple scoring is another way to help the perfect-bound book to open and lay flat. Lay-flat binding is much better than comb or spiral binding because the title of the book can be printed on the spine. Another benefit is that narrower gutter (inside) margins are possible with lay-flat, which means you can get more type on a page. Lay-flat, however, is not durable enough for thick books. Get samples from your printer.

•◆ **Cloth binding** (case binding or hard binding) usually consists of *Smyth sewing*, or *side stitching*, individual signatures together. Then they are installed (and glued) between two hard paperboards. Some hardcover books today are manufactured with just an adhesive rather than sewing and hold up quite well. A glue-only hard binding (called *perfect bound case bound*) can also have the glued area of the spine scored with notches (*notch-binding*) so that the glue can run down into the notches for more glue coverage and strength.

•◆ **Wire stitches** are staples and can be used in binding thin paperback booklets. Wire stitches can be *saddle stitched* (the staple is on the fold) or *side stitched* (the staple is driven through from the front to back cover). Saddle stitching will handle 80 pages (20 full sheets) or less, depending on the thickness of the stock, because of the amount of paper lost in wrapping around the spine. On the other hand, side stitching can be used to bind even several hundred pages. Side-stitched books won't open to lie flat, so this method shouldn't be used in manuals. The stitches come from a roll of wire and are adjustable in length. Wire-stitched booklets do not have a spine for printing the title, and they have a low perceived value, so I do not recommend this method.

•◆ **Spiral wire binding** will allow books (such as automotive manuals and cookbooks) to open and lie flat, but spiral looks cheap. Spiral-bound books do not sell well in bookstores because the title doesn't show on the spine, and libraries don't care for them, because the pages are easy to remove. It is possible to spiral bind pages inside a heavy cover stock that wraps over the spiral (called *concealed spiral binding*) so that the spine can be printed. Some computer manuals are bound this way. But spiral still costs more. A better alternative is lay-flat binding (see above).

- **Plastic comb binding** allows the book to open and lie flat and is often used for mail order books directed at professionals, short-run academic texts and industry manuals. This system may be used on books up to 1.5 inches thick. Comb binding is relatively expensive, and the plastic spine can be imprinted, however, it still looks cheap, the pages tear out, and comb-bound books don't stack well, making shipping a chore. Again, a better alternative is lay-flat binding.

- **Velo-Bind** is similar to side wire stitches but uses melted plastic rivets. This method is very strong and can be used to install either special Velo-Bind hardcovers or soft document covers. The books will not lie flat when opened.

- **Notebooks or binders** are sometimes used for very expensive manuals directed toward professionals, especially as a mail-order product. They have the usual advantages of a binder, pages can be removed and added, but the binders are expensive, hard to ship and their pages tear out easily. It is better to choose between hardcover and softcover.

THE PRINTING PROCESS

The printer will photograph your laser output (camera-ready pages) or disk file and the negatives will be stripped into a *flat*. Then a bright light will be used to burn the thin *printing plate* through the flat. Alternatively, the printer may skip the flat and go directly from disk to plate, which can be less expensive.

The stripped-in printing flat

PRINT RUN: An economical number for most first runs is 3,000 copies. Do not print more unless you have presold some of your book, such as to a book club or dealer. Ask for prices on two or three quantities so you will be able to see what a difference in price the various print runs make. Each printer has a unique mix of machinery, so their quotations for various quantities will be quite different.

SELECTING A BOOK PRINTER: Each printer is set up differently. Some specialize in case binding (hardcover) and some in perfect binding (softcover). Some are equipped for very short runs (under 500), short runs (3,000 to 5,000), long runs (100,000), and on up. Any item in your specifications varying from their system will drive up their costs and your quotation. When they have to take a book off the assembly line to shift it to the other side of the factory or send it out to a binder, costs go up.

As a publisher, you don't have to learn printer capabilities and printing equipment. Just send out a Request For Quotation (RFQ), describing your book to the book printers listed in Appendix 2. Then accept the lowest bid. If your next book has similar specifications, you will probably deal with the same printer. Once you establish a relationship with the printer, your costs will probably go down further because you will require less handholding and the printer may extend you complete credit. But also send out RFQs to other printers from time to time to make sure your printer is still giving you a good price.

Beware of "job printers" soliciting book printing. Many printers are looking for new territory and are attracted to books, a big-ticket item. There are some 45 genuine book printers in the U.S. and Canada. These printers print only books, have set up streamlined operations, have specialized equipment, use teams to handle the prepress functions and often run two and three shifts on their equipment. Their quality is consistently good because they don't have to spend time figuring out how to lay up the negatives in the flats so that the pages come out in the right order and right side up. They want to do a good job, and they have to; they can't suddenly decide to switch to printing posters, labels or business cards.

For best quality, lowest price and on-time service, stick with printers who print nothing but books. How can you tell? Just ask what they print. See the list in Appendix 2.

REQUEST FOR QUOTATION: To calculate book production costs, send an RFQ to a number of printers. In the RFQ pictured below, specification examples and hints are in bold.

Request for Quotation

Please quote your best price and delivery in printing and binding the following book:

Identification

Title of book:	*Sex and the Single Publisher*
Author:	**Dan Hunter**

Specifications

Quantity:	**3,000 and 5,000**
Number of pages including front matter:	**144**
Trim size:	**5.5 x 8.5- Full**
Method of printing:	**Web press OK**
Copy:	**Customer to provide PDF file**
Illustrations:	**7 JPG images, no bleeds**
Cover:	**Print sides 1 and 4 only. Customer to supply color composite film and match print**
Paper	
Text:	**60# white offset book. Paper shall be recycled, acid free and neutral pH**

Cover:	10 pt. C1S. Cover stock shall be acid free with lay-flat film lamination
Ink Text:	Black throughout
Cover:	Four colors
Proofs:	Complete bluelines
Binding:	Perfect
Packaging:	Shrink-wrapped in stacks of six. Cartons shall be tightly packed and sealed and shall weigh no more than 40 lbs. each
Terms:	Net 30 days. Credit references available on request
Deadline:	Please quote by _____

Your quote for 3000 $
 Overruns: $
 Reprint of 3,000: $

Your quote for 5,000: $
 Overruns: $
 Reprint of 5,000: $

Price per halftone: $
Delivery charges: $

Discount for prompt payment:
Delivery time:
Other miscellaneous charges:

Remarks:

Signed: _____
For: _____
Date: _____

Quote valid for:

Are there any minor specification changes that will result in a lower price? Please explain.

Any item in this RFQ takes precedence over any industry convention. The disk, flats and all artwork shall be returned to the customer on completion of the job.

Sample Request for Quotation

 Shipping is not very expensive, because trucking companies give special rates for bound books. Your printer may even be willing to drop ship large case-quantities for you directly to major customers, your distributor and fulfillment service.

Simply make up an RFQ like the one pictured, make enough photocopies and mail them to all the printers on the list. Also send the RFQ to a couple of local print shops for comparison. Don't send your RFQ to just a few; the inquiry will not result in enough comparative data. The only way you will know you are getting the best price is if you get quotations from all the printers. Don't worry about their reception of a photocopied RFQ; printers are used to making competitive quotes.

When the RFQs are returned to you, spread them out for comparison and interpretation. Examine any items that you did not request, and add up all the miscellaneous prices. Some printers will have filled out your sheet, but others will have used their own form. Make sure the quotes are "FOB destination," that is, that trucking to you is figured in. You may find that the distant printers quote much lower prices even with the trucking costs.

Don't be concerned about hurting the feelings of your local printers. If their bids are not the lowest, show them the other bids. This is your excuse for not giving them the work. They will be interested in what the competition is quoting and will appreciate your openness.

Asking for estimates for both printing and trucking, levels the quotation playing field. Compare the *delivered* prices.

SHRINK-WRAPPING: Have the printer shrink-wrap your books in stacks of two or more; the cost is about 20¢ per shrink. Shrink-wrapping will protect your book by providing a moisture/dust barrier while preventing scuffing. If you shrink -wrap the books individually, the stores usually will not break the wrap. Then the customer can't look inside, and that usually results in a lost sale. If you wrap the books in larger increments, you may have to break the wrap for small orders, losing the benefits of the protective plastic. The best compromise is twos.

BLUELINE PROOFING: Always insist on blueline (or equiv-alent) proofs prior to printing. This is your last chance to check the printer's work prior to its going on the press. At bluelines you are checking that all pages are straight and in sequential order, photos and graphs are placed and reproduced correctly, and there are no dirt spots or negative scratches on the pages. You should not start extensively revising or rewriting your book at bluelines as the printer will charge you for each page you replace that is not a printer mistake.

GET IT IN WRITING: Get *everything* in writing. You are new to publishing, and what *you* assume may not be the same as what your *printer* assumes. Good faith, trust and friendship are fine until the books arrive. Many printers do not read or retain written documents. Cover yourself. Never rely on oral directions.

Ask for samples and show the printer what you like, what you expect. Get an estimate explaining exactly what each part of the job will cost. Then if you have two more photos than you planned or want to make minor author alterations and have pages reshot, you and the printer will arrive at the same added figure. Submit detailed printing instructions along with your page and cover pre-print materials. Count the books you pick up, and get copies of the receiving slips.

Make sure your RFQ includes a clause that states, "Any item in this RFQ takes precedence over any industry convention." You aren't familiar with the printing industry and aren't interested in how business is normally done. You simply want an attractive book and you want to know what it will cost.

KEEP YOUR ARTWORK: Maintain a file with a couple of clean copies of the book and all your reproduction materials. If you need them again (and you do hope for many happy reprintings), you don't want to have to regenerate lost material.

Put all the artwork, photos, drawings, etc., into a large envelope. You want to be able to find them easily if you contract for a translation or other foreign edition. Keep the disks and negatives of all promotional material, such as brochures and order forms.

The art and disk for the book are the publisher's property. Many job printers will tell you that the large, thin metal printing plates, stripped-in negatives (flats) and even your disk belong to them, because they are the product of the printer's craftsmanship. Printers who argue this point simply want to ensure that you return to them for reprints, whereas in fact the plates are difficult to store and printers usually throw them out.

Fortunately, most book printers do not want to keep your flats and will even charge you for storage if they have not been reused or returned within three years.

WHEN THE BOOKS ARRIVE from the printer, count the cartons. Compare the carton count with the number on the bill of lading. Your cartons should be shipped together to each destination, or if a large quantity, the boxes should be strapped on wooden pallets and covered with plastic sheeting. However, books sometime disappear in transit. Open random cartons and check for damage. If the books were loose in the carton, the top ones will be scuffed. You may also find your extra covers that were inadvertently packed in a book box.

For more information on printing, see Document 603, *Book Printing at the Best Price* and/or Special Report *Book Printing* at http://ParaPublishing.com.

Be accurate with facts. You will be repeated. When you write a book, you are committing history. Steal ideas, steal facts, but do not steal words.

Para Publishing is a unique book business. It does not operate like a big traditional publisher, and it does not lose money. Dan Poynter lays out the following reasons for the success of his company:

- Publish your own material. Do not waste your time on, or split the money with, other authors.

- Perform every publishing and business function yourself. After your first book, farm out those tasks you do not wish to perform.

- Operate as a sole proprietorship, not a corporation, and keep your books on a (modified) cash basis.

- Do not mimic the big traditional New York publishers. Many are not making a sufficient return on their investment. Some of their procedures exist for a good reason, while others are just convention (also known as a rut). The trick is to know the difference.

- If you cannot find a need and fill it, then *create* a need and fill it. Decide on your market before you write the book, and write to that market.

- Market your books like breakfast food, not like a film. This is not one-shot entertainment; go after a market share and keep selling that book year after year.

- You will have to spend more time selling than you will writing. Concentrate on marketing rather than editorial functions.

- Produce valuable information, aimed at a small target audience, and charge a fair price.

- Stay in a single field and produce more information for it.

Write what you love—and love what you write.

5
Announcing Your Book
Telling the World
You Are an Author and a Publisher
Getting Listed

Before you run off to promote your book to potential readers, you should announce it to the book industry and register it with government offices. (Make your book and your company easy to find.) Some of these announcements must be made before you go to press. For a clear understanding of when each of the following should be done, see Appendix 1, "Your Book's Calendar."

As you use this chapter, remember, if the people at some registration offices and directories reject your application, do not give up. Try to figure a way around their objection and file a new form. It is very doubtful they will remember rejecting your initial application.

Since these people may not have a lot of confidence in publishers with a single title (who may never publish again), it is best to represent yourself as being larger. After all, this will not be your only book. Use different names for your company, publisher and author. "Burgett Publishing, Gordon Burgett Publisher and book by Gordon Burgett" is a sure tip-off that you are small and new.

Names and numbers change as people and companies move. For a free, current list of contacts, see Document 112, *Poynter's Secret List,* at http://ParaPublishing.com.

INTERNATIONAL STANDARD BOOK NUMBER (ISBN)

The ISBN is a worldwide identification system that has been in use since the late 1960s. Use a different ISBN for each edition of the work: softcover, hardcover, audiotape, CD, online version, etc. The number's use avoids errors in identifying the products ordered, shipped, invoiced and received. The ISBN makes the books and tapes flow faster and more accurately through the book industry. Many of your dealers will not accept your book without an ISBN.

INTERNATIONAL STANDARD BOOK NUMBER--UNITED STATES AGENCY
International Standard Numbering System for the Information Industry
121 Chanlon Road, New Providence, New Jersey 07974
TEL: 877-310-7333 FAX: 908-665-2895 Email: isbn-san@bowker.com

International Standard ISO 2108

R.R. Bowker, A division of Reed Elsevier Inc.

APPLICATION FOR AN ISBN PUBLISHER PREFIX

FOR AGENCY USE ONLY

SYMBOL: _____

PREFIX: _____

PLEASE PRINT OR TYPE:

Company/Publisher Name: _____

Address: _____

Phone Number: _____ Fax Number: _____

Toll Free Number _____ Telex Number _____

E-MAIL _____ Web Site: _____

Fax-on-Demand: _____ Toll Free Fax: _____

If P.O Box Indicated, Local Street Addre ss is Required:

Company Position _____ Phone Number _____

Name of Rights & and Permissions Contact

Title _____ Phone Number _____

Name of ISBN Coordinator/Contact _____

Title _____ Phone Number _____

Division or Subsidiary of _____

Imprints _____

An ISBN Application

A typical ISBN might be 0-915516-21-7. Here, the initial "0" or a "1" indicates a book originating in an English-speaking country. The "915516" identifies the publisher. The suffix "21" identifies this particular title and edition of the book. The last number, "7," is a check digit, that is, a mathematical function, to make sure the rest of the numbers are correct and that they haven't been miscopied or transposed.

The ISBN is printed on the copyright page of the book and at the bottom of the back cover or jacket, above or below the bar code.

Contact the International Standard Book Number, United States Agency, R.R. Bowker, 121 Chanlon Road, New Providence, NJ 07974, 877-310-7333 ext. 6770 or 888-269-5372 (fax 908-665-3502), and ask for an ISBN application; they will send all the information you need to fill it out. Or you can print the forms off the R.R. Bowker Web site at http://www.bowker.com/standards/ or http://www.isbn.org.

For a fee ISBNs are available in blocks of 10, 100, 1000 and 10,000 numbers. Rush service is also available.

1-56860-800-0	1-56860-825-8
1-56860-801-9	1-56863-425-4
1-56860-802-7	1-56860-827-2
1-56860-803-5	1-56860-828-0
1-56860-804-3	1-56860-829-9
1-56860-805-1	1-56860-830-2
1-56860-806-X	1-56860-831-0
1-56860-807-8	1-56860-832-9
1-56860-808-6	1-56860-833-7
1-56860-809-4	1-56860-834-5
1-56860-810-6	1-56860-835-3
1-56860-811-6	1-56860-836-1
1-56860-812-4	1-56860-837-X
1-56860-813-2	1-56860-838-8
1-56860-814-0	1-56860-839-6
1-56860-815-9	1-56860-840-X
1-56860-816-7	1-56860-841-8
1-56860-817-5	1-56860-841-6
1-56860-818-3	1-56860-842-4
1-56860-819-1	1-56860-843-2
1-56860-820-6	1-56860-845-0
1-56860-821-3	1-56860-846-9
1-56860-822-1	1-56860-847-7
1-56860-823-X	1-56860-848-5
1-56860-824-3	1-56860-849-3

ISBN log sheet

Most beginning publishers will need 10 or 100 numbers. You will need enough numbers for each edition of each book: hardcover, softcover, audio, CD, download, eBook/PDF, eBook/XML-OEB, eBook LIT, etc.

If you ask for 10, your publisher identifier number will be seven digits long and your suffix will be just one digit. If you ask for 1,000, your publisher identifier will be five digits, leaving you with three in the suffix. The ISBN people will mail or email you a logbook sheet with enough room for listing 10 (or more) different book editions.

Once started in the system, you will assign each of your new editions an ISBN suffix from your ISBN log book. You do not have to start at the beginning of the log. The only requirement is that each title, revision and binding has a different number. If you use the first number on the logbook sheet, the "0" at the end will tip off those in the industry that this is a first book. When you fill up the sheet and run out of numbers, buy some more. Because of the expansion of eBook and on-demand publishing, the ISBN Agency plans to increase the number of available ISBNs by adding digits within a few years.

INTERNATIONAL STANDARD SERIAL NUMBER (ISSN)

The ISSN is for *serials*. Publications issued in parts, such as magazines, newspapers, annuals, directories, proceedings and any publication expected to continue indefinitely, are called serials. For an ISSN application (Form 67-60), contact the Library of Congress, National Serials Data Program, Washington, DC 20540; 202-707-6452 (fax 202-707-6333), or download the form plus instructions from the Library of Congress Web site at http://lcweb.loc.gov/issn.

R.R. BOWKER COMPANY

Bowker is a subsidiary of Reed Elsevier Inc., which publishes many source documents and performs many services for the publishing industry. Bowker administers the ISBN and SAN programs, and publishes the magazines *Publishers Weekly, Library Journal* and *School Library Journal* and reference books such as *Books in Print, American Book Publishing Record, Literary Market Place, Publishers Trade List Annual* and many more. Treat each Bowker office separately, as though it were in a different building, so your mail won't get misdirected or lost.

Once you sign up for the ISBN program, you will probably get a call from Bowker suggesting you pay for an annotated listing in *Books in Print*. Most publishers agree this is a complete waste of money.

BAR CODES

The bar code on a book identifies the ISBN, which in turn identifies the publisher, title, author and edition (hardcover, etc.). The wholesalers, chains and other bookstores will not accept your book or audio without a bar code. If your book arrives at a distributor or wholesaler without a bar code (or without a price included in the bar code), they will sticker one on and charge you for it.

You must have a bar code even if you think you won't be selling many books through bookstores, because some people will order your book through stores. Since most books have bar codes, your book will not appear to be mainstream if you do not have one. It will look odd without one—and it will not be taken seriously. It will look like kitchen table publishing, loving hands at home, not quite ready for real publishing.

The bar code you want is the **Bookland EAN** with the Price Code extension, and it should be printed on the lower half of cover 4 (the outside back cover) on hardcover and softcover books and on cover 2 (the inside of the front cover) on mass-market paperback books. Your cover designer will order the bar code (about $30 each) or use a software program to generate it.

On mass-market paperbacks (usually sold in drug and grocery stores), an additional bar code (the **Universal Product Code,** or **UPC**) is required. The cost of the UPC starts at $300. To obtain one, see the Uniform Code Council Inc.'s Web site at http://www.uccouncil.org. Ask for the Price Point UPC with ISBN Add On Code. Most hardbound and trade paper books use only an EAN Bar code, however, if your book will be sold in retail outlets other than bookstores, you may need a UPC Bar code in addition to the bookstore EAN Bar code.

Use the ISBN on invoices, catalogs, order forms, packing lists and the book itself. A bar code printed on your sales flyer allows the bookstore buyer to simply scan the code when ordering your book.

ISBN 1-56860-046-1

9 781568 600468

51495

**The Bookland EAN bar code
(for bookstores)**

Beginning from the lower left, the first three digits (978) identify this number as being a Bookland bar code and the product as being a book. The next nine digits (156860046) correspond to the ISBN for the book (as noted at the top of the bar code). The last figure is a bar code check digit. In the smaller price extension bar code to the right, the first digit indicates the type of currency, such as U.S. dollars. The next four digits indicate the retail price of the book ($14.95).

Order a copy of *Machine-Readable Coding Guidelines for the U.S. Book Industry* ($7.50) from the Book Industry Study Group Inc., 160 Fifth Avenue, New York, NY 1001-7000; 212-929-1393; fax 212-989-7542. See its Web site at http://www.bisg.org.

Bar code/ISBN prints and negatives are available from the suppliers listed in Appendix 2 under Bar Code/ISBN Suppliers. To order a bar code, call one of the suppliers and tell them you want a Bookland EAN bar code with Price Code (the smaller one) and then provide the ISBN, price, title of the book and any other information (e.g., hardcover edition) they may need to identify the negative they will send you. The bar code negative will be delivered in a couple of days. Bar codes should be in black, printed on a white (or very light colored) background so that they will scan properly. A red background behind a black bar code may confuse the scanner.

STANDARD ADDRESS NUMBER (SAN)

The SAN identifies each separate address of every firm in the book publishing industry, including publishers, wholesalers, libraries and bookstores. SANs sort out the billing and shipping addresses and help to determine which Book Nook an order is going to.

STANDARD ADDRESS NUMBER--UNITED STATES AGENCY
International Standard Numbering System for the Information Industry
121 Chanlon Road, New Providence, New Jersey 07974
TEL: 908-665-6770 FAX: 908-665-2895 Email: isbn-san@bowker.com
R.R. Bowker * A Unit of Cahners Business Information

ANSI/NISO Z39.43-1993

APPLICATION FOR A SAN ASSIGNMENT FOR A BOOKSTORE, PUBLISHER, DISTRIBUTOR, etc

Please assign a SAN to the following address:

STORE OR COMPANY NAME: _____

ADDRESS: _____

_____

CITY: _____ STATE: _____ ZIP: _____

PHONE NUMBER: _____ FAX NUMBER: _____

E-MAIL: _____ WEB SITE: _____

FAX-ON-DEMAND: _____ TOLL-FREE FAX: _____

CONTACT NAME: _____

TYPE OF BUSINESS: (Please check one)

    Bookstore   Publisher

    Book Distributor   _____ Library

    Book Wholesaler

    Other, Please clarify: _____

PAYMENT: **A One Time Service Charge of $100 Per SAN For Each**

    Check/Money Order enclosed. Make payable to "R. R. Bowker."

___ Charge: American Express Visa Master Card

Card Holder Name: _____

    Account #: _____ Expiration Date: _____

Total amount enclosed or charged:

Our Company hereby applies to the ISBN/SAN U.S. Agency for a SAN Assignment

Authorized signature: _____

SAN application

A SAN can be requested when you apply for an ISBN. The cost is $125 and the seven-digit number should be printed on all stationery, purchase orders, invoices, etc. See the ISBN-SAN Agency Web site: http//www.ISBN.org for an online application form. Standard Address Number (SAN)—U.S. Agency, 121 Chanlon Road, New Providence, NJ 07974), 877-310-7333 or

877-310-7333, 908-665-2895 (fax), email: ISBN-SAN@ Bowker. com.

ADVANCE BOOK INFORMATION (ABI)

Advance Book Information is another Bowker service. By filling out their online ABI form, your book will be listed in *Books in Print* and several other specialized directories. *Books in Print* is published in October of each year and is one of the most important reference book in the industry.

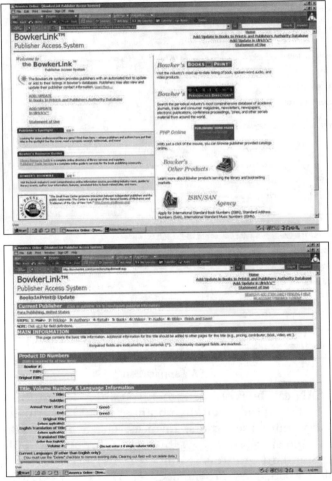

ABI application

An ABI form printout should also accompany your application for an ISBN number to show that you are indeed publishing a book. You are not expected to have all the information that is requested on the form (e.g., ISBN number, Library of Congress Control number).

Go to the Bowker web site to register your titles online: http://www. bowkerlink.com.

You should fill out an ABI form about six months before your book comes off the press. See a further discussion in Chapter 7.

Bowker makes your book listing available on their Web site: http://www.bowkerlink.com. You must periodically check to see that your listing is correct and make any necessary updates and revisions.

LIBRARY OF CONGRESS CONTROL NUMBER (LCCN)

Library of Congress Control numbers appear on the copyright page of each book and are included in the lists and reviews of the leading journals of the book trade. The control number differs from the ISBN in that one ISBN is assigned to each different edition of a work (hardcover, softcover, etc.), but the Library of Congress number is assigned to the work itself, no matter how the work is published. Use of the number enables subscribers to the Library of Congress catalog card service to order cards by number and thus eliminate the searching fee. Library of Congress numbers are essential if you want to sell to libraries. About 20,000 libraries all over the world subscribe to this service and some of them order almost every cataloged book. Additionally, most of the books are listed in *The National Union Catalogue*, issued several times a year in four editions. Most public and private libraries subscribe to it.

The Library of Congress number must be printed on the copyright page of your book, so you have to apply for the number before your book is published through the Library's Preassigned Control Number program. (They do not preassign numbers to books that are already in print because it is too late to print the number in the book.)

Preassigned Control numbers are given only to books that the Library of Congress assumes will be added to library collections or for which they anticipate substantial demand for Library of Congress printed cards. The types of material that the Library collects, only in a very limited way and for which catalog card numbers are generally not available, include calendars, laboratory manuals, booklets of less than 50 pages, brochures, advertisements, bank publications designed for customers, blueprints, certain kinds of light fiction, privately printed books of poems, religious materials for students in Bible schools, catechisms, instructions in devotions, individual sermons and prayers, question and answer books, most elementary and secondary school textbooks, tests except for standard examinations, teachers' manuals, correspondence school lessons, translations from English into foreign languages, picture books, comic strip and coloring books, diaries, log and appointment books, prospectuses and preliminary editions, workbooks and vanity press publications.

Since the staff at the Library of Congress sometimes confuse self-publishing with vanity publishing, it may be best to fill out the forms using different names for author, publisher, etc.

Contact the Cataloging in Publication Division, Library of Congress, 101 Independence Ave., S.E., Washington, DC 20540-4320, 202-707-6372. Ask for "Procedures for Securing Preassigned Library of Congress Control Numbers" and a "Request for Preassignment of LCC Number" application (Form 607-7). The forms can also be accessed, filled out and submitted via the Library of Congress Web site at http://pcn.loc.gov/pcn. Prior to filling out the form online, you must submit an online application to participate, which is simply a record of your name and address as publisher.

The Library of Congress will send you a catalog card number along with the author, title, imprint and publication date.

REQUEST FOR PREASSIGNMENT OF LIBRARY OF CONGRESS CATALOG CARD NUMBER

NOTE: Card numbers cannot be preassigned to books which are already published.

DATE: _____

PUBLISHER'S NAME ON TITLE PAGE: _____

CONTACT PERSON: _____ PHONE NUMBER: _____

Type or print clearly the complete address to which the preassigned card number should be sent.
(This will be your return mailing label.)

FOR CIP OFFICE USE

Library of Congress Catalog
Card Number preassigned is:

Transcribe the information in items 1-6 exactly in the form and order in which it will appear on the title or copyright pages of the printed book. Use only those abbreviations which will actually appear on these pages. (Please attach a copy of the proposed title page, if available.)

1. Author(s) _____

2. Editor(s) _____

3. Title and subtitle(s) _____

4. Edition statement (exactly as printed in the publication, e.g. second edition, revised edition, etc.) _____

5. U.S. place of publication: City _____ State _____

Any copublisher (s) and place _____

6. Other information found on title page _____

7. Series title (s) and numbering, exactly as printed in the publication _____

8. Approximate number of pages _____ No. of volumes _____

9. ISBN _____ Binding: ☐ Hardcover ☐ Paperback

10. Proposed date of publication: Month _____ Year _____

11. Does (or will) the title in item 3 appear at periodic intervals, e.g. annually, quarterly, etc? ☐ Yes ☐ No

12. Will this publication be submitted later for CIP data? ☐ Yes ☐ No

For each title which receives a preassigned LC catalog card number, the Library of Congress requires one copy of the best edition of the published book. If selected for the Library's collections, the book will be cataloged. A postage-free, self-addressed label will be sent with the preassigned card number for your convenience in mailing the required advance copy of the work as soon as printed. This copy is in addition to copyright deposit copies.

Send this form to: Library of Congress
Cataloging in Publication Division
Washington, D.C. 20540

FOR CIP OFFICE USE ONLY. DO NOT WRITE BELOW THIS LINE

Searching notes

607-7 (rev 2/84)

RECD:

ASGN:

SENT:

APIF:

LCC number application form 607-7

The first four digits of the Control number indicate the year in which the card number is preassigned, not the year of publication. But if you apply after January 1, your book will appear to be a year newer. Ever wonder why the dates on films are in Roman numerals?

The Cataloging in Publication (CIP) Office of the Library of Congress must be advised of all subsequent changes in titles, authors, etc., and cancellations. This notification is important because it prevents duplication of numbers. A new number is not necessary when changes are made. Confirmations of changes will not be acknowledged unless you request them.

There is no charge for the preassignment of a card number. A complimentary copy of each publication must be sent to the CIP Office, Library of Congress, Washington, DC 20540. This copy is used for final cataloging so that cards can be printed before the book is released. The CIP Office provides postage-free mailing labels for use in sending these advance publications. The book is only for checking, so send the less expensive, softcover edition.

The U.S. Copyright Office is operationally separate from the CIP Office, but the CIP and LC Control Number offices are the same. Control card numbers may be applied for per the above information or when applying for cataloging-in-publication data.

CIP data block application form 607-6

Apply for your numbers and listings in this order: ISBN, Library of Congress Control Number and then file the completed ABI form. (See Appendix 1, "Your Book's Calendar.")

CATALOGING IN PUBLICATION (CIP)

Cataloging in Publication is a separate program for publishers of multiple books that enables them to print detailed Library of Congress cataloging information on the copyright page of their books. Because the data block is already printed in the book, librarians are able to process new titles for library users rapidly and economically. Printing the CIP data block on the copyright page of your book will make you look more established and aid librarians.

First you must be accepted into the program, and then you must request cataloging data for each new book. For information on the CIP program, write the CIP Office, Library of Congress, Washington, DC 20540, 202-707-6372, and request "Cataloging in Publication—Information for Participating Publishers" and some "Publisher's Response" forms. The CIP people are eager to help. They even provide postage-paid mailing labels for the materials you are expected to send back.

To be eligible for the CIP program, you must have published at least three books. Until you have, Quality Books, the library supplier, will fill in for the Library of Congress with Publisher's Cataloging in Publication (PCIP) data blocks. A staff librarian will catalog your forthcoming title and send you a camera-ready data block. Contact Quality Books for an application: 1003 West Pines Road, Oregon, IL 61061-9680, 800-323-4241 or 815-732-4450; fax 815-732-4499. See Quality Books' Web site at http://www.quality-books.com.

The Library of Congress CIP office and Control Number office are the same. Control numbers may be applied for as indicated above or when applying for CIP Data. See http://www.l cweb.loc.gov/loc/infopub.

Here is a line-by-line explanation of the CIP data block:

- ❶ The heading is made distinctive by setting in bold typeface.
- ❷ The author's name
- ❸ The title of the book.
- ❹ ISBN.
- ❺ Library of Congress subject headings
- ❻ "Z285.5"is the LC classification number. "P69" is keyed into the last name of the author, in this case "Poynter."

"070.5'93" is the Dewey Decimal Classification Number (see the *Dewey Decimal Classification and Relative Index* at your public library), and "99-57841" is the LC catalog card number.

---

❶ **Library of Congress Cataloging-in-Publication Data**
❷ Poynter, Dan
   ❸ The self-publishing manual : how to write, print and sell your own book / by Dan Poynter. — 13th ed.
      P.   cm.
   Includes bibliographical references and index.
❹ ISBN 1-56860-073-9 (pbk.)
❺ 1. Self-publishing—United States.   I. Title.
   2. Desktop Publishing—Computer publishing, etc.
   3. Publishers and Publishing—Handbooks, manuals, etc.
   4. Printing, Practical—Handbooks, manuals, etc.
   5. Authorship—Handbooks, manuals, etc.
❻ Z285.5.P69   2000
   070.5'93—dc20   99-57841 CIP

Typical CIP data block

The CIP copy is taken from the Anglo-American Cataloging Rules, the Library of Congress Subject Headings (the big red book) and the *Dewey Decimal Classification and Relative Index*. See them at your public library.

Once you are accepted into the CIP program, you will submit information on each book prior to printing. Send a printout of the front matter of your book and a filled-out LCC data sheet to the CIP Office. This enables them to select the proper classification numbers. They also like to have any other information you might have, such as a descriptive brochure on the book, a photocopy of your ABI form and a biographical sketch of the author. Within 10 business days, the Office will send the CIP data and the catalog card number.

Sometimes titles are misleading, and the CIP Office does not catalog the book correctly. For example, is *What Color is Your Parachute?* about job hunting or skydiving? If your book is miscataloged in every library across the country, readers may never find it. Give the CIP Office as much information on your new book as possible, and read their "Information For Participating Publishers" carefully. You may even supply suggested data. Pay particular attention to the "subject tracings" (line 4 in the CIP data block illustration). How a book is cataloged can be just as important as how it is reviewed or advertised.

COPYRIGHT

A Copyright may be registered before your manuscript is published, but unless you are passing a lot of copies around for technical proofing and comment, you might just as well do as most publishers do: wait for books to come off the press. Your work is automatically copyright *protected* under common law because you created it; it just isn't copyright *registered* yet.

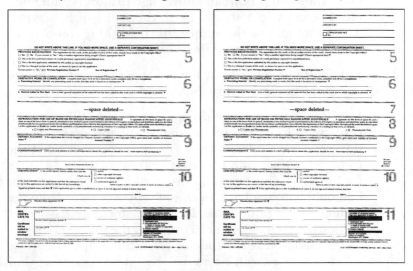

Copyright Form TX

Contact the Copyright Office, Library of Congress, 101 Independence Avenue, S.E., Washington, DC 20559-6000, 202-707-3000 or 202-707-9100 (hotline) or 202-707-5959 (information specialist). Request copyright package 109. Upon receipt, read over these publications and order any others you feel you need. The Copyright Office will also send you some business reply mailing labels so that you can send them the copyright form, your cheque and the book for registration. You can also access information and fill out Form TX from the Copyright Office's Web site at http://loc.gov/ copyright.

To register your copyright, follow these three steps:

1.   **Print the copyright notice on the copyright page** (title page verso). The notice takes the following form: "© 2001 by Robert Howard." You may use the word "copyright" but "©" says the same thing and is necessary for international protection. Also add "All rights reserved" and expand on this if you like. Check other books. The copyright notice must appear in all copies of the book to protect you, so double check it and all the numbers on the copyright page every time you proofread copy, page printouts, bluelines, etc. The copyright should be in the name of the owner. The owner may be the author, the publishing company or whoever created or paid for the work.

2.   **Publish the book.** Check for the copyright notice before any of the books are distributed.

3.   **Register your claim with the Copyright Office within three months of the book coming off the press.** To do this, send a completed Form TX, two copies of what the Copyright Office calls the "best edition" of the book and a fee of $30. The best edition would be the hardcover edition if both the hardcover and softcover came from the printer at the same time. However, since the hardcover edition often takes longer to produce, the softcover may be the best edition at the time of publication. If you enclose softcover copies with Form TX, be sure to note that they were produced first.

The Copyright Office will add a registration number and date to the form and send you a photocopy containing a seal and the Registrar's signature.

The new copyright term is for the author's life plus 50 years. Your ownership of the book is now a valuable part of your estate, so be certain your copyrighted material is mentioned in your will.

Copyrights protect you like a patent, but they are cheaper and much easier to secure. Like a patent, however, you must always be on the lookout for infringers. The copyright protects your text, photographs, drawings, maps—everything in the book except the title.

DIRECTORY LISTINGS

You have many opportunities to list your book in directories and with associations that are referred to by thousands of people. The following pages include the most important of the directories and associations. I suggest you list your book in as many of them as possible.

With listings in *Books in Print*, the *Small Press Record* and *Literary Market Place*, a membership in the Publishers Marketing Association and subscriptions to *Publishers Weekly* and *Writer's Digest*, you will begin to receive a lot of writing and publishing mail.

1. *ABA Book Buyer's Handbook* is used by bookstores to find your shipping, discount, STOP and returns policies. To be listed, your company must be at least a year old and you must have published at least three titles. Contact the American Booksellers Association for an application at 828 S. Broadway, Tarrytown, NY 10591, 800-637-0037 or 914-591-2665; fax 914-591-2720; http://www.bookweb.org.

2. *The Book Buyer's Manual* is published by the National Association of College Stores. For an application, contact NACS, 500 East Lorrain Street, Oberlin, OH 44074, 440-622-7498; fax 440-775-4769; http://www.nacs.org.

3. *Book Dealers Drop Ship Directory* will list your book for individual, drop ship sales. Contact Al Galasso at North American Bookdealers Exchange, Box 606-PT, Cottage Grove, OR 97424, 541-942-7455; fax 561-258-2625; nabe@bookmarketingprofits.com.

4. *Book Trade in Canada* is the *Literary Market Place* of the Canadian book publishing industry. If you are located in Canada, contact Quill & Quire, 70 The Esplanade, #210, Toronto, ON M5E 1R2, Canada, 416-360-0044; fax 416-955-0794; info@quillandquire.com; http://www.quilland quire.com.

5. *Canadian Books in Print* is the *Books in Print* of the Canadian book publishing industry. If your book is being printed in Canada, contact Marian Butler, University of Toronto Press, 10 St. Mary's Street, #700, Toronto, ON,

M4Y 2W8, Canada, 416-978-2239; http://www.utpress.
utoronto.com.

6. **Canadian Publishers Directory.** If you are located in Canada, request an application from Quill and Quire, 70 The Esplanade, #210, Toronto, ON, M5E 1R2, Canada, 416-360-0044; fax 416-955-0794; http://www.quilland quire.com.

7. **College Store Executive.** *The National News and Merchandising Magazine of the College Store Industry.* If your book might be sold in college bookstores, send for a *Book Announcement Form* and other information from *College Store Executive,* PO Box 1500, 825 Old Country Road, Westbury, NY 11590-0812, 516-334-3030; fax 516-334-3059. See http://www.ebmpubs.com.

8. **Contemporary Authors** is a large reference book containing over 100,000 biographical sketches. Authors of technical and vanity press books are not eligible. Request a form from *Contemporary Authors,* Gale Group, 27500 Drake Road, Farmington Hills, MI 48331, 800-347-GALE or 248-699-4253; fax 800-414-5043; http://www.galegroup.com. Don't be modest. The more you write on the form, the more space you get in the book. After you fill out the application, make a few photocopies so you will be ready when someone else asks for extensive biographical information. The listing is free.

9. **Directories In Print** will accept your book listing if it has an extensive appendix. Request a form from Gale Group, 27500 Drake Road, Farmington Hills, MI 48331, 800-347-GALE or 248-699-4253; fax 800-414-5043; http://www.galegroup.com.

10. **Directory of Mail Order Catalogs** and the **Directory of Business-to-Business Catalogs**. If you have several books and offer them in your own brochure or catalog, send for an application form for these directories. Grey House Publishing, 185 Millerton Rd., Millerton, NY 12546; 800-562-2139; fax 518-789-0545; books@ greyhouse.com; http://www.greyhouse.com.

11. *International Directory of Little Magazines and Small Presses* is another place you will want to list your new firm. For an application, contact Dustbooks, PO Box 100, Paradise, CA 95967-9999; 800-477-6110 or 530-877-6110; fax 530-877-0222; dustbooks@dcsi.net. Request information on their other directories. See http://www. dustbooks.com.

12. *Law Books in Print.* If you are publishing books for the legal profession, get a listing in *Law Books in Print.* Send for an application to Oceana Publishers, Inc., 75 Main Street, Dobbs Ferry, NY 10522; 914-693-8100; fax 914-693-0402; info@oceanalaw.com; http://www. oceanalaw.com.

13. *Literary Market Place (LMP)* is one of the most important reference books in the publishing industry. It lists every major publisher, publicity outlet and supplier. An inclusion here will help your customers and suppliers to find you. To be listed in this annual reference, you must publish at least three books a year. Send for an application form to Literary Market Place/Reed Elsevier, Inc., 121 Chanlon Road, New Providence, NJ 07974; 888-269-5372 or 908-464-6800; fax 908-665-3502; info@bowker.com; http://www.literarymarketplace.com.

14. *National Directory of Catalogs.* If you have several books and offer them in your own brochure or catalog, send for an application form for this directory. Oxbridge Communications, Inc., 150 Fifth Avenue, #302, New York, NY 10011; 800-955-0231 or 212-741-0231; fax 212-633-2938; info@oxbridge.com; http://www.mediafinder.com.

15. **Online bookstores.** Some of the following online bookstores allow you to register your book online. Contact them regarding information for publishers. Annotate your listings by sending cover art, table of contents, back cover copy, etc.
    http://www.amazon.com
    http://www.bn.com
    http://www.borders.com
    http://www.booksamillion.com
    http://www.eCampus.com

http://www.seekbooks.com
http://www.elgrande.com

16. **Publishers Directory** is a directory in which you may have a free listing. For an application form, contact Gale Group, 27500 Drake Road, Farmington Hills, MI 48331, 800-347-GALE or 248-699-4253; fax 800-414-5043; http://www.galegroup.com.

17. **Publishers, Distributors, Wholesalers of the United States.** Once you secure an ISBN, you are automatically included in this directory. Contact Reed Elsevier, Inc., 121 Chanlon Road, New Providence, NJ 07974; 800-521-8110 or 908-464-6800; fax 908-665-6688; http://www.reedref.com.

18. **Publishers' International ISBN Directory** is published by the R.R. Bowker Company, 121 Chanlon Road, New Providence, NJ 07974. Call for information: 888-269-5372; fax 908-665-3502; http://www.bowker.com.

19. **Publishers Marketing Association (PMA)** is an international association of more than 3,500 publishers who band together to promote their books in a cooperative manner. PMA holds educational seminars, buys and shares advertising space, makes cooperative mailings and operates booths at major book fairs. Local affiliates of PMA are located all over North America. Annual membership for a publishing company with under 10 employees is $95. Contact PMA for a sample newsletter and a membership application: 627 Aviation Way, Manhattan Beach, CA 90266; 310-372-2732; fax 310-374-3342; pma-online @aol.com and see http://www. Pma-online.org.

20. **Quill & Quire Spring and Fall Announcements.** If your books are being produced in Canada, request an application from Quill and Quire, 70 The Esplanade, #210, Toronto, ON, M5E 1R2, Canada; 416-360-0044; fax 416-955-0794; http://www.quillandquire.com.

21. **Small Press Record of Books in Print** is a special *Books in Print* for smaller publishers. For an application, contact Dustbooks, PO Box 100, Paradise, CA 95967-9999;

800-477-6110 or 530-877-6110; fax 530-877-0222; dustbooks@dcsi.net. Request information on their other directories. See http://www.dustbooks.com.

22. *Software Encyclopedia.* If you are publishing software, send for an application for this directory. Reed Elsevier, Inc., 121 Chanlon Road, New Providence, NJ 07974; 800-521-8110 or 908-665-6714; fax 908-771-8699. See http://www. bowker.com.

23. *Vertical File Index* lists lower-cost items (usually under $10) such as pamphlets, posters, maps and reports. Send one book to Eloise Morehouse, H.W. Wilson Co., 950 University Avenue, Bronx, NY 10452; 800-367-6770 or 718-588-8400; fax 800-590-1617 or outside U.S. and Canada, 718-590-1617; custserv@hwilson.com; http:// www.hwwilson .com.

24. *Writer's Market.* A listing here means you want manuscript submissions from authors. For an application, write *Writer's Market,* Writer's Digest Books, 1507 Dana Avenue, Cincinnati, OH 45207; 800-289-0963 or 513-531-2222; fax 513-531-4082. See http://www.writersdigest.com.

FORMS: For a complete set of forms, including all those mentioned in this chapter, see *Publishing Forms* under Para Publishing Special Reports in Appendix 2 or order it from Para Publishing's Web site: http://ParaPublishing.com.

If you want a response, you have to ask for it.
— **John Huenefeld**

Writing a book is an adventure. To begin with, it is a toy and an amusement. Then it becomes a mistress, then it becomes a master, then it becomes a tyrant. The last phase is that just as you are about to be reconciled to your servitude, you kill the monster and fling him to the public.
— **Winston Churchill**

6
What is Your Book Worth?

Prices, Discounts, Terms, Collections and Returns

Book pricing is a complicated affair that strikes a compromise between a price high enough for the publisher to stay in business and low enough to overcome customer price resistance. There are perhaps three major reasons people write books: reward (fame and/or fortune), love of writing and a desire to disseminate important material. While you may want to get the word out, your first book is usually for recognition, and once that is out of your system, the second is for money. Consequently, the author is likely to under price the first book but work with a very sharp pencil on the price of the next.

The higher your price, the more mistakes you can afford.

THE LIST PRICE

Many first-time author-publishers ask themselves whether they want maximum financial return or maximum distribution, feeling they can't have both. Usually they wind up with a price on the cover that is too low. As a result, many small publishers have a garage full of books that they cannot afford to market effectively. Without a high enough price, there is not enough money for promotion, and without promotion, the book will not sell. If the book fails to sell, there is no money for promotion, or even to pay the printing bill.

One major reason small publishers stay small is their failure to think objectively about pricing their books. Low prices make you work harder for less and limit your growth. You must also consider that the price printed on the cover is not what you will receive for the book. Dealers require a percentage for their selling efforts. Everyone in the book-selling process takes a cut: distributors, wholesalers, bookstores and other book sales outlets.

Your promotion costs—to let people know the book exists—are likely to be much higher than you originally anticipated—around 25% of the list price. Some 10% to 20% of the books may be shipped out as review copies, and 10% may come back from bookstores damaged. Discounts, advertising and returns take a big chunk out of the list price.

It is normal to invest 20% to 30% of the gross back into letting the world know your book is available. Depending upon the subject matter and the size of the potential audience, we often send out more than 500 review copies to appropriate magazines, newsletters, newspaper columns, news syndicates and opinion molders. Reviews are the most effective and least expensive promotion you can do for your book.

Books are becoming more and more expensive; visit a bookstore and compare prices.

In a how-to book, you are selling exclusive information, not entertainment or stacks of paper. Your book is unique. Like you, it is one of a kind. While customers will not pay more than what they figure is a fair price, if your book is a good one and they want it badly enough, they will pay what you ask. The selling price is not nearly so frightening to the buyer as it is to the author.

Under pricing a book to increase sales is a big mistake. In fact, it may even undermine the credibility of the book. And remember, price has a reverse impact when a book is purchased as a gift.

According to *Publishers Weekly*, women are more resistant to book prices than men. Women buy most of the books on cooking, health, diet and gardening, as well as fiction. In fact, women buy 68% of all trade books.

THE PRICING FORMULA

Here is a formula for pricing your book. You must look at price from the bottom up and from the top down.

BOTTOM UP: Books you intend to sell through bookstores and mail order should be priced at a minimum of 8 times production cost, textbooks at 5 times. Production costs include typesetting, printing and trucking in.

The 8 times formula does not fit every case; there may be a few exceptions. Consider your audience and the cost of reaching them. If you write a pictorial history of your town, and the chamber of commerce is buying all the books to give to tourists, your promotion and distribution costs will be much lower. For nonfiction aimed at a small target audience that continuously sells, you may be able to justify 7 times. If 8 times seems like a lot, you should know that audiovisual materials are often marked up 11 times.

Direct Mail: If you plan to sell your book through direct mail advertising, you will get the full price of the book by avoiding book trade discounts. However, your list price will have to be higher, not lower, because direct mail is so expensive. A direct mail offer will cost more than 50¢ each for bulk rate postage, envelope, cover letter, mailing house stuffing, etc. Your expected response may be 2% or less. Conventional direct mail industry wisdom says you can't profitably sell a book through direct mail advertising unless it is priced over $35.

Yes, I know, your book has no competition...however, *all* authors feel their book is unique.

TOP DOWN: The price you put on your back cover, embed in your bar code, put on the order blank on the last page of your book and list in all your promotion should be as much as the traffic will bear. Visit a bookstore and check other books like yours. Look for other books on the same subject that would be purchased by the same type of person.

Yes, I know, you think your book is for everyone. Look, I publish books on skydiving. I want everyone to jump—to have fun, to skydive safely and to come back, make more jumps, join the club, buy equipment and (hopefully) buy more books. But, I am realistic. I know skydiving is not for everyone. Just because you spent the last year pouring your heart, soul and credit limit into your tome does not mean everyone is interested enough to buy it and read it. Now, that said, what is the profile of the typical potential purchaser for your book?

You want to find out what your potential buyer is willing to spend. If you are selling to teenagers, your price will have to be low and the book in softcover. If yours is a business book, $34.95 and hardcover with a dust jacket might be right. If this is a professional book aimed at doctors or lawyers, a hardcover book without a jacket at $90 would not be out of line.

Before you can sell a person anything, you have to make him or her want it more than the money it costs.

Looking at the range of prices in your category on a bookstore shelf, the price for your book must be right in the middle. If you poll bookstore managers on pricing, remember their perspective is that lower prices will sell more books, so they will often advise a price which may be too low. Also look at the formats of other books like yours: hardcover, softcover, size, shape, color printing and so on. And remember books with old copyright dates will many times have inordinately low prices, as their prices have not increased along with normal inflation.

Book buyers are less influenced by price differentials than almost any category of customer.
—John Huenefeld, *Huenefeld's Guide to Book Publishing*

COMPARE UP AND DOWN: Now, hopefully, your bottom-up price (8X) is lower than your top-down price. If there is an overlap, you will have to reformulate your book.

If the cover price is too high, you will price your book out of the market. If it is too low, the book will not be credible; potential buyers will think there is something wrong with it. If your book is priced too high for its class of buyer, it won't sell well; your potential customer will resist. If it is priced too low, you won't make enough to invest in further promotion.

Pricing the book any lower than 8X is courting financial disaster. If the projected list price seems too high, consider cutting out some of the copy or photographs, or selecting a smaller type size and narrower leading (space between the lines) to get more text on each page and reduce the total number of pages. If your book has a huge number of pages, you might consider dividing it into two volumes. Check with your printer for other ways to reduce costs. Now, if the customer still won't pay that much, you picked the wrong subject to write about. See

Document 604, *How to Price Your Book,* at http://ParaPublishing. com.

Retail price should depend more upon the value the buyer places on the product than the cost to the producer.
Leonard Shatzkin, *In Cold Type*

REVISED EDITIONS: You can price revised editions a bit higher. When updating a book and going back to press, there is an advantage: your book has been out there working for you. A revised edition is a new book—with a track record. It has a reputation and can command more attention and more money. Price the revision toward the top of the range of the books on its shelf.

OTHER PRICING CONSIDERATIONS

RAISING THE PRICE: If you do raise the price, remember to change your ads, brochures, Web site, etc., and send off a news release about the reprint to *Publishers Weekly.* (Every little mention helps.) To ease the blow to your better dealers, who have listed your book in their catalogs, consider offering them a one-time buy on the new edition at the old price to protect their catalog listing. This offer will also generate quick cash to help you pay your printing bill.

The book How to Beat Inflation *has just gone from $14.95 to $19.95.*

ALWAYS CHARGE X.95: It may seem old and silly, but $19.95 still seems a lot cheaper to the subconscious mind than $20, and there is no good argument for a mid-price like $19.50.

REVISE THE ABI FORM: If you have already sent in the ABI form, do not worry. Just go to the Bowker (Books in Print) Web site at http://www.bowkerlink.com. Click on "add/update" in Books in Print to Register. Bowker will email you your user name and password so you can update your listing (and submit new-title ABI forms on line) any time.

PRICE ON COVER: Your book *must* have a price on the cover—for three reasons.

1. If you do not print your price on the back cover of a softcover book or on the jacket front flap of a hardcover book, the distributor or the bookstores will sticker it. If the book comes back, you will not be able to remove the sticker, so you have to destroy the book or replace the jacket.

2. The price is reflected in the price extension of the bar code on the back cover, and any savvy buyer can decipher the code.

3. Your book should have an order blank on the last page—facing out. For example, see the last page of this book. We sell more books each week on these order blanks than on any other promotion we do.

So, if you are pricing your book on the order blank and on the back cover in the bar code, why not also print the price on the back cover in Arabic numerals?

The price should be printed at the bottom of the back cover on a softcover book. Do not place the price at the top of the back cover where it may turn off potential buyers before they read down through the sales copy. On a hardcover book, the price should be placed near the upper right corner of the jacket front flap.

HOW MANY BOOKS TO PRINT?

You must consider both your purpose for writing the book and how many you can expect to sell. Do you want just a few books for family and friends? Will it be a high-priced, mail order book with a small target audience? Or will it be a popular book, with a wide audience, that should sell well in bookstores? How many books will be used for review copies, gifts and other freebies? Make a list.

INITIAL PRESS RUNS should normally be limited to the number of books one can reasonably estimate will be sold in the first year. Unless you have a substantial number of prepublication sales (such as to a book club or large corporation), it is a good idea to limit the first printing to 3,000 books. No matter how diligently you proofread, some errors will not surface until they appear in ink. Also, once you see the book in its final state, you will wish you had done some things differently—especially on a first book. By printing a smaller number, you can use the next few months to catch your errors and make some design changes. Then you will be much happier about the *revised* second edition.

Set the first press run conservatively. It is better to sell out and have to go back to press than to find yourself with a garage full of unsold books. You will be spending a lot of money on promotion, so it is best to hedge your bets by tying up less money in the book, even though you have to pay a slight premium in printing costs to do so.

But do not be too conservative. All the books will not be sold; many will be used for promotion. If you print 1,000 copies and send 500 out to newspapers and magazines for review, there will be only 500 copies left to sell. Reviews are your least expensive and most effective form of promotion, and 500 review copies is a realistic figure (see Chapter 7). Many publishers figure 10% or even more of their print run will be used for review copies and promotion. Except for highly specialized topics, 3,000 makes a good initial print run.

The economics of printing are as follows: the greater the quantity of books, the higher your bill, but the less each book will cost you. The start-up costs make the first press run much more expensive than reprints. The major expenses are the start-up costs of composition, layout, camera work, stripping, press setup, etc. Once the type is set, you only pay for the paper, binding and press time. The more copies printed at one time, the lower the price per copy.

Economy of scale is only true up to a point, since the differences become smaller and smaller as the press runs increase. Each next thousand books become cheaper. The price breaks fail to maintain significance after about 9,000 copies. Normally, between 9,000 and 10,000 copies, you save so little that it isn't worth the storage space or the price of borrowing money. Therefore you do not want to print over 9,000 unless you have some presold and are certain that number will move out within the year.

For example, depending on the size of the book, you might receive printing/binding quotes such as:

No. of copies:	500	1,000	3,000	5,000	7,000	9,000	10,000
Total cost:	$1,495	1,784	4,485	6,778	8,750	10,530	11,300
Unit cost:	$2.99	1.78	1.49	1.36	1.25	1.17	1.13

So it is to your advantage to order as many books as you can sell in order to get the best unit price. And you want the best price, as long as you are fairly sure you can sell the higher number.

Remember that a printer makes money on printing. Do not let them talk you into more books than you need. There is economy in scale, but there are no savings in paying for books you can't turn into cash. Consider the total printing bill as well.

PRINT RUNS ARE NEVER EXACT: Printers always run a few extra pages, expecting some to be spoiled. When all the sheets are gathered, there are still some that must be thrown away. Accordingly, it is customary in the trade to have overruns and underruns, and your bill may be adjusted higher or lower, up to 10%. A print run of 3,000 could wind up anywhere between 2,700 and 3,300.

ESTIMATING SALES

Projecting sales that first year will be difficult with your initial book, because you don't have personal sales experience in its field. You may be able to find out how similar books have done by calling their publishers. For comparative sales figures, call Ingram's automated stock sales system (known as FREDDIE) at 615-213-6803. Just punch in the ISBN (found on the copyright page) to check the rate of sale for the various books you have located on your subject. The automated voice will tell you how many books are stocked in each of the Ingram warehouses, how many copies Ingram sold last year and how many they have sold so far this year. These numbers are not total sales figures, but since Ingram handles more than half of the books in the U.S., the figures will give you an idea of the rate of sale and are good for comparison.

Remember that bigger publishers have more clout in the bookstores, as well as other outlets, and already have the connections for promoting and placing their titles; your book will not do as well until you learn the ropes and have had time to effectively promote it.

Get a copy of *Financial Feasibility in Book Publishing* by Robert Follet. It contains guidelines, worksheets and rules of thumb for estimating sales. Find it under Para Publishing Special Reports in Appendix 2 or order it from http://ParaPublishing.com.

Do some market research. How many associations, magazines and conventions are there participating in this activity? How many people care about this subject? If you cannot objectively project moving 3,000 copies in the first year, you will have to raise the price to justify printing a shorter run of the book.

With proper promotion, any reasonably good nonfiction book, aimed at all but the tiniest markets, should sell 2,500 copies in its first year (plus up to 500 promotional copies).

REPRINTS

Reprints should be well timed. If you order a reprint too early, you may tie up more money before the first run is paid for, and many of those books from the earlier run could be sitting on the shelves in the stores—unsold. It is a good idea to make some telephone calls to find out if the book is actually moving. On the other hand, if you wait too long to reprint, you run the risk of being out of stock and losing the all-important sales momentum the book is enjoying. Reprints usually take three to five weeks. Coordinate with your printer so you can get a fast reprint if necessary. It is much better to be out of books for a few weeks than to have the truck arrive with 5,000 more as bookstores are returning copies.

REVISION VS. REPRINT: A "reprint" means there are no changes; a "revision" means you have made updating content corrections. As the publisher, you decide how many changes are necessary for the book to qualify as a revision. Books may be "revised" or "completely revised." See the copyright page of this book as an example. Always include a new ISBN when you publish a revision so the book industry will treat the book as new. Your distributor will put it back in the front of the catalog ("front list") as a new book.

The book trade is new-product driven. Make a legitimate revision, assign a new ISBN and bar code and keep your book *new*.

SIZE OF INVENTORY

When your stock is running low, consider printing time (reprints take three to five weeks), trucking time (two to six days), seasonal demand for this title, etc. Then, considering the size of your storage space, the amount of money you can invest, need for future revisions, inventory tax dates (if your state has one), etc., print a one- to two-year supply of books. One great advantage of these nearly annual printings is the ability to make revisions, thus keeping the text up to date.

The demand for some books continues on and on; others have a definite life. The trick is to know when the sales cycle is over. It is nice to run out of stock just before the demand curve ends in a cliff. Watch your sales and do not reorder until the last minute.

PRINT-ON-DEMAND (POD): If your sales are down to three or four per month, you do not want to invest the money and inventory space in 3,000 copies. With POD, you can print one book at a time, but the cost per unit is much higher. See Chapter 4 on printing.

DISCOUNTS

Discounts must be set down in a definite policy right from the beginning. Discount structures have to be clear to both you and your customers to avoid any misunderstanding.

END-USER CONSUMERS placing individual orders usually pay the **full retail price** (they do not get a discount) and they send cash with their order (CWO). When an order is received without a cheque, it is best to return the order with a copy of your brochure and a short note requesting payment in advance. Circle your prices and terms on the brochure. Some people order asking to be billed, because they don't know what the full price will be. By asking for payment in advance you will lose a few orders, but it will stop credit losses and cut billing costs. See the order blank at the end of this book for an example. Avoid COD shipments. They require too much paperwork for a small sale, and the collection charges often upset the customer.

Retail your books for full list price. Do not compete with your dealers or cheapen your product.

DEALER DISCOUNTS: The terms publishers extend to booksellers vary so much from firm to firm that the American Booksellers Association publishes a loose-leaf handbook that tries to list them all. Discounts are supposed to be based on the theory that there is a saving in bulk shipments. However, book-selling tradition bases the discount rate on the *category of the wholesale customer,* arguing that certain intermediaries need a greater discount because they are providing a service and are passing on part of the discount.

- **National Distributors** usually take 25% to 30% of the net (what they collect from the stores and wholesalers). That may work out to be around 66% off the list (cover) price. That 66% may sound like a lot, and it is. But distributors have sales reps that visit the stores and chain buyers to take orders. It is virtually impossible to get books into stores without a personal visit to the appropriate buyer.

  Distributors want an exclusive but most handle only the book trade (wholesalers and bookstores). You can turn that portion of the business over to them, forget about the stores and go on to the nontraditional markets, which are easier, more lucrative and more fun. You will pay the freight to your distributor (FOB destination), but you will usually ship directly from your printer. See the distributor discussion in Chapter 8.

- **Wholesalers** get 50% to 60% off the list (cover) price on the theory that they purchase large quantities for resale to retailers and libraries. Often they are regional suppliers providing stores with both one-stop shopping and a short supply line for quick and easy restocking. Wholesalers, in turn, usually allow bookstores 40% to 45% off the list price, depending on the size of the order. Stores are allowed to mix titles to get a larger discount. Wholesalers usually extend discounts of 20% to 33% to libraries. Wholesalers sometimes pay the shipping (FOB origin) when purchasing from the publisher.

  The largest wholesaler in the country is Ingram Book Company. Based in Nashville, Ingram has five warehouses. They have a warehouse within one-day UPS service of 95% of the bookstores in the U.S.

- **Retail bookstores:** Discounts to bookstores start at 40% for single-title orders. This comes as a shock to many new publishers, but one has to consider the high overhead of retail outlets for rent, taxes, salaries, utilities, insurance, etc. They need at least 40% to stay in business. Incidentally, bookstores enjoy a smaller markup than gift, sporting goods and many other stores, which often get 50% or more. The publishing industry has been able to justify the lower discount by making the books returnable if they aren't sold. Fortunately, books are uniform in size, easy to store, simple to ship and unbreakable. Shipping charges are added to the bookstore's invoice (FOB origin).

- **College bookstores** get 20% to 25% off list price on (text) books to be sold to students. The quantity is often large, and any books not sold after the school term begins are returned. There is very little risk to the store, because the store is only acting as an order taker. The "short discount" results in a lower price to the consuming student.

    These *short discounts* are sometimes applied to regular (trade) books, and when this is done, all sales literature should be clearly marked. The book trade will not be too enthusiastic about the poor discount, but they can't complain if they are buying in ones and twos and have been informed of the short discount in advance.

- **Online bookstores** were so eager to build market share that they often bought even at zero discount. Contact each of the online bookstores (see the listing in Appendix 2) for their information for publishers. Some have special programs requiring a higher discount such as the Amazon Advantage at 55%.

- **Libraries:** Some publishers give libraries a 20% discount, but most libraries do not expect a discount and many orders will arrive with a cheque made out for the full list price. Libraries are only ordering one book for an end-user, so there is no justification for a discount. Most small publishers charge libraries full list price.

FEDERAL TRADE COMMISSION RULES: The FTC requires that the discounts you offer one dealer be offered to all dealers who are purchasing the same quantity on the same terms. You are not required to extend credit, but if dealers are paying cash and want the same quantity, you must sell at the same discount. Search for "price discrimination" and the "Robinson-Patman Act" at http://www.ftc.gov.

Your distributor will order by the carton, usually 1,000 to 2,000 books. The wholesaler will in turn order 10 to 50 books from the distributor, and the bookstores will usually take 1 to 3 books from the wholesaler. If you sign with a distributor, you will have few direct sales to wholesalers or bookstores.

DISCOUNTS OUTSIDE THE BOOK TRADE: No single discount schedule fits all types of publishers. For example, if you have one book or a single small line of specialized books, cater primarily to a specific segment of people, and expect to have several large dealers who purchase hundreds of books at a time, you may wish to consider a simplified discount schedule. The simplified schedule works best for sales to stores other than bookstores.

1-2	No discount
3-199	-40%
200-499	-50%
500 and up	-40%, -25%

Simplified discount schedule

"Less 40%, less 25%" amounts to 55% off. First you deduct 40% and then take 25% off what is left. Wholesalers reselling to retailers make 25% on their investment, which is a good amount.

The simplified schedule gives every dealer the 40% they need, allows you to serve the nonbook industry with large orders while not upsetting the book trade with its small orders, and leaves you with just three figures to remember. Whatever discount schedule you choose, make it simple. You will have to use it to compute each order.

Normally titles can be mixed to achieve higher discounts, except where there is a great difference in price. You wouldn't mix a $1.50 title, normally wholesaled 500 at a time, with a $40 book usually purchased three at a time.

Your discounts and terms should be printed in your dealer bulletins, the ABA *Book Buyer's Handbook* (http://www.bookweb.org), and where requested in other listing forms. A sample of a dealer bulletin is given on the following page.

Don't confuse "discount" with "markup." A discount of 50% from $2 to $1 is the same as a 100% markup from $1 to $2.

When figuring your discounts, total the order and then subtract the discount. You will come out with a slightly higher figure than if you figure the discount per book and then extend it out. For example, 200 $5.95 books at 50% off = $595.00 but $5.95 - 50% = $2.97 x 200 = $594.00, a $1 difference.

Once you have published your prices and terms, stick to them. Besides the need to obey the FTC rules, it just is not profitable to deviate from those figures that took you so long to calculate. Some dealers will be asking for a better deal, and some publishers feel that any sale above their cost is a good one. But it is not fair to give one customer a better deal than another. You have to draw the line somewhere.

CONSIGNMENTS are when the dealer takes delivery of the books but doesn't pay the publisher until they are sold. Most distributors operate on consignment inventory and pay 90 to 120 days after they sell the books to the bookstore or wholesaler. While publishers should avoid selling to small accounts on consignment, there are good arguments for these terms with major distributors. Book manufactures require large print runs, so part of your inventory might just as well sit in another warehouse as well as your own.

The publisher is financing the author on one end and the bookstore's inventory at the other. We are in a consignment business that pretends it is not.

—Sol Stein, president, Stein and Day

Resale Prices For Books & Tapes on
Book Writing and Book Publishing

Dealer Bulletin   **January 1, 2002**

Featuring new and better discounts as well as a greater selection. See our brochures and Web site for descriptions and list prices. Please order using full title and/or ISBN for identification.

Terms are 30 days from date of invoice. A finance charge of 1.5% per month will be added to all balances over 30 days.

Discounts:		
1	book	No discount
2-4	books	20% off
5-9	books	30% off
10-24	books	40% off
25-49	books	42% off
50-74	books	44% off
100-199	books	48% off
200	Or more books	50% off

Credit: Orders over $50 must be prepaid or send bank and three trade references.

Shipping: Books are best shipped via UPS or USPS Priority Mail. We can ship via truck or Federal Express but do not recommend them for long distances because the rates are considerably higher. Shipping is FOB Santa Barbara.

We dislike **drop shipping** individual books but will do it at list less 40% plus $4.

Shortages or nonreceipt must be reported to us within 15 days of the ship date.

Resale Numbers: California dealers must mention their resale number with their order.

Promotional materials: We can supply photographs of all our publications for your catalog work. See the press room on our Web site.

Book Trade: Our books are available from major wholesalers such as Baker & Taylor, Ingram, Bookpeople and others. Our distributor to the book trade is Publishers Group West. **STOP orders** are accepted for individual books at list less 40% plus $4.

Orders may be sent to the address below. Telephone orders may be made to 800-PARAPUB, 9:00 am to 5:00 pm, Monday through Friday, Pacific Time (or to the answering machine after hours). Purchase orders may be faxed to 805-968-1379 or emailed to orders@ParaPublishing.com at any time.

A universal discount schedule

SHIPPING CHARGES are usually charged in addition to the price of the book for wholesale and retail sales and direct sales to individual customers (FOB origin).

HANDLING CHARGES upset many customers because they feel that *handling* is a cost of business. If you charge for *postage* and it is not the same as the amount on the package, you will also hear about it, especially from bookstores. So if you do plan to tack on a little extra to pay for the invoice and shipping supplies, call the "postage and handling" charge "shipping."

Those dealers who object to any figures higher than the actual postage on the carton usually just scratch it off the invoice when paying the bill. Invoice altering becomes more frequent after each postal rate hike.

A STOP order

STOP (Single Title Order Plan): Like SCOP (Single Copy Order Plan), "Stop" is an easy method for bookstores to order single books for their customers. A "stop order" consists of a special multipart order form that arrives with a cheque. Because the store is paying in advance, they assume a discount of 20% to 40%. The cheque may be filled in or blank and restricted to a certain maximum amount. Sometimes the order asks that the book be shipped directly to the customer and other times to the store. Part of the order form may be used as a shipping label.

Contact the American Booksellers Association for an application form for a listing in their ABA *Book Buyer's Handbook*. When you fill it out, indicate that you wish to participate in STOP and list your terms. Many publishers agree to accept STOP orders based on the list price less a 40% discount, plus $4 for shipping.

TERMS and credit are different in the book trade. Most wholesalers and bookstores routinely take 60 days to pay, many take 90, and some get around to mailing out cheques in six or eight months. This forces the publisher into a frustrating banking situation. There are very few small publishers who can afford to finance the inventories of their dealers.

The customary terms for the book industry are that invoices should be paid within 30 days of an end-of-the-month statement (30 EOM). This is up to 30 days longer than "net 30-day" terms. Some publishers, eyeing other industries, offer "2% 10-day" terms, but the dealer usually pays late and still takes the 2%. Another way to get most of your money faster is to offer 5% for "cash [or cheque] with order" (CWO). Unfortunately, this offer is usually taken by the financially sound good-pay store that would pay on time anyway, not by the slow-pay store you will have to chase for months. Many of the newer small publishers don't subscribe to the 30 EOM terms or discounts for fast pay; they quote strictly "net 30 days."

"Advance dating" of invoices is sometimes done for seasonal businesses and catalog houses. The invoice is dated a couple of months after the books are shipped. This provides the dealer with the opportunity to get the books into stock in advance before the rush—important where timing is critical and sales are not immediate.

Ship your invoices separately via first class mail; don't just enclose them in the carton with the books as invoices can be misplaced at the receiving dock. The longer it takes the invoice to reach the accounting department, the longer accounting will take to pay it.

Once you have decided on your terms and have published them, stick to them religiously. Any sign of relaxation will be evidence that you don't mean what you say, and some dealers will take advantage of you. You are a publisher, not a banker, and if you were in the loan business, you would charge interest.

CREDIT: It is only practical to extend credit and ship quickly to new accounts. You will receive all sorts of small orders from distant stores, and it is not worth the time and effort to run a credit check on each one. It may cost $50 or more to run a credit check, even if you do it all yourself by telephone, and it will take a lot of time. On one- and two-book orders, credit checks are not worth the effort for the occasional bad pay or bankruptcy.

If a large order out of nowhere seems too good to be true, it probably is. A few people have ordered large quantities of books (200 of a title) from small publishers without ever intending to pay for them. They turn around and sell the books to stores and remainder houses at a great discount.

In 1982, I suffered a serious accident just prior to the ABA book fair. I was in the hospital for five weeks and could not work for almost six months. While in the hospital, I received a very large order from someone who pretended to be a big wholesaler in Michigan. The buyer even had the nerve to write across the bottom of the purchase order: "Missed you at the ABA, get well soon." It took several years to put him out of business, and at last report even his bankruptcy trustee couldn't collect from him.

Set a limit of, say, $50 for any dealer order coming in on a letterhead or purchase order. Enclose your brochure, statement of terms and return policy with the invoice. You could even slip in a form letter welcoming their account, explaining that you are happy to extend credit and that prompt payment of this invoice will raise their limit to $100. Beyond that, you will require trade and bank references. Those who do not stand your test, or who are awaiting a credit check for a large purchase, can be urged to pay in advance via a **pro forma invoice** (you make out a complete invoice to include shipping charges, but you don't ship the books until the invoice is paid). Another clever trick is to ask for 50% of a large invoice in advance—then ship just 50% of the order.

Schools, libraries and state and federal governments are good pay but often slow pay. Just make sure their request comes on their purchase order. Too often someone in the parks department will write to you on city letterhead asking for a book, with no mention of money. This may well be an unauthorized order.

Sometimes schools or government agencies will telephone or fax an order and then follow with a written purchase order. If you are lucky, they will mark the second message "Confirming order—do not duplicate." Otherwise, you might wind up shipping twice.

Join a local publishing association and meet some of the people in other book firms. If you question an account, often a call to one of your contemporaries will provide the credit information you seek.

> Recently a business publisher used a "sure-fire" credit gimmick to increase his mail order sales. He offered an expensive business materials kit to large businesses on a "free trial" basis. They could use the materials for 14 days at "no risk," then either pay for them and receive a free bonus-disk, or return them. He figured most large businesses would buy the materials once they started using them. The orders came in and he shipped hundreds of kits...(you finish the story)... Hint: since the businesses had already received the kits—hardly any were paid for or sent back.

Foreign orders can be treated in the same way as domestic ones. There will be a difference in shipping charges, sometimes higher and sometimes lower. Unless they pay in dollars drawn on a U.S. bank, there may be a cheque cashing (currency conversion) charge. Foreigners have about the same payment history as U.S. Customers. The simplest way to avoid extra bank charges is to specify that all orders are payable in U.S. Funds drawn on a U.S. bank.

Some publishers place a surcharge on foreign orders, and it might be appropriate to add a small paperwork fee to very large orders requiring customs forms, but since most foreign orders do not require more work than domestic shipments, a surcharge discourages foreign sales and insults foreign customers.

STATEMENTS: Wholesalers and bookstores are accustomed to receiving end-of-the-month statements of their accounts; they want a recapitulation of the many small orders they have placed. Statements are not a requirement, but they may speed payment when these customers are waiting for one. Your accounting program can generate statements or you can photocopy the invoices and mail them.

Hand-write your collection message on the copy. The collection messages might include:

- Is there any reason why this past due bill has not been paid?

- If you are unable to pay the whole bill, won't you evidence your good faith by sending us a partial payment?

- We subscribe to Dun & Bradstreet's Commercial Collection service.

- If payment is not received within 10 days, we will be forced to turn this matter over to our attorney for collection.

Enclose brochures on new books with the statements. You might as well fill up the envelope to its full postage limit.

COLLECTIONS

When the money does not come in on time, you have to exercise your collection process.

When addressing invoices, always include the name of the person signing the book order. This focuses your claim on a specific individual, where it will have more impact than if you simply send invoices and statements to the company. Now pen a nice personal note to this particular person on the bottom of the statement.

If the account goes another month without a response, pen a stronger note on the bottom of the statement. Then wait two weeks and make a telephone call. If they don't pay in 90 days, cut them off. You don't need customers like them. In most other industries, 30 days would be the limit; the book industry is much slower pay.

After this, there are a couple of options. You can arrange with your attorney to send a standard collection letter. The charge might be $10 to $15 each for a quantity of collections. You might also consider a collection agency. Your local agency (see the yellow pages under "Collection Agencies") will have affiliates all over North America, or you might contact a large firm with many offices, such as Dun & Bradstreet. Collection agencies usually take one-third as their collection fee, and they prefer the easy cases. They have little power and usually get their money through a personal visit, which embarrasses the bookseller. They will threaten legal action and will turn the case over to a local attorney if they fail to collect. Generally, the older the debt, the harder it is to collect.

SKO-Brenner-American is a collection agency that specializes in the book trade. They publish a monthly confidential list of delinquent bookstores and wholesalers. They will also handle collections. For information on their services and a subscription to their newsletter, see http://www.skobrenner.com.

The telephone is a powerful collection instrument and a good supplement to dunning notices. Many callers use scripts to make sure they get their complete message across quickly.

Remember, it is better to have the books returned unsold than to have the books sold and not get paid.

If a customer has been bouncing large cheques on you, put the next one in "for collection." Your bank will send it to the customer's bank with instructions to hold the cheque until there is enough money in the account to pay it.

To collect a large bill from a foreign customer, try calling the cultural attaché at the nearest embassy or consulate. Often the attaché will relay your message, and this puts pressure on the foreign debtor.

Whatever collection system you select, make it automatic, so that you can be objective and will not allow deadbeats to negotiate delays. Let customers know you mean business. See *Business Letters for Publishers* in the Para Publishing Special Reports in Appendix 2 or at http://ParaPublishing.com for some suggested collection letters.

ACCOUNTS RECEIVABLE

This is one of the most pleasant operations, because it is fun to count your money. As the cheques arrive to pay for due bills, match them with the invoices. (If only everyone would note the invoice numbers on their cheques!) Mark the invoice with a date stamp to indicate when the payment was credited. Put this file copy in a record storage box or binder. See the invoice handling discussion in Chapter 10.

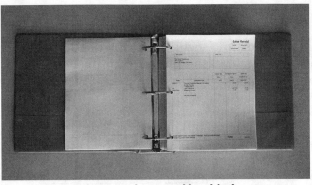

Invoices may be stored in a binder

Cheques will be made out to the publishing company, the author or the name of the book. List them all on your cheque deposit rubber stamp. Pay a little extra for a self-inking stamp; it will save you a lot of time.

Bank deposits can be made up every few days. If you do not use a computerized bookkeeping system, add the cheques up and submit your adding machine tape with your deposit slip. If your bank wants you to list each cheque individually on the deposit slip, threaten to go to another bank. Big corporations do not have to do this, and you won't either if you are assertive. Keep it simple!

RETURNS

Returned books are one of the biggest controversies in the publishing business amounting to over $7 billion annually. Distributors, wholesalers and bookstores expect to be able to return all books they do not sell. Bookstores return over 18% of the books they order to the distributor, but the distributor returns just 2% to the publisher and they are shelf worn. If this still sounds like a lot, then consider that the returns are so high for mass-market paperbacks that the dealers save shipping costs by "stripping" the books and sending back only the covers for credit.

The returns system almost amounts to *consignment*, and you are caught in a bind, because if the booksellers did not have the return privilege, they would be far less likely to carry your books. You want your books displayed and so you have to take the chance of having several of them come back. Therefore, there is little difference between consignment and a no-strings return policy. Returns result in zero profit transactions (ZPTs). The books went out with costly paperwork and came back with paperwork; everyone was busy, but nothing was sold.

From time to time, people in the book industry suggest changes to the system of returns. One popular recommendation is to eliminate the returns and pass the savings on to the bookstore in the form of higher discounts. Because we operate in a free-market economy with a lot of competition, none of these suggestions have ever caught on.

Make up a **return policy** and send it to anyone who requests it. Baker & Taylor and some of the other wholesalers will probably ask for your return policy when they first open an account with you. Also send the policy when a bookstore or wholesaler requests permission to return some books.

Most publishers will allow returns between 90 days and one year of the invoice date. They specify 90 days because they want to make sure the books were given a fair trial on the shelves, but one year because they do not want the books sitting around too long; the title may go into a new printing.

Most publishers require the bookseller to request permission and specific shipping instructions first, but few stores do. They just ship the books back.

The paperwork that comes with the return should identify the original invoice number under which the books were purchased. You want to credit the bookseller with the correct amount they paid. You also want to make sure the books came directly from you. If the books were purchased from a wholesaler, they should be returned to the wholesaler.

Books must arrive back at the publisher in good, unblemished, resalable condition so that they may be returned to stock. This is the biggest failing of the bookstores. They almost never pack the books properly. They just throw them in a carton, often without cushioning material, and send them back. During the long trip, the books chafe against each other and the carton and consequently arrive in a scuffed, unsalable condition.

Large publishing firms usually do not send refunds on returns. They issue *credits*, because they are dealing with the bookstore on a continuing basis. Small publishers, with few other titles to offer, should send a refund cheque.

BOOK RETURN AUTHORIZATION

1. OUR BOOKS ARE RETURNABLE. If a title isn't moving in your market, we want to get it back before a new edition makes it obsolete. Thank you for giving it a chance on your valuable shelf space. Our return period is normally between 90 DAYS AND ONE YEAR of the publisher's invoice date; however, we will accept the book for return after one year as long as the edition is still in print. To keep our products current, we update our titles every one and a half to two years.

2. RETURN PERMISSION MUST BE REQUESTED so that we can issue detailed packing and shipping instructions. This is your authorization and the instructions are below.

3. NOTICE OF SHORTAGE OR NONRECEIPT must be made within 30 days of the shipping/invoice date for domestic shipments, 60 days for foreign.

4. BOOKS DAMAGED IN TRANSIT are not the responsibility of the publisher. Please make claim to the carrier.

5. Returns must be accompanied by your packing slip listing QUANTITY, TITLE, AUTHOR, ORIGINAL INVOICE NUMBER and INVOICE DATE. Books returned with this information will be credited with 100% of the invoice price minus shipping. Otherwise, it will be assumed that the original discount was 60%. Some books have been returned to us when they should have been directed to one of our wholesalers; books should be returned to their source.

6. ROUTING: Ship books via parcel post (book rate) prepaid or UPS prepaid to Para Publishing, Attn: D. Poynter, 530 Ellwood Ridge, Santa Barbara, CA 93117-1047. Note: This is not the same as our order address.

7. To qualify for a refund, returned books must arrive here in good RESALABLE CONDITION. If they are not now resalable, please don't bother to return them. If you are not willing to package them properly for the return trip, please don't waste your time and postage.

   To package the books so that they will survive the trip, we suggest you wrap them the same way they were sent to you. There are two important steps in successful book packaging: Keep them clean and immobilize them. Place the stacked books in a plastic bag. This will separate the dirty newsprint and greasy "peanuts" from the book edges and will prevent grit from creeping between the covers. To keep the books from shifting (which causes scuffing), cut a shipping carton to the right size and stuff it tightly with padding.

   Since it has been our experience that books shipped loose in oversize Jiffy bags always arrive scuffed, it is now our policy to simply REFUSE them at the post office so that they will be returned to the bookstore. DO NOT USE JIFFY BAGS!

8. A credit memo will be issued toward future purchases.

9. Industry tells us that it now costs more than $8 to write a letter. Correspondence, packaging and postage cost us all a great deal in money and time (and time is money.) Years ago, when postage was cheap, it made sense to return slow-moving books. Today, however, many bookstores are finding it is far more cost effective to simply mark down the books and move them out.

Sample returns policy statement

7
Promoting Your Book

Making the Public Aware of Your Book
Without Spending for Advertising

If you intend to be a successful author, you will measure your success with money. To make a profit, you will depend on good promotion. This chapter covers promotion: those methods that require some time and effort but no big advertising dollars. Of course, there will be a certain amount of overlap.

It does not matter if you sell out to a publisher or publish yourself; the author must do the promotion.

Your most important reference book will be *Literary Market Place*. Although you can use the copy in your local library, this book will be used so often that you should buy one for use at your desk or get an on-line subscription to it.

The secrets to book sales are (1) to produce a good product that has a market and (2) to let people know about it. Many small publishers receive very little publicity for their books. This lack of attention is not because of any great conspiracy between the big (New York) publishers and the media; it is simply because the neophytes do not ask for coverage. Many small publishers are good at publishing but haven't any experience in promoting. They seem to have little interest in their books beyond the editorial work and production. They do not want to promote; they just want to create. Some beginning publishers feel the marketing end of publishing is too "commercial," and this becomes their excuse for neglecting the most important part of any business: informing the buying public of their wares. For, obviously, if you don't sell your product, you will not be able to afford to produce more editorial material.

Being an author is 5% writing and 95% promotion.
—**Russ Marano,** *Hi-Tek Newsletter*

THE COST OF ADVERTISING

Selling books through space advertising is expensive, because books are a "low ticket" (low selling-price) item. If you were selling airplanes, one sale would pay for a lot of ad space, and if you were selling something less expensive like candy, you would sell so much to so many people that the ads might pay. It is tougher to break even when advertising a low-priced product to a small and scattered group of people. For example, a half page ad in a national book-oriented magazine might cost $1,850. Using round numbers and assuming you printed the book for $2 and are selling it for $20, you would have to sell 102 books at retail, or 308 books at wholesale, just to break even on the ad. Experience tells us you will be lucky to get five orders.

Do not spend money on advertising until you have exhausted all the free publicity.

Use free publicity to find out which magazines are right for your book. Then spend your advertising money there. Always test before you spend money. Too many publishers start with large ads and blow their promotion money in the wrong places.

ADVERTISING VS. PUBLICITY

The major differences between advertising and publicity are cost and control. Publicity is free, but advertising is not. On the other hand, you can control your advertising, but your news release (publicity) might be rewritten by an editor, drastically changed or not run at all.

Generally, book promotion is less expensive and more successful when you use book reviews, news releases and, if appropriate to your book, a limited amount of highly targeted direct mail advertising. Book reviews are "editorial copy" that is far less expensive and far more credible than space advertising. For most nonfiction books, there are over 500 appropriate magazines and newspaper columns that receive and review books, and the number of review sources is growing with the proliferation of online reviewers. Then you should follow up with news releases every month to the very same magazines and newspapers (especially when you can tie into your book a national breaking news story). Let these opinion-molding editors know what you are doing and why your book has the information their readers need.

Just as a parent's responsibilities do not end with giving birth, an author's do not end with publication. The *child* must be raised and the *book* must be promoted.

EDITORIAL COPY VS. ADVERTISING COPY: On the average, people spend seven minutes with their magazines. Obviously, they see very few of the ads. Of those ads they do see, they read very few. Of those ads they read, they believe very few. Of those ads they believe, they act on very few. People are skeptical of advertisements. On the other hand, readers tend to believe editorial copy. Now ask yourself: How much advertising space can you buy for $1,500? Not much—and it won't sell many books anyway. For the same amount, you can send out 500 review copies, many of which will result in editorial copy (articles and reviews) that people will believe. The public is usually more receptive to publicity because editorial copy is viewed as news and advertising is perceived as self-serving. An industry rule of thumb is that editorial coverage is seven times as valuable as paid coverage.

> The main difference between marketing a book and marketing soap is that a book is a one-shot deal.... A book usually has only 90 days to make it or it is dead.
> **—Carole Dolph, promotional director, Doubleday & Co.**

However, competition for free space is a tough proposition. Three hundred new titles are published each day, and with the growth of purely electronic books, the daily output may be considerably higher. More books are published in the fall than the spring. You have to compete for attention in a crowded field and against much larger, more knowledgeable firms. But you will be surprised at how successful you can be when you jump into the fray, exploiting the media through news releases, review copies, radio and TV appearances, feature stories, interviews and pre-sensation—especially when you target specific audiences.

Large publishers are lucky if 40% of their titles make money, and remember that they have whole departments of experts to launch their promotions. They also have built up thousands of key contacts during their many years in the business. You have only one book, your first, and therefore you have only one chance to make it. But look at the brighter side. The big firms often work by routine and without imagination, spending only a short time promoting a book before moving on to the next line. They do not have anyone on the staff who knows anything about either the subject matter of the book or specialized promotion. They do not know which groups of people care about this particular subject.

And your overhead is much lower. You cut out the intermediaries by publishing yourself. You will do a more effective job of promotion because you have a greater interest in your book than a publisher who is looking after several titles (or several hundred titles) at one time. There is a lot of room for the very small independent publisher with imagination, initiative and a well-defined target market.

By doing the promotion yourself, you avoid the most common problem in author-publisher relationships: differing on the amount of effort that should be invested in each area of promotion and advertising. The author cannot be objective about his or her product and is convinced that the book would sell better if only the publisher would spend money to promote it. The publisher, on the other hand, needs more sales to convince him or her that it is worth investing more dollars in promotion. As both author and publisher, you see both perspectives and make the final decisions.

Many, many times, I have said, "This is too hard. I am getting out of this business," but then something good will happen and my enthusiasm is replenished.
—Patricia Gallagher, *For All the Write Reasons*

BOOK PROMOTION TAKES TIME: Writing the book is the easy part—the tip of the iceberg. The real work begins when you switch hats to expend time and money on promoting the book.

Book reviews take three months to three years to appear, because magazines and even daily newspapers have long lead times. Do not get discouraged. The easiest mistake is to send out books for review, email news releases on your book or post a direct mail offer, and then sit back and wait for the results. The secret of savvy book promotion is to keep up the pressure: keep sending out the packets and keep making the telephone calls.

BEGINNING THE PROMOTION

FIRST ANALYZE THE MARKET by determining who might purchase your book, and then figure out the best way to reach them. Your buyer must be *identifiable* and *locatable*. Ask yourself what stores they frequent, what magazines they read, what associations they join, what conventions or events they attend, what channels they watch, what Listservs they join and so on. Where can you find a high concentration of people interested in your book?

Analyze carefully the type of person who is a prospective purchaser of your book. This is perhaps the single most important thing to consider.

If your book is on auto repair for the car owner, one prospect is the car enthusiast. What do they read? You will want to send news releases, review copies and maybe even articles to auto magazines. Since there will be few women who will purchase such a book, you won't send review copies to women's magazines. Where do car enthusiasts congregate? Auto supply stores, car rallies, auto shows? If this repair manual covers one type of car, you may be able to find a highly targeted mailing list of owners of that type of car. Check the Internet for Listservs and chat groups for auto repair. The trick is to think about who the buyer might be and then think about where this type of person can be found. Rarely is the answer bookstores or libraries.

Show me a publisher who says you can never tell which book will make it and I will show you a publisher who evaluates manuscripts without considering the market.

As you read through the next few chapters, think about your book and its market. Make a list of, or underline, those ideas mentioned that best fit your book. Then go back and work out a promotional schedule, by the week, for several months. Set a schedule so you won't lose sight of it later when you are busy keyboarding orders and stuffing cartons.

One reason the demand for books is constant is that the book-buying public is not static. It is constantly changing. New readers are entering the bookshops all the time, while old readers are going to that big library in the sky.

—Max Alth

If you are approaching general bookstores, college bookstores, public libraries or school libraries, you will want to determine their seasonal buying patterns. If you are pursuing direct-mail sales, you will want to set up a system of mailings and emphasize the program in higher response seasons. The keys to your promotion are market "targeting and timing." More on all these later.

If your book fails to sell, you don't know your market.

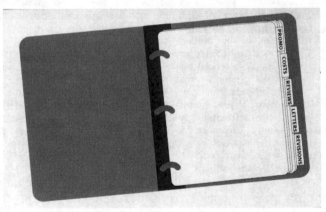

Set up a promotion binder for each book

ASSEMBLE A BINDER: Organize your promotion thoughts and record your work by setting up a binder for your book. Use a 2" or 3" three-ring binder with dividers for five sections. Slant-ring binders with inside pockets are best. Now set up each section as follows:

➤ **Section 1** is where you record your **promotional plan.** Type up your initial plan and check off the items when completed. Whenever you have a new idea, turn to the second page of Section 1 and make a note. Use the balance of this section to store every news release you write, every mailing you make and every brochure you design. Date each promotional piece and record the results. In the back of Section 1, store copies of the publishing forms you file. You may have to subdivide Section 1 as the amount of your promotion increases so that you can easily file and locate your materials in each marketing category.

●◆ **Section 2** is for all your **costing information**. Store copies of all the printing, artist, trucking, etc., bills as well as all the printing quotations. With this information all in one place, even after six printings, you will know exactly how many books have been printed and what each edition cost.

●◆ **Section 3** is where you store the **reviews**, **testimonials** and **other publicity** you have generated. All the good things that have been said about your book are kept in one place, so that when you want to make a list of testimonials, they will be easy to find.

●◆ **Section 4** is for any **important correspondence**. Here you will store some of the more interesting letters that do not fit in the other sections.

●◆ **Section 5** is the **revision section**. As you come across new material or think of something that should be included in the next edition, make a note and store it here.

You will appreciate the promotion binders even more after you publish several books. All your costing, promotion, review and revision information will be easy to find.

KEEP TRACK OF CORRECTIONS: Also take one copy of the book, mark it "Correction Copy," and keep it near your desk. Cut off a corner of the front cover so that it won't walk out of your office or find its way back into stock. As you find small errors or want to make changes, mark this book. Then when it comes time to return to press, all your revision information will be in the correction copy and the fifth section of your binder.

PATTERN OF SALES: You can expect your sales to take on an airfoil shape if your promotion is well organized. For most books, sales will climb rapidly, level out, taper off and become steady.

Thereafter, you will notice bumps in response to seasonal changes or when your advertising or promotional work is successful. The big initial jump is due to your prepublication publicity.

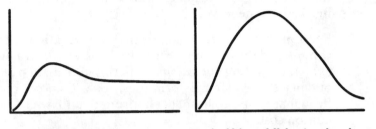

Your sales chart   **Typical big publisher's sales chart**

The big New York publishers promote books in the same way Hollywood publicizes a motion picture: they throw it out on the market to see if anyone likes it. If it gets a response, they dump in some promotional money. Then they may push it for a couple of months. When the interest cools, they bring out another product and start the process all over. As a small publisher, it makes more sense to market your book like breakfast food or soap. Develop your product, pour on the promotion, establish a niche in the market and then continue to sell at the same level for years. This can be done with a nonfiction book that is revised and kept "fresh" at each printing.

"BEST-SELLERS" are only a name, a myth. This is not like a gold record in the music industry or another service to the trade run by Bowker. National best-seller lists (there are several, and they do not often agree) are assembled from certain bookstore and other sales reports. Even if you move a million books via mail order distribution, you won't make a best-seller list, because the list may only track bookstore sales. On the other hand, you may calculate that your book is the best-selling book in its field, and there is no reason you can't mention this in your advertising. For example, *Parachuting Manual with Log* is the best-selling skydiving book of all time. For more information on the various best-seller lists, advice on how to make them and scores of great promotional ideas, see Document 612,

Best-Sellers: What They Are and How to Make Them, at http://Para Publishing.com.

PROMOTION IS UP TO THE AUTHOR: Large publishers do not effectively promote books. One of the biggest misconceptions in traditional publishing is that the publisher will take care of all the promotion. Publishers actually do little promoting, and by the time the author figures this out, the book is not new, making any further promotional efforts too late. The media is geared toward reporting about the latest current releases (front list titles), they rarely pay attention to older books.

A self-publisher who had his book acquired by a major publisher at a recent BEA convention, was promised a 20-city author tour and much specialized promotion. The reality: the book had a limited print-run, was dumped into the bookstores, there was no special promotion to his target market, and he was allowed one-day in three cities and had to share expenses for the mini author tour.

Bookstores make your book available, but they do not promote it. These outlets provide availability, but you must encourage people to go into the stores. If your book is a hot seller, the bookstores will want to carry it. If no one asks for it, the stores will not touch it. Authors must create the demand.

Authors need to be assertive and take control of the book's promotion. Start by searching for mailing lists, sending for ad rate cards and drafting news releases (more on these later). There is a lot to learn from this chapter even if you aren't self-publishing.

KEY CONTACTS are those people who can help you move the greatest volume of books with the least expenditure of time and money. These contacts must be developed if you are going to promote your book properly. The only difference between you and a professional book publicist is that the professional already has media contacts. There are many wholesalers, TV people and subsidiary rights buyers who are just waiting to discover you and your book. Even though most are very busy, they want you; that is what their job is all about. You will meet a great number of nice, helpful people, but only a few key contacts will do you a great amount of good. What you have to do is locate them and then carefully cultivate them. Some of the people will be listed in *Literary Market Place* and other directories available at your library. For others, you may have to call the company and ask for the name of the buyer or acquisitions person, for example. Tell the company operator (or even better, someone in the special division you are targeting) who you are and ask who you should properly correspond with. Write, email or call this contact and field your sales pitch; establish a rapport, but also be brief, as they are usually very busy. Maintain credibility, and remember that they are everyone else's key contact too. Do not expect them to return calls. Send review copies of your book and follow up in a few days with a telephone call asking, "Have you received it?"

Start files on these key contacts and fill the folders with letters and notes of your telephone conversations. Track them with a contact-management software program such as ACT!, Goldmine, TELEMagic and Maximizer. Note the personal likes and dislikes of your contacts so you can bring them up in future conversations. Treat contacts well, and with intelligence, and they will be there to help you with your next book too.

ADDRESS CODES

Tracing each order you receive back to a specific promotional effort or paid advertisement provides you with important business intelligence. Without this information, you may be unknowingly spending your energy and money in the wrong places. Waste becomes tragedy when you continue blind promotional spending because you are not certain which promotions are paying off. Both your time and money are limited; you must spend them in those places that will bring maximum return. The trick is to add a code to your address.

To code your address, just add an extra letter or number to your street address or PO box. Code everything! Every brochure, ad, order blank, news release, directory listing, everything. Then you will receive only a few orders you cannot trace to a specific effort. Some people will be influenced by your promotion and instead of buying through your ad or mailer, will look for your book at their library or bookstore. But coding will indicate the source of most of your orders.

List your address as *4759 Walker Street, Suite 712*, or in a classified ad where every word costs, *4759-712 Walker* (the code part is 712). Many customers figure out the obvious codes and, knowing they aren't important to the address, leave them off. So if you are advertising in *Popular Science* in August 2002, don't use

4759 Walker Street, Dept. PS-8-2. Use a plain number or a suite number; they appear important to the address. Never use a department number—that is an obvious code. Careful coding is even more important with news releases and those items not going directly to the general public, because the media are conscious of these codes and often won't repeat them. An address code is of no value to you if it doesn't get used.

List all the places where you are mailing news releases and other promotional material, and give a short code to each. Letters are good for a start, but there aren't enough of them and some can be confused when rendered in script on an envelope. Avoid "I" and "1," "u" and "v," "G" and "6," "Z" and "2," "0" and "O," and "4" and "H."

> People often ask, "But won't the post office object to all this added information?" The answer is no, as long as the essential addressing information is there so they can easily determine where to direct your mail. On the other hand, you may confuse visiting customers who drive down your street looking for a building tall enough for a Suite 712.

Add a field to your order-entry software program and record the source-code of the orders as you generate invoices.

Total the responses periodically and record them by code letter or number on a ledger sheet. Also enter on the sheet when certain advertising and promotion was generated and when you receive your first response; so you can better visualize the timing and results. Where some of your orders originated can be quite revealing. How else would you know, for example, that a mention in a *Changing Times* article brought in 140 orders? Or that most foreign bookstores find you in *Books in Print*? Or that a book to one review source was actually passed to another magazine for review? With this information, you will be able to assess what works and where you can most effectively spend your time and money to generate more sales. After a few months, you will wonder why address coding wasn't obvious to you from the beginning. Coding is especially important if you are placing coupon ads in multiple specialized magazines.

PROMOTIONAL MATERIALS

"Promotional materials" can take many forms. Initially they may include photocopies of your manuscript, folded and gathered pages from the printer, page printouts, overruns on covers, etc.

Consider combining the jacket of your book with a cover letter and an order blank for a mailing. Another successful and popular promotional package consists of press kit folders made from overruns of the cover. Just ask the printer to print a few hundred extra covers. Then fold them, tuck in your promotional materials and mail them out. The result is an inexpensive yet impressive, professional-looking press kit. Or, cut out the front cover and paste or double-stick tape it to the front of "pocket-portfolios" available in various colors at stationery stores.

> *Hiring a publicist isn't a vanity; it is a realistic commercial decision.*
> —**Paul Cowan**, *Mixed Blessing*

PROFESSIONAL BOOK PUBLICITY/MARKETING SERVICES are available if you don't have the time or desire to organize your own promotion. Book publicists primarily write and place news releases, organize autograph parties and place authors on TV and radio. Marketing services, on the other hand, specialize in securing distribution, promoting to libraries and special-sales sources, sending out galleys and review books, organizing co-op marketing, Internet promotion, exhibits, advertising, and creating promotional materials and sales brochures. A few target new sales outlets, specialty stores, and sell foreign and sub-rights.

Some publicists/marketers will have an expertise in specific markets—cookbooks, computer books, fiction, Christian, Spanish-language, etc.

More and more authors who are published by large New York publishers are hiring their own PR firms to promote their books, knowing that the publisher will do little to promote.

Publicity companies usually work on a retainer basis, some on a per-placement basis, rarely do they work by the hour. The average monthly retainer is between $2,000 and $4,000. Publicity takes time; you must hire the publicist for several months. Many ask for a six-month contract.

For an author tour (radio, TV, print media and bookstore autographings), a publicist might ask for $1,500 plus expenses for the first city they serve and $500, for each additional city. In each city, you might do four or more appearances each day for two days.

If you decide to hire a professional publicist or marketing service, start early. Do not wait until your publication date. However, your book should be readily available in bookstores before you start appearing on radio or TV.

Publishers Weekly estimates there are close to 200 independent book publicists. Some are listed in Appendix 2 under Publicists/Marketing, and more may be found in *Literary Market Place* under Public Relations Services.

Publicists are very expensive. Most self-publishers are better advised to follow this book and promote the book themselves.

Books do not sell themselves. People sell books.

TESTIMONIALS AND ENDORSEMENTS: Testimonials sell books because many people feel that there is no greater credibility than a recommendation from a satisfied customer. Testimonials and endorsements will be used in two places: on the back cover of the book and in your sales literature.

Endorsements for your **Back Cover** may be gathered from "peer reviewers" who read and comment on your complete manuscript or individual chapters. Initially, you want their comments as peer reviewers to double-check your work, and then you want to quote their praise. Therefore, they must be "opinion molders." This means you want people known in the book's field or known to the general public. They should be people with recognizable names or recognizable titles, are connected to well known companies or organizations, or have professional credentials (doctor, lawyer, professor, author, politician, etc.).

For example, you might ask me to endorse your book if it is on writing, publishing or skydiving. My endorsement on other subjects would not be appropriate or valuable since I am not known outside these fields.

You will want to add testimonials and excerpts from your reviews to all your **Sales Literature**, brochures and Web site, as well as to your "review and testimonial sheet." The review and testimonial sheet is an important part of your publicity package, because it indicates that other people like your book. This sheet should be assembled from in-coming reviews, and sent to later reviewers, prospective dealers and anyone else you are trying to convince that the book is a winner.

You may need endorsements on a particular point, or you may need a variety of endorsements. You do not want all the blurbs to say the same thing, or to be very general, such as "It is a great book." After someone has reviewed your manuscript, approach them again. Write out an endorsement making a particular point (relating your book to *their* audience), and ask the peer reviewer to look it over and edit it. Say that you need a quotation in this area. Editing is much easier than creating, and most people will accept the prompting quickly or just go with your version of the endorsement.

The best way to collect testimonials is to ask for them. It is easier than you think, because people like to see their name in print. As long as your book is good, experts in the field will jump at the chance to be mentioned. If they sell products or consulting, the exposure is valuable to them. Whether due to vanity or possible financial gain, high-profile people want to have their names in print. Stephen King seems to endorse (and get his name on) every book he can. Do not pay for endorsements; quotations cannot be considered valid if payments are involved.

Shoot high. Solicit testimonials from the most important and most recognizable people in your industry or activity. You may be able to locate their office address, their agent or someone who knows them.

Unsolicited testimonials will arrive after the book is published. They should be acknowledged and filed for future use. For more information, see Document 609, *Blurbs for Your Books: Testimonials, Endorsements and Quotations*, at http://ParaPublishing.com.

PUBLICATION DATE

The publication date is a place in the future, well after your books are off the press, when your books are available in the stores and your promotion hits. The publication date is a means of focusing attention. The idea is to have the product accessible when public attention peaks in response to your promotion. You want to time book reviews, TV appearances, autograph parties, etc., to hit after your book is in the bookstores and readily available.

The publication date has nothing to do with the date your book is published (the day it comes off the press and you have finished books in hand). It is the date you list on the ABI (Advance Book Information) form, but it is not the *day of publication* you list on the copyright form. The publication date is a *fiction* for the benefit of a few big important prepublication review magazines such as *Publishers Weekly*. There is nothing to stop you from selling or shipping books before the "pub-date." Sometimes entire print runs are sold out prior to the publication date.

After your publication date has passed, remove mention of it from your review slip, news release, etc. There is no need to remind the media that your book is no longer new. Let them focus on the issues and the quality of the book.

The big important prepublication reviewers need three to four months of lead-time. *Publishers Weekly* and the other wholesale trade review magazines need this time to evaluate your book, assign it to a reviewer, write the review and get it into print for the benefit of the stores. Monthly and bimonthly magazines such as *Kirkus Reviews* need even more lead-time (five months). The stores, in turn, need time to order the book and receive it into stock so it will be available to the public on or before your publication date (known in the bookstore as your "in-store" date). When planning your publication date, remember that book rate shipping can take three weeks from coast to coast.

Newspapers have shorter lead times than magazines. Since they are dailies or weeklies, they require books just a few weeks prior to the publication date.

Production is always subject to delay, so it is recommended that for your first book, and until you learn the challenges exacted by the printing trade, you wait until the book is off the press before you set your publication date.

If you have achieved sufficient prepublication momentum, you should make a significant amount of sales before the printing bill arrives. It is a matter of planning, scheduling, timing and work. The big publishers expend 90% of their promotional effort before the publication date. You, of course, will keep up the pressure.

The best publication dates are probably in the first quarter of the year. Most of the big publishers aim for October and

November to take advantage of the Christmas gift-buying season. Avoiding the last quarter of the year will decrease your competition for publicity. But get your book to market; never hold it back for a better release date. Sell fresh information.

Some publishers tie their publication date to a significant date to hitch on to publicity naturally occurring on that date. For example, if you have a book on an aspect of World War II, you might tie in to D-Day. People will be thinking about the war on this date, so your book will benefit from the memorial publicity. If you know your book and its subject area well, finding a date to link to should be easy. If you need help, check Chase's *Annual Events,* Kremer's *Celebrate Today* and Beam's *Directory of International Tourist Events.*

It is always smart to take advantage of a prime selling season. A book on a summer sport should come out in early spring, when people are making plans for the summer, but not in summer, when they are outside and not reading. A book on skiing should come out in the fall.

For a fuller explanation and a chart, see Document 608, *Your Publication Date*, at http://ParaPublishing.com.

The **ship date** is the month your book arrives from the printer and will be available to your distributor and dealers. It is preferably four to five months prior to the publication date.

BOOK REVIEWS

Reviews sell books. They are the least expensive and most effective promotion you can possibly do for your book. Considering the cost of producing the book, promotional materials, mailing packaging and postage, each promotional package usually costs less than $3 as it goes out the door. That means you can send review copies to over 300 magazines for around $900. If you are writing on a subject of interest to business people, your book should be of interest to over 1,000 business-oriented magazines, newsletters and newspaper columns in the U.S. Unfortunately, most large New York publishers are very cheap with review copies—sending out less than 50. Reviews are not difficult to get, and they cost you very little in time and money.

Because nonfiction books are news, we get our products reviewed free.

There are two major types of book review media: "prepublication date" or wholesale reviews and "postpublication date" or retail reviews. They cater to separate markets, and the approach to each is different. In addition, there are early reviews and continuing reviews. The book review order and breakdown look like this:

- **Prepublication date reviews** aimed at the wholesale book market.

- **Early reviews,** copyright and directory listings.

- **Postpublication date reviews** aimed at the retail market. These include:
    - **sure bets:** those that *will probably* review the book.
    - **the rest:** those that *might possibly* review the book.

- **Continuing review program.**

PREPUBLICATION REVIEWS are directed toward the book industry. Certain magazines will review your book prior to publication so that the bookstores and libraries will have the opportunity to stock it before patrons start asking for it. Since over 300 new titles are published each day, there is no way a store can stock every book. In fact, booksellers can't even spend the time to evaluate them all. Consequently, many book dealers and librarians depend on the summaries in industry review magazines when making their purchasing choices. Prepublication reviews are directed at the trade and should not be confused with the regular book reviews aimed at the consumer/reader. Good reviews in the prepublication review magazines will bring you more good reviews in other publications later, because many reviewers want to review books that are already starting to get recognition and have been pre-selected by others.

There is no way anything you send to PW can be too early.
—John Baker, editorial director, *Publishers Weekly*

Prepublication reviewers expect to receive **bound galleys.** Galleys can be the same as the laser output you sent to your book printer (each bookpage centered in the middle of an 8.5 x 11 inch sheet of paper), but you stand a much better chance of review if the pages are trimmed to the final size and perfect-bound with a plain typeset cover. If you send a finished book with a finished cover to a prepublication reviewer, it will not be reviewed, because it is obviously not "prepublication." For instructions on preparing galleys or Cranes, see *Book Reviews* in Para Publishing Special Reports in Appendix 2 or at http://.Para Publishing.com.

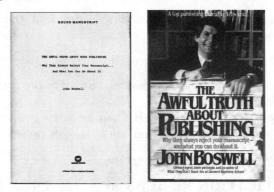

Bound galley and finished book

F&Gs are the Folded and Gathered signatures of the printed book ready for binding. F&Gs formerly were sent to the publisher for final approval prior to binding the print run. Bound galleys are F&Gs with a generic perfect-bound cover added.

Four to five months prior to your publication date, send bound galleys with a cover letter and a news release to the following prepublication reviewers, then send a follow-up copy of the finished book one to two months after sending the galley. But you *must* send the galley first.

1. *Publishers Weekly*, Forecasts, 360 Park Avenue So., New York, NY 10010-1710; 646-746-6758; fax 646-746-6631. *PW* is directed at the book trade (bookstores, wholesalers, libraries and publishers). A good review here will result in many bookstore orders; most will come through wholesalers. PW gives priority to books with broad general appeal. They review about 7,600 new books each year. They do not review reprints, reissues or revised editions. Send galleys between 12 and 16 weeks of your publication date. Circulation: 38,000. Contact *PW* for their "Forecast Submission Guidelines," and see the first page of the

Forecasts section for recent submission details. See http://www.publishersweekly.com/about/forecast-guid elines.asp.

2. *Library Journal,* Book Review Editor, 360 Park Avenue So., New York, NY 10010-1710; 888-800-5473 or 646-746-6818; fax: 646-746-6734; bkrev@lj.cahners.com. *LJ* is a magazine directed to general public librarians. They review over 6,000 books each year, from the 30,000 received, specifically to assess their value to the library market. For many nonfiction books, a good review in *LJ* will sell over 1,000 copies. A rave review on a high demand topic may move 5,000. Most of these library orders will come through a library wholesaler, and some 80% of these through Baker & Taylor. Therefore, it is important to let the wholesalers know about your book too. *LJ* will review from galleys or the finished book. Circulation: 28,000. See http://www.libraryjournal.com /about/submission.asp.

3. *Kirkus Reviews,* Library Advance Information Service, 770 Broadway, New York, NY 10003-9597. Tel: 646-654-4602; kirkusrev@kirkusreviews.com; fax 646-654-4706. *KR* is a book review magazine directed toward libraries and bookstores. They review about 4,800 books annually; most any fiction and nonfiction except poetry, mass-market paperbacks and children's books for toddlers. *KR* likes to see two copies of the galley four to five months prior to publication of the book. Circulation: about 5,400.

4. ALA *Booklist,* Up Front, Advance Reviews, 50 East Huron St., Chicago, IL 60611; 800-545-2433 or 312-944-6780; fax 312-337-6787. *Booklist,* published by the American Library Association, reviews books for small- and medium -sized public libraries. They review fiction, nonfiction, reference, young adult and children's books; over 8,000 reviews per year. This does not include textbooks, workbooks, pamphlets or coloring materials. Send galleys or finished books. Circulation: 31,500. See http://www. ala.org.

5. *New York Times Book Review,* Charles McGrath, 229 West 43rd St., New York, NY 10036; 212-556-1234; fax

212-556-1320. The *New York Times* is one of the most prestigious of review publications, publishing about 2,200 reviews annually. *Times* reviews are also syndicated, so a review there may appear in papers throughout the country. The *Times* does not review very technical, specialized or juvenile books. Send galleys and then send follow-up books when printed. Circulation: 1,600,000. See http://www.nytimes.com/books.

6. *Los Angeles Times Book Review*, Steve Wasserman, 202 West 1st St., Los Angeles, CA 90012; 213-237-7778; fax 213-237-4712; steve.wasserman@latimes.com. *Times* editors look for books that are of general interest to their newspaper readers, reviewing over 2,100 per year. Circulation: 1,100,000 daily, 1,300,000 Sunday. See http:// www.latimes.com.

7. *School Library Journal* (two copies), Attn: Trevelyn Jones, 360 Park Avenue So., New York, NY 10010-1710; 212-463-6759; fax: 646-746-6689; tjones@cahners.com. *SLJ* prints over 4,000 reviews annually by school and public librarians of new books for children and young adults. They will consider for review any book appropriate for school library use. This monthly (except June and July) has a circulation of 43,000. See http://www.slj.com.

8. **Quality Books, Inc.**, New Title Acquisitions, 1003 W. Pines Rd., Oregon, IL 61061-9680; 800-323-4241 or 815-732-4450; fax 815-732-4499. Quality is a distributor of small press titles to libraries. They want to know about your nonfiction books and tapes early. Contact them for application forms. See http://www.quality-books.com.

9. **Major book clubs.** Send bound galleys to the major clubs, such as Book-of-the-Month and Literary Guild and those specializing in the book's field. See *Literary Market Place* for a list of book clubs. See http://www.literarymarketplace. com.

10. *Foreword Magazine*, 104 So. Union St. #207, Traverse City, MI 49684; 231-933-3699; http://www.forewordmag azine.com.

11. Presentation copies to **opinion molders.** The best way to get sales moving is to get the book talked about by the right people. This group may amount to anywhere from just a very few people to hundreds. Sometimes a publisher will send special bound galleys to opinion molders to get the public talking about the book. Many people feel that receiving an advance bound galley is much more impressive than receiving the actual book. Some opinion molders should get bound galleys, but others should receive the finished product.

EARLY REVIEWS, COPYRIGHT AND LISTINGS: In anticipation of your new book coming off the press, address shipping bags to those places listed below and stuff them, as appropriate, with cover letter, review slips, photocopied Advance Book Information (ABI) form, and a 4" x 6" or larger photograph of the book's cover. Stuff in brochures, copies of early reviews and other materials to convince reviewers the book has been accepted by others. Do not skimp here. Then when the truck arrives from the printer, stuff the books into the bags and ship them off.

Take note what is said about each of the addressees below, because some may not be appropriate to your book. If yours is an adult scientific text, do not bother to send it to the *Horn Book* magazine, which reviews children's books.

1. *American Book Review,* Rebecca Kaiser, Illinois State University, Campus Box 4241, Normal, IL 61790; 309-438-3026; fax 309-438-3523. This bimonthly, with a circulation of 15,000, reviews 240 books each year.

2. **Baker & Taylor.** To establish a business relationship with Baker & Taylor, contact Robin Bright, Publishers Services, PO Box 6885, Bridgewater, NJ 08807; 908-541-7000; brightr@btol.com; http://www.btol.com.

3. *Booklist,* American Library Association, 50 East Huron St., Chicago, IL 60611; 800-545-2433 or 312-944-6780; fax 312-440-9374; http://www.ala.org/booklist. You should have sent bound galleys to *Booklist* some months earlier.

4. *Chicago Tribune Books,* Elizabeth Taylor, 435 North Michigan Ave., Chicago, IL 60611 312-222-3232; fax 312-222-0234. See http://chicagotribune.com/leisure/books.

5. *Choice,* Editorial Dept., 100 Riverview Center, Middletown, CT 06457; 860-347-6933; fax 860-704-0465; choicemag @ala-choice.org; http://www.ala.org/acrl/choice. *Choice* is a publication of the Association of College and Research Libraries, a division of the American Library Association. *Choice* reviews 7,200 books annually for the $300 million academic library market: high school, college and special libraries. Monthly except August. Circulation: 4,800.

6. **Feature News Service,** Jim White, PO Box 19852, St. Louis, MO 63144-2096; 314-961-9827. Reviews books for 87 weekly papers.

7. **Gale Group,** Attn: *Contemporary Authors,* 27500 Drake Rd., Farmington Hills, MI 48331; 800-877-GALE or outside the United States and Canada 248-699-4253; fax 248-699-8054; ca-content.editor@galegroup.com. *Contemporary Authors* will not list you in their directory if they think your books are self-published. See http://www.gale group. com.

8. *Horn Book magazine,* 56 Roland St., #200, Boston, MA 02129; 800-325-1170 or 617-628-0225; fax 617-628-0882. *Horn Book* reviews about 420 books each year for children and young adults. It is published bimonthly and has a circulation of 24,000. See http://www.hbook.com.

9. *Ruminator Review,* Margaret Todd Maitland, 1648 Grand Ave., St. Paul, MN 55105; 651-699-2610; fax 651-699-7190; review@ruminator.com. *Ruminator Review* (formerly *Hungry Mind Review*) is a quarterly book review magazine founded in 1986 and distributed free in more than 600 independent bookstores around the country. Each print issue is built around a particular theme and includes reviews and essays by some of America's finest writers. See http://www.Ruminator.com.

There are only two phases to the promotion of your book: The first 90 days and everything else.

—Joel Roberts, broadcast media coach

10. **H.W. Wilson Co.**, Attn: Nancy Wong, *Cumulative Book Index*, 950 University Avenue, Bronx, NY 10452; 800-367-6770 or 718-588-8400; fax 800-590-1617 or outside U.S. and Canada, 718-590-1617; custserv@ hwwilson.com; http://www.hwwilson.com. Books must have at least 100 pages and a print run of at least 500 copies.

11. *Independent Publisher*, Jenkins Group, 400 West Front St., Suite 4A, Traverse City, MI 49684; 800-706-4636 or 231-933-0445; fax 231-933-0448; jenkinsgroup@ publishing.com. Bimonthly, *Independent Publisher* reviews 75-100 titles every issue. Circulation: 7,000. See http:// www.Bookpublishing.com.

12. **Ingram Book Company**, Ingram Express Program, Publisher Relations Dept., One Ingram Blvd., La Vergne, TN 37086-1986; pubrel@ingrambook.com. The book must not be marked or identified as a promotional copy. Enclose your brochure and discount schedule (a higher discount on single orders will allow them to give stores a discount that will increase sales). Contact them for application forms. See http://www.ingrambookgroup. com.

13. *Kirkus Reviews*, 770 Broadway, NYC, NY 10003-9597. Tel: 646-654-4602; kirkusrev@kirkusreviews.com; fax 646-654- 4706. You should have sent bound galleys to *Kirkus* some months earlier. This is a confirmation copy to show the book has been published.

14. *KLIATT Young Adult Paperback Book Guide,* Paula Rohrlick, 33 Bay State Rd., Wellesley, MA 02481; 781-237-7577; fax 781-237-7577; kliatt@aol.com; http://hometown.aol.com/ kliatt. *KLIATT* annually reviews some 1,600 softcover books for young adults. The magazine is bimonthly and has a circulation of 2,300.

15. *Library Journal,* Barbara Hoffert, 360 Park Avenue So., New York, NY 10010-1710; 888-800-5473 or 646-746-6819; fax 646-746-6734. Again, you should have sent bound galleys some months earlier. This is a confirmation copy to show the book has been published.

16. **Library of Congress, Acquisitions and Processing Division**, Washington, DC 20540, along with your brochure and dealer discount schedule. See http://www.loc.gov.

17. **Library of Congress Cataloging in Publication Division,** Washington, DC 20540. Send one complimentary copy of your book. Once you have published three books, you are eligible to participate in the CIP program and receive library-cataloging data for printing on your copyright page. See Chapter 5. The Cataloging in Publication Office supplies postpaid mailing labels once you have been admitted to the CIP program. See http://www.loc.gov.

18. **Library of Congress Copyright Division** (two copies), Library of Congress, 101 Independence Ave. SE, Washington, DC 20559-6000, for copyright registration, along with your cheque for $30 and copyright form TX. See Chapter 5 and http://www.loc.gov.

19. **Library of Congress Exchange and Gift Division**, Gift Section, Washington, DC 20540. See http://www.loc.gov.

20. *Los Angeles Times Book Review,* Steve Wasserman, 202 West 1st St., Los Angeles, CA 90012; 213-237-7778; fax 213-237-4712; steve.wasserman@latimes.com. See http://www.latimes.com. This is a follow-up confirmation. Book galleys should have been sent earlier.

21. *Midwest Book Review,* James A. Cox, 278 Orchard Dr., Oregon, WI 53575; 608-835-7937; mwbookrevw@aol.com. They receive about 1,500 books each month and review about 450 of them both in print and online. See http://www.execpc.com/~mbr/bookwatch.

22. *Newsday,* Laurie Muchnick, Two Park Ave., New York, NY 10016; 212-251-6623; fax 212-696-0590; email to:

muchnick@newsday.com. *Newsday* reviews general-interest books such as fiction, history, politics, biographies and poetry. They do not review how-to books. Send books to the appropriate departmental editor. Circulation: 800,000 daily, 950,000 Sunday. See http://www.newsday.com.

23. *New York Review of Books*, 1755 Broadway, Floor 5, New York, NY 10019; 212-757-8070; fax 212-333-5374; nyrev@nybooks.com; http://www.nybooks.com. This bi-weekly (except January, July, August and September, when it is monthly) magazine publishes reviews, prints excerpts and buys serial rights. They review over 400 books each year, and the circulation is 130,000.

24. *New York Times,* Daily Book Review Section, 229 West 43rd St., New York, NY 10036; 212-556-1234; fax 212-556-1320. See http://www.nytimes.com/books.

25. **Patrician Productions,** Victor Kassery, 145 West 58th St., New York, NY 10019; telephone 212-265-5612. Some 500 books are reviewed annually for radio and TV.

26. **Dan Poynter,** PO Box 8206-380, Santa Barbara, CA 93118-8206, autographed. Yes, we receive around 20 books each week. That is why *The Self-Publishing Manual* has been called "the book that has launched a thousand books" (actually many more). All books are acknowledged.

27. *Publishers Weekly,* Attn: *Weekly Record*, 360 Park Avenue So., New York, NY 10010-1710; 646-746-6758; fax 212-463-6631. You should have sent bound galleys to *PW* some months earlier. This is a confirmation copy to show the book has been published.

28. *Rainbo Electronic Reviews,* Maggie Ramirez, 8 Duran Court, Pacifica, CA 94044; 650-359-0221; http://www.rainboreviews.com. Reviews 300 books annually and publishes them on GEnie online service.

29. **Reader's Digest Select Editions,** Tanis Erdmann, Editor-in-Chief, Pleasantville, NY 10570; 914-244-1000, ext. 5396; fax 914-244-7565; http://www. readersdigest.com.

30. *Reference and Research Book News,* Jane Erskine, 5739 NE Sumner St., Portland, OR 97218; 503-281-9230; fax 503-287-4485; booknews@booknews.com; http://www. booknews.com. This quarterly, with a circulation of 1,700, reviews some 1,200 books per issue.

31. *Reference Book Review,* Cameron Northouse, PO Box 190954, Dallas, TX 75219; 972-690-5882. This semi-annual has a circulation of 1,000 and reviews some 200 books per year.

32. *Romantic Times,* Nancy Collazo, 55 Bergen St., Brooklyn, NY 11201; 718-237-1097; fax 718-624-2526; info@ro mantictimes.com. *Romanic Times* is a monthly aimed at consumers and focuses on nonfiction best-sellers and all genres of fiction except childrens' books and poetry. Over 150 reviews are printed in each edition. See http://www. romantictimes.com.

33. *San Francisco Chronicle,* Attn: David Kipen, Book Editor, 901 Mission, San Francisco, CA 94103; 415-777-6232; fax 415-957-8737. Circulation: 570,000 daily, 715,000 Sunday. See http://www.sfgate.com/eguide/books.

34. *School Library Journal,* Attn: Trevelyn Jones, 360 Park Avenue So., New York, NY 10010-1710; 646-746-6759; fax: 646-746-6689; tjones@cahners.com. This is a confirmation copy to show the book has been published.

35. *Small Press Review,* Attn: Len Fulton, PO Box 100, Paradise, CA 95967-9999; 800-477-6110 or 530-877-6110; fax 530-877-0222; dustbooks@dcsi.net; http://www.dustbooks.com. This monthly publication has a circulation of 3,500 and specializes in fiction and poetry.

36. *USA Today,* Diedre Donahue, 1000 Wilson Blvd., Arlington, VA 22209; 703-276-3400 or 703-276-5494; ddonahue@usatoday.com. This daily national newspaper prints reviews every Friday and other times under special

subject areas such as sports, money, lifestyle, or art and entertainment. Circulation: 1.9 million. See http://www. usatoday.com.

37. *Voice Literary Supplement*, *Village Voice*, Joy Press, 36 Cooper Square, New York, NY 10003; 212-475-3300; fax 212-475-8944; editor@villagevoice.com or jpress@village voice.com. They review 500 books each year in 10 issues. Circulation: 180,000. See http://www.villagevoice.com.

38. *Washington Post*, Marie Arana, *Book World*, 1150 15th St., NW, Washington, DC 20071; 202-334-6000; fax 202-334-5059; aranam@washpost.com. Circulation: 780,000 daily, 1,100,000 Sunday. The *Post* reviews about 1,500 general fiction and nonfiction books each year. A favorable review in the *New York Times* or the *Washington Post* tends to stimulate good reviews in the book sections of smaller newspapers. See http://www.washingtonpost.com.

39. **Contact the online bookstores,** such as Amazon.com and BarnesAndNoble.com, about carrying your books. See the listing under Bookstores: Online in Appendix 2.

40. **One copy to each of the 8 to 10 major wholesalers.** See Chapter 8 and Wholesalers in Appendix 2

41. **One copy to each of the 6 to 10 most important opinion molders** in your field. If these people talk up your book, you will be off to a good start. Autograph the books.

These early review copies must be sent out as soon as the truck arrives from the printer. Reviewers like *new* books, and books are dated, so it is easy to tell when they are not new. Equally important, most of your initial sales will come from these reviews, so if you do not get moving with your review copy program, that inventory will not move out. Meanwhile, the dated books are getting older every day.

REVIEWS TO THE ULTIMATE CONSUMER: Now that the prepublication and early review packages have been sent, it is time to get to the *retail* reviewers. These are the rest of the book review magazines, newspapers with book review columns, general interest magazines that review all types of books, freelance book reviewers, radio and TV stations with talk shows and book programs and, last but not least, special interest periodicals that cater to the book's field(s).

It would be very expensive and terribly inefficient to send review copies to every reviewer, and yet some publishers do this. Many of the larger publishers automate their review book process. The result of taking the human touch out of the loop is that some reviewers get more than one package, while others receive large numbers of books they do not review. Big publishers often ignore reviewers who request a specific title, because the promotion people are by now concentrating on a new line of books. Smaller publishers tend to be smart enough to always send out a "requested title," knowing there is a very good chance of its being reviewed.

Since book reviews are very effective and review copies are very inexpensive, it makes sense to spend more time and effort on reviews than on most other forms of promotion or paid advertising. For most books, it is not unusual to send out 300 to 500 review copies. This may seem like a lot, because many large publishers circulate less than 50, but it is a sound investment. The complete review package will probably cost you around $3 for the book, promotional material, shipping bag and postage. Several inches of review space in magazines, major and minor, is extremely valuable. And this is editorial copy, far more credible than advertising puffery. For example, 94% of the librarians rely on reviews they read in *Library Journal*, but only 35% believe the ads. The more reviews you receive, the more likely that librarians will see the reviews and buy your book. And, of course, you will repeat the best reviews on all of your library flyers

If only 30% of the magazines you target review your book, you are way ahead on your investment. Considering that reviews return so much, it is wise to follow these two simple rules:

1. Do not be stingy with review copies, but do not waste your money either.

2. When in doubt, ship it out.

UNDERSTANDING THE REVIEWER: There are two basic types of reviews. A *summary* review relates the contents of the work without issuing an opinion on its value. These reviews help potential readers select books for their particular needs. An *evaluative* review decides whether the author has covered the topic and compares the book with similar works. It usually ends with a favorable or unfavorable recommendation, and may be brief or long.

Your book is a product of yourself. You poured your time, heart and soul into it. But just because you were interested enough to take the time to write it doesn't mean a reviewer will be interested enough to take the time to read it all. A book critic will read your entire book, but a book reviewer will probably only check the front matter. Some reviewers write reviews on 10 to 15 books a week. Most of the reviewer's comments will come from your news release and other enclosures. Make them good. Also consider this: if a reviewer elects to use large portions of your superbly written news release in the review, then to some degree, you are actually controlling the content of the review.

It helps to understand the lot of the editor and/or reviewer. Whether they are full-time or freelance, they have one thing in common: they are extremely busy. Neither time nor room is available to review all the books that come in, and there just aren't enough book review columns to go around. Even the prestigious and prolific Sunday supplement of the *New York Times* can only cover about 10% of the books received. All books are not assigned; most reviewers select the ones they want to review. You can't change the situation, so you might as well understand and take advantage of it.

A few years ago, I was dropping off a batch of books at the loading dock in back of the post office in Santa Barbara. I saw a young man (not in a postal uniform) with a cart full of packages near the dumpster, and my curiosity mounted. As I watched, the man ripped open the cartons, took out what appeared to be books and placed them in a large carton. Then he threw the wrappers in the trash. Unable to stand it any longer, I approached the man and asked if these were *lost-in-the-mail* books. Turns out the packages were for Los Angeles book critic Robert Kirsch. This gigantic load of books was being received at his home address (imagine what showed up at work), and he not only didn't have time to pick up the books himself, he didn't have room for the wrappers. There is a second lesson here too: Much of the material you ship with review copies is likely to become separated from the books.

Ruth Coughlin of the *Detroit News* says, "I arrive at my office each Monday morning to find 200 books in unopened mailing envelopes stacked outside my door." Alice Digilio of the *Washington Post* says, "We have somebody here 20 hours a week whose only job is to tear open book packages."

If your book has special-area appeal, you can greatly increase your chances for review by submitting your book to the special publications reaching that particular group. For example, if your book is on hang gliding, you would send review copies to all the hang gliding magazines and newsletters worldwide. Then you would consider every aviation, outdoor, sport, recreation, do-it-yourself, teen, men's, etc., magazines you could find. There are some 60,000 magazines being printed in the U.S. today (and a lot more foreign). There must be some reaching the groups you want to target.

Be prepared for delays with publications from the smaller associations. They may want to review your book, but they have staff and budget limitations. Usually they rely on outside free help for book reviews. Typically, the editor will only scan a book before sending it off to an appropriate expert requesting him or her to review it. Often, the reviewer is very busy too.

SELECTING REVIEW PERIODICALS

For lists of appropriate media, visit the reference desk of a large public library and ask to see the periodical directories. There are at least two for magazines, two for newsletters and several for newspaper columns. (Stop by the bank first for a roll of coins for the copy machine.) Copy just the pages you need and bring them home to enter the addresses of the periodicals into your computer; you will use these addresses over and over again. Some of the periodicals you will consult are:

1. *Standard Periodicals Directory:* thousands of magazines. http://www.mediafinder.com.

2. *Ulrich's International Periodicals Directory:* many U.S. and foreign periodicals. http://www.ulrichsweb.com.

3. Hudson's *Subscription Newsletter Directory.* PO Box 311, Rhinebeck, NY 12572; 845-876-2081; hphudson@aol. com; http://www.newsletter-clearinghse.com.

4. Gale's *Newsletters in Print.* http://www.galegroup.com.

5. *Literary Market Place:* many good lists such as book review syndicates, book review periodicals, book columnists, cable networks, radio and TV stations with book programs, book clubs, news services and newspapers with book sections: http://www.literarymarketplace. com.

6. **Bacon's Directories:** http://www.Bacons.com.

7. *Gebbie's All-in-One Media Directory:* http://www.gebbie inc.com.

8. *Editor and Publisher International Yearbook:* the key radio and TV personnel. http://www.mediainfo.com/store/yearbook.htm.

9. *Working Press of the Nation:* lists media people at newspapers, magazines, radio, television, syndicated columnists, etc. http://www.bowker.com.

10. *Directory of Literary Magazines* by the Council of Literary Magazines & Presses, 154 Christopher St., #3-C, New York, NY 10014-2839; 212-741-9110; fax 212-741-9112.

11. *Writer's Market:* directed at writers in search of magazine publishers: http://www.writersdigest.com/catalog/index. htm.

12. *Encyclopedia of Associations* directory: lists 18,000 special-interest trade and professional organizations: http://www.galegroup.com.

13. *National Trade and Professional Associations:* 7,600 associations, unions and societies: http://www.columbia books. com.

14. *The Pocket Media Guide:* lists major trade, business and general interest magazines and newspapers. 33 pages. Free from Media Distribution Service (MDS), 307 West 36th St., New York, NY 10018.

15. **ParaLists** maintains several up-to-date lists if you do not have time to go through the exercise of compiling your own. Some lists may be rented—ready to go. See current list counts and prices at http://ParaPublish ing.com.

Address review books to a *specific person* or your book may get ripped off by someone else on the staff. When this happens, you not only waste a book, you lose out on a review. Also address review books to the *position*, not just the name, of the editor or reporter. If your recipient is on vacation, your mailing might be pigeonholed for weeks—and no longer considered news once rediscovered upon his or her return. If you cannot find the editor's name in one of the above-listed references, call and ask, or address the package to the Review Editor.

Depending on your subject, you may find 400 to 500 potential reviewers for your book. Don't be surprised if you come up with 600. On the other hand, if the topic is very specialized, the print run is short, and the cover price is high, you may find there are only a few dozen interested and qualified potential reviewers. The best rule is to contact everyone who might possibly review the book. Divide the periodicals into two groups:

- **The good bets:** those you have heard of, good matches that are published regularly and have a large circulation. These periodicals should and probably will review the book.

- **The rest:** those you have not heard of, the title does not sound as though the periodical matches your book, it is published quarterly and has a circulation of 600. These periodicals might possibly review the book.

Some magazines will be perfect matches for your subject, and some, although more general, will have such a large circulation that they cannot be ignored. Send books to the group of good bets, but send only the promotional literature and a "Review Book Request" postcard to most of the rest. When the cards come back, send out the books and the review literature. You are fishing at this point; you won't hook a fish with every cast, but you have narrowed your odds with the postcard responses.

Go through the directories and make up lists of newspapers, weekly magazines, review journals and specialized periodicals. Many smaller newspapers do not have reviewers on their staffs; they use syndicated columns. Be sure to send review copies to all syndicated reviewers.

Reviewer addresses should be entered into the computer so they can be reproduced for use again. A simple mailing list program will do the job, but a database software program such as Microsoft Access will allow much more flexibility. Add a code to each record in the address file to indicate what type of review publication it is (e.g., aviation magazines, parachuting magazines, ballooning magazines, in-flight magazines, soaring magazines, etc.). The narrower your classifications, the more valuable your lists.

Most label programs will allow you to print three-across pressure-sensitive labels through your laser printer.

REVIEW PACKAGE

The review package sent to reviewers should include a book, brochure, review slip, sample review/news release, reprints of other reviews, cover letter, reply card and a photograph of the book. Here are the details:

1. BOOK: Do not send a damaged book or *selected second* as some publishers do. You want to put your best foot forward, hoping to get the attention of the reviewer. Pack the book as you normally do so that it will arrive in good condition.

Some reviewers still assume that in real publishing, the hardcover edition comes out several months prior to the softcover. If they receive a paperback, they assume the title is old. Today, with the increasing dominance of the *quality* or *trade paperback,* this barrier is beginning to be breached, and many books are being selected for review on their own merits, rather than being sorted by their wrapper. If you are publishing in softcover only, make sure the point is clear in your review package.

Use a rubber stamp to mark the review copies. Rubber-stamp the *edges* of the pages (side of the book) so that the marking is visible without lifting the cover. It is embarrassing when a marked review copy finds its way back into your for-sale stock.

WOW! A review copy
Review book rubber stamp

The rubber stamping will not stop the sale of a review book, but it will ensure the book will not be returned to you by a bookstore for credit.

In mid-1979, the newspaper and book industries were scandalized when 10 newspaper book reviewers were accused of selling review books to the Strand bookstore in New York. Apparently, several bookstores sent form letters to reviewers soliciting books. The stores typically buy the books at 25% of list price and resell them at 50% of list. One reviewer estimated he received 30,000 review copies in seven years. Many periodicals have a policy of donating review copies philanthropically: to hospitals, charitable book fairs, foreign libraries, etc.

Certainly the ability to easily sell review copies may promote the requesting of more books with no intention of ever considering them for review. There is nothing wrong with a reviewer requesting a book if he or she plans to review it. But it is wrong if they plan to sell the book without first considering it for review. It has recently been noted that along with the burgeoning growth of Web-based book reviewers, more and more brand new books are being offered for sale as "slightly used books" on the web, many times before their publication dates and at inflated prices. So the practice of requesting review copies, primarily to be sold, may be with us again.

2. BROCHURE: Use the brochure you have produced for the retail buyer, and make sure it looks professional. There is no need to print a special brochure for the reviewer. This brochure simply provides more information about the book and your company.

3. REVIEW SLIP: Many books are sent with book review slips listing vital information, and some books also have the title, publication date and price rubber-stamped on the inside of the front cover. Most publishers slip the loose sheets into the book. However, pasting the book review slip inside the cover with a spot of rubber cement or double-sided tape will make sure it stays with the book. Review slips may also be made by computer-generating the information on mailing labels and pasting them on the inside front cover or flyleaf of each book.

Review copies are the least expensive and most effective way to promote your book.

≡✈➤≡Para Publishing Presents for Review

Title: *The Self-Publishing Manual*
Author: Dan Poynter
Edition: 13th, completely revised. (A new book with a track record).
Number in print: Over 157,000
CIP/LC: 99-057841
ISBN: 1-56860-073-9
Pages: 432
Price: $19.95
Season: Fall 2001
Publication date: September 2001
Rights:
  a. Book clubs: Writer's Digest Book Club, Independent Book Club, Small Press Book Club.
  b. Condensations: Publishing Trade, Income Opportunities.

A copy of your review to the address below will be appreciated.

Para Publishing
Reviewer Relations Department
PO Box 8206
Santa Barbara, CA 93118-8206
Tel: 805-968-7277; Fax: 805-968-1379
info@ParaPublishing.com

Book review slip

4. SAMPLE REVIEW in the form of a **news release.** Many reviewers use releases verbatim. In fact, it won't hurt to write up two samples, a short one and a long one.

Book review for *Choices: A Teen Woman's Journal for Self-awareness and Personal Planning*
  by Mindy Bingham, Judy Edmondson and Sandy Stryker.

For Immediate Release:

"As a little girl, did you ever wonder what became of Snow White, Cinderella, and Sleeping Beauty after they married their princes and retired to their respective castles?"

And so begins a revolutionary new book, *Choices: A Teen Woman's Journal of Self-awareness and Personal Planning* by Mindy Bingham, Judy Edmondson and Sandy Stryker (Advocacy Press). This refreshing book is a welcome change from the traditional offerings for teenage girls. While the publishing industry continues to produce more and more romance novels for adolescent girls that reinforce the "they-lived-happily-ever-after" Cinderella syndrome, *Choices* gives the message, at a critical time, that the teenage girl has to take charge of her life—that she can't just drift and hope for some Prince Charming who will take all her burdens away.

Sample review

5. OTHER REVIEWS: Reviewers are cautious people. They are more apt to review your book if big-name reviewers have treated it favorably in prepublication reviews. One way to convince them your book is worthy of their attention is to include copies of these early reviews. Cut out or scan each review, paste it on a piece of plain paper, and cut out or scan the masthead or title of the magazine and paste it in for source and date identification. Underline or yellow mark the best parts of the review to draw attention to them. Make photocopies for your review kit.

Take advantage of a good review. Besides being very good for the ego, it can be used to further stimulate your promotion and sales program. You want your distributors and wholesalers to know you are promoting the book, so send them a copy. If a review appears in a local newspaper, send copies to the local bookstores. Keep these pasted-up reviews on file in your red promotion binder and send them out with future review copies, letters to foreign-rights buyers or for use any time you need more promotion. When you set up a booth at a bookfair, enlarge the reviews as part of your booth dressing and counter display.

Pasted-up prepublication and early reviews

6. COVER LETTER: The cover letter should be short and to the point. If you plead for a review, you demean both you and your product. Make your letter sound like you are helping the reviewer find something his or her readers will be interested in. Mention that you are enclosing a review copy. Suggest an interesting or unique (perhaps local) angle. Introduce the book and its contents. Stress benefits to the recipient, not to you. Tell why the book is important to today's reader, and ask for a review.

> Some public relations people like to get very personal in review copy mailings. They jot a little personal note to the reviewer, hoping to snow them into thinking they have met before, or that the reviewer may have made some long-forgotten promise at a cocktail party. This technique should only be used with great caution as it can easily backfire and destroy the relationship.

7. REPLY CARD: Some publishers like to include a self-addressed reply postcard for the reviewer's response. The reply card is optional. The return rate is not high. Some cards take a long time to come back, and others are not returned at all. Many reviewers simply don't know when the review will appear.

It is not necessary to use business reply indicia or a stamp on the reply postcard. Reviewers at significant periodicals do not buy their own stamps. They throw outgoing mail in the basket for the mailroom to handle.

```
                        PLEASE ACKNOWLEDGE

    We have received the complimentary review book or galleys you sent of
    Book title: _____

    ☐ We expect to review this book on (date): _____
    ☐ Please send a photograph of the book
    ☐ Please send a photograph of the author
    ☐ We did not find this book suitable for our review.


    Name of reviewer: _____
    Full job title: _____
    Name of publication or broadcast station: _____
    Mailing address: _____
    _____ Zip: _____
    Comments (optional): _____
```

Review book acknowledgment postcard

8. COVER PHOTOGRAPH: Artwork will command much more space and make the review more attractive, resulting in a higher degree of readership. Enclose a color photograph of the book cover and, if the book is well illustrated, samples of the interior artwork. Send photos of the book whenever you feel they might be used, and always note in your cover letter and news release that photos are available. A clearly typed, taped-on identifying caption should hang below the photograph or be affixed to the back.

When placing the order for prints, specify that they are for reproduction, glossies, and 4" x 6" (or larger) in size. Unless you have a readily recognizable face, send a photograph of the book, not of yourself. Remember what you are selling.

REVIEW/TESTIMONIAL SHEET: The "rev/test" sheet lists excerpts from reviews and testimonials along with pertinent printing and rights information.

UNSOLICITED TESTIMONIALS: There is no better promotion than a recommendation from a satisfied customer that is unsolicited.

Save all those voluntary testimonials and nice letters; bank them for future use. When you have 10 to 20 of them, photocopy them, cut them apart and arrange their best, most quotable parts in a logical order. Put duplicate praise aside and try to arrange the testimonials so that they flow, tell a story and follow one another. Then either get permission to use their signatures or paste the testimonials to a sheet of blank paper, omitting the names and addresses of the writers. Start the page off with "What readers are saying about [title of the book]." Since all the printed and handwritten styles are different, the page will have good credibility.

ADDITIONAL REVIEW SOURCES

Now that you have mailed books to the good bets—those periodicals that match your subject and are very likely to review the book—it is time to approach others. Your second list may total 1,000 or more.

Send a cover letter, brochure, news release and a "Review Book Request" card. The reviewers can request a review copy if the book looks like it might interest their readers. Some will print your release without even asking for a book.

Read what others are saying about

Parachuting,
The Skydiver's Handbook

This is only up-to-date basic sport parachuting handbook and it is highly recommended. —The Next Whole Earth Catalog.

For a lesson or just some vicarious thrills, read Parachuting, The Skydiver's Handbook. —New York Post.

A valuable collection of information and a good first look at the sport.—Library Journal.

Dan's strength as a writer lies in his technical descriptions of equipment; these are faultless. —British Sport Parachutist magazine.

This handy volume falls into the "Everything you need to know about..." category and is required reading for everyone who wants to jump out of an aeroplane. —Flight International.

All aspects are covered in a clear and authoritative fashion. —Air International.

Poynter's latest fills the bill of educating while entertaining. He says it well. —Parachutist magazine.

Chapters cover an overview of the sport, detailed discussion of each facet of the first jump, the history of parachuting, and an in-depth study of parachuting emergencies. Other sections discuss specialized jumping and equipment. Appendix contains a glossary and a list of drop zones, books, magazines and films. —Sporting Goods Business.

Well-written, this volume is profusely illustrated with photos and drawings. A useful addition to the public library collection. —Choice magazine.

Dan Poynter has done it again. —Spotter NewsMagazine.

Dan Poynter has generously guided thousands to authorship. Their books make this a better world. —Dr. Robert Müller, Past Assistant Secretary General of the United Nations and author of *2000 Ideas & Dreams for a Better World.*

After eight revised editions, **over 70,000 copies are in print.**

➤ **Honored** with an Award of Excellence by the Aviation/Space Writers Association. Named the best technical/training book of the year.
➤ **Selected** by the U.S. Parachute Association, the Canadian Sport Parachuting Association, and other national organizations for sale to their members.
➤ **Serialized** in *Parachutist* (USA), *Free Fall Kiwi* (New Zealand), *Fritt Fall* (Norway), and *CanPara* (Canada).
➤ **Mentioned** in *Joint effort, Aviation/Space, SAFE Journal, Flyv* (Denmark), *Soldier of Fortune, Thrill Sports Catalog,* Alaska Flying, Skydiver Magazin (Germany) and many more.
➤ **Selected** for transcription for the blind by the Milwaukee Public Library and the Florida Department of Education.
➤ **Translated** and published in Spanish by Editorial Paraninfo of Madrid.

Parachuting, The Skydiver's Handbook by Dan Poynter & Mike Turoff. All new, completely revised, eighth edition. 5.5 x 8.5, 400 pages, 260 illustrations. ISBN 1-56860-062-3, LC 97-22061. $19.95. Publication: Winter 1999-2000.

Para Publishing, PO Box 8206, Santa Barbara, CA 93118-8206 USA. Tel: (805) 968-7277, Fax: (805) 968-1379. Email: DanPoynter@ParaPublishing.com; Web site: http://www.ParaPublishing.com

Review/Testimonial sheet

Mailing to 1,000 reviewers may bring a response from 200 or so. The mailing and the resulting book shipment will be less costly than sending books to the original 1,000. This is an inexpensive way to "fish" for those interested in reviewing your book.

CONTINUING REVIEW PROGRAM: Your review copy program will not end at the publication date. Requests will come in as other reviewers hear of your book, and you should be on the lookout for new reviewers. For example, keep an eye on the Media section in *Publishers Weekly*.

There were 1,733 daily newspapers in the U.S. at last count: 458 are morning and 1,275 are evening; 783 newspapers publish on Sunday. Only three papers have Sunday book review sections: the *New York Times,* the *Washington Post* and the *Los Angeles Times*. They were discussed earlier under prepublication reviews. There are approximately 7,700 weekly newspapers. Then there are monthly newspapers, newsletters, magazines, journals and other types of periodicals—a lot of review possibilities.

Three to four months after your initial review copy mailing, hit those who were sent the cover letter, news release and Review Book Request card again. Send them the same package (deleting any reference to the publication date), but this time hand-write across the top of the release: "This book is available for review." A lot of reviewers will have missed your first mailing, may decide to look at your book because they have read about it elsewhere, or they may be writing an upcoming column about the subject. You will be amazed at the response. A year later, reslant your release and try this again. If your book ties into a national holiday or news event, send out another release with that news angle, prior to the event.

Here are some response numbers: Some years ago, 19 publishers joined in a "Books for Review" program. A very attractive brochure offering 29 books was sent to 1,800 reviewers. The participation cost was $46 per book, or about 2.5¢ per contact. Approximately 8% of the reviewers responded by requesting some 700 books. Over 50 requests were received for some of the more popular titles. The publishers were able to approach reviewers inexpensively while not wasting books or material on reviewers who were not interested. The Books for Review program is a good example of how publishers can band together to exploit free publicity while keeping their promotion costs down. Books for Review was turned over to the Publishers Marketing Association (PMA) and is currently being mailed to 4,500 daily and weekly metropolitan newspapers.

▼▲▼ *Para Publishing*

DanPoynter@ParaPublishing.com

Dear Book Reviewer:

Are any of your readers frustrated authors? How would you like to help them, by revealing the secrets of breaking into print?

The Self-Publishing Manual has just been published in an all-new, expanded edition. Known as the book that has launched thousands of books, it brings publishing within the reach of nearly everyone.

Help all your readers, who have a book inside them, by returning the enclosed postcard today. You might encourage a future Zane Grey, Mary Baker Eddy, Whitman, Poe, Thoreau, Shaw, Paine, Kipling, Sandburg or Twain (all self-published.)

Sincerely,

PARA PUBLISHING

Dan Poynter

Dan Poynter
Publisher

DFP/ms

REVIEW BOOK REQUEST

I would like to receive a review/examination copy of:

Book title: _____

PLEASE SEND THE BOOK(S) TO:

Name of publication or broadcast station: _____

Name of reviewer: _____

Full job title: _____

Mailing Address: _____

_____ Zip: _____

Circulation: _____ Frequency: _____ Av. No. of Pages: _____

Brief description of publication: _____

Audience profile: _____

Comments (optional): _____

---

http://ParaPublishing.com; PO Box 8206, Santa Barbara, CA 93118-8206 USA
Tel: 805- 968-7277; Fax: 805- 968-1379; Cellular: 805- 448-9009

Cover letter and book request postcard

Be on the lookout for review possibilities outside the book pages of magazines and newspapers. Depending upon your subject, contact newspapers: cookbook editors, lifestyle editors, sports page editors, business editors, etc. Watch for special sections.

UNSOLICITED REQUESTS: From time to time, you will receive unsolicited requests for review copies. You might want to look up the periodical for its frequency, circulation and audience match, as well as whether this person is really on the staff or a bona fide stringer. However, since the review package costs you so little, the better procedure is probably just to respond cordially. Certainly the free publicity a review can provide is worth many times the cost of the book. When in doubt, ship it out.

PRESS CLIPPING SERVICES employ people who regularly read all major publications and clip out mentions of their clients. You can subscribe to one of these services (see listings in *Literary Market Place*), but it probably is not worth the expense. The clipping services cannot read every periodical; they often send clippings that mention your key word but not you, and you do not need all these clippings anyway. Many smaller periodicals will send you copies of their magazine containing the review. Some people enclose a clipping with their order. There will be very few reviews you do not hear about.

TRADING ADVERTISING FOR REVIEW: Never suggest to an editor that you might be willing to advertise in the magazine as a way of gaining a review. Most editors do not sell advertising—that is the job of the advertising department. Petty bribery will repel most review editors, who view themselves as independent. On the other hand, when the ad sales representative calls, it is OK to say that you are "waiting for the review to appear to test the match between your book and the magazine's audience."

Once you receive a card notifying you that a review will appear in a given publication, you might like to advertise in it too. Some publishers feel this double impact is worth their while, though others do not. Many like to see how the review pulls before investing in an ad. They let the review test the medium, and then they quote the review in the follow-up ad in a future edition. The major advantage of the ad is that it is more likely to have specific ordering information.

BAD REVIEWS: Some of your reviews may be negative, and one reason (but not the only reason) is that some reviewers are negative. Some of these critics are frustrated writers who try to bring all other published authors down to their level. They take cheap shots or use the book as a springboard for lofting their own views.

Reviewers tend to be very cautious people. Even a very favorable review will probably contain one negative sentence or paragraph. This is a cover to save the reputation of the reviewer in case the book turns out to be a loser.

> *Many book reviews are mean spirited. Even if a reviewer likes a book, he or she must find fault and write snide and/or patronizing little asides about the author's character or motives that demonstrate the reviewer's intellectual and moral superiority.*
> **—Andrew Greeley in *Publishers Weekly***

In smaller publications aimed at a select target audience, the author will probably know every qualified reviewer. For example, skydiving books have to be reviewed by experienced parachutists.

In an effort to find a qualified reviewer, the editor will look for someone with a background in a book's subject. Books are sometimes unknowingly assigned to a reviewer who has an axe to grind with the author. (Some reviewers write negative reviews on purpose.)

Don't worry about a negative review. Any review is better than no review, because people tend to remember the subject more than the details of the critique. Even a bad review will arouse reader curiosity. Libraries must cover every subject, and acquisition librarians are always searching for something new.

> *There is nothing like a good negative review to sell a book.*
> **—Hugh R. Barbour, bookseller**

When you quote the negative review, just use the good parts. If there are no good parts, just say "as reviewed in the *Washington Post*" or "find out why *Consumer Reports* hated this book." Do not edit out the bad words so that the review appears to be favorable.

> *Ellipses are often the enemy of truth.*
> **—Brigitte Weeks, editor, *Washington Post Book World***

It is flagrant misrepresentation to edit out less desirable phrases if they change the meaning and intention of the review. Reviewers and editors are writers too, and most have excellent memories. If you misquote them, they will probably catch you and will certainly remember you when next you send a book for review.

Learn from negative reviews. Perhaps your promotional approach is misleading. Think about changing your news release. Help the reviewers understand the book. Try to direct their thinking. The same goes for good reviews. Focus on the praise—the parts of the book reviewers like. Emphasize these parts in your updated news release.

> *Someone once remarked that we have the power of life and death over a book. Life perhaps, but not death. We could devote our entire section to loathing the latest Sidney Sheldon, and it would make no difference.*
>
> **—Stefan Kanfer in** *Time*

WHY REVIEWERS REVIEW BOOKS: Many reviewers will spend some 10 hours reading a book, a couple of days thinking about it, and perhaps 6 hours writing up the review. Some reviewers are paid a small amount and often get a short description at the end of the review (which may be helpful in promoting their own book or agenda), however, many do not get paid at all. They get the book and the satisfaction of being on the inside of publishing and/or their area of expertise. To add insult to injury, the IRS has attempted to tax some reviewers for the value of the books they have received.

> *Book reviewing is one of the few activities in the world that could be said to depend largely on love.*
>
> **—Jack Beatty, literary editor,** *New Republic*

Your local newspapers, magazines and radio and television stations almost have to cover you, because you and your book are local news. Get out the *Yellow Pages* and make up a list of local media. You will probably find more than you expected. Send a review package to each periodical, addressed to a particular features editor. They may not have a book review section, but you would rather have a half-page feature on yourself and your book anyway. Follow up in a few days with a telephone call to the most important ones. Next, do the same for local radio and television stations.

If you know a freelance or staff reviewer personally, send him or her a review copy. Use every possible connection you might have. Hit all your hometowns—where you live now, where you grew up, where you went to school—all of them. You may get not only a nice review, but a special feature story as well.

FOLLOW-UP CALLS increase your chances for a review. Don't be a pest, but it is acceptable to call to see if your book *has been received.* You may find your package has not been received or that your book or news release should have gone to another editor. Make your calls brief and to the point.

ACKNOWLEDGE ALL REVIEWS with a personal note; praise and thank the reviewer. They will remember you when you send your next book. The easiest way is to photocopy the review and write a short message on it. A small amount of time spent on letters here is an investment in the future. Annotate your computerized list of reviewers to indicate that this reviewer has performed for you.

HOW TO SHIP: Review copies can be sent to most reviewers via USPS Media Mail. If you live near any of the reviewers on your list, hand delivery never hurts.

> When the *Frisbee Player's Handbook* rolled off the press, I made up a list of reviewers in zip code order. New York coauthor Mark Danna made the systematic rounds of reviewers in Manhattan and threw the book at them. The unique circular book was brought to their attention, made an impression and was very well reviewed.

If the reviewer requested the book on one of your Review Book Request cards or on letterhead, make a photocopy of the card for your file and place the card on top of the book. Everyone recognizes and takes an interest in his or her own handwriting. Seeing their writing reminds reviewers the book was requested. Also reference that the book has been requested in your cover letter to the reviewer so that they don't think your's is just a "blind submission."

CREDIT THE REVIEWER: Reviewers like credit for their work, so mention their name as well as that of the publication. For example, end the review with: "Kevin Gibson, *Parachutist Magazine.*" In fact, if the reviewer really likes the book, he or she will try to provide a few quotable lines, hoping for a mention.

PERMISSION TO QUOTE: Reviews are written to be quoted. Normally, you do not have to contact the reviewer or periodical for permission. However, in the last few years, a few isolated review publications have begun requesting payment for reprinting their reviews. This is a new development.

Put a lot of effort into reviews. Far less expensive than display advertising, they are the best promotional investment you can make. For more details on setting up your review program, see *Book Reviews* in Para Publishing Special Reports in Appendix 2 or at http://ParaPublishing.com.

NEWS RELEASES

Releases are used to announce products, promotions and events. They accompany galleys and review copies of books and are included in promotional kits to radio, television, and print media. Sometimes a release accompanies other promotional or informational material, and sometimes a release is sent alone.

"News Release" is the modern term for "press release." Your message will be sent to all forms of media such as radio, television and other opinion molders, not just the print media.

The media are in the news-gathering and publishing business; they want to hear from you. Publicity is not like *expensive* advertising, instead it involves the use of *inexpensive* news releases. News items receive a much higher degree of readership than advertising, and greater readership leads to more response (sales). News releases generate publicity and invite book reviews. Releases may be used to announce publication of your new book to newspapers, magazines, libraries, radio and TV. In fact, they should be sent to anyone who will listen.

The people mentioned in them wrote many of the articles and news items you read. Editors might use only one news release in 10, but news releases are responsible for 20% to 25% of the editorial space in many newspapers and magazines. Some of the smaller, more highly targeted publications use an even higher percentage of news release input.

Editors would use even more news release material if the news releases they received were more interesting. Your challenge is to draft copy that is irresistible to the editor—to come up with interesting information the editor will want to pass on to his or her readers. You want the editor to open your monthly mailings first while thinking, "I wonder what good material John/Jane is sending me today?"

If you make life easy for editors, they will give you coverage.
—**Terri Lonier,** *Working Solo*

Remember, you are providing a service to busy editors. As an author-publisher, you are an expert in your field and a great information source. You are providing important, timely and interesting information to the editor and his or her readers.

The four steps to placing your news releases are:

1. Develop an interesting "angle" that shows how your book will benefit the reader. You need a "hook," an issue.

2. Locate and cultivate the appropriate media contacts.

3. Deliver the information in the proper form.

4. Be persistent and follow up.

Give the editors what they want and need; deliver the information in such a way that it is useful and newsworthy. The less rewriting your release requires, the more chance that it will be used.

TAILORING NEWS RELEASES: You will draft some releases specifically for distribution to a single publication. Study the publication, imitate the writing style and follow the same article layout. The secrets are to know what the editor considers good news value and to know how to write in good press style.

Computers make news release tailoring easy. Most of your release will remain the same, but you will tailor the headline and lead paragraph to the target audience. For a book on publishing, we would have different pitches for releases sent to magazines for publishers, writers or printers. Just change the headline and lead paragraph and let the machine copy the rest of the previous release.

(Letterhead)

For Immediate Release. . .

Contact: Joyce Ready Tel: 800-PARAPUB
Fax: 805-968-1379
eMail: AlwaysReady@ParaPub.com

Headline
Type a descriptive, clever and catchy headline in capital letters and center it. Lure the editor to read more. Then space down four lines and get into the body of the release.

Issue or problem
The lead paragraph is designed to invite the largest number of people to read the article. It must have broad appeal; make it interesting. The release should be *issue oriented*; write about the *problem*, not the book. The release should begin by stating the problem and telling why this is an important subject. Make it provocative.

Development
Spend a second paragraph developing the message. Put the most interesting information first to keep the reader reading. Recite the most important items in descending order so that if some are cut from the end, the most important will remain. Provide interesting facts and statistics.

How the book solves the problem
Now move from a *what* orientation to the *how* orientation. It is not necessary to dwell on the book. Anyone who finishes the article will be interested in the book. Then describe the contents of the book; mention it as a resource. Continue with some background on the topic and show why your book is unique, useful and timely. Recite benefits to the reader.

Author
Spend a short paragraph on the author and tell why the author is an expert on the subject.

Ordering information
Give the price and mention that the book is available from the publisher as well as the stores. List your address so the reader will know where to send the money. Code your address.

End the release with the newspaper termination sign: -30-.

News release layout

FORMAT AND LAYOUT: The format of the release is standardized. The easiest way to design it is simply to type "NEWS RELEASE" on your own letterhead stationery. Then just type in the date the release is to be used ("For Use the Week of September 17th" or "For Immediate Release").

Place a contact name with telephone number in the upper right-hand corner. If your name is Greg Godek, the book is

---

For immediate release . . .

Fmi: Patricia Finn, tel: 805-968-7277

"This book is so reduced, so concise, so easy to grasp—so if you're really serious about writing grab it." —Barnaby Conrad, Founder and Director, Santa Barbara Writers Conference.

Bet You Can't Read Just One

Writers love writing and they love reading—especially when it is about writing. This is a book about writing for writers and it is in sound bites. Dan Poynter has taken the whole business of writing nonfiction books and distilled it down to the most important tips or rules. *Successful Nonfiction: Tips & Inspiration for Getting Published* could well be described as *Life's Little Instruction Book* meets *Chicken Soup for the Writer's Soul*.

Each page contains a writing tip, a pertinent illustration, an explanation, a relevant story and a quotation on the point from someone in history. This book could be much longer but Poynter has distilled the 109 inspirational tips into memorable and thought-provoking bite-sized pieces.

Sound bite books seem to be all the rage now. Maybe it is because people are so short of time. Some books are just groupings of quotations. This book goes much farther.

This 144-page gift book is beautifully designed with French flaps, gold stamping, embossed letters, contrasting end sheets and matte lamination. It is a treasure both inside and out.

Dan Poynter is the author of 77 previous books, many of them on writing and publishing. He is best known for *The Self-Publishing Manual, How to Write, Print & Sell Your Own Book*, now in its 12th revised edition in 21 years.

Successful Nonfiction is available for $14.95 in most bookstores or by calling Para Publishing at 800-PARAPUB.

-30-

Successful Nonfiction; Tips & Inspiration for Getting Published by Dan Poynter. Original edition. 5½ x 8½, 144 pages, 110 illustrations. ISBN 1-56860-061-5. $14.95. Publication: Winter 1999-2000.

Para Publishing, PO Box 8206, Santa Barbara, CA 93118-8206 USA. Tel: (805) 968-7277, Fax: (805) 968-1379. DanPoynter@ParaPublishing.com **http://ParaPublishing.com**

News release example

authored by Greg Godek and the book is published by Greg Godek Publishing, make your company look like a larger publisher by selecting another (pen or PR) name for the contact person.

Double-space on 8.5" x 11" paper. Some publicists use legal-size paper, which has the advantage of sticking out of a pile of papers and is more easily noticed. Begin a third of the way down from the top and leave 1" margins on the sides and bottom.

The release can be any length, but one page is usually best. If the release runs more than one page, identify the story with a header in the upper left-hand corner of the second page. Or excerpt a portion and place it in a separate release featuring background on the book's subject or an author biography. One way to condense a release to a single page is to use the computer's ability to change from double space to 1.8- or even 1.5-line spacing. Do not use a staple to bind pages together; use a paper clip. Never type on the back of the sheet. If more than one page in length, put "more" at the bottom so the reader will know to go to the next page.

More and more news releases are being submitted via email. Editors are more likely to use a news release they do not have to retype.

JOURNALISTIC STYLE: Observe basic journalistic style: Keep your sentences to 23 words or less; use 3 p.m., not 3:00 P.M.; commas and periods inside closed quotation marks; no capital letters for anything in the text but initials, first letters of proper names and first characters of sentences (exception: TV, not tv); no extra space between paragraphs (double space, same as the rest of the text); the first mention of the author should include first name, middle initial and last name (subsequent mentions should include last name only). Magazines like book titles in italics, while newspapers place quotation marks around them.

> *Releases should, like all writing, be accurate, consistent, clear, concise, persuasive, interesting and, above all, correct in spelling, punctuation and grammar. (I did not say this would be easy*
> **—Rose Adkins, past assistant editor, *Writer's Digest***

Use the fewest number of words to communicate any thought. Cut unnecessary words. Circle all repeated words in a paragraph and select alternates. Never use a less common word when a familiar one will convey your meaning. Use simple sentences; complex sentences can be hard to read. Do not make judgments. If you say the book is "the most important contribution to literature since the Bible," the editor will cut it out or just trash your release. On the other hand, it does not hurt to quote someone else who says something nice about your book. Proofread and re-proofread!

Take your time and compose a good release. Not all news gatherers do their own work all the time, so your release may appear verbatim in print. It may even be reprinted word for word as a book review or wind up syndicated in several magazines.

A release that starts out, "Festival Publications is happy to announce..." is self-serving. There is a much better chance your release will be used if the headline begins "Breakthrough found in..." The release is being written for the readers of the periodical; it isn't an announcement for your company picnic. When drafting a news release for a specific section, such as *Publishers Weekly's* Back to Press column, write it in the same format and style as the column you are targeting. Do not make the editors rewrite the release; they may round-file it instead.

If possible, include a photograph. One from the book illustrating the point you are making in the release is best. Remember, you want the release to push your *issue*; the book is secondary, almost subliminal.

MAILING (EMAILING) THE RELEASE: Print out the releases and ship them off with a photo of the book, and enclose a response card for the reviewer. Or email the release with an offer to send a photo, or invite the editor to lift a photo from your Web site.

PLEASE ACKNOWLEDGE

We have received your News Release about (book title): _____
We will take the following action:
☐ Your book will be featured on (date): _____
☐ Your book will be featured in the near future
☐ Please send a photograph of the book
☐ Please send a photograph of the author
☐ Please send a complimentary copy of the book

Name: _____
Full job title: _____
Name of publication or broadcast station: _____
Mailing address: _____
_____ Zip: _____
Comments optional): _____

Release response reply card

An enclosed **Release Response Reply Card** will provide instant feedback. The cards will tell you if you are writing good releases and if you are sending them to the right people. You won't have to wait months wondering if the articles will appear.

You will be ready to collect clippings, and the responses will provide leads for possible book reviews.

Send the releases to all appropriate magazines, newletters, book clubs (see "Book Club Rights" in Chapter 8), subsidiary rights contacts ("Subsidiary Rights" in Chapter 8), wholesalers, libraries, sales representatives, hometown papers, etc. Don't forget your connections with alumni, fraternal, trade or church publications. Spread them around. Follow up with a telephone call to the most important periodicals.

News releases to local periodicals may be hand delivered. Personal delivery not only receives more attention, but meeting editors will be a great education for you.

Use news releases liberally. Every time you go back to press, or revise the book, issue a release to herald it. Magazines such as the prestigious *Publishers Weekly* will give you a few lines if you just let them know. Releases should also be issued to announce speaking engagements, TV appearances, autograph parties awards won and any other newsworthy event. If business slows down, think up a newsworthy event and write a release about it.

Always respond to *PW's* requests for information for their spring and fall announcements issues. Once you register for an ISBN, you will be on R.R. Bowker's mailing list and should receive these requests automatically. You must follow the *PW* submission guidelines in order to be listed. If you are going on tour, send a short release, listing the places and dates, to *PW's* Author Publicity column. Also be on the lookout for special editions of *PW* and other magazines. Some of the special editions are on cookbooks, travel books, sports books, etc. Listings are usually free.

Foreword Magazine has four announcement issues per year for independent and university publishers. See their Web site for submission guidelines: http//www.forewordmagazine.com. Tel: 231-933-3699, Fax: 231-933-3899.

Remember that media people work in a pressure-cooker world. Be polite; they won't expect it. You will get a lot of mileage out of one kind word.

For more information on news releases and paint-by-the-number instructions for drafting and using them, see *News Releases and Book Publicity* in Para Publishing Special Reports in Appendix 2 or at http://ParaPublishing.com.

PRESS KITS: Some publishers like to get fancy and assemble a press kit or media kit. While it isn't necessary to send a kit with a review book (they usually get discarded by the reviewer), there are other events where you might like to hand a kit to a reporter. The press kit is a pocket-portfolio folder with your book cover glued or taped to the front. It contains news releases, early reviews and testimonials, letters of endorsement, an author biography, a cover letter, touring dates, publicity plans, book and author photographs, questions to ask the author, a business card, etc. The folder can come from a stationery store, or if the book measures 8.5" x 11", it can be made from book cover overruns.

While publicity misused can be nothing but an ego trip for the author, well used it can be a powerful sales tool.

—**Al Lind**

USE COVER OVERRUNS for book promotion. Print your promotion copy on the other side and mail them out. If your book is 8.5" x 11", fold and trim the extra covers into file folders and hand them out at appropriate conventions. Delegates will carry your folder around, using it to collect other papers, for days. If you have a hardcover book, get extra jackets—not just for promotion but for replacements on the book. Jackets become shelf-worn quickly in the stores. A new jacket will make the book look crisp again. Also, distributors and sales reps need extra covers for their presentations to book buyers. Always ask your printer for the overruns and order a few hundred extra. Run-on printing is very inexpensive, whereas reprinting the cover/jacket later or using color copying can be quite costly.

NOTIFY YOUR FRIENDS of your new book by mailing them a news release or brochure and an order blank. Send these mailings to friends, relatives and influential people in the field covered by the book. They are prime prospects and will help to promote your book by just talking about it. For those mentioned in the book, send a flyer with a rubber-stamped message, "You are mentioned in this book." A very high percentage will respond.

Influential people in the field should receive a complimentary copy; you want these opinion molders on your side.

RADIO AND TELEVISION TALK SHOWS

Every day, more than 10,200 guests appear on 988 television stations that broadcast 4,250 local interview and talk shows across the U.S. Roughly 94% of the author-guests do not even have recognizable names.

Many people love to go on radio and television. In fact, I think some people write books just to get on the air.

Authors are interesting people. Most people think that authors are experts and celebrities. Radio and television talk shows constantly need interesting guests to attract listeners and viewers. The fact that you wrote a book will get you on; then you must have something interesting to say that is unique, controversial or fascinating.

Most of the guests booked by the shows are authors, so your book is your entrée to the airwaves. However, you are appearing on the show as interesting, entertaining "talent," not to overtly promote your book. The host will promote your book (or may allow you to plug it), but your function is to impart exciting information about your subject. If you come across as dull or unprepared the host can always reduce your segment or edit you out later.

Do talk shows sell books? Sometimes, oftentimes, but not all the time. We hear when a show works, but we usually do not hear the rest of the stories. If you enjoy talk shows, do them; if you do not like talk shows, do not feel obligated to go on the air.

FOR-PAY INTERVIEWS: Never pay a station for an interview. If a radio station is charging you, it must be because they don't have advertisers or listeners. Conversely, stations do not pay you for an interview. They are giving you exposure.

Start with telephone interviews on "talk-radio." They are fast, easy, inexpensive, and you do not have to get dressed up or travel. You just talk from your own telephone to the radio host who is probably miles away. Begin with local radio shows and work your way up. Then graduate to local television shows and work your way to national shows. Do not try to start out with *Oprah* or *Regis*. You have only one shot at these top shows, and if you blow one, you will not only not be invited back, you won't be invited to any of the others. They monitor each other. On the other hand, if you are a dynamic guest, others will notice and want to book you.

HOW TO GET ON: There are several ways to get on the shows. You can book yourself, advertise your subject and expertise in the publications the producers read, or hire a public relations agency to contact the producers for you. For a complete explanation and the very latest in contact names and addresses, see Instant Report #602, *Interviews, How Authors Get on Radio and TV*, at http://ParaPublishing.com. You can also take out a listing in the *Radio-TV Interview Report*. For a sample copy, advertising rates and an application, contact Bradley Communications, 135 East Plumstead Ave., Lansdowne, PA 19050-8206; 800-989-1400, ext. 119, or 610-259-1070; fax 610-284-3704; rtirmag@aol.com; http://www.rtir.com.

MEDIA FLYER: Another way to let the talk shows know you are available is by sending them a catchy media flyer. The media flyer stresses an interesting issue and offers you as an expert to explain the subject. The back of the flyer can describe the book. The book is not the subject of the pitch; it simply gives credibility to the expert.

TELEVISION: The big television shows are best, of course, because they reach more people. *Today, The Tonight Show, Oprah* and *60 Minutes* are the most influential in book selling. The best plug for a book is when Oprah Winfrey takes a personal interest. According to *TV Guide*, an appearance on *Today* can sell 3,000 copies of a book, but a few minutes on *Oprah* have moved 50,000.

Do not overlook the smaller and local shows and cable stations. They are much easier to get on, and you can use them to work your way up. Many stations have special shows for interviewing authors, and most have at least one talk show. Your local station will want you on its community affairs program. Depending on your subject, the station may even produce a short clip for their news broadcast. Once you have appeared on one local station, don't give up on the others. Use another interesting angle.

To get on a show, find out who the producer is. Locally, you can simply call the station and ask the switchboard operator. For other stations, call the station or consult the directories in your library.

When you are on a television tour, try to book print media too. Make the most of your time by granting interviews to the newspapers and magazines in the same city. Don't forget college newspapers if appropriate. Also try to schedule author signings at bookstores and appearances at clubs, organizations and writer's groups. The fact that you are appearing on radio or television will tell them you are important, and they can promote your in-store-signings in conjunction with your other appearances and events.

Once you appear on television, you may want a "clipping" of the show. Some services tape everything on the air and will sell you a copy. Contact Video Monitoring Services of America at 323-993-0111 (LA) or 212-736-2010 (NY). Or if you ask, the TV station may tape the show for you if you supply the video tape.

RADIO: There are 700 U.S. and Canadian radio talk shows that will interview you by telephone. With telephone interviews, you do not have to get dressed up or leave home, and because the scheduling is tighter, you can conduct a dozen interviews a day. Radio stations like telephone interviews because they make even very busy celebrity authors available at very low cost.

Some shows will tape you during the day but air in the middle of the night, so if you have a popular topic the best shows may be live call-in programs scheduled during morning and evening "drive-time" when people are in their cars or in the kitchen listening to the radio. Other specialized subjects, such as new age/metaphysical, romantic relationships and certain political issues may play better to "night owls." Try to book shows scheduled at the appropriate times for your book.

YOU'RE ON THE AIR: The show's producer will call you to set up an appointment and then will call you at the appointed time. (Always clarify whether they will be calling at 7:00 a.m. your time or their time.) Respond by sending a copy of the book and media kit containing your news release, author bio and photocopies of any reviews you have received. If you send a list of questions or interesting facts about your topic that can trigger questions, most hosts will use it.

PARACHUTING/SKYDIVING

YOU CAN FLY LIKE A BIRD ! ! !

Skydiving is not just falling out of an airplane in a vertical tumble for thousands of feet — it is also exhilarating horizontal flight.
Leonardo da Vinci and how many others have dreamed of flying? Skydiving is an unforgettable dream come true.

Nearly everyone flies in his or her dreams; the young idolize Superman, while adults admire birds. Parachuting is more than an experience, more than a sport. To some it is recreation, to others an adrenalin rush, and to many it becomes a total involvement, an all-encompassing, personal commitment to the exclusion of every other activity.

Find out why so many seek the thrill of flying:

Dan Poynter is a well-known, widely-read aviation author with 26 books and more than 500 magazine articles to his credit. A pilot, master parachute rigger, parachuting Instructor/Examiner with over 1,200 jumps, and now a professional author, Poynter is past chairman of the Board of the U.S. Parachute Association. He is one of parachuting's most experienced and respected leaders.

His first book, *The Parachute Manual, a Technical Treatise on Aerodynamic Decelerators,* covers everything there is to know about the parachute. The Manual is known as the "Bible" to parachute riggers everywhere; it is in use by all branches of the U.S. Armed Services, the forest Service and many foreign governments.

Additionally, Dan has six other popular and technical parachuting/skydiving books to his credit, two of which have been translated into other languages.

● Just as airline travel has changed dramatically since its beginnings, advances in parachuting techniques and equipment have made the sport relatively safe and thoroughly fun!

● A new training technique, **tandem jumping,** involves strapping a passenger to an experienced instructor. The first jump is a freefall "skydive" in tandum all the way to flying the "canopy" to a soft, comfortable landing.

● Today's novice parachutists find an ever-growing variety of skydiving challenges and thrills waiting for them after they complete their student training.

● Relative work (forming circular "stars" and other formations in freefall) is an important part of national and world parachute competition.

● Everyone can jump: There are jumping doctors, lawyers, government officials, engineers, pilots, business executives, police officers and students.

● There are jumpers with one leg, and some with no legs; some with only one eye and, yes, even blind.

● The age minimum for parachuting is 16 and there are many jumpers in their 80's.

● Because of the rapid expansion of the sport, many permanent commercial sport parachuting centers, similar to ski areas, have been established to cater to public parachuting needs.

● Like other action sports, parachuting is not without its "routine" injuries; however, the vast majority of accidents occur during deviations from accepted safe jumping practices.

When doing a story on any aspect of PARACHUTING/SKYDIVING:

Contact Dan Poynter, Para Publishing, P.O. Box 40500-602, Santa Barbara, CA 93140-0500, or call (805) 968-7277. Upon your request you will be sent a complete press package, including books.

A media flyer

When you go on the air, be prepared. Disable your call waiting if you have it on your telephone. (The clicking is annoying.) Several months have passed since you wrote the book, so review it. Practice public speaking. Think about the best answers to the questions most likely to be asked. Rehearse your stock answers and use high-impact words or brief "grabber" comments that are suitable for a sound bite. Make a list of the main points you want to make, and slip them in no matter what the questions are. The talk show host may frustrate you by bouncing from subject to subject, so don't be caught with nothing to say. Push the subject, not your book. Do not mention the book at every opportunity—it only turns off listeners and wears out your welcome.

Before you start the interview, make sure that the show host, producer, and switch-board operator all have a card with your complete ordering information—phone, fax, and email address numbers, and the fact that your book is available in bookstores. When you start doing a heavy schedule of radio-TV, your book must be in as many bookstores as possible, because people are creatures of habit, they buy books where they always buy books regardless of your prompting.

On the big morning shows, you will be lucky to have 60 seconds on the air. Later in the day, you might have four to eight minutes. Evening shows may run an hour.

A few years ago, I was listening to a local radio station while running errands. I heard a disc jockey talking about making his first parachute jump. Since I had written several books on skydiving, I called the disc jockey, who spoke to me during record plays. An invitation was extended, and I dropped by the radio station for an impromptu interview that lasted all afternoon.

Media people are busy and under a lot of deadline pressures. Even though your book is the most important thing that has happened to you lately, it is just another news item to them. They are not easily impressed; they deal with news-making personalities all the time. Be polite; they won't expect it. Everyone around them is tough and short. A kind word from you will go a long way. A thank-you note afterwards will leave a nice memory, and you will receive great treatment for your second book.

The biggest challenge all authors face with media interviews is that their books are not in all the stores. Listeners may make one attempt to buy the book and then forget about it. One way to handle this potential disaster is to tell the host you will send a free information kit to any listener who will drop you a card. Talk show hosts love to give things to their audience, and most will repeat your message, phone number and address again and again. Now the responses will come directly to you, so you can add these hot prospects to your mailing list and send them a brochure and other information on the subject.

AUTHOR PROMOTION

AUTHOR TOURS are the way you promote your book at events and on television out of town, and they are very hard work. There was a time when all authors had to do was deliver their manuscript to the publisher and then go home to await the royalty cheques. However, with the advent of TV and more hype in the book business, the major promotion effort for the writer now is in criss-crossing the country speaking and selling the book.

> *For the publisher it is publicity at low cost. For the author it is an endurance test.*
>
> *—Wall Street Journal*

Author tours are a tough, grueling experience from sun-up to sun-down, and they are not inexpensive (air travel, food, lodging, clothing, car and driver, etc.), but there is no more effective way of reaching huge masses of the book-buying public.

Tours mean going on as many radio and TV shows as possible, interviewing with print media and visiting bookstores and other author events between shows. It is terribly discouraging to find that most of the stores do not have your book in stock. Some authors fill their van with books so they can make store deliveries before going on the air.

When you know you are going to be on a show, try doing a postcard mailing to all the bookstores in the broadcast area (often your distributor will aid you in this by giving you the lists of important stores). Let the stores know who your distributor or wholesalers are so they can easily order in anticipation of your appearance.

Before appearing at a bookstore for a reading or a signing, send an email message to all your friends, relatives and associates within driving distance of the store. The store will drum up a few attendees, but if you want a crowd, the turnout is up to you.

Advertise your itinerary in the American Booksellers Association's *Bookselling This Week* several weeks before you are scheduled to leave. The ABA publishes this newsletter so that bookstores can prepare for authors appearing in their cities. They will order your book and anticipate your visit to their area.

RADIO-TV GIVEAWAY PROGRAMS will provide you with great exposure, and all you have to do is donate a book. These programs are presented to raise funds for charitable organizations or as "pledge drives" for nonprofit radio-TV stations. Be on the lookout for them.

NEWS CONFERENCES are often staged by big publishing firms by hosting a lavish party and presentation for the press. But there is nothing wrong with a small gathering. If you have something provocative to say on a timely subject, and if it would normally be mentioned as a news item, you may be able to draw out the media. You do not have to rent a hotel suite. News conferences can be called in a friend's home or in a public meeting place. Press people just want the information as quickly as possible. Be prepared with press kits.

News conferences are held hourly throughout the annual three-day Book Expo America (BEA) convention, however, as the print and electronic media are so busy interviewing authors and covering events in the convention exhibit halls, only the biggest names or hottest topics can pull reporters away to the news conference areas.

When promoting your book, speak proudly about it. You worked hard on it and should be proud. False modesty will get you nowhere.
—Mark Danna, coauthor, *Frisbee Player's Handbook*

FEATURE ARTICLES: Local papers, company magazines, alumni and association publications, etc., are always looking for interesting news about their people. Let them do a story on you and they will mention your greatest accomplishment—your book. You are now an expert, an interesting person, and a celebrity just because you are a published author. It's the "magic" of being an author.

You are news to every publication you are connected with, from national associations to local newspapers. Take advantage of them. Remember, book reviews sell books, but feature stories sell more books.

MAGAZINE ARTICLES are a way to gain publicity for your book while furthering your writing career. It is easy to spin off articles from the chapters of your book. You can sell the articles, build your reputation and help to sell the book too.

First of all, you will be pleased to find that you will have less difficulty selling articles to magazines now that you are a published author. You are an expert, and magazines want authoritative material. Of course, you will want to end the article with: "Editor's note: Ed Rigsbee is the author of... that is available from...," and type the notice just as you want it to appear. Do not leave this up to the editor. Those who read your article are interested in the subject or they wouldn't be reading about it. Many will want to know more and will seek out your book.

Most national magazines do not pay a great deal for articles—usually just a few hundred dollars. However, the exposure is more important to you than the money. And if you offer the article for free, you have a better chance of its seeing print. Write to the editor, enclosing a few pages from your book that would be suitable for that particular magazine, and offer to write an article with the magazine's editorial slant. Offer to send an outline, or include it with this first mailing. It is easy to extract a section, add an introduction and a conclusion, and edit it down slightly.

SPEAKING ENGAGEMENTS: As an expert on your subject, you are in demand by service organizations, adult education programs, church groups, PTAs, businesses, conventions, the chamber of commerce and others. Many of these groups feature a guest speaker at every meeting. Sometimes they rotate the responsibility among the membership to find a speaker. Your call to them might actually get someone off the hook.

The possibilities will become obvious once you begin to think of your topic from the marketing standpoint. If yours is a carpentry how-to book, a hardware store or lumberyard might like to build a seminar around you. Your presentation might turn into an annual affair. Think of the nurseries that hold pruning classes every spring. You will make good contacts and develop new ideas; it is stimulating.

When you make your speaking appearance, always mention your book. Have one on display, and make several copies available for sale and for autographs in the back of the room. Authors often make more from "back-of-the-room" book sales than they do from the presentation itself. Prepare a short, powerful speech on one small, very interesting related item, and leave plenty of time for questions and answers. Always write out your personal introduction so the host won't stumble around trying to explain who you are.

Speaking engagements will do three things for you: they promote and sell your book, you might receive a fee for speaking and they add to your professional portfolio. Now, in addition to being an author and a publisher, you are a presenter too. You must be an expert!

SEMINARS are speaking engagements you organize yourself. You set up the daylong program and collect the admissions. A General Motors study found that approximately 40,000 seminars are given in North America each year and generate revenues of $100 million to $160 million.

Use your book as a text for the seminar and include it in the admission fee. Display related books in the back of the room and sell tapes of your lecture. If you have an idea, you can get $20 for the book, $80 for the audio, $200/hour for private consultation and $300 or more for the seminar. For information on setting up seminars, write to Gordon Burgett, Communications Unlimited, at Gordon@sops.com.

AUTOGRAPH PARTIES are a good ego trip when they are successful and can help to make your other advertising more effective. Normally, these events are scheduled by the publisher for the benefit of the author. However, unless the author is well known, the autograph party rarely pays. The best scheduling ties in with a radio or TV appearance and some local promotion.

When my parents taught me not to write in books, they did not know they were raising an author who would autograph them.

Contact a local bookstore and ask if you may set up a table, erect a sign and provide some refreshments. The bookstore may be reluctant to sponsor such an event unless you are willing to underwrite some of the cost. The expense won't be small, because in addition to the refreshments and sign, you will have to consider a good deal of advertising via email, postcards and even local newspaper ads. But the store might pay half. Even if the store fails to sell a lot of your books, this event you are staging will bring new customers into their shop. Once customers are introduced to the bookstore, they are more likely to return in the future.

Do seminars not signings. Attract buyers to your autograph parties.
—**Terri Lonier**, *Working Solo*

The store will provide the place, but you must get the people in. Do not rely on the regular customers to buy your book. Mail announcements of your appearance to every friend, relative, acquaintance and prospect in the area. Make the event sound big and important. Make everyone in town think that everyone else is going, and that if they don't go, they will be the only one not there.

Once you know that a local paper is going to review your book or do a feature article on you, visit the bookstores. Suggest to the manager that they might like to place an ad in several editions to draw readers into their store. Offer to stage an autograph party—another fine tie-in.

Don't overlook fund-raising event autograph parties. Here you do the selling and donate part to the club or organization.

When traveling, drop in on bookstores, and when you find your books on display, offer to autograph them. An autograph makes the book more valuable, and this will provide an opportunity for the staff to become familiar with you and your book. Bookstores will often feature "signed books" in a special sales area. Sometimes you will wind up doing an impromptu presentation.

For more information on author tours, see Document 639, *Autograph Parties & Signing Books*, at http://ParaPublishing.com.

BOOK AWARDS: There is probably no greater satisfaction to a writer than having their book selected for an award. Some book awards are big and well known, and some are obscure. There are those that are general, while others are quite specialized, but all are awards, and just being nominated for one looks good in your advertising.

Awards can be mentioned in advertising, and announcement stickers (such as gold medallions or stars) with the name of the award printed on them and applied to the books. These stickers are a bit of extra work, but they get attention. If the organization making the award does not sell the stickers, have them made by a lable printer, quick-print shop or make them yourself with a laser printer. In later editions, the "sticker" can be printed right on the book.

According to *Publishers Weekly,* the big publishers say that awards do not sell books. By the time the award is received, the book has been pulled from the stores and the publishers are promoting newer books. So what is the effect of an award? "It makes the author cost more when contracting for their next book," said one large publisher. Fortunately, smaller publishers benefit from awards, because they keep their books alive longer.

After Alan Gadney and Carolyn Porter's book won "Outstanding Reference Book of the Year" in their category from the American Library Association, they reaped the following benefits: Because of ALA publicity and their award promotion, library sales went through the roof. They managed to place a "Revised Award Edition" with seven national book clubs. With an award sticker on the cover they took a booth at the ABA convention, landed national distribution, regional distributors and wholesalers, and came out with 22 major publishers interested in publishing a new edition. Then they went to the ALA convention in New York where the book was on special display. While there, they negotiated a co-publishing contract, not just for one book, but for a series of 16 books... So awards do count, and if you win one, then promote it as far as possible.

Book awards, contests and grants are listed in *Literary Market Place* and *Writer's Market* (available at your library) and in a book titled *Grants and Awards Available to American Writers,* published by PEN American Center. See http://www.pen.org/grants.html.

EXCHANGES BETWEEN PUBLISHERS: Mail order customers interested in a certain subject tend to purchase every book on that subject. Unfortunately, many small publishers do not have enough titles on any particular topic. When two or more publishers of like material handle each other's books, their customers get a wider range of choices and the publishers get an improved response rate to their advertising because they are selling multiple titles. This cross-distribution partnering, formerly available only in other sales channels, is now becoming more common in mail order book marketing.

Approach publishers with books that complement yours. You can do this by telephone or in person at bookfairs. Smaller publishers displaying at the BEA and ALA conventions are usually quite receptive. You can find them in the less expensive main-hall booths and in the small press section.

Trade cartons of books based on their list price, and add them to your brochure. If you do not wish to take on products from other publishers, at least make an agreement to stuff each other's brochures into outgoing packages (called "Flyer-Swapping").

BOOK LISTS can be used to plug your other books. Each of your books should carry a list of all your books, and these lists should be updated at each reprinting. The list can also be in the appendix of the book. This is a way to get your sales message to potential buyers in the same field at little cost.

KEEP ACTIVE: Be prepared to move into action when your book takes off. Have your promotional plan organized so you will be able to gain maximum mileage from your publicity. Capitalize on each piece of promotion. Have your releases, ads and letters drafted.

Take advantage of every possible market. Pursue the most lucrative, but don't overlook the marginal ones—move in as many directions as possible. It costs very little to serve more markets once you have done the initial organization.

No matter what else you do, do at least five things to market each and every one of your important books each and every day.

—John Kremer

See *Book Promotion Made Easy: Event Planning, Presentation Skills & Product Marketing* by Eric Gelb. http://www.Small BusinessAdvice.com.

WHO BUYS BOOKS?

Over $25 billion a year is spent on books in the U.S. This figure is projected to reach $38 billion by 2004. About 1.4 million active titles are listed in *Books in Print*, with 78% from small and independent publishers.

Book buying is increasing among the growing market for older-aged customers (50+ years) and decreasing in the mid-age market (30-49) because of competing interests.

Households headed by college graduates account for 18% of the adult market (although 42% of college graduates and 58% of high school graduates never read another book after graduation).

U.S. families that do not buy or read books (80%); U.S. adults that have not been in a bookstore in five years (70%).

The total amount of knowledge is doubling every three years.

WHERE DO THEY BUY BOOKS?

Large Chain Bookstores 24.6%
Small Chain/Independent
   Bookstores 15.2%
Book Clubs 17.7%
E-Commerce/Internet 5.4%
Warehouse Clubs 6%
Mass Merchandisers 6%

Mail Order 5%
Food/Drug Stores 4%
Discount/Variety Stores 3%
Used Bookstores 3%
Multi-Media 1%
Other Outlets 9.1%

Growing markets: Internet, Book Clubs, Discounters and Warehouse Clubs because of the discount pricing.

Declining markets: Independent Bookstores which have been severely impacted by the growth of the Large Chains; and Mail Order sales due to the availability of books on the internet and at discount outlets.

MOST POPULAR CATEGORIES OF BOOKS

Popular Fiction 53.3%
Cooking/Crafts 10%
Religion 9.3%
General Nonfiction 7.8%
Psychology/Recovery 5.2%

Technical/Science/Education 5.8%
Art/Literature/Poetry 3.3%
Reference 2.2%
Travel/Regional 1.4%
All Others 1.7%

Courtesy: American Booksellers Association, Association of American Publishers and Book Industry Study Group.

8
Who Will Buy Your Book?

Markets
Distribution Channels

Most people think of bookstores when they ponder the idea of selling books. Bookstores are one outlet and there are ways to reach them effectively. But there are many additional places to sell books. First we have to identify the people most likely to purchase a given title and then we have to locate them. We have to make our books available wherever our potential customer may be shopping. It also helps to know who is buying books and where they are buying them, (see chart on previous page).

The pessimist might say the market is small and there is too much content. The optimist might tell you to look at the size of the untapped potential market.

In terms of where people buy books, no figures are available for book sales outside the book trade. It is suspected that a very large, unreported number are sold through specialty shops (e.g., parachute books in parachute stores, other special interest books in health food, office supply, computer, auto, garden and toy stores), catalogs, as premiums, etc. These nontraditional sales are usually easier to make, very large and much more lucrative.

The chain superstores have grown and stabilized somewhat (they build new stores and close others), the chain mall stores (with smaller selections) are shrinking, and many independent bookstores are being killed off by the chains (for now, the very largest and also the small specialized independent bookstores seem to be surviving). More and more specialty stores are carrying books, as are grocery and drug stores, newsstands, hotels and airports. College chain and franchise bookstores are growing, taking the place of independent college stores. The largest growth has been among Internet book sites such as Amazon.com and BarnesAndNoble.com. The Internet is now about 6% of the market.

Selection is directly related to sales.
—Jon Glazer, Little Professor Book Centers

TARGET YOUR MARKETS

Audience specialization is accomplished by concentrating your promotional efforts on those most likely to buy. Before you wrote your book, you analyzed your potential audience, and then you slanted your text toward them. In producing your book, you considered how it might be marketed and made your product attractive in this medium. Perhaps you put extra effort into the cover. The selection of your marketing channels is very important. For example, the chains seem to concentrate on fast-moving books. If your book is very technical and is aimed at a very narrow audience, you do not want to send them to the chains. The unsold books will only come back. Even if you get your book into a nonbook market where there aren't any returns, you want the books to sell, not to sit on the shelves forever. You want dealers who are repeat customers. So consider who patronizes each of the various outlets, and be objective in considering whether they are your buying audience.

There is no secret formula. It is simply a good item for which there is a need, at the right price, offered to the right market.

In analyzing the market, you will consider your principal marketing concerns, your customers (individuals, schools, libraries, international markets, subsidiary rights, industry, government, etc.) and your distribution channels (distributors, wholesalers, bookstores, specialty stores, book clubs and catalogs). Your marketing tools are book reviews, news releases, direct mail advertising, exhibits, sales representation, etc.

With a specialized nonfiction book, you can avoid the expensive, traditional, big-publisher methods of marketing to everyone, by identifying and locating only those people vitally interested in your subject matter. Work smarter, not harder. Define your core audience, and then get to work. Select your special audience and find a way to reach them. You will find that magazines, stores, catalogs, broadcast interviewers, specialized book clubs, columnists, associations, conventions and others serve your target group. For example, if your book is on skydiving, you know you can reach your customers through the U.S. Parachute Association, the Para-Gear catalog, *Skydiving* magazine and at the national championships. Who are your customers? What is their profile? Where can you find them? Where do they congregate with others who have like interests? Where is your customer?

You do not have to attack the whole group; you can go after just the cream off the top. Mail to the libraries with the biggest purchasing budgets; visit the buyers of the larger chain stores and select the wealthiest of the direct email purchasers. Mailing lists can be rented selectively by region, category, gender, income level, past purchasing history and other criteria; you do not have to buy the whole country or an entire category.

Hedge your bets by balancing your markets. Put most of your energy into selling your primary target group. Send out review copies, new releases, broadcast email messages and so on. Then attack your secondary group and your tertiary group and so on. Sell to anyone outside those groups who approaches you too, but don't spend a lot of time courting him or her. Invest your time and money where they will bring the greatest return.

Focusing on where you can sell the most books most effectively is the same strategy used by many of the national book distributors who primarily court buyers at the major bookstore chains and wholesale operations, where a single order can be placed for hundreds or thousands of copies. Then, smaller book outlets that buy only a few copies are called on maybe once or twice a year or just sent a catalog and contacted by telephone.

REPETITIVE AUDIENCE CONTACT is your mission once you have identified your marketing area. A repeated promotion in direct mail advertising, space ads, etc., will normally bring the same response as it did the first time. Naturally, the returns will drop off if the ad is repeated too often (many agree that six weeks is sufficient spacing). And there is some value to repetitive exposure. After a while, people begin to recognize and become comfortable with your product and message. It is also wise to change your message occasionally, because some in your audience will pass over it after having seen it several times. But don't change for the sake of change. Repeat what works until it doesn't work; go with a winner.

It helps, as well, to have more than one product, because each customer who buys is a prime target for similar books and products. People who buy how-to books on a specialized subject often collect them all. Slowly build your clientele and your product line.

MULTIPLE MARKETS will cost more in time and money but will stabilize your financial position by smoothing out the income peaks and valleys. It is wise not to have all your eggs in one basket. With a how-to nonfiction book, you might concentrate, for example, on a distributor to the book trade, product catalogs and direct email, then move on to other marketing channels such as co-op programs, exhibits and promotional mailings. Some of your marketing efforts will depend on your preferences. If you like personal contact, you might do more talk shows and visit more stores. If you like your privacy, you might use more review copies, news releases and email. Book promotion should be fun, so do what you enjoy most.

SEASONS AFFECT YOUR SALES

You should plan your major marketing efforts around the prime selling seasons. The big publishers bring out most of their new titles in the fall, targeting them at the December holidays. Their second major season is in the spring. June graduates are a good market. Business books move best in the late spring and late fall, not during the summer. Outdoor books do best in late winter, when people are confined indoors and are thinking about the activities of the coming summer. Travel books will do well a few months before the applicable travel season.

Most publishers find December and late August to be slow. December because of the many competing end-of-the-year activities; late August because people are concentrating on the transition from summer vacation/play to fall work/school.

Business picks up again after the first of the year and after Labor Day.

WHOLESALE VS. RETAIL SALES

Since it is only a bit more work to ship a carton of books than a single book, you want to pursue *quantity* orders. If you are selling more, you can print more and achieve a lower per unit cost. You will use distributors and wholesalers and will sell to stores, catalogs, etc. You will give them a percentage of the retail price but will sell in greater numbers.

On the other hand, the advantage of selling directly to the ultimate consumer (the reader) is the elimination of the distributor/wholesaler intermediaries; you keep the entire list price for yourself. But approaching the reader requires greater effort, and the books are sold *one* at a time. Books have been sold door to door, at street fairs, flea markets, and hawked on street corners. Individual sales are not normally efficient.

With the rise of the Internet, the intermediaries are being cut out naturally. Publishers and authors are dealing directly with their consumers, the end-user readers. The Web allows the party seeking information to find the party creating the information—quickly, easily, accurately and inexpensively.

The Internet allows us to substitute inexpensive direct email broadcasting for expensive traditional direct (postal) mail advertising. It has become less expensive and less time consuming to alert potential customers of new information products.

MULTIPLE DATABASES: The traditional bibliographic database is *Books in Print*, a multivolume reference book available in print, on CD and online. See http://www.bowker.com/bip. *Books in Print* lists the 1.3 million books that are currently available, or *in print*, in the U.S.

Today, many people find the databases maintained by Amazon.com and other online bookstores easier and less expensive to use and they provide more information about the books.

While you cannot physically place your book in every bookstore, you can make it available through every store by listing in these databases.

DISTRIBUTORS AND WHOLESALERS

We used to recommend that nonfiction book publishers serve the book trade (mostly bookstores) through wholesalers. We went on to suggest that you place your books with as many wholesalers as possible so as not to place all your eggs in one basket. However, in recent years "National Distributors," led by Publishers Group West, have carved out a large niche in the distribution of books by making sales calls and generating large orders from chain and independent bookstores, and then stocking the books with wholesalers so that the stores can easily order them.

Bookstores would rather order from wholesalers for several reasons. Historically, publishers have been slow to fill orders. Stores would rather write 15 cheques to wholesalers at the end of the month, not 15,000 to individual publishers. And stores prefer to deal with a limited number of suppliers they know and with whom they have established accounts. Also, bar codes make instant inventory control and just-in-time delivery possible. One wholesaler, Ingram, has warehouses within one-day UPS delivery of 95% of the bookstores in the country. Store buyers know they can pick up a telephone, call a toll-free number, consolidate an order and get delivery tomorrow.

Bookstores will order from a wholesaler first before they will consider a distributor or a publisher since the selection of titles is greater. Wholesalers provide one-stop book selection. They act as warehouses for bookstores. With quick service from wholesalers, stores can carry more titles on their shelves because they need fewer copies of each book. When they run low, bookstores can get additional copies overnight.

Currently, I recommend that publishers select a single national distributor on an exclusive basis (to the book trade). Let that distributor sell books to the bookstores and wholesalers so you can concentrate on specialty stores, catalogs, individual mail order sales and other markets.

THE COST OF DISTRIBUTION: Most distributors take 25% to 30% of the net (that is, what they collect from the stores—which varies according to how many books the store orders). A 30% net deal can translate to about 66% off of the list (cover) price. For example, if the distributor's discount to all buyers (wholesalers, chain and independent bookstores and other sales outlets) averages 50%, then the publisher's 70% of a

"30/70 net deal" will equate to 35% of the full 100% list price. As a "rule of thumb," the publisher receives about one-third of the list price of the book, and the distributor about two-thirds, out of which they give 40% to 60% discounts to the bookstores/wholesalers, and pay for sales reps, warehouse, staff, accounting, administration and overhead. After all discounts are given and everyone is paid, distributors usually operate on thin profit margins, which is one reason some occasionally go out of business.

The distributor's services to you include warehousing, cataloging, sales representation (to the independent bookstores and chains), shipping, billing, collections, marketing and editorial consultation. Many distributors provide other services at additional cost. Some of those services include an exhibit at the BEA book fair, filling individual (retail) orders, co-op advertising in book trade publications, postcard mailings to bookstores in areas where you are appearing on radio or TV, etc.

The only successful way to get both independent and chain stores to buy is through a face-to-face visit. Publishers have tried less expensive methods such as mailings and telephone calls, but none have worked as well as in-person sales calls. Large publishers have their own group of sales reps. Small publishers use distributors that also have sales reps. You need a distributor both to effectively sell to bookstores and then to make books available through as many wholesalers as possible.

Sixty-six percent may sound like a lot to give away and it is. But most distributors handle only the book trade (wholesalers and bookstores). So you can turn that portion of the business over to them, forget about the bookstores, and go on to the nontraditional markets that are easier, more lucrative and more fun. Your distributor will send you a nice cheque each month and will move a lot of books into the stores. You will be able to print larger quantities and achieve a lower-per-unit cost. So while you are sharing around two-thirds with your distributor, they are providing many services and are helping you move more books.

More and more of the chains and larger independent stores are requiring electronic ordering systems (EDI). Few publishers can afford them, so here is another reason to use a distributor. Book reviewers are more likely to review books that have national bookstore distribution and are readily available to their readers (always mention your distributor in your review kit and promo materials). Having a distributor means that a professional book trade organization has selected *your book* for sale out of all the thousands of other books available. Distribution legitimizes your book, separates it from the pack and gives it credibility in the marketplace.

THE DISTRIBUTION PROCESS: To help you understand the book supply pipeline, the following is a listing of the various intermediaries between the publisher and the bookstore. Several of the companies are evolving and growing. Some started off in one category and changed.

A distributor is a surrogate sales department for a group of independent publishers.
—Julie Bennett, publisher

National distributors act as the exclusive sales and fulfillment department for their publisher clients. They are publisher-driven (in other words, they "push" the product into the stores), and their mission is to create store demand for orders. They usually represent each publisher's entire line of books. Most have a catalog and sales reps who visit buyers at the chains and independent stores. They also supply the wholesalers. Your distributors will launch your books each season in a catalog. Typically, distributors pay you 90-120 days after they ship the books.

Your distributor serves the wholesalers (especially Ingram and Baker & Taylor), sends their sales reps to the independent bookstores and other sales outlets, and sells your books to the chains. The primary difference between national distributors and the various wholesalers listed below is that only one distributor will sell your books on an *exclusive* basis to the book trade through sales reps that sell to bookstore and wholesaler buyers, usually through a face-to-face meeting.

Remember, while distributors replace part of your shipping department, they *do not* replace your marketing department. You must always do the marketing yourself.

Wholesalers perform a valuable order-consolidation and distribution service but they don't market individual titles.
—Mark Sexton

Wholesalers are more demand-driven or bookstore-driven. They wait for the orders (they wait for someone to "pull" the product from them); they do not generate orders. But they respond quickly. They carry just those books that are in demand and fill orders when received; some do not even stock the books. They carry books from most publishers non-exclusively, because their main service is delivering books quickly. While many wholesalers may call themselves "distributors," they are actually wholesalers, because they do not have sales reps.

More than 30% of the bookstores buy from wholesalers regularly and most depend on wholesalers for some of their stock. These wholesalers ask for a 50% to 60% discount from you or your distributor and then sell to their stores at 40% to 45% off, depending upon quantity (titles can be mixed to get a higher discount). Even the big chains make use of wholesalers when they run out and are desperate for a book.

Wholesalers can be sub-divided as follows:

●◆ **National Wholesalers:** there are two national wholesalers that have multiple warehouses in various parts of the country so that they can quickly ship books to every library and bookstore in the United States. Baker & Taylor has four regional service centers (warehouses) and does about 80% of its business serving the "institutional" market (public libraries, schools, colleges, universities, specialized libraries, etc.), and about 20% serving the "retail" market (bookstores and other retail outlets). Ingram Book Co. has five regional warehouses and focuses its business exactly the opposite of Baker & Taylor—approximately 80% store and 20% institutional.

●◆ **Regional wholesalers:** These wholesalers focus primarily in one region of the country and some have active marketing programs and specialized sales representation. They include The Bookmen (Midwest), Bookazine (New York), Koen Book Distributors (East Coast and Northwest), Southern Book Service (Southeast), Sunbelt Publications (Southwest), Washington Book Distributors (Mid-Atlantic), and others. There are about a dozen significant regional wholesalers.

●❖ **Specialized Wholesalers:** A larger number of wholesalers offer books in specific categories—children, computers, cookbooks, gift books, health, legal, medical, music, new age, outdoor, religious, scientific, travel and so forth. Some serve specific types of sales outlets, such as college stores, golf shops, school supply stores and truck stops. Advanced Marketing Services and Anderson are two that serve discount stores, warehouse clubs, and mass merchandisers.

●❖ **Library Wholesalers:** These companies find books for libraries. Up to 90% of the libraries buy from wholesalers. These wholesalers provide a valuable service by combining orders and saving librarians from thousands of single-title orders. Larger library wholesalers stock some books, but most order from publishers only when filling an order.

While there are many library wholesalers, only about a dozen do substantial business. Bordart, in Williamsport, Pennsylvania, is the largest of the library wholesalers with a warehouse stocking over 100,000 titles. Other library wholesalers ranked by the approximate size of their warehouses are: Emery-Pratt company (100,000 titles), Ambassador Book Service (75,000), Midwest Library Service (75,000), Coutts Library Service (35,000), Blackwell Book Services (25,000), Academic Book Center (20,000), Book House (20,000), and Eastern Book Company (15,000).

Independent Distributors (IDs) carry magazines, trade books, and mass-market paperbacks to serve drugstores, supermarkets, newsstands, hotels and some airport outlets. IDs are really magazine wholesalers who treat books the same as magazines: the books go on the rack for one month. Then if they do not sell, the IDs replace the selection and return only the covers from unsold books for credit. You probably will not deal with many IDs, although your national distributor may. The larger IDs are Anderson News Co., headquartered in Knoxville, Tennessee; The News Group; Charles Levy Circulating Co. and Hudson-RPM Distributors. Through consolidation and attrition, the number of IDs has dwindled from over 1500 several years ago, to less than 300 today.

Library Distributors: There are two library distributors, Quality Books and Unique Books. Both have traveling sales reps that actively sell books to libraries.

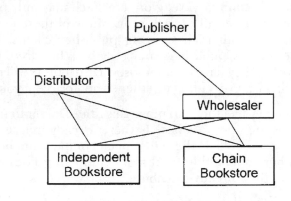

The Book Trade sales process

Most publishers sell to either national distributors or directly to wholesalers that serve both the chain and independent bookstores. Chain bookstores are stores that are related to each other and usually have a single central buying office. For lists of distributors and wholesalers, see Appendix 2.

SELECTING A DISTRIBUTOR

Now the question is, how do you find the right national distributor? The secret is to match your book (or line of books) with a distributor that already offers titles of the same type. They will have a relationship with stores that have major sections of that type of book, and they may be serving other appropriate stores outside the book trade. For example, if you have a business book, you might approach Publishers Group West or NBN. If you have a traditional religion or new age book, you might contact a specialized wholesaler like Bookpeople, DeVorss or New Leaf. If you have a health and fitness book, you might check with Nutri-Books. If you strike a deal with Nutri- Books/Royal, for example, they will get your book into book- stores with significant health and fitness sections and into health food stores. You want a distributor or sometimes a wholesaler that is already plugged into the right markets for your book.

SELECTION CRITERIA: Distributors are very selective. There are only about 15 national distributors who carry broad lines of books, and an additional few who specialize in cookbooks, fiction, new age, military, religion, etc. Each may only present a couple hundred new titles each year. Many of these new "front list" titles are from their existing publisher clients, so their acceptance of new publishers may only be a hundred, more or less, per year. They have to be choosey! Distributors will consider the following when deciding whether or not to accept your book:

- Do they feel they can move this title? Does it fit into their existing line of books? Is there a ready market for this type of book? Is there too much competition, both from other similar titles and from competing lines of books that they already distribute?

- Is the book manufactured to accepted industry standards in terms of binding, page and cover design, typestyle, size and so on? Cover design and a professional interior design and typesetting are especially important.

- Is the book backed by an advertising or promotion budget and marketing plan that will bring the book to the attention of readers, libraries and/or bookstores? A substantial budget for marketing and promotion is important. A distributor can convince trade buyers to make the book available in bookstores, but the publisher in turn must make readers aware of the book and motivate them to buy.

- Does the publisher have more than one product? Distributors like to open accounts with established, ongoing businesses. Many distributors are hesitant to deal with one-book publishers who may never publish again.

- Do they perceive the publisher to be a "problem client," that is someone who will tie up their time with constant phone calls and naïve questions, not really market or promote, ask for constant explanations of the distribution process and sales reports, nit-pick their contract terms, and generally be more of a nuisance than the value of their potential book sales.

Your next move is to contact the distributors that appear to best match your book(s) and request submission procedures. For a current list of distributors and the categories of books they want and do not want, see Document 605, *Locating the Right Distributor,* at http://ParaPublishing.com.

If a distributor turns down your book, it may be because the book is not right for their particular market, the book may be poorly written or produced, or, in their brief evaluation, they fail to see its sales potential. Distributors, like bookstore buyers, have little time to evaluate the dozens of books they receive every day. Try again. Wait a few months to build up a track record. Then resubmit the book and send along sales figures, reviews, endorsements, your marketing and promotion success— anything that will demonstrate that the book is selling and that customers are responding. If the book is moving, the distributors may want to get in on the action.

Distributors are often reluctant to open an account with a one-book publisher. Therefore, if you are new or small, you must be persistent. You must convince them this is the first book of many and that this book will move.

If you call a distributor and they do not feel your book is right for their line, ask them for a recommendation of another distributor or specialized wholesaler. They know the industry and will not consider noncompeting distributors as a threat.

PMA TRADE DISTRIBUTION PROGRAM: Started in 1992, this is a special book program sponsored by Publishers Marketing Association (PMA) and Independent Publishers Group (IPG), a national distributor. Twice each year (in January and July), PMA members may submit books to a selection committee. Books are screened for suitability for general interest bookstores by buyers from Borders, Barnes & Noble, Baker & Taylor, Ingram, Independent Publishers Group and independent bookstores. IPG has agreed to carry all the books selected. This is a great service for the chains, because they get access to pre-selected, pre-screened (otherwise unseen) books. It is also a great program for the smaller and newer publisher because it provides access to the chains, wholesalers, and independent book sellers. See PMA's Web site at http://www. pma-online.org.

EXCLUSIVES are necessary in the book trade because sales reps want credit for their efforts. Stores prefer single vendors of record so they can cycle books back (returns) and forth (orders). This exclusive territory is only for the outlets covered by the national distributors. The sales outlets are usually wholesalers and bookstores, or what we call the "book trade." Give your distributor an exclusive to the book trade and then concentrate your time and money pursuing other areas such as the gift trade, catalogs and other outlets.

CONSIGNMENT: Most distributors operate on consignment inventory and pay you 90-120 days after they ship the books to the bookstore or wholesaler. This means they have very little invested in their operation. While publishers should avoid selling to small accounts on consignment, there are good arguments for these terms with national distributors. Book manufacture requires large print runs, so part of your inventory might just as well sit in another warehouse as your own.

Remember, however, title (ownership) to the books is still yours. If the books are lost or damaged and if the distributor does not have insurance, the loss could be yours.

MAJOR WHOLESALERS (See Appendix 2 for a complete listing)

BAKER & TAYLOR is headquartered in Bridgewater, New Jersey, with warehouses in Somerville, New Jersey; Reno, Nevada; Momence, Illinois and Commerce, Georgia. All buying is done from Somerville. The company has an additional 100,000 square foot consolidation center in Franklin, New Jersey, that stocks 15,000 titles and acts as a backup for the other regional warehouses.

Although the company is education oriented and much of their effort is directed toward finding books for libraries and schools, the bookstore market is also served. B&T is a mirror of library demand. If you receive a good review in Library Journal, some 75% of your library orders will come through B&T.

B&T stocks more than 120,000 different titles, over 3 million books in all. They have 1.4 million titles listed on their CD-ROM database. On heavy days, they receive over 90,000 books and ship over 90,000 books. In a recent year, they returned 2 million overstock books to publishers. They added 3,000 new publishers last year and currently solicit new title information from some 14,000 publishers. The company employs over 1,700 people and grosses about $800 million annually. Its 38 salespeople call on more than 105,000 libraries across the U.S., and its representatives attend more than 500 library meetings each year.

B&T wants a 55% discount, net 90-day payment terms, FOB destination (free freight) and fully returnable. If you do not choose to be in the B&T system, you may allow them any discount you wish. Since they are usually waiting for your book to complete a large order, they won't quibble over the discount and will even pay a pro forma invoice (in advance). However, being a "stock" publisher with a listing on their database makes your books available to many more stores and buyers, which is easily worth the 55%. B&T says publishers dictate the terms and that they will carry trade books at 50% off, no free freight (still returnable), but they will special order only—they will not stock the title. If you do not agree to their terms, they will not make you a stock publisher and they will only buy from you when they have to (when they want to serve a good customer).

B&T charges a one-time $125 setup fee for new vendors (they will waive this fee if you are a PMA member). In return, B&T will enter the publisher and all books into their database and CD-ROM product. If you sign with a distributor, that distributor will have an existing relationship with B&T so you will also avoid the $125 setup fee.

B&T offers several book marketing opportunities. One is the *Independent Press Quarterly,* a direct mail piece that goes to 12,000 retailers and public libraries. Each mailing has 10 to 20 flyers prepared by the publisher. For a sample of the mailing package and details, contact Brenda Larson in Bridgewater at 908-218-3860 or larsonb@btol.com. Also ask her about other promotional tools.

B&T's first notice of new books often comes from the Library of Congress, so make sure you apply for a Library of Congress control number for each title. And about half the orders received by B&T come in electronically and reference the ISBN. Make sure your numbers are correct in all brochures and listings. But they want to hear from you as soon as possible— don't wait for them to find you.

Contact B&T's Publishers Services in Bridgewater and ask for a copy of their *Information Outline For Publishers*. This multipage document explains all B&T's programs. Fill out and return their Vendor Profile Questionnaire and their New Title Information Sheet. Work with Publishers Services in Bridgewater but also contact the facilities in Somerville, Commerce, Momence and Reno for a stocking order.

INGRAM BOOK CO. is the largest wholesaler to independent (nonchain) bookstores. It has been growing very rapidly. Headquartered in Nashville, Tennessee, Ingram has five regional warehouses and a returns center in La Vergne, Tennessee; Fort Wayne, Indiana; East Windsor, Connecticut; Roseburg, Oregon; Chambersburg, Pennsylvania and Petersburg, Virginia. With this spread of warehouses, Ingram can provide next-day delivery to over 95% of its bookstore and library customers. Ingram stocks fewer titles (some 100,000 in each warehouse) than Baker & Taylor but stocks the books in greater depth. Ingram sells over $2 billion in books each year from some 2,000 publishers and distributors to 18,000 bookstores and libraries. Ingram does not promote books; they make them available to retailers.

Normally, Ingram wants to buy your books from a national distributor they already deal with. Your distributor will present your book(s) to Ingram. Then you can work with your distributor to take part in some of Ingram's promotional programs. A few smaller and newer publishers with a line of books have been successful at approaching Ingram directly.

Ingram is very business oriented; they want to know about your promotion. You must convince them there will be demand for your books. Be prepared to answer their questions about what you plan to do to make your book sell. Their decision to buy or not to buy your book will be based on your promotional plans as much as on the quality of the book itself. Most of the buying for the regional warehouses is controlled from Nashville. Ingram wants a 50% discount and pays the freight, though some new publishers have been unable to negotiate a deal better than 55% FOB destination.

Ingram mails its listings to over 9,000 bookstores each week. Getting in the listings is a respected accomplishment, but staying on the list through reorders is more difficult and a more accurate measure of your book's success.

Ingram runs special promotions. For around $1,200, your book can be featured in a circular mailed with their monthly statements to stores, or for about $1,500, the book can be mentioned by the order operators. Ingram also publishes *Advance* magazine and *Paperback Advance*.

If you have a distributor, the distributor will present your book, but you may also submit a sample copy to Ingram (and to other wholesalers to make as many as possible aware of your book). However, make sure you stress that the book is available through your national distributor. Send a copy of the book, with a brochure and any other promotional materials, to: Ingram Book Company, Linda Curtis, Publisher Relations, One Ingram Blvd., LaVergne, TN 37086-1986, Tel: 800-937-8100 (new accounts), Tel: 800-937-8200 (customer service), Fax: 800-876-0186 (ordering) http://www.ingrambook.com. There are many trade buyers, and Linda Curtis will direct your materials to the appropriate one.

INGRAM EXPRESS PROGRAM: This is a special direct-relationship program for publishers with 10 titles or more and no national distributor. For publishers with less than ten titles, Ingram suggests that they sign with a national distributor that sells to Ingram. Contact Ingram Express for a list of these distributors at 615-793-5000 or the phone numbers in the previous paragraph.

Publishers who are accepted into Ingram Express will be listed in the Ingram database and will have their books stocked in Ingram's four super warehouses (in Tennessee, Oregon, Connecticut and Virginia). It is then up to the publishers to generate orders from as many chain and independent bookstores, libraries and schools as possible so that the books move out of the Ingram warehouses. If there are only minimal sales, after a period of time, Ingram may eliminate that publisher from the program.

Most bookstores do business with Ingram, and the Ingram Express Program makes ordering independently published titles easy for the stores (they just add the titles to their next large order to Ingram). Ingram Express publishers can make bookstores aware of their titles through sales flyer mailings, co-op catalogs, trade magazine advertising, sample copies sent to bookstores, telephone calls and even trips to see local bookstore buyers.

To be acceptable to Ingram Express, all books must be perfectbound or hardbound (no spiral or comb) with an ISBN, EAN bar code and price printed on the back cover. Ingram requires a 55% discount, publisher-paid freight, a signed contract and extensive marketing information. For further details, their contract, Publisher Information Form and Marketing Strategy Questionnaire, see the Ingram Web site: http://www.ingrambook.com.

BOOKSTORE CHAINS (See Appendix 2 for a complete listing.)

The large bookstore chains are important to publishers because they control the majority of the bookstore market. That means that a limited number of buyers control most of the books sold in bookstores. Chains are easier to reach since they have single central buying offices. Visiting one chain buyer to sell hundreds of copies is more efficient than sending sales reps to hundreds of individual stores.

The chain stores have their cash registers tied to the central computer to monitor sales. They purchase by category and demographics, matching books to the store's neighborhood clientele. Often the computer will throw a large number of books out to stores as a test, only to be sent back if unsold after a period of time. This instant access to sales information enables the headquarters to stay on top of fast-breaking books. They can reorder quickly to maintain inventory levels.

> *What really interests us are print runs and promotions. We want to know what is the publisher going to print? What is it going to put behind the book? Is the author good on talk shows? And is there going to be a tour?*
> —**Harry Hoffman, former CEO, Waldenbooks**

Although most chain buying is centralized, many local stores are authorized to make small purchases, and they are especially receptive to regional books and local authors. Walden does not permit local managers to make purchases, but headquarters does listen to them when they request a local publisher's book. Most chains expect a 40% discount, FOB origin, and many pay in 60 to 90 days.

The larger chains have stopped buying directly from smaller and newer publishers. However, you can still reach them through your distributor. So find a distributor and then let the distributor pitch the chains. You can also place your books with the various wholesalers (see Ingram Express program for those with 10 titles or more) and then encourage bookstores to order via the wholesalers.

The major bookstore chains account for over 60% of national bookstore sales. If you add to that the percentage of books sold through warehouse and discount stores, the Internet, book clubs, mail order and other outlets (see chart facing the beginning of this chapter), then independent bookstores and small chains (those with six or fewer stores in the chain) now make up only 15% or less of the total dollar volume of books sold. (This is why some distributors send reps only to the chains and major wholesalers, and then sell to the remaining independent bookstore market via catalogs and the telephone.)

Bookstore sales patterns are radically different today than only a few years ago when independent bookstores were still riding high. Then books were also sold through department stores. Today department stores generally do not carry books. Chains close stores and open new stores literally month by month. More and more independent bookstores are being forced out of business by chains, especially those indys that are not niche-oriented. The general sales trend is to the major chains, discounters, warehouse clubs, book clubs, special markets and Internet book sales.

Here is a break down of the major types of bookstore chains:

SUPER STORE CHAINS: The three largest bookstore chains control the majority of the bookstore business.

> ☞ **Barnes & Noble,** headquartered in New York, is a national chain affiliated with B. Dalton, BookStar, Bookstop, Doubleday and Scribner stores. They have over 1,500 bookstores, and are increasing their superstores, while decreasing the B. Dalton stores. B&N had $3.55 billion in sales in the fiscal year 2001.

B&N buys by format and publisher rather than by subject category. This approach fosters and permits the establishment of a publisher-buyer relationship, so get to know your buyer. Your distributor should contact B&N for you or you can visit on your own (but clear it with your distributor first). Send books and catalogs and call ahead to obtain a current contact name.

• **Borders,** based in Ann Arbor, Michigan and affiliated with Waldenbooks, Brentanos and Library Ltd., is one of the most successful mall-based booksellers in the U.S. with more than 1,100 stores. Borders purchases books from approximately 7,500 publishers, but they prefer to deal with (fewer) distributors. They had $3.24 billion in sales in the fiscal year 2001, and are growing world wide. Their average return rate is 21%.

Borders buys by category. Your distributor should contact Borders for you or you can visit yourself (clear it with your distributor first). Send review copies, news releases and catalogs to the appropriate buyer.

• **Books-A-Million,** Birmingham, Alabama, has over 100 stores, 26 are superstores. Many are combination book and greeting card stores operating under the Bookland name. BAM had $418 million in sales in fiscal 2001.

NATIONAL CHAINS: These include two chains that sell not only books, but also music and videos—Hastings (with about 150 stores) and Media Play (with about 80 outlets, including the Musicland and On Que stores). Other national bookstore chains include Little Professor Book Centers, Virgin Megastores (about 20 stores, also selling music and videos), Rizzoli and Waterstone's (about 20 stores in airports). Little Professor, based in Ann Arbor, Michigan, has no central buying. Each store buys individually.

REGIONAL CHAINS: These include chain bookstores that serve specific regions of the country, such as Joseph Beck (including Davis-Kidd) and Reader's World in the Midwest, Harry Schwartz in the Upper Midwest, Chapter 11 in the Southeast, Olsson's in the Central Atlantic area, and Books Inc., Tower and Powell's on the West Coast.

CHILDREN'S BOOKSTORE CHAINS: Chains that sell books, toys and other children's products, such as Books "R" Us, FAO Schwarz, Hammet's Learning World, Kidsmith and lots of stores with the word "Learning" in the name—Learning House, Fun, Place, Shop, Smith, etc.

INDIVIDUAL BOOKSTORES, individual but not necessarily independent, are a diverse group of retailers. They include the downtown bookstore, the college store, the religious bookstore and others. There are over 15,000 stores that carry books. They come in all sizes: some sell books exclusively, while others carry books as a sideline; some stores are general and some are specialized (computer, movies/TV, mystery, new age, science fiction, women's etc.); and some are attached to museums or libraries.

BOOKSTORE PATRONS

Bookstore patron profiles consist of the book addict and the occasional buyer. These recreational readers are used to plunking down $24.95 for hardcover fiction. Fifty percent of the customers in a bookstore are looking for a particular book. These particular-book seekers are more likely to be younger and female. About 47% are looking for a nonfiction title, 27% for a particular book of fiction and 28% want textbooks. Although 20% do not find the book they are looking for, 54% buy one or more books before they leave. Then there are those people who never visit a bookstore.

Bookstores are a lousy place to sell books.

Modern booksellers are faced with trying to attract and sell to all these people. To do so, they have to locate in high-rent, heavy-traffic areas. Stores report an inventory turnover of 2 to 5 times a year, with an average of 3.3 times. If a book hasn't moved in four months on the shelf, it is usually returned. The newer and smaller publisher is trapped between the Scylla of wide exposure and the Charybdis of massive returns.

Bookstores are the frosting, not the cake.

Many small publishers tolerate, but don't pursue, small individual bookstores. The major challenges with stores are that they order just a few books at a time, complain about the 40%

discount, seldom pay in 30 days and often return the books for a refund—damaged. You wind up processing a lot of paperwork for many small orders and returns while making very few sales. The best approach is to let your distributor handle the stores.

If selling books through bookstores was good business, the bookstores might be paying their bills.

Try visiting nearby bookstores; it will be a good education. Tell them you are a local author and, therefore, local people will be interested in your book. Mention any local publicity such as talk shows that are planned. Stores want to know if the book is readily available through a wholesaler and if it will be promoted. Reviews and author appearances are more important than advertising. If the book is professionally produced, a sale should not be difficult. Be ready with the stock phrase "I can offer you the books at a full 40% discount, without delivery charges, and they are fully returnable, of course." The whole pitch will probably run 5 to 10 minutes. You can also offer to do an author signing or reading and participate in any in-store promotions, such as window displays, front-of-store exhibits, or end-of-aisle posters.

COLLEGE, SCHOOL AND TEXTBOOK STORES also respond best to face-to-face sales calls. There are roughly 2,800 college stores serving 2,200 U.S. colleges and universities with over 11 million students. Some of the major college store chains are: Follett College stores (about 600 stores), Barnes & Noble (315), Wallaces' (60), Nebraska Book (50), Founders (20) and Dekalb (15).

College stores are on their own schedule, depending upon whether they are on the semester, quarter or early semester system. Don't put too much energy into college stores. Many of them primarily stock text books and reference materials. Students generally don't spend money on much more than assigned texts, CDs and beer. Large textbook orders go to the publisher. About one-third of school store orders are through wholesalers, so wholesalers might be a better way to reach this market.

Many librarians view the publisher as the money-grubber between the author and the reader.

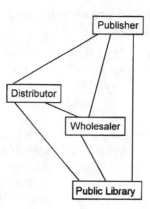

The library trade

THE LIBRARY TRADE

Even though orders are for smaller quantities, libraries offer greater potential to the small publisher than bookstores.

Libraries come in several types. There are almost 16,000 public libraries (8,937 public library systems, some with branches). There are 50,000 libraries in elementary schools, 20,000 in high schools, and 15,000 special libraries (including 1,700 law libraries). Other libraries include: more than 3,000 in colleges, 1,897 governmental, 363 military and over 1,000 formal libraries exist in larger churches.

The Library of Congress shelves 24 million books, Harvard University has 14 million and the New York Public Library has 11.5 million. For more statistics, see http://www.ala.org.

Over 90% of the libraries that respond to your mailings or a review in *Library Journal* or the other library magazines will order from a library wholesaler, and 75% of those orders go to Baker & Taylor. Rather than place thousands of orders with individual publishers for single titles, libraries (just like the bookstores) save time by bundling the orders together and sending them all to a wholesaler. They are extended a 20% to 33% discount by the wholesaler, so they are not only saving time but are receiving both price and service.

Their challenge is money. The cost of ordering and processing a new title can cost as much as the book itself. Many libraries are spreading their already tight budgets even thinner now by adding audiovisual and other non-print items. Most of the library budget goes for personnel; only about 15% is spent on books and other media.

LIBRARY MARKET SIZE: Libraries spend around $1.5 billion each year for books, buying some 14% of the books published. Of those, public libraries buy 23%, el-hi school libraries 33%, college libraries 27% and special (e.g., law, medical) libraries 17%. Many library purchases are for books with press runs under 5,000, which would not get published without their support.

If libraries bought one copy of every book published in the U.S., they would each need a budget of over $2 million per year. Yet only about 2,600 public libraries have an annual book budget of $25,000 or more, and most have much less. They have to be selective in their purchases. Contact only those libraries that can afford to buy your book. Do not waste your energy and money pursuing the rest.

As could be expected, children's books and fiction aren't of any great interest to college libraries. Send your brochures to the right type of library. If you have a special-interest book, target those libraries (and bookstores) with an interest in your subject.

Libraries do not buy "fill-in-the blanks" type books because librarians do not want people writing in their books. If your book has to be filled in, you must accept the fact that libraries will not buy it. Some fill-ins can be changed to lists. Or you might suggest that readers photocopy the page.

Many libraries are also adverse to buying spiral or comb bound books, because patrons can easily rip out the pages. Additionally, spiral/comb bound books must have a printed spine so they can be shelved "spine out." Libraries almost never buy books in ring binders, and if they do, they rebind them for permanence.

Many libraries buy more for topic than quality. They have to justify their budgets to the community (if public) and try to offer something for everyone. It is said that better judgment is shown in the purchasing of children's books and fiction. One librarian recently explained, "When material is scarce on a topic and interest is high, we will often buy any reasonably priced new book through an ad in *Library Journal* or even a flyer. However, we usually don't buy if the book receives a bad review."

DO LIBRARY ORDERS KILL SALES? Some book publishers question the wisdom of selling to libraries, on the theory that this one sale will kill several others when many people read the book free. They note that some magazines charge libraries a higher price for a subscription on the theory that more people will read the periodical.

Other book publishers feel that libraries are showcasing their book—and are paying to do it. At least four orders for *The Self-Publishing Manual* are received each week with a letter starting, "The library will not let me check the book out again so I want to buy my own copy."

Library loans may hurt sales of fiction (because they are only read once), but not reference books (they are used over and over and people need a personal copy). Mailing a free copy of a new book to the central buyer of major library systems (those with many branches) might even be a good promotional investment.

APPROVAL PLANS: Some wholesalers serve their library accounts automatically by sending collections of books in specific categories *on approval*, allowing the library to return the unwanted titles. Because the wholesaler has prescreened the books and matched them to the library's special collections, few are returned. Academic and special libraries might buy 30% of their books this way, whereas public libraries buy some 10% of their books through approval plans. Obviously, it is to your great advantage to have your book included in these computer-matched offerings, especially in the Baker & Taylor system.

ORDERING CYCLES: Libraries tend to do most of their ordering around the beginning or end of their fiscal year (usually December 31 or June 30), when they try to use up their old budget or break into a new one. This is when they may show slightly less buying discrimination. Your book might be selected at this time even if it is an afterthought, not a first choice. At the three-quarter point in their fiscal year, libraries are often out of book purchasing funds. School libraries usually use the slow summer months to work on ordering.

ACQUISITION LIBRARIANS: Some libraries have acquisition librarians, while committees select books in others. Because more than one person is often involved in acquisitions in the larger libraries, it is wise to send more than one copy of your promotional material.

Do not send your promotional material to the head librarian or acquisition librarian. In large libraries, it is best to direct mailings to the subject area supervisor who makes the actual buying decisions. These supervisors are in charge of areas such as children's books, adult fiction, reference, etc. Ask about these categories at your local library, and always list the category at the top of your sales flyer.

Since libraries want to order from wholesalers, you must let them know which wholesalers carry your book by listing them on your sales flyer. Make ordering easy. Librarians want all the numbers: ISBN, LC control number, Dewey classification, copyright date, number of pages, trim size, binding, etc.

It helps if you build consumer demand, because most libraries respond when a library patron requests a title. For example, school libraries are responsive to the wishes of their faculty. Mailings to teachers often result in school library orders.

BOOKS WEAR OUT: They can be lent out only so many times. A softcover book is good for about 18 cycles. The life span of most books is 1.5 to 2 years. Unless a worn-out title has seen a lot of recent use, it usually isn't reordered. On the other hand, if the book has been very popular, the library may order several copies. Books are also stolen. Despite electronic security systems, about 20% of a library's collection is lost each year. So many books are kept past the due date that librarians do not have time to look up the fines. Many libraries have a flat fee, say $10, for any overdue or lost book.

> In 1979, when *The Self-Publishing Manual* was first presented to a librarian in Santa Barbara, she said, "We will have to order several of these. This is the type of book our patrons keep." During the next few years, the library went through more than 30 copies, despite the fact that the book is available for sale in several bookstores, instant print shops and office supply stores around town.

HARDCOVER OR SOFTCOVER BOOKS? Do libraries want hardcover or softcover book? Neither; more and more, they want electronic books, because they do not have shelf space for books. Fiction is still being stocked in print form, but reference materials are on CD-ROM or are accessed online. Now when people want to take research material home from a library, they do not photocopy or print out a hard copy; they download it onto a floppy. The world of electronic books is not coming; it is here!

DEALING DIRECTLY: Some publishers have elected to deal directly with libraries instead of using wholesalers. Most of these publishers specialize in higher priced reference books, for which libraries are their largest market. They make regular mailings to libraries, count on getting full price and like to stay close to their market. But most librarians prefer to use wholesalers.

Librarians are likely to purchase only one book per branch. It is hard to justify a mailing when more often than not the library will order it through a library wholesaler to whom you give a 40% to 60% discount.

The librarians say they buy to cover a subject; they will buy a higher priced book if it meets the need and is the only one available. Libraries do not expect a discount unless they order several copies. Some publishers follow a universal discount schedule, giving 10% for an order of 5, 20% for 20, etc. Some big-city public libraries take advantage of quantity deals because they are buying for several branches simultaneously.

LOCAL SALES: Your local library should buy your book just because you are part of the community. Some even have a special private room for books by indigenous writers. If so, it would be appropriate for you to donate a copy to this reference section. If you do make such a donation, be sure the local paper is notified with a news release, so you can get some promotional mileage out of your largess.

> I donated a couple of my new books to the local public library when I lived in Quincy, Massachusetts. The books were placed in a special room reserved for local books. This was quite an unexpected honor in the hometown of two U.S. Presidents.

LIBRARY MARKETING PLAN

The best way to handle the library market is to strike a deal with Quality Books, become a stock publisher with Baker & Taylor, let all the library wholesalers know where to find you by sending them a brochure, join the PMA library mailings, make your own mailings to libraries with special collections, patronize selected library co-op exhibits, and prepare a great review package for *Library Journal*. Here are the details:

QUALITY BOOKS uses sales reps to sell books to libraries. In the business over 35 years, they have approximately 6,000 active library accounts. Quality needs 100 new titles each month and actively seeks new books. They sell to libraries at list price or at a 20% discount. Quality wants 55% off, a consignment contract, fully returnable and 90 days to pay. If you will agree to a 60% discount, they will pay in 60 days; 62.5% discount pays in 30 days. Fifty-five percent may sound like a lot, but Quality buys by the carton and pays on time. Returns to publishers average 2% to 3%, and Quality pays the return shipping.

Quality wants books on business, travel, making money (doing anything), reference books that are not too highly priced or too technical, and hardcover children's books. They do not want fiction or poetry. They warehouse approximately 15,000 titles and the normal sales life of books carried by Quality is 12-18 months.

Contact Quality for a New Book Information form and a sample Distribution to Libraries Agreement at 815-732-4450 or at http://www.quality-books.com.

> Quality rejected *Parachuting: The Skydiver's Handbook* when it was initially published. The selection committee just didn't believe the library market was large enough for such a specialized sport. Quality was handling a number of my other books and gave the handbook another look soon after Tom Drewes (then owner) took up skydiving in 1983. Everyone was pleasantly surprised—Quality moved several hundred copies.

The Quality Books Selection Committee looks for the following when evaluating a book for library use:

•◆ **Adult nonfiction and selected children's titles.**

•◆ **New** (copyright in current year). The book must not have been exposed to the library market previously. The publisher's primary market must be outside the library market. The book must be submitted to Quality Books prior to the official publication date.

➬ The book is well organized:

■ **Good title and subtitle.** Must be informative, not cute. Must clearly and instantly convey the book's purpose. Title must be the same on the cover, spine and title page.

■ **Includes a table of contents and index.**

■ **The book is clearly different** from others in its field. Librarians like to fill information gaps.

■ **The information is readily accessible**—the book is user friendly.

➬ No fill-in-the-blanks books. Several customers must use the book.

➬ ISBN, LCCN and bar code to aid identification of the book. Quality prefers a cataloging in publication data block to help librarians in cataloging the book. However, this is not mandatory for selection. If you have not yet published three books and, therefore, do not qualify for the CIP program, Quality can supply you with a data block. Contact them for this CIP data before you go to press.

➬ Binding. Libraries prefer a hardcover binding for reference books and books for their permanent collection. Academic libraries prefer hardcover; special libraries have no preference. Thirty-four percent of the books purchased by libraries today are softcover, which allows librarians to order more books from the same budget. However, the perfect binding must be durable. The book must have a spine to display the title and must be shaped to fit a library shelf, not long, low or round.

➬ A topical subject. The book must be the type customers want to borrow from the library.

➬ Sales aids. The publisher must supply 30 extra covers for the reps to show to the libraries.

Think about these criteria when writing and designing your next book.

The secret to having your book accepted by Quality Books is to notify them of the new title early. Quality has to get the jump on the regular wholesalers if they are to be effective in moving books for you. The selection committee turns down 700-800 titles each month. Some books do not meet the selection criteria described above, but most rejects are older books from larger publishers.

The ideal time to send in the New Book Information form along with a sample copy and promotional materials, is before you go to press. Then books can be shipped directly to Quality directly from the printer. It is a great feeling to go to press knowing some books are already sold. If you cannot submit an advance sample copy prior to printing then submit the book, forms, and pro- motional materials immediately after printing. The sooner the better. An initial stocking order from Quality is usually 50-100 books.

UNIQUE BOOKS: Unique Books operates like Quality Books but on a somewhat smaller scale. They have been in business about 15 years, warehouse about 5,000 titles and accept not only adult non-fiction and children's books, but also fiction and university press titles. Like Quality, they send sales reps to libraries and exhibit at library conferences. Your book can be carried by both Unique and Quality—a usual opening order from Unique is 30-60 books.

BAKER & TAYLOR: Become a *stock publisher.* Library sales account for 68% of B&T's business. You should have made contact as you worked through the previous bookstore section.

OTHER LIBRARY WHOLESALERS: Notify other library wholesalers through a mailing. Some of the larger library wholesalers include Academic, Ambassador, Blackwell, Book House, Brodart, Coutts, Eastern, Emery-Pratt, Midwest and Yankee Book Peddler.

BOOK REVIEWS in library review magazines. Since a good review in *Library Journal* or *ALA Booklist* will move around 1,200 copies of most books, book reviews are worth some extra effort.

Book reviews are the librarians' overwhelmingly most popular tool for making selection decisions. Acquisition librarians just do not have time to read and evaluate all the new books.

They rely mostly on *Publishers Weekly, Library Journal, Booklist, Kirkus Reviews, Choice* and the *New York Times Book Review.* Ninety-four percent of the librarians rely on reviews in *Library Journal,* while 91% read the reviews in *Booklist.* Only 44% believe the ads in *LJ,* and only 35% have confidence in the ads in *Booklist.* The figures for *Publishers Weekly* are 75% and 53%. See the addresses for the magazines in Appendix 2 under Magazines for Publishers. Also see the Book Review, Magazines and Serials sections of *Literary Market Place.*

Follow up on review packet mailings to the above-mentioned library review magazines with a telephone call. Never ask if they plan to review the book but rather if they have received the book. If not, or they can't find it, get a name and send another book.

PMA CO-OP LIBRARY MAILINGS: At the end of each month, PMA (Publishers Marketing Association) mails a flat envelope containing individual book flyers to 2,600 public libraries across the U.S. that have a purchasing budget of $25,000 or more. These are just public libraries, and then only those that can afford to buy. Cost for participation is $145 plus your flat (unfolded) flyer on one or more books. PMA also makes co-op mailings to 3200 K-12 libraries, 3300 colleges and university libraries, and 2,600 special interest libraries for $165 per mailing. See http://www.pma-online.org.

Consider the type of library that is most likely to buy your book. Maybe you just want school, medical or law libraries, or maybe you have a regional book and just want public libraries in New England. Make mailings either alone or in cooperation with other publishers.

SPECIAL COLLECTIONS: Look for special libraries or regular libraries with special collections. If yours is an aviation book, send brochures to libraries with an aviation section. Do not go to the expense of mailing to all libraries when you can isolate those that have a particular interest in your topic. Gale Research rents lists of libraries with special collections. See their Web site at http://www.galegroup.com.

For a list of special libraries, contact the Special Library Association at http://www.sla.org.

Many individual library associations rent their mailing lists. For example, the American Association of Law Libraries can supply a list of 2,300 law libraries on labels. For more information on contacting special libraries, send for *Marketing to Libraries Through Library Associations* from the American Library Associa- tion at http://www.ala.org.

When you plan to make a mailing to specialized libraries, invite other publishers to join you. Co-op promotions can save a lot of money and help justify otherwise marginal mailings. Contacting other publishers is easy. Just send a notice of your proposed mailing for listing in the *Publishers Marketing Association Newsletter.* See their Web site at http://www.pma-online.org.

LIBRARY REVIEW MAGAZINES: *Library Journal, ALA Booklist* and other trade magazines run special editions and special sections throughout the year. Areas covered are travel books, children's books, metaphysical books, cookbooks, religious books, etc. Book listings (a few sentences about your book) are usually free. Advertising and listings should be planned for these special editions where attention is being drawn to a particular subject.

Contact each magazine for a list of upcoming special issues, ad rates and information about how to list your book. The addresses are in Appendix 2 under Magazines for Publishers.

SCHOOL MARKET

The school market spends over a billion dollars each year for textbooks, and while most of these books are developed especially for certain courses, many are regular books developed for other markets but adopted as supplementary educational aids. Educators are the most price conscious of all the book markets. Textbook publishers respond by keeping their prices lower than normal and extending only a 20% (short) discount to school bookstores.

ELEMENTARY AND SECONDARY SCHOOLS: In the U.S., there are approximately 64,000 public elementary, 24,000 public high and 1,800 combined schools in 18,000 school districts. Additionally, there are some 14,000 private elementary and 4,000 private high schools. Together they employ 2.3 million teachers.

In 22 states, schools purchase texts under a state adoption system, where a board approves titles for a five-year period. State adoption is a hunting license and allows the salespeople to try to sell the book to the schools. Even where there is no state adoption system, planning seems to follow a five-year cycle. In some areas, publishers have to ship to central depositories, where the schools draw on books as needed. This usually means a consignment inventory, and the publishers aren't paid for the books until requisitioned by the schools. The school market is tough and very competitive.

To reach the home school market, see *The Authentic Jane Williams Home School Market Guide* from Bluestocking Press (800-959-8586; fax 530-642-9222; uncleric@jps.net).

COLLEGES AND UNIVERSITIES: Colleges are changing. There are more students over 25, more women are going back to school, and more people are turning to continuing education courses in their specialty.

There are three types of college bookstores: those that are owned by the institution, those that are private and those college stores with a private lessee. As in the general book store business, large chain franchises are devouring independent college stores.

Textbook publishers concentrate on wooing the instructors, who select books for their courses in more than 3,000 schools. This decision is easy for some professors, because they pen their own textbooks. Normally, the purchasing is done by the local bookstore, and the instructor notifies them of his or her choice by April for the fall term. Of course, there are challenges. Sometimes the choice is made too late or the estimated number that will be needed is wrong. Some students avoid buying the text by sharing or making repeated visits to the school library. The result is a store return rate on textbooks of more than 20%.

Teachers expect to get free examination copies of books, and while some treat this privilege with respect, others just collect books or sell them to the bookstore. The bookstore, in turn, sells the book to a student or returns it to the publisher for a refund. The bookstores even supply teachers with blank Desk Copy Request forms designed to be sent to the publisher for freebies. Often, young instructors are trying to build up their libraries. Older professors, who have more say in book selection, do much less collecting.

To check the validity of these requests for examination copies, some publishers request information about the size of the course, the requester's academic position, etc.

During the last 30 years, I have sent out scores of requested desk copies and so far only two have resulted in large school bookstore orders.

To attack the college market, analyze your book's subject and decide which course might find it useful. The teachers are easy to find, and direct mail advertising is the most effective method of reaching them. In fact, some publishers find the lists so specialized that they use them to send free, unsolicited examination copies.

More and more college students are avoiding the college bookstore. They are getting a better deal from online textbook dealers.

PREPUBLICATION SALES

These sales will bring in some money early and help you pay the printing bill. But it isn't wise to start too soon on the prepublication publicity for your first book. The first time around is a learning experience, and there will be countless delays in the writing, production and printing process. You do not want to find yourself spending all your time answering the question, "Where is the book I ordered?" On your first book, hold the announcement until it is on the press. The next time, adjust and start earlier.

Once you learn the promotion ropes, you should be able to sell enough books through prepublication sales, to both wholesale and retail customers, to pay the print bill.

Write up a news release, send in your ads and make a mailing. Offer an early wholesale deal ("to be shipped directly from the printer") to associations and specialty dealers. It is nice to have a pile of orders on the desk when the book comes off the press. But timing is important; these orders must not pour in too early and should not arrive too late.

If your book is specialized and you are able to find an appropriate mailing list, you should consider a prepublication retail offer. Tell the potential buyer the book is being printed, and if they want one hot off the press, they should send their money now because you will be shipping on a first-come, first-served basis. Include an early order deal such as "postage free if you order from this ad." This mailing should also be sent to all your friends and acquaintances; many will respond and will be pleased that you thought of them. If a prospect is mentioned in the text or the acknowledgments, that person is sure to buy one. You can also autograph selected copies.

Never discount a brand new book! Many new publishers feel they have to offer a deal to readers. Discounting a new book makes you appear to be in a distress situation. You are in a very strong position—you have a new book. You need every penny of profit; do not give it away.

NONTRADITIONAL MARKETS

Specialty (non-book) outlets offer many nonfiction publishers their largest market. For example, a book on mountain climbing will sell better in backpacking shops than in bookstores, and the size of the store's purchases will be larger. Sales to stores other than bookstores are often called "nontraditional sales" or "special sales."

Warner Publishing cracked a new market in 1978 when Karen Lustgarten's *Disco Dancing* was sold in record stores.

The only relationship between nonfiction books is their packaging, the subject matter of each book is unique. Nonfiction should be sold where customers for it can be found. Boating books should be placed in nautical shops, tourist books in tourist shops and football books in sporting goods stores. Sell your books where the highest concentration of potential customers can be found. Most of your prospects probably never go into a bookstore. So make your books available through bookstores, but do not confine your sales efforts to these shops.

At Para Publishing, we tolerate, but do not pursue, bookstores.

SELLING TO SPECIALTY STORES: Many specialty stores will want a 40%, 50% or more discount, but they usually buy outright. There are no returns.

In these shops, it is very important to establish, cultivate and maintain as close a personal relationship as possible with the management. It is of the utmost importance that they like you and your book so they will promote it at every opportunity. Selling them the first time often requires a personal visit to prove the sales potential of the book. When making a direct mail promotion to these shops, remember their peak selling seasons and the required lead time.

> *The smaller houses were relatively more successful in using non-book retail outlets than the largest houses were.*
> **—Judith Appelbaum,** *How to Get Happily Published*

One innovative book marketer is Bruce Lansky of Meadowbrook Press. He is good because he markets books the way he used to market candy. His (then) wife Vicki wrote a book on nutrition for babies called *Feed Me, I'm Yours,* and the Lanskys decided to publish it themselves.

First Bruce tried a local children's clothing store. They bought, so he approached a wholesaler of infant items but was turned down flat. He had to offer consignment and counter racks to let the wholesaler prove to himself the books would move. The wholesaler called three days later and ordered 12 dozen more—they were in business. Next Bruce created a mailing stuffer for the wholesaler to enclose with the statements he sent to his 1,000 accounts. Sales soared.

Bruce's secrets to special sales are:

- **Play dumb.** Visit the account and learn all about their terms, key accounts, their store or warehouse and the reps in their field. Think as the specialty wholesaler and retail outlet does.

- **Don't act like a publisher.** Pretend you are in their business. Bruce was in infant accessories that day. Act as they do. Your book is a "specialty product."

- **Use success to breed more success**. Do your research, run small tests and learn the industry. Subscribe to their magazines, join their associations, exhibit at their trade shows and get to know the players. Make a mailing to distributors and retailers and follow up with calls.

Other non-book retail channels include gift shops, hardware stores, garden shops, auto supply stores, etc. Many are establishing book corners for an additional profit center, as well as to lend prestige to their line.

Run a test in a few local shops. Develop your approach (posters, counter displays, price, etc.) before rolling out in a wider promotion. Just as there are distributors and wholesalers serving the bookstores, there are distributors and wholesalers catering to the non-book outlets. Check these stores and look for books. Find out who distributes them to the store. That distributor could get your books to other stores of the same type in their territory.

Those stores that do not carry books will have to be accessed through direct mail, advertising in their magazines or through sales reps of other types of products. Search for lists of the category of stores you are interested in. Ask the local store manager for names of hot sales reps and rep groups who handle other lines of products. These sales reps may take on your book. They will want a sales commission of 10% to 15% of the net-billed amount (that is, a commission on the books after discount and not including the shipping charges).

If the specialty shop is a franchise, make a pitch to the headquarters. Many franchisers do not control the buying of their individual franchisees, and even if they do, the sale will not be easy. However, the hope of making one large sale to the whole chain is worth some of your sales time.

Several years ago, I was in a local instant print shop when the owner began asking about *The Self-Publishing Manual*. Forty percent off sounded good, and the printer wanted to put some books on the counter. I doubted the books would sell, but brought in eight copies in a counter display (cut-down carton) to humor the printer. Three days later, the printer called for more. Apparently, the type of people who frequent copy shops are the type who work with the written word—a good market after all. This lesson resulted in an expansion into other instant print shops and a book on how to paste up. Some outlets for books may not be obvious at first.

If you receive an inquiry from a market you never thought would be interested in your book, draft a letter to similar stores or groups saying, "This [store or group] ordered the book and we thought you might be interested too." The mailing might be just 100 pieces—no great investment—and there is a good chance of a payoff.

A few years later, I thought I might capitalize on desktop publishing by selling *The Self-Publishing Manual* through computer stores. I placed books in several stores and there they sat. Very few were sold. Sometimes the seemingly obvious outlets for a book don't work.

If the appendix of your book has a source directory, do a mailing to each firm, saying, "You are mentioned in the book. We thought you would like to know and that you might like to offer this book to your customers." Build up a strong, reliable dealer network.

SELLING TO THE GOVERNMENT AND MILITARY

There are 2,300 libraries in the federal government library system and 80 agencies that purchase books, according to *Publishers Weekly*. Most of the libraries come under the Department of Defense.

Some of the Army's libraries must be approached through central offices, but others can be approached directly. For example, the Army Library Program procures hardcover books for Army libraries around the world and softcover (or paperbacks) for distribution in the field. Of the about 60 hardcover titles chosen monthly, some 60% are nonfiction. About 100 softcover titles are procured each month and distributed in 900 kits; selections are highly recreational. Centralized purchases are made under annual contracts with wholesalers.

Navy libraries spend over $3 million each year on books. The International Communications Agency (formerly the U.S. Information Agency) runs 129 libraries in 110 countries with 6,000 to 25,000 volumes each and devotes about $2 million each year to procurement. They like to see brochures and review copies.

Sending brochures to military buying offices is not nearly as successful as sending information to *specifiers*. For example, a brochure on a parachute book should be sent to parachute lofts in the Army, Air Force, Navy, Coast Guard and Marine Corps. The parachute riggers in lofts know how useful the book can be and will tell the buying offices how many they want.

For more detailed information see Document 637, *Selling Books to the Military Market*, by Michael Sedge at http:// ParaPublishing.com and U.S. Government Procurement Offices in Appendix 2.

PREMIUMS AND INCENTIVES

Premiums are products that are given away or sold at a discount to promote business. Premiums may be given away by a store or other business to attract customers, while *incentives* are given to salespeople as prizes for achieving sales goals. (An ad specialty is an imprinted product, such as a pen or key chain, which is given away.) The premium/incentive market is a $20 billion per year business. Books are in eighth place with $500 million in sales. According to *Potentials in Marketing* magazine, 16.8% of the companies using premiums also use books. Books make especially good premiums and incentives because you can customize their covers and they have a higher perceived value than some other premium trinkets. In fact, in some areas, regulated industries such as banks are prohibited from giving away certain items or the value of those items is limited.

Look for a company with products or services that closely match the book's subject matter. If your book covers a regional topic, try local businesses. Books can be digitally imprinted with "Compliments of...," for example. If you cover a subject with wider appeal, such as a book on beer can collecting, contact the beer, aluminum, steel, can and packaging companies. Such a book would make an ideal corporate gift or could be worked into a promotion. A tour guidebook might be sold to a motel chain.

Judy Dugan was working in a graphic arts shop when the first edition of *The Self-Publishing Manual* was being typeset. As she pasted up the pages, she read the book and became increasingly interested. She had been toying with two manuscripts (one on Santa Barbara highlights and history, the other a children's book) for years. She began asking me all sorts of questions about the possibilities for her books. One challenge she had was a lack of money to invest.

I noticed that Valley Federal Savings was moving into downtown Santa Barbara. I explained that it was a prime candidate for a regional book such as her Santa Barbara book, because it would tie the out-of-town bank to the local community. A premium could be used to lure potential patrons into the bank.

In two short visits, she walked out with a purchase order for 5,000 copies in softcover and 1,000 copies in hardcover. She was paid one-half on signing and one-half on delivery—at full list price. The money allowed her to print 11,000 books so she could serve the local tourist market with her own 5,000.

The bank's copies had special back cover printing that said, "Compliments of Valley Federal Savings" and the bank advertised in newspapers, on radio and television. They invited people to come into the bank for a free, autographed copy of the book. They set up Judy with a table and a sign and she spent the week greeting people and signing her name.

Publishers have sold premium books to doctors, dentists, chiropractors and other health care professionals (both individual and group practices), and to those in the finance, real estate, insurance and other fields. The possibilities are endless. The books can be imprinted or stickered with the name of the company, and a foreword or sales pitch from the buyer can be added to the front matter. In return, premium buyers buy in large quantities.

Premium orders are large, usually 1,000 or more books, and the customer can ask for 60% off. Such a discount can be justified for a large order that eliminates the problems of financing, storage and individual shipping. A typical premium discount schedule might look like this:

# copies	Discounts
25-99	20%
100-499	40%
500-999	50%
1,000-14,999	60%
15,000 up	Cost of printing plus 10% of list price

Terms: Non-returnable, net 30 days, FOB warehouse/printing plant, freight collect.

Discount schedule for premiums

If you can strike some premium deals before going to (or back to) press, you might increase your press run and achieve a lower per unit cost. Premium sales are tough and time consuming, but the payoff is big.

Do not forget to capitalize on a premium sale. For example, you might use "Official Recipe Book of the Pillsbury Company" or "Recommended by Radio Shack." Premium deals are not just sales; they are also endorsements for the quality of your book.

SPONSORED BOOKS are those you are almost commissioned to write. There may be an institution that wants your book printed and will offer a large advance order. For example, if you wrote a book on the Frisbee and there were no others on the subject, the Wham-O Manufacturing Co., which makes flying disks, might want the book published because the publicity would help their sales. With this sponsorship, they might want some sort of cover credit, such as, "Published in association with Wham-O." Such an endorsement is to your advantage, because it lends credibility to the book.

Some industries need favorable publicity and find that sponsoring a book is much less expensive than placing full-page ads. They may pay for much of your production, printing, marketing and publicity. A book is also much more effective promotion because it appears to be more objective. When you approach these large companies, make sure you have your book or manuscript copyright protected and that you establish a "paper trail" of your contacts and meetings in order to diffuse any thoughts they might have about ripping off your ideas.

FUND RAISERS: Nonprofit organizations are always running sales to raise money for their cause. These flea markets, bake sales, street fairs, etc., promoted by church and civic groups can provide you with an opportunity to move some books.

Every nonprofit has a constitution and bylaws. In the document is a mission statement. The primary mission will be education: to spread the word on what the organization does. All you have to do is match your book to their mission statement.

Unless the organization is the National Association of Cookie Products, a "bake sale" does not match their mission statement.

Find a group that agrees with the subject of your book. Offer to sell them books by the carton at 40% off. They can sell them at list price (or offer a slight discount to their members) and put the money into the club's treasury.

Leila Albala of Quebec wrote and published *Easy Halloween Costumes for Children*. When writing the book, she included a short chapter on UNICEF, since it is traditionally connected with Halloween. After the book was printed, she sent copies to the UNICEF branch in Calgary. The branch liked it and ordered 10 copies, on consignment. Leila capitalized on the order by sending a press kit to the *Calgary Herald*. The story on the book mentioned UNICEF, and 400 copies were sold in just a few days.

Next she contacted UNICEF Canada. They were impressed and agreed to take the book for the whole country. Then she sent press kits to all the major daily newspapers. UNICEF Canada has sold over 3,000 copies in English and 1,000 copies in French. Leila is now concentrating sales efforts on UNICEF in the U.S., a market 10 times larger.

Leila thought of a market that was not so obvious, placed the books and then created the demand for them. Who cares that UNICEF had never sold books before?

Try approaching some local organizations first to get a feel for the way they operate. A gardening club might sell a gardening book, for example. If you are successful, consider a mailing to similar groups nationwide. Don't forget to tell them of your past good track record for sales and assure them that the unsold books can be returned—they can't lose! When an organization buys your book, they are giving it an implied endorsement. You can mention this in your promotion materials.

SUBSIDIARY RIGHTS

Essentially, subsidiary rights give someone else permission to reproduce (repackage) your material. They include book clubs, mass-market paperbacks, film rights, translations, etc. The two major classes of subsidiary rights are *print rights* and rights to *non-print adaptations.*

The bottom line makes it abundantly clear: subsidiary rights have become less and less subsidiary.
—Nancy Evans

Subsidiary rights are so important to the big publishers that the rights are often auctioned off before the original book is printed. However, most publishers report that less than 2% of their income is derived from subsidiary rights sales. A condensation or small book club sale usually brings more fame than fortune. Such a sale is also a great morale booster for both the author and the publisher, not only because of the money but also because someone else obviously likes the book.

The main reason publishers can sell the subsidiary rights for so little is that they are not paying production costs to their printers or, more important, royalties to their authors. Most author-publisher contracts call for a 50/50 split of subsidiary rights revenues. Some contracts give 90% of revenues to the author on any non-print (e.g., film) subsidiary rights. The publisher gets 10% as an agent.

Some subsidiary rights require only a continuation of the same printing (some book club rights), but don't let your customer get away with just paying for the additional press time. They should pay for all your setup and overhead costs. If a book club or other subsidiary rights buyer becomes serious and you aren't familiar with negotiating rights, get a literary agent or an attorney who understands the book publishing business. The agent will get 10% to 15% of whatever he or she brings in, and the lawyer will usually work for a percentage or a straight hourly fee for checking the contract. Agents are listed in *Literary Market Place*. For a list of book attorneys, see Document 113, *Book Publishing Attorneys*, at http://ParaPublishing.com.

> *A publisher's attitude toward a manuscript ought to be similar to a coal mine operator's attitude toward coal: get every last bit of value out of it.*
> **—Sol Stein, president, Stein and Day**

MASS-MARKET REPRINT RIGHTS are for those pocket-sized books selling from $1 to $5 in the supermarkets. This is the one market where it is easier to sell fiction than nonfiction. Mass-market publishers like seven-year contracts with renewal options and initial print runs of 30,000 to 50,000 copies. Mass-market publishers offer 4% to 7.5% in royalties; the cover price is low and the royalty scale does not slide up until sales reach 150,000 copies. Advances are usually just a few thousand dollars. Unless you have a *very* popular book, the mass-market firms won't be interested.

The secret is to match your book with a publisher that has experience with that type of material. Look at other books and search for publishers who have produced the same subject matter. Not every editor in every house is interested in everything. Mass-market publishers can be contacted after your book has been out for a year or so.

> *Without subsidiary rights, publishers would operate in the hole.*
> **—John Dessauer, *Book Publishing: The Basic Introduction***

PERIODICAL RIGHTS: Serializations and excerpts by magazines and newspapers may be *first serial rights*, if before publication, or *second serial rights*, if afterward. Both generate a lot of good publicity. Big periodicals pay more than small ones, and first rights are more valuable than second rights. The subject matter has to be of great interest to the periodical's readers.

Serializations help generate sales for the original book. Always request that the periodical include the ordering information for your book in the article. Place the exact wording in your contract or letter as well as on the material submitted, such as:

> Reprinted with permission from *The Self-Publishing Manual* by Dan Poynter, copyright © 2001. Available from Para Publishing, for $23.95 postpaid. Tel: 800-PARAPUB; http://ParaPublishing.com

Such a notice will generate a lot of individual mail order sales. Anyone who reads the whole article will be a prime prospect.

Magazines will probably contact you regarding serializations after receiving a review copy of the book. However, you should make the offer to the most appropriate magazines prior to going to press. Send advance information to those magazines most closely related to the topic of your book.

CONDENSATION RIGHTS: Book condensations in magazines do not normally pay a lot, but the publicity they provide will sell more books. Make sure the magazine is a quality product, one you will be proud to be associated with. Check their past condensation work, and call the publishers of the subject books. Ask if they are happy with the way they were treated and with the quality of the condensation, and compare the price they were paid with the one you have been offered.

The magazine normally farms out the rewrite, and the work should be a true condensation, not a reprint of two meaty chapters. You can expect them to offer a couple of hundred dollars, up to several thousand, depending upon the publication and circulation. Expect an offer of $600. Remember, they have to rewrite the text and that costs money. Sell the condensation rights on a nonexclusive basis; the magazine will be first in print, but you want to retain the right to sell again to other publications. Always retain text approval, because their writer could completely miss your point when making the condensation. Read the draft over carefully and make corrections; your name is on the piece, and the condensation will be a major sales tool for your book. You want it to be right. Make sure the condensation includes information about where the original book can be purchased, complete with price and address. See the example in "Periodical Rights" above.

Magazines will probably contact you regarding condensations after receiving a review copy of the book. However, you should make the offer to the most appropriate magazines prior to going to press. Approach just a few magazines with a good book-to-readership match.

ANTHOLOGY RIGHTS: An anthology is a collection of writing selections from one or more authors, usually on the same theme. You may be able to sell a chapter or two of your book for a compilation. Editors of anthologies may offer you a flat fee or a percentage of a normal royalty. If 10 authors are each contributing a chapter, each might be offered 1% of the list price or one-tenth of a 10% royalty.

You could also spin off a piece of your book into your own anthology by contacting other authors in your field for submissions. Many times "experts" in a field who have not authored many books, will contribute a chapter to an anthology for only a small fee or even free copies of the final book that they can use for promotion and to impress their peers.

BOOK CLUB RIGHTS: Book clubs offer you some money and a great deal of prestige. Since they were established in the mid-1920s, the Book-of-the-Month Club (BOMC) (3.5 million members) and the Literary Guild have been helping their members by selecting the best books of the thousands available, at lower than normal prices. Now there are more than 200 national book clubs moving over $500 million worth of books each year, most of which cater to highly specialized groups. There are also a growing number of community book clubs or *reading groups* serving specific regions and cities. Some local book clubs have several thousand members.

A book not submitted is a book not chosen.

The usual book club royalty is 10% of the list price plus production expenses. For example, say it costs you $2 to print the book and the list price is $20. The clubs like to discount the book to their members, so knock off 20% and you have $16 as the membership price. You will receive $3.60 per book, representing $2 for production and $1.60 as a 10% royalty on the $16 membership selling price. If the book club invests in the printing, you get just the *royalty* of 10% of the club's selling price. Book club purchases are usually non-returnable.

Larger clubs will make their own printing or join you in your original print run. Smaller clubs will want to buy from your finished stock. Those doing their own printing or joining yours should benefit from a 10% royalty deal. Book clubs buying 500 to 1,000 books from your stock should be treated as a large dealer and be given a discount of 55% or 60%.

However, some smaller special-interest book clubs that buy limited quantities of books, may only offer to pay a maximum of 25% of the discounted member price as they need the remaining 75% to cover their club mailings, overhead and profit. Thus, if the "member price" is your "list price" less 20%, and you are being paid 25% of the remainder, then you are actually receiving only 20% of list (with printing costs and royalties included in your 20%). Also consider, the terms of payment: is there a partial advance payment on signing (to cover your printing) and the rest on delivery (or 30, 60 or 90 days after delivery)—or does the club want to pay you the rest semi-annually as the books sell, which could stretch the payments out over a year or more. You may decide to refuse orders from the small book clubs.

The larger clubs usually want an exclusive; they don't want other clubs to carry the book too, at least not at the same time. Smaller and specialized clubs aren't so particular, because their memberships do not overlap.

When Alan Gadney and Carolyn Porter placed their contest/grant book with seven national book clubs, they were able to separate the clubs by specialty—film and video, writing and photography book clubs. Each group did not care about the others because there was little overlap. The two large photography book clubs also agreed to split the book itself—one took hardbound, the other softbound (they considered them separate books at separate prices). And they each offered the book as a Special "ALA Award Winning" Book Club Selection, which meant featured promotion in the club mailings. All of this took considerable negotiation among the seven clubs—that's where the fun came in...

A book club sale is an important endorsement. If you can make the sale before going to press, the endorsement can be noted on the back cover as well as on all your promotional materials. For example, on the back cover of *Is There a Book Inside You?* it says, "Writer's Digest Book Club, Main Selection."

Do sales to book clubs hurt regular sales? Absolutely not! They help you start off with a large number sold, provide you with a valuable endorsement, and draw a lot of attention to the book via the book club promotions. Your per-unit printing cost is lower because of the additional book club copies added to the print run, and you can make some money on the deal.

Approach book clubs when you have a completed manuscript or galleys to show them. If they don't respond, write them again after publication and enclose photocopies of your reviews. They have to be convinced it is a desirable book, and that is where clippings of reviews can help. Send a letter to every club that might possibly be interested. Check *Literary Market Place* for book clubs and make up a list for a mailing. See Book Clubs in Appendix 2.

PERFORMING RIGHTS cover stage, motion pictures, radio and television.

The usual royalty rate is 15% of the *net,* and this is usually a bad deal. Film companies are notorious for their creative accounting procedures that result in a very small net if any; some have been known to write off everything possible against the film. Always insist on a smaller percentage of the *gross.* The gross figure is much more objective. Another possibility is a fixed fee or percentage each time the book or film reaches certain pre-established performance levels. For example, when the book becomes a best seller or receives a major award; the film is sold to television, major cable, video, foreign or achieves high box office grosses.

Performing rights involve complex contracts and should not be negotiated without advice from a book attorney. If you receive a firm offer, see one immediately.

It is easier to sell another edition of an existing book than to write a new book.

TRANSLATION RIGHTS: A publisher in another country may wish to buy the translation rights. The foreign publisher will pay you a royalty and take care of everything. Normally, you supply the photos and a couple of copies of the book with late changes noted. They translate the text, change the measurements to metric and take care of all the printing, distribution, etc. Royalties might be 5% to 7% for hardcover rights and 5% to 10% for softcover.

Foreign publishers and foreign rights representatives are listed in *International Literary Market Place*.

When negotiating a foreign rights contract, consider the number of copies to be printed, the printing schedule, cover price, royalties for both hardcover and softcover editions, the advance and the government tax, if any. Some countries impose a tax on exported royalties. Japan, for example, charges 10% of the remitted amount. Generally, you should negotiate as high an advance payment as possible, because with certain publishers in certain foreign countries, policing your royalty payments and actually getting paid may prove difficult. Always get references on foreign publishers, distributors or wholesalers you are not familiar with.

For complete details on foreign sales, see *Exports/Foreign Rights: Selling U.S. Books Abroad* under Para Publishing Special Reports in Appendix 2 or at http://ParaPublishing.com.

MERCHANDISING RIGHTS: If the subject of your book suddenly becomes hot, customers will beat a path to your door with offers to make T-shirts, decals and coffee mugs. They will want to license your title or logo to put on their products.

RECORDINGS AND BRAILLE EDITIONS are published for the visually impaired. If your book is well received, you may be approached for permission to translate your book into Braille or put it on tape. When you fill out the copyright form for your book, you will have the opportunity to give the Library of Congress a nonexclusive right to reproduce your book in recorded or Braille form. In fiscal 1997, Recordings for the Blind & Dyslexic distributed nearly 225,000 recorded and computerized books to 45,000 members. See their Web site at http://www.rfbd.org.

See *Literary Market Place* for more subsidiary rights possibilities. For subsidiary rights wording, see *Publishing Contracts* on disk under Para Publishing Special Reports in Appendix 2 or at http://ParaPublishing.com.

OPPORTUNITIES WITH OTHER PUBLISHERS

CO-PUBLISHING is a way for two firms to spread the risk and the reward in a new book. Usually, one publisher is large and the other small, or the two concentrate on different markets. The larger publisher usually handles the bookstores and libraries, while the smaller publisher sells directly to user groups and fills the individual mail order sales.

Get an agreement on who decides, performs and pays for the following: book and cover design, page and cover production, printing, marketing strategy, promotion and sales to the book trade versus special markets, fulfillment and accounting. Be wary of supposed co-publishing deals where you pay for everything, and the co-publisher uses their ISBN (so all sales go to them). And they market the book and handle accounting without you being able to monitor their performance or break the contract. Do not let a co-publisher take advantage of you.

SELLING OUT: Many new author-publishers publish their first book and then sell out to a large publisher—and many sell too cheaply. Acquisition editors from major houses make the rounds of the booths at book fairs such as Book Expo America in the spring. These editors are hunting for good books to add to their lines. Small publishers are usually thrilled to be courted by a big house and often make the mistake of selling for the same 10% (or less) royalty an author gets for a manuscript.

Ten percent of the net receipts is small reward after expending so much time and money to package and promote a book as well as to test the market. The big publisher is exploiting the little publisher at 10% because all the risk has been removed. Successful books should cost more. The large publisher must understand that even though your company is small, the book is coming from another "publisher;" this is not just an untested manuscript from an author. A fee should be paid to the small publisher for packaging, market exploration and establishing a sales record, as well as a royalty to the author.

When a large publisher buys a book from a small publisher, the price should be two or three times the production costs, plus 10% of projected sales. They should pay for all your time, work and financial risk. The deal should be made "royalty inclusive," which means receiving your money up front—not waiting until months after their books are sold.

Sell only the *North American rights* to the *book trade*. Retain all rights except those to bookstores and libraries in the U.S. and Canada. Always keep the nonexclusive individual sale, mail order rights. The big publisher will not be interested in individual sales anyway. Make sure you can buy books for resale for the printing cost plus 10%. Normally, you will be required to buy in lots of 500 or more, but this is a bargain, because you do not have to invest in a large print run. Make sure all rights revert to you once the publisher lets the book go out of print. In evaluating a contract, consider the advance, the royalty, when you will get paid, who gets what part of other subsidiary rights, the duration of the contract and free copies to the author.

Give the publisher the rights for only what they are publishing in-house. For example, if they publish audio, give them the audio rights. But if they try to tie up the electronic (eBook, online, etc.) rights but only intend to look for a buyer, give them a 90-day option on the electronic rights.

Small publishers and self-publishers are better off cutting a distribution deal or co-publishing with a larger publisher. In a distribution arrangement, the big publisher buys several thousand books for 60% to 70% off list price on a nonreturnable basis with an advance to cover your printing, the remaining payment upon delivery or 30 days after delivery and has an exclusive in the book trade: bookstores and libraries. Insist on a large quantity so the large publisher is in deep and has to promote the books.

With the book trade covered, the author-publisher is now free to concentrate on retail mail order sales and the non-book markets. But be forewarned: If you do sell out, you will probably make less money and lose control of your book.

BOOKSHELF BOOKS: Offering other books in the same line as your anchor product will spread costs and make you the "information center" for your interest area. See Document 632, *Bookshelf: Selling Books from Other Publishers*, at http://Para Publishing.com.

Keep your bookshelf focused on a particular topic. Most of your orders will be for your own books. The bookshelf books will sell well, but they will not approach the sales of your own books.

You can also place your book in "bookshelves" run by other publishers, magazines and newsletters

FLYER EXCHANGES: Some publishers in your specialty field may be interested, not in buying and reselling copies of your books, but rather in a simple cross-promotion—you include their sales flyers in your consumer mailings and/or book shipments, and they do the same with your sales flyers. You can locate similar publishers in *Literary Market Place, Publisher's Marketing Association Resource Directory, Writers' Market* and at book fairs and publishing events.

THE INTERNATIONAL MARKET

Foreign sales of American language books exceed $1.8 billion annually, with most going to Canada, Great Britain, Japan, Australia, Mexico, Singapore, Netherlands, South Korea, Taiwan and Germany—in that order.

The most common way to cater to the international market is to fill and mail foreign orders the same way you fill domestic ones. Most of your export sales will come with the daily mail. They will be just like your domestic orders except for their lighter weight stationery, strange addresses and pretty stamps. Most of the foreign bookstores get your address from R.R. Bowker's *Books in Print*.

Postal rates for foreign shipments may be higher or lower than domestic rates, depending on which rate has been raised most recently.

Be advised that adding a country to your U.S. distribution will not double your sales. For example, expanding from the U.S. to Canada may increase sales only 7% to 10%. You must compare the sizes of the English-speaking populations.

For more details, tips and contracts, see *Exports/Foreign Rights: Selling U.S. Books Abroad* in Para Publishing Special Reports in Appendix 2 and at http://ParaPublishing.com.

BOOK EXHIBITS

Specialty shows, such as sport and boat exhibitions and trade shows, are rarely worthwhile for a small author-publisher with a single title, because the costs to exhibit (booth space and dressing, travel, food, lodging and shipping) are too expensive. However, you can make sure that your book is carried and offered for sale by someone in the show. Find a booth(s) with related merchandise and offer them some books on consignment; sign them up as a dealer. Give them a carton of books and an examination copy for the table. They will get a 40% piece of the action and you get the exposure while moving your books. Place your book in as many booths around the show as possible.

BOOK FAIRS provide important exposure to your book. The major national U.S. shows are sponsored by the following:

- **Book Expo America:** the most important book trade convention in North America, held often in late May with an attendance around 30,000. This is a book industry event, not open to the general public. inquiry@bookexpo. reedexpo.com; http://www.bookexpo. reedexpo.com.

- **American Library Association Book Fair:** the major library conference, held in late June with an annual attendance of about 25,000. The ALA also holds a midwinter exhibit in January, attendance 10,000. pio@ala.org; http:// www.ala.org.

- **National Association of College Stores Book Fair:** usually mid-spring and attended by college bookstore managers. info@nacs.org; http://www.nacs.org.

- **Christian Booksellers Association Book Fair:** usually in July with a mid-year expo in January. info@cba-intl.org; http://www.cbaonline.org.

- **Frankfurt Book Fair** is the world's largest international rights convention usually held in early October in Frankfurt, Germany. http://www.frankfurt-book-fair.com.

Contact these organizations about the fairs and then attend a nearby one yourself to assess how you might fit in to your advantage. The big associations sponsor regional and local book fairs. Also many cities throughout North America sponsor book fairs open to the general (buying) public. The *Los Angeles Times* Festival of Books held at UCLA each April is becoming one of the largest with a 150,000 weekend attendance.

International book fairs are held all over the world, the most important being in London and Frankfurt for all types of books and in Bologna, Italy, for children's books. They can give good exposure and may lead to foreign rights sales, but probably are not worth your own exhibiting effort. Use a co-op exhibit service instead.

Conventions and conferences of professional, academic and trade associations will present you with a "qualified" audience for your books if you match your subject matter to the show. Educational books do well at educational exhibits, and these conferences are especially fun because they provide you with an opportunity to meet with authors as well as customers. For more ideas, consult *National Trade & Professional Associations of the U.S. and Canada Directory* and *Gale's Encyclopedia of Associations*, available in your library.

Exhibiting at a book fair is often an inspiring experience; it will recharge your batteries. You will learn more about the industry, meet some great people, make valuable contacts (distributors, wholesalers, retailers, reviewers and the media), sell a few books, and perhaps even sell some subsidiary rights. Typically, the show's management provides a space measuring about 10' x 10', a draped table, curtained side and back panels, a sign, carpet and a chair or two. Check their brochure closely. Get some book stands, mounted blow-ups of your book covers, and take a good supply of books and brochures.

> Find out what promotional opportunities the book fair offers: One-On-One Book Marketing was able to secure a 10x30 foot book-banner space for their publisher clients above the main entrance to the BEA in Chicago. They reserved the space in advance, after hearing that, because of construction, all 30,000 people attending would enter the BEA main hall through one set of escalators past the banner. With traffic in and out six to eight times a day for three days, they estimated well over a half-million advertising impressions during the show. And they know the banner worked. There was constant activity at the booth, buzz around the floor, and the authors were mobbed at their book signings. The banner turned heretofore unknown authors (and books) into stars of the convention.

EXHIBITING SERVICES will put your books on display with those of other publishers very inexpensively, and some do a very good job of representing your wares. Some of the larger co-op exhibit services are: Combined Book Exhibit (CBE) and PMA for library and booktrade events, Association Book Exhibit (ABE) for professional conferences and Academia Book Exhibit and Scholar's Choice for academic meetings. Write to several of them to compare prices and see which fairs they plan to attend; some offer package deals if you sign up for the whole season.

For more information on book fairs, see *Book Fairs: An Exhibiting Guide for Publishers* under Para Publishing Books & Reports: Book Promotion & Marketing in Appendix 2 or at http://ParaPublishing.com.

> *It's much better to have reps selling the list to 1,000 buyers across the country, making independent decisions, than having five buyers at the chains deciding what is or isn't a worthwhile or viable book.*
>
> **—Sales Director of a major publishing company in** *Publishers Weekly*

9
Advertising Your Book

Direct Mail, Print, Broadcast

It is said that advertising will make a good book sell better, but it can't turn a poor one into a success. First we will talk about advertising in general, and then we will discuss the details of your brochure, direct email advertising, classifieds, space ads and radio/TV. Much of the information is overlapping and can be applied to more than one area of advertising, so I advise you to read the entire chapter.

Remember, we do not recommend spending money on advertising until all the free publicity is exhausted. Advertising is just too expensive and rarely pays when selling books. When in doubt, do not advertise.

In each ad campaign, run a small test ad and then figure the cost of the campaign "per sale," that is, how many books did this ad sell?

The cost "per contact" is interesting, but it is the cost per sale that tells you if you are winning or losing. Ads placed in magazines that will send buyers to bookstores must generate more sales than ads directing the orders to you (mail order). The difference is that you are giving your bookstore distributor 66% of the list (cover) price, whereas the mail sales come directly to you at full price. Do not run unprofitable ads! They waste money and make you work for nothing.

The people selling advertising talk about the "number of impressions" and "cumulative impact" when they try to get you to spend more on ads (or try to explain why your ad wasn't successful). A series of good, consistent ads are of some help, because prospects remember that they heard of the book before. But remember, you are selling a $20 or $30 book, not a $20,000 or $30,000 automobile. You have to sell a lot more product to pay for the ad and you can't even justify as much need to your buyer.

The secret to successful publishing is not to publish more and more books but to effectively market those books already published.

DIRECT MARKETING

Direct response marketing is any promotion or advertising that provokes a measurable response or order from the individual it was targeted to. In book publishing, direct marketing consists of order blanks in books, catalogs, package inserts, radio, TV and direct mail.

Every household in the U.S. receives 84 pounds of direct (bulk) mail each year. We each use three working days to sort and decide what to do with it.

One book out of four is sold via direct mail advertising. Most of this volume goes to book clubs, but they don't get all the business; there are over a half billion dollars left. Direct mail offers the small publisher an opportunity to sell to the customer without competing with the big publishers. Mail provides equal treatment. However, savvy smaller publishers are abandoning traditional postal mail for faster and cheaper email.

Don't confuse "direct mail" with "mail order." Direct mail is a form of advertising that competes with space ads and television spots, whereas mail order is a delivery method or form of distribution that competes with storefronts.

TARGET MARKETING: This is the Age of Specialization, of the narrow focus. For example, years ago, we had general weekly magazines such as *Look, Colliers* and *The Saturday Evening Post.* They are gone. Today we have specialized magazines such as *Graphic Arts Monthly, Publishers Weekly* and *Parachutist* magazine. We also have specialized newsletters, Web sites, ezines and cable TV shows. As consumers, we have the advantage of buying only those products that are specific to our wants and needs. As entrepreneurs, we *tailor* our products to special segments of the population and then we *tailor* our pitch to bring the product to their attention.

A book will not sell unless people know about it.
—**Bob Greene,** *Esquire*

Direct mail (including email) advertising allows you to pinpoint your target market with a specialized pitch. For example, the people you target with your mailing might be skydiving instructors. Skydiving instructors have different needs and desires than skydiving students, or jump pilots, or parachute riggers, or drop zone owners. Each is involved in skydiving in general, but each requires a different pitch.

Direct mail advertising is a targeted shot at the customer. This is not a shotgun blast at every household in the neighborhood, hoping to find a couple of people interested in your books.

ECONOMICS OF DIRECT MAIL

Unless you have several related titles, priced over $35 each, to share your brochure, you won't make money regularly in direct postal mail advertising. The smaller and newer publisher is only successful using direct mail for prepublication offers and occasional mailings to (often smaller) highly targeted lists.

One must understand the economics to put direct mail advertising of books into perspective. If you tell enough people about your book, a certain "percentage" will buy it. The challenge is to keep costs down by telling just that certain "buying percentage." A general-interest book advertised to a general consumer audience is lucky to generate a return of 1.5% to 2%. That is just 15 to 20 orders per 1,000 pieces mailed. In fact, only 10% of the recipients will even remember the mailing piece.

The cost, on the other hand, may be quite high (probably around $450 per thousand or 45¢ per piece). The amount depends upon the price of the list (the more selective ones cost more), the postage and the type and number of inserts and other expenses, such as mailing house stuffing fees. A high response rate is required just to break even. So it is tough to make a living selling a single title through direct mail. But now you have a customer who may buy again. And that means you need more than one product.

Think long term. Very few mailings make a killing from outright sales the first time out. With each mailing, you are trying to add qualified buyers to your house list for future orders. A *qualified buyer* is someone who has sent money to you before; this person is more likely to respond again and again. The objective is to develop a customer, not just to make a sale.

Direct mail marketing is a process of looking where you have been, seeing how you got there and deciding where to go next. Past mailings and testing are the tools for future decisions. Profit (or loss) is determined by taking your book sales, less returns, less your cost of books and fulfillment and less your direct marketing costs.

EMAIL IS FASTER: You do not have to wait several days for the mail house to assemble the packages and for the Postal Service to deliver them. Email is cheaper. You do not have to spend money on envelopes, stuffing or postage. Email provides feedback sooner. Responses often start within 30 minutes. Then you can test another pitch. Most broadcast email costs you some time but little money.

Your house email and postal lists also become valuable assets and a new profit center, because you will be able to rent them to other firms. More on renting your own lists later.

DIRECT MARKETING TECHNIQUES

What makes direct marketing successful is the offer of the right products via the right medium with the most enticing propositions, presented in the most effective formats, proven successful as a result of the right tests. The successful direct mail campaign is made up of planning, list selection, copy, layout, timing and testing.

CREATING AD COPY: You will need a good, basic description of the book that will appeal to the consumer. This material, altered as required, will then be used over and over. Come up with very few words to describe the book. This becomes its "handle" and can even be the subtitle for the book. This handle will be expanded for brochures and catalogs while it is directed toward the intended audience. Some small ads will only have space for the handle and a small amount of hard-hitting copy. But once this is done, the future copywriting is easier because you are not starting from scratch each time.

REPETITION: One rule of direct mail is that if you remail to the same list after a couple of months or longer, the response will be almost as great as the results from the first mailing. Many marketing people use a list four times a year, and when it fails to break-even or better, it is time to change the list. They say that repetitive mailings have a cumulative effect and the message is strengthened. Good lists have a certain amount of turnover. Names are continually being added and deleted.

Many entrepreneurs send a weekly email memo to their clients. The memos contain news and often some humor. These periodic messages help to keep in touch.

TIMING: The best time for your mailing and email to arrive is mid-week, on a Tuesday, Wednesday or Thursday. A lot of mail arrives on Mondays and the day after holidays, and your piece could be lost in the clutter. Friday's mail is often put aside because the recipient is about to leave for the weekend.

Fortunately, it is easier to time the delivery of email than it is with bulk rate postal mail.

The best times of year for offers to arrive, according to some experts, are after the New Year and after Labor Day. The Direct Marketing Association compares the months for response (assuming your book is not season-related, such as a Christmas book or a year-end holiday gift offer) as follows:

January	100.0%	July	73.3%
February	96.3%	August	87.0%
March	71.0%	September	79.0%
April	71.5%	October	89.9%
May	71.5%	November	81.0%
June	67.0%	December	79.0%

Best response months based on January

Some say that March to April (income tax time?) and May to June are the worst months. Other experts warn against the summer months, when people are away and the mail piles up. Most agree December is bad because the potential customer is busy with family and holiday activities.

The subject of your books will determine the best months. For example, if your books are on outdoor sports, the best months are January through May, with a peak in March, and September through November. During the summer, the prospects are out doing what they were reading about during the winter. The best time to email to federal libraries is March and April, when they are preparing for their next fiscal year. May appears to be the best month for schools. Professional books seem to sell better in the first quarter of the year. The third quarter is second best. All factors must be considered in relation to your specialized subject and audience. On the other hand, you may have a reference book that people need throughout the year.

INTERNATIONAL MAILINGS: The U.S. is a culturally influencing country. The world consumes great quantities of U.S. information and thought. With the increase in both the standard of living and purchasing power in many other countries, the potential for book sales world wide is increasingly good. There is a demand for books on leading edge subjects.

English became a world language in the last century. In fact, although 3,000 languages are spoken in the world, over 40% of the knowledge base is in the English language. English has replaced German as the scientific and technical language, replaced French as the diplomatic language and is the international language of aviation, business, computers and the Internet. Business books from the U.S. have done very well in the last few years with the surge of worldwide interest in U.S. management thought.

Naturally, books in English should be promoted with messages and brochures in English, and prices should be quoted in U.S. dollars (with cheques drawn on a U.S. Bank) since it is customary to settle international accounts in U.S. currency. Converting foreign money into dollars is expensive.

SINGLE LINE OF BOOKS: Publishers should concentrate on a single line of books, such as aviation, regional subjects or wastewater treatment. Then all the books in your brochure or catalog will relate to each other. There is no need to make up a separate brochure for each book. Think like a specialized book club and define your audience. Stay in one field with your books, related products and services.

ORDER BLANK: Every book should have an order blank for the same and/or other books. Place it on the last page—facing out. (Turn to the last page in this book as an example.) It is important to ask for an order, and that is what order blanks are designed to do. It is not enough to hope a potential buyer might find your address on the copyright page, because he or she still won't know how much to include for shipping and sales tax. The order blank says, "Yes, we accept orders, we will take your cheque or credit card and here is exactly what the total order will cost."

> Why would anyone buy a book they already have? For a friend! At Para Publishing, we receive more orders on our back-of-the-book order blank than from any other direct response effort we make. We have over a million books out there, and each is selling more of our books.

TOLL-FREE PHONE NUMBERS AND CREDIT CARDS: It is generally accepted that a toll-free order number will increase the response to an offer. Some clients will respond to your solicitation via fax or email, but some would rather call than send their credit card numbers into cyberspace. Toll-free numbers raise the confidence level and the level of customer service.

Toll-free numbers work best when paired with credit card charge arrangements. Today, people are prepared to place a call and charge a product to a credit card. Credit cards make buying much easier and will bring both more and larger sales. See the discussion of credit cards in Chapter 10.

ECHO EFFECT: Every promotion campaign you wage for a book will bring in some sales that are not directly attributable to that campaign. Some people find it easier or faster to buy your product somewhere else, such as dropping by a retailer's store. There are many ways people can get the book besides return mail or email. College professors who receive interesting mailings often request their libraries to order the book. The "echo effect" is difficult to measure, but some direct marketers claim these indirect orders often exceed the direct orders.

Since over 75% of libraries use wholesalers, most of the orders from an emailing to libraries will come to you through Baker & Taylor, and you won't know the name of the actual purchasers. Sometimes publishers even help the potential customer in this direction and, in effect, give him or her a choice of purchasing by mail or visiting a bookstore. The message on the brochure might say, "Available at your local Waldenbooks or direct from the publisher."

WHITE MAIL: Orders not traceable to any promotional effort or source are called "white mail." The longer you are in business, the more orders you will receive that are not traceable to any specific promotion. The market place is a vast web of connections. A brochure sent to one source generates a multi-book order from another. A review book sent to single reviewer winds up syndicated in newspapers across the country. That's what makes the book business so constantly exciting—the always unexpected response.

MAILING LISTS

While many elements are required for a successful direct mail or email message, the list is the most important part. The best sales copy sent to the wrong list can't do well and if emailed will probably trigger a nasty spam response. Conversely, the worst sales copy mailed to the best list often does acceptably well. Obviously, the goal is to mail a good message to a good list.

The list must target the appropriate group and be up to date. You want quality, not quantity. People get new jobs, move, die, lose interest in certain fads and trends, forget hobbies, etc. Yesterday's prime prospect may have other interests today, or may have changed their address.

"Spam" is an unsolicited email message sent to many recipients at one time and is the electronic equivalent of junk mail. People dislike spam emailings. You should be discriminating in assembling or renting lists and careful in how you use them. Use *very targeted lists* and direct your message to that type of person. This is where targeted email can be very effective, because you are honing in on your exact customer (far less expensive than renting broad lists since there is little waste). One example would be offering a parachute book to a list of skydivers and starting off the message with "Dear Fellow Skydiver..."

LIST CATEGORIES: Direct mail mailing lists fall into three categories, sometimes called yours, theirs and compiled:

- **House list:** comprised of (1) "sales," which are past buyers—a *premier* house list consists of multiple-order past buyers—and (2) "prospects" who have inquired about your book, stopped by your book fair booth, attended your seminars, etc.

●◆ **Mail response list:** list of people who have responded to offers similar to yours. You rent this list from list owners or list brokers.

●◆ **Compiled list:** developed from membership lists, directories, people attending events, etc. You rent this list from list owners or list brokers, or compile it yourself.

YOUR HOUSE LIST: The highest quality list is normally your own. This is your list of customers—those who have contacted you. Your house list should pull 2 to 10 times better than any you might rent. The people on your list know you and your product; they look to you as an old friend; they feel comfortable doing business with you and have done business with you before.

New customers have to be bought (through list rental); existing customers are free.

The people who were your best customers last month are most likely to be your best customers this month. They should be contacted repeatedly. These customers will buy from you again and again as they experience changes in their needs, moods and financial condition. Hopefully you will have something new to sell them.

It costs more to sell a book to a new customer than to an existing customer.

Think of using your house list in three ways:

1. Identify the best customers on the list.

2. Find more customers for your house list by using outside lists.

3. Sell books to your house list at a maximum profit with minimum waste.

You should maintain two house lists: a *sales list* (those who have bought something) and an *inquiries list* (those who have contacted you for information but have not sent money). All other lists from other sources contain only prospects.

Your sales list is by far the most important. The only people who should be added to it are those who have paid to get on it by buying something.

There are several ways to build your house list. The most common way is to rent another list, make a mailing, and then add the names of those who respond to your own list. Just be sure to segregate all responses into the sales or inquiries lists, as appropriate. Do not corrupt your lists with untested names. One source of email lists and services is JazzMail: http://www.bookjazz.com.

You can begin compiling your own retail prospect mailing list by going through your personal phone book and Christmas card list. Include all family, friends, business associates and acquaintances. Include anyone who might conceivably purchase your book.

Add a line for the email address to your book's order blank and telephone order forms. Always ask callers for their email address. Start collecting now.

- Also start your **commercial lists:** bookstores, libraries, wholesalers, big non-book accounts, people and companies in your industry.

- And work on your **promotion mailing lists:** magazines, newspapers, newsletters, radio and TV stations. Check reference books such as *Literary Market Place*.

Keep your lists for your next book so you will be prepared when it comes time to send out prepublication announcements, review copies and other promotion.

LIST MAINTENANCE: Lists must be kept up to date if they are to keep pace with our mobile society and remain valid. This means continually being alert for address changes and returned email.

Lists, whether yours, theirs or compiled, must be recent. Any list not mailed within the last three months will result in a lot of returned email. When renting, ask when the list was last *cleaned*. You may not want to use an old list unless it is so specific to your target market that even with many "nixies" (bad addresses), the results will pay off.

Lists go out of date fast because people move. Over 20% of our gypsy-like population moves each year, and younger people move even more often. Almost 47% of the population is not living in the same home they occupied five years ago. In the western U.S., the figure is over 56%.

FINDING LISTS: As a small publisher, you are probably also the author. You are a participant in the subject you write about. While a book is just a product to a large New York publisher, you have a mission and are closer to the book's subject matter. If, for example, your book is on skydiving, you know there are two magazines, one national organization and one national champ-ionship in the United States catering to your group. You know how to reach your readers because you are one of them. Associations have direct lines to people interested in their mission. Most have a membership list, magazine, newsletter, Web site, annual function, etc. Contact associations for their mail and email lists. You may also spot list sources in specialized magazines.

Your competitors may not be interested in renting their house list to you, but they may be willing to trade for *your* house list on a name-for-name basis.

LIST BROKERS: List brokers specialize in bringing list owners and list renters together. The broker receives a fee (usually 20%) from the list owner. Brokers can be a good source of direct mail advice. More and more list brokers are handling email lists now.

Lists and list brokers can be found in *Direct Marketing* magazine, *Direct Marketing List Sources*, *Klein's Directory*, *Literary Market Place* and your local *Yellow Pages*. Request catalogs from all of them. One thing you will find is that the same lists are handled by many different brokers. You will see the same lists in catalog after catalog. Many lists are small, and some brokers have a minimum.

PUBLICITY DISTRIBUTION SERVICES: Direct Contact Media Services will send out your custom news release via fax or email. Paul Krupin has assembled targeted media lists for the book publishing industry. See this Web site at http://www.book-publicity.com. Also see his site for tips on drafting your email solicitation.

COPYING LISTS: Copying lists violates the rental agreement and normal business ethics, is against the law and is a waste of money. List *rentals* are for one-time use only, and you are obligated not to add the list to your file. The list owner guards against second usage by sprinkling (seeding) the list with decoy

290 — The Self-Publishing Manual

names (plants). Stealing an unproven name from a list will only dilute the quality of your own house list. You are, however, authorized to add a name to your list once you have qualified it (once it has resulted in an order). So, rent a list, mail to it and add those that respond to your house list.

PARTIAL LISTS: You don't have to rent the entire list. Why send to all libraries when you are likely to get a better return from those with a higher book acquisition budget?

I know half my advertising is wasted but I don't know which half.

—**William Wrigley**

"Hotline Names" are new additions to the list. If you are selling books on "beginning" skydiving, why rent the whole membership list from the U.S. Parachute Association when you can rent names of just the new "beginning" members? Hotline lists tend to be 60 to 90 days old.

Most small press publishers lack an understanding of mailing lists. So many firms waste so much money on lousy lists. They buy "mail order" lists not knowing what those people bought, when they bought, how much they paid, what their profile is, how many times the list has been rented and on and on.

—**Galen Stilson,** *Direct Response Specialist* **newsletter**

TESTING A LIST: The big direct mailers test before investing large sums of money in renting a mailing list. Testing is a preliminary mailing or distribution intended as a preview or pilot before a major campaign. Test mailings are used to determine probable acceptance of a product or service and are usually made to a specially selected list.

Testing is done by renting just part of the list and sending your mailing to every nth (e.g., tenth) name. Nth-name testing provides a better sample than renting names from A through D, because you are testing names throughout the list as opposed to those in only one section.

A minimum sample should be 3,000 names (some experts say 5,000). Remember that you are testing the mailing message as well as the list; they both affect the results. If a mailing to a sample group produces a 2% response, statistics show that a mailing to the entire list will result in a 1.4% to 2.6% response, and it is usually just under 2%. Realizing these probability limits will help you evaluate a list and make the decision whether to risk a larger and more expensive mailing to the full list.

A lot of things can go wrong after a test mailing. A list can be non-representative or out of date, or your book could be bad, and the word may have circulated between your test and the big mailing. Keep good records; only with statistics can you effectively evaluate a mailing. Note all your costs. If a test is inconclusive, run another test. Most tests fail; expect it. When one fails, be thankful you didn't rent the whole list. Then drop that list and don't try it again.

Rollout mailings to the entire list do not always reflect your test results. There are just too many variables, such as time lapse, season, change in economics, weather, consumer behavior and many more. The test mailing benefits from pass-along readership, where some recipients, who are not buying, forward the message on to a friend they know has an interest in this book. When you mail or email to the entire list, you also hit the pass-along readership, and they have already seen your offer.

SELL YOUR MAILING LIST: If you maintain your mailing lists by noting which book or subject area the customer purchased, it becomes very selective and quite valuable. These are people who have taken the time to send away for a book. They are very good prospects for similar offers.

You can handle your own list or work through a broker. Most brokers are interested in handling your list when you reach 20,000 names; some want 50,000.

Start by getting listed in *Direct Marketing List Source*. This directory provides the details on over 80,000 lists. See their Web site at http://www.srds.com.

YOUR WEB SITE

Your web site lies at the heart of your promotional campaign, and it can be set up long before your book is off the press. All your promotion should guide people to your site. Print the URL on your brochures, email signature, letterhead, business cards, etc.

Include on your web site a color shot of the cover, a complete description of the book and backup materials such as the back cover sales copy, table of contents, reviews, testimonials, promotional materials and related content. Do not forget ordering instructions.

BROCHURE

You will still need a brochure to hand out at book fairs and other events.

When you are ready to draft a brochure, stimulate your creative juices by reading a couple of articles or a couple of chapters on copywriting.

The brochure, like the Web site, should describe the book, tell something about you, and answer most of the recipient's potential questions. The basics are the book's measurements (trim size), number of pages, number and type of illustrations (drawings, photos, charts, etc.), binding and price. The contents should be summarized to provide a clear understanding of the book's coverage. Use bullets to outline and emphasize the main points (primary benefits to the buyer). Do not use too much detail, or the buyer may find material he or she does not want—sell the sizzle, not the steak. Excerpts from reviews will demonstrate that others like your book too. Follow the proven, standard formats.

See competitive books at Amazon.com and print out their pages. The descriptions will contain buzz words, sound bites and other important phrases you will want to include in your promotional copy.

Brochures provide you with an opportunity to say nice things about yourself that you can't say in face-to-face selling. It should sound like someone else wrote the copy. Be direct and clear, and give the reader as much to-the-point information as possible.

It takes hard writing to make easy reading.
—Robert Louis Stevenson

People like to see what they are buying, so a photo of the book should appear in the brochure. Ask your cover artist to attach an image file of your front cover to an email. Store it in your computer and drop it into your brochure. Also post it on your web site and send it to the online bookstores. You can print out small quantities of flyers with color images of the cover with an inkjet or color laser printer.

The ad worked because it attracted the right audience,... because it aroused curiosity and because it offered a reward.
—John Caples

At this point, you may not know exactly how many pages the book will have, but you can estimate and then use a description such as "over 180 jam-packed pages."

BROCHURE PRINTING: Printers specialize, and a number of them print only four-color catalog sheets. Catalog sheets are called "flyers" if flat and "brochures" if folded. These specialists buy large quantities of paper at a low price and have all their equipment set up for greater operating efficiency. They use standardized 8.5" x 11" on 70-pound to 100-pound white, slick gloss paper, with four colors on one side and one color on the other, or four colors on both sides. You can also use 11" x 17" stock and fold it to 8.5" x 11" for a 4-page brochure. Most will print directly from your digital disk files, thus avoiding having to make expensive separation negatives and a match print. Some also print color post cards, posters and other promotional material.

8.5" x 11" Color Flyer, 100# Gloss Stock		
Quantity	Color (1 side)	Color (2 sides)
1,000	18¢	33¢
2,500	9¢	16¢
5,000	6¢	10¢
10,000	5¢	7¢

Sample prices for color digital printing

You can also print a large quantity of only the front of the flyer (with your book cover, description and ordering information) in color, leaving the backside blank. Then you can print the backs of a few flyers for a small special mailing. This allows you to tailor your text to each mailing, add reviews, sales copy, special offers, etc. For very short runs of 50, consider using your computer's color printer.

Once the brochures arrive, use them everywhere. Stuff them in every package, letter, news release, mailing, etc. Carry some in the car; leave them at the barbershop, in the seat pocket on the airplane, at the dentist's office, etc., and carry some with you at all times. Pack one in with every book you mail out. A brochure has to be distributed widely to do any good.

When you are ready to work on your brochure, see *Brochures for Book Publishers* under Para Publishing Special Reports in Appendix 2 or at http://ParaPublishing. com.

AVOIDING SALES TAX ON PRINTING: Some states, such as California, do not charge sales tax on the printing of direct mail packages, but the brochures must be delivered directly to the mailing house by the printer to qualify. This can be quite a saving, so it is worth checking the laws in your own state for sales tax exclusions

California also does not charge sales tax on shipping supplies such as cartons, bags and tape. Presumably, the purpose of the exemption is to create jobs and promote exports.

PREPUBLICATION MAILING: While your book is being printed, start looking for sales with a prepublication offer. Use benefit copy; tell what the book will do for the recipient. Include "And if you will order by return mail, we will pay the postage and send the book as soon as it comes off the press." On prepublication offers, emphasize that the book is on the press, and assure them you won't process their credit card until the book is shipped. Mention an expected shipping date, but give yourself an extra month to six weeks.

Tell not what the recipient can do for you, tell what you can do for the recipient.

End your sales letter by telling the reader exactly what you want him or her to do. "Grab your credit card right now and fill in the order blank. We absolutely guarantee your satisfaction. The book must meet your expectations or your money back. You can't lose!"

At Para Publishing, we offer an unconditional money-back guarantee at any time, no questions asked. We want customers to be happy with their purchases. If they return a book, we are glad they took the time to look it over. The theory behind the no-time-limit guarantee is that without a deadline, such as 10 days, a customer may never get around to making the return. Either the theory is valid or we have very good products, because we have very few returns.

TESTIMONIALS: People today are overwhelmed with exaggerated claims and hype from the media. Therefore, it is important to incorporate a confidence factor into your promotional copy.

Testimonials from readers and reviewers will help justify your claims for the book and draw attention to your customer service. Testimonials help build the reader's perception of believability, stability, honesty and value. Shorter testimonials can be placed in your email letter, promotional materials and on the book itself. Longer ones should be on your Web site.

Your book is a success when people who haven't read it pretend they have.

To be valuable, the endorsement must be from someone who has a name or title recognizable and important to the reader. For example, if you have a book on golf, you might want a few nice words penned by Tiger Woods or a testimonial from the executive director of the PGA. Buyers respond first to quotations from well known people (if appropriate) then to people who have professional credentials (doctor, lawyer, educator, author, Ph.D., etc.) or are connected with well known organizations.

For more information on gathering testimonials, see Document 603, *Blurbs for Your Books: Testimonials, Endorsements and Quotations*, at http://ParaPublishing.com.

BROADCAST ADVERTISING

There are many ways to get time on radio and television. You can buy time, make a "per inquiry" deal, run an infomercial and/or be interviewed.

- **Buying time.** Many of the principles of buying print advertising apply to buying broadcast time. Both are just too expensive for books.

- **Infomercials** can propel you to the big time, but they are expensive to make and many of them fail. Work with an experienced infomercial producer.

- **Interviews.** Now that you are a published author, talk shows will want to interview you. See the discussion in Chapter 7. Also see Document 602, *Interviews: How Authors Get on Radio and TV*, at http://ParaPublishing.com.

- **Per Inquiry (PI)** ads require no investment and are a good way for you to try out new advertising media. Many smaller newspapers, magazines, newsletters, radio and television stations will run your ad for a share of the results. The orders are sent to them with the cheques made out to you, thus giving you both a check on each other. Their cut is usually 33% to 50% of the order, or about what you would give any retailer. They do this to fill unused space or time and generate some income.

Normally, you have to prepare the ad. This means camera-ready or digital artwork for newspapers and magazines or tapes for radio and television. A one-minute videotape may run $100 originally and about $25 for each duplicate. Many authors (and other entrepreneurs) prefer doing their own shows to hiring an actor at $100 or more. The author is very much a part of their book, and the personal touch can go a long way.

The best approach is to contact the station, paper, etc., describing your book and asking if they accept PI advertising. Stations want sure deals, so if you have done this before, recite your good track record.

If you have already tested a medium and experienced a good return, it may not be worthwhile to offer them a PI deal. It is usually better to pay for your ads and get all the money than to go PI and take only part. On the other hand, even free advertising is wasted if it fails to generate business; it is a waste of your time and energy.

CO-OP ADVERTISING

Co-op ads are a popular way the big publishers direct sales to bookstores with local space advertising. Typically, the publisher pays 75% of the ad cost (but no more than 10% of the value of the books shipped to the store), and the bookstore pays 25%. If the store is a regular advertiser in the local papers, they usually get a slightly better rate. The procedure is to have the store place the ads, but the tear sheets of the ads and bills go to the publisher. Then the publisher credits the store with 75% of the ad bill toward book purchases.

To justify co-op advertising, you have to anticipate that the store will move a lot of books. And, while the stores may be a major outlet for a big publisher, they are usually a minor one for a small firm that concentrates on mail order sales.

The Federal Trade Commission (FTC) regulations insist that any deal offered to one dealer must be made available to all.

Small publishers who test co-op ads with one store could find themselves in great financial difficulty, being obligated to advertise for everyone else.

Many small firms feel that co-op advertising is just too complicated and too time consuming, and they routinely answer all inquiries in the negative. This saves time, money and stays away from the FTC.

POINT-OF-PURCHASE SALES AIDS

These include bookmarks, dumps, posters, etc. Posters can be very useful in specialty shops and at exhibits, but there just isn't any room for them in a bookstore where every inch of space is used as efficiently as possible. Librarians like posters, but they rarely buy more than one book. Free bookmarks with advertising printed on them are used 30% to 38% of the time by bookstores. Dumps are special shipping cartons/display units, which are used by 38% to 40% of the stores, depending on the available counter and floor space. Many larger stores suggest and request them. Some clever publishers have designed small table top dumps with directions for detecting counterfeit bills on the back. This ensures premium display space on the counter near the cash register.

Dumps can often be found in trash bins behind bookstores. Many publishers ship their books in counter dumps, floor dumps and shippers (cartons). Bookstores do not need the dumps because they have shelves, so they toss both the dump and the shipper into the dumpster. You will find a variety of colors, sizes and shapes. Use the dumps for testing new (nontraditional) markets.

CATALOGS

Over 7,000 print catalogs are published in the U.S., and each year 11.8 billion are mailed. For our purposes, there are two types of catalogs: general book catalogs, which are not interesting, and special interest catalogs, which are. Catalogs can move a lot of books and they are committed to you for the life of the catalog—usually one year, and if your book sells well, it may appear in issue after issue.

Special merchandise catalogs feature a line of merchandise but devote a page or two to related books. Since you are already in the field (having written about it), you probably know who they are. See the various catalog directories at your public library.

For more information on catalogs, see Document 625, *Selling Books to Catalogs*, at http://ParaPublishing.com.

REMAINDERS

Remainders are overstock books that are sold off to remainder dealers at greatly reduced prices. The big publishers are only interested in books while they are maintaining a certain level of sales. When the demand drops, out they go. Your situation is different, because you are storing the books at home, have a lower overhead, like the prestige of having a current book and can get by on the occasional sales. Initially, each book in your brochure adds to your size. You will have to have several titles before you drop any. You can always run off another 1,000 copies or print single copies (on demand); there is no reason to go out of print. If it is a good how-to book and you have kept it up to date with revisions at each printing, it should continue to sell indefinitely.

Typically, a remainder dealer will offer you 1% to 3% of the list (cover) price of the book. On a $19.95 book, that would be just 20¢ to 60¢ each. Do not remainder a book until the value of your storage space exceeds these amounts.

John Huenefeld offers this rule of thumb for determining when to drop a title: Multiply the quantity on hand by the list price. Then divide by 20 to get 5% of the list price value of the stock. Now compare this 5% figure with the net sales for the last 12 months. If the sales were not greater than this 5% figure, it's time to call the truck.

Remaindering is big business. Almost 20,000 titles go out of print each year, and 25 million copies are remaindered. A lot of big firms are in this business. Many wholesalers carry remainders or "bargain books," which can account for one-third of a bookstore's gross. Some books see their sales pick up once they have been remaindered. The new price and marketing effort have turned books completely around. Remaindered books have sold out and then gone back to press.

Notify your distributor before remaindering a book and offer to take back their stock.

Lists of remainder dealers can be found in *Publishers Weekly, Literary Market Place* and the *American Book Trade Directory* at your library. Write to a number of remainder dealers (some of them specialize in certain types of books, sold to special markets), indicating the quantity, list price, title, hardbound or paperback, condition, location, whether they are prepackaged, and if so, in what increments. Enclose a copy of the book and your sales materials. Establish a closing date and announce that you will accept the best offer for any quantity. Shipping is FOB your warehouse, terms are net 30 days and the books are not returnable. Once you have selected the highest bidder, call them and make sure you have a deal.

Most remainder dealers want 1,000 to 5,000 books, minimum, and they want your entire stock so they have an exclusive. Some will take your slightly damaged stock or "hurts" (scratched copies returned by bookstores).

HURT BOOKS: Remainder or donate damaged returns (hurts) to a charity. You can deduct the value of the book at its original acquisition cost plus your storage and handling costs and the postage out. Prisons, foreign libraries and church bazaars will be very happy to accept your books. By donating your scuffed books, you recover your original investment in them.

For detailed information on remainders and other forms of inventory reduction, see Document 633, *Beyond Remainders*, at http://ParaPublishing.com. Hopefully, you won't have to deal in remainders.

WHITE SALES: Another possibility is to offer your remainders and over-stocked books directly to the national and regional chain bookstores through a one-time only "white sale." Contact the remainder or bargain-book buyer at the chains and send them a sample book and promotional materials. Chain bookstores (retailers) will pay slightly more than remainder dealers (wholesalers)—about 5% of list, possibly more depending on the book.

If you include a FREE offer, be sure there are no strings attached. People get mighty fed up with "free" offers that wind up costing them money.

A strong book market must rely on the prospect that many different writers may have their works appraised and published by numerous competing firms and sold by numerous competing bookstores in diverse markets.
—Richard Howorth, president
Amercian Booksellers Association

10
Fulfillment

Moving Your Book Out the Door

Book order fulfillment consists of invoicing, inventory storage, picking, packaging and shipping. These routines involve opening the mail, sorting it, gathering the email, fax and telephone orders, keyboarding the invoices, wrapping the books, affixing the shipping label, applying postage to the package, making the trip to the post office (or other delivery system) and maintaining a record of the sale. Inventory management includes storage and stock monitoring, so you will know when to order another printing.

Fulfillment is expensive. According to John Huenefeld, most small- to medium-sized publishers spend about 10.5% of their gross on fulfillment. All costs, including labor, storage and shipping materials, average $2.44 per order handled, or 66 cents per book. If your business is mostly wholesale (many copies of the same book to fewer customers), you may be able to drop your fulfillment percentage to 6% or 7%. If all your orders are for individual books at retail, your fulfillment costs may be as high as 14%.

MAIL ORDER SELLING offers you the opportunity to run a high-volume, worldwide business without a large cash investment in multiple facilities. To compete with larger companies, all you need is a better product and more efficient promotion. Since we are far from most of our customers, book publishing is primarily a mail order business.

Mail order businesses deal with their customers at a distance, without face-to-face delivery. The product might be delivered by the post office or a large shipment might go by truck. Mail order is particularly appropriate for the distribution of books. In fact, over half the business and professional books are sold and shipped directly from the publisher to the ultimate consumer.

Smaller publishers are attracted to mail order selling because it is easier than getting into bookstores. They ship to wholesalers and stores, but they don't spend money visiting them. In fact, there are many stories about books that had done poorly in the bookstores but, when properly promoted, sold well through mail order.

Mail order buyers probably do not frequent bookstores, and it is likely they do not even think of themselves as book buyers. Some of these customers are ordering from online bookstores and some get their books directly from the publishers. A *Publishers Weekly* article about Bantam noted that, geographically, mail orders equate proportionally to population figures. The majority of orders come from the most populated states, California and New York, not from the states with fewer bookstores. Mail order purchasing is a habit. Many people prefer to buy informational books this way. Once they begin, they often collect everything they can find on the subject.

ORDER TAKING

Initially, you will take, process and fill orders by yourself to keep it simple. You want to streamline the workload to avoid any duplication of effort. For example, keyboarding an invoice and then typing a separate label is a waste of time and money (cost of label, etc.). Just print out three copies of each invoice and use one copy for the shipping label/packing slip. This one-time writing also avoids transposition errors in figures and addresses. Once your business grows to the point where you have several titles and employees, you will require a more elaborate fulfillment system.

To enable you to visualize the distribution system, the fulfillment process will be discussed in sequence.

ELECTRONIC ORDERS: Most of your orders will arrive electronically via telephone, fax and email. These orders are usually charged to a credit card. A few orders will arrive in the mail with enclosed checks or money orders. Since many orders will be received electronically, you will need "merchant status:" the ability to accept credit cards.

Many of your orders will be generated by your *Web site*. If most of your promotional efforts are on the Web, most of your orders will arrive via email and most of your correspondence will be via email.

Draft stock paragraphs that can be cut and pasted into an email to answer questions, announce new products and services and take care of routine business matters.

POSTAL ORDERS: Open the mail and check the contents, but do not take the orders and cheques out of their envelopes. Sort the stuffed envelopes into piles according to whether they are individual retail sales, book dealers (stores or distributors), libraries or special accounts (associations, sport centers, etc.). Make up a separate pile for inquiries—you will want to send these people a brochure. Other piles will be for accounts receivable, letters to be answered, etc.

When a retail order arrives without a cheque, make a note of the omission (such as "cheque not enclosed") on the envelope. Then send a brochure with a note requesting money in the correct amount. Occasionally, you will get a letter back, saying that a cheque was enclosed with the original order. But you will have your note on that envelope to confirm your suspicions and jog your memory. Make a photocopy of the envelope with the notation and request that the sender either recheck his or her records or send you a photocopy of the canceled cheque.

TELEPHONE ORDERS: Today, more and more people use the telephone to order. Not only is it easier and faster, if they are paying 10 cent/minute for telephone service, a three-minute call is cheaper than a stamp.

Telephone contacts are important opportunities for sales and increased sales. They take place when you have the attention of the prospect and they are (usually) paying for the call. Consequently, an untrained employee should not handle telephone calls. Make sure everyone knows who is to take calls, except in case of overflow, or train every staff member to take calls. Have an order form ready, or route orders to the order-entry computer operator for direct punch-up. Order forms prompt questions, making it easier to obtain all the necessary information (such as the *ship to* address).

Be sure to ask for their email address. Retain it for your mailing list and use it if there is a question about their order.

For a free copy of our telephone order form, see Document 147 at http://ParaPublishing.com.

Toll-free numbers (800/888/877/866) are expected of businesses today. See the discussion in Chapter 9.

ANSWERING MACHINE ORDERS: Answering machines are very useful in business because they can take orders after business hours. They are a great convenience to both you and the customer. Clients do not expect you to answer after hours but they do expect to be able to leave a message at any time. It is nice when you return after a weekend away to find a number of orders waiting for you on your answering machine.

> Many people like our recording, which says: "Para Publishing, this is Dan Poynter. If you would like an information kit on publishing or parachuting, please leave your name and address. If you would like to charge a book to your VISA, MasterCard, Discover or American Express card, please leave your name, address, telephone number, the name of the book, type of charge card, the card number and the expiration date. Thank you." *(beep)*

FAX ORDERS: Facsimile transmissions do not replace the telephone; they replace the Postal Service for delivering letters, purchase orders and drawings. Some of your orders will come in by fax.

Get a fax machine and install it on a separate telephone line. List your fax number on your letterhead, business card and order blanks. Without a fax, people will wonder if you are really in business. Get a plain-paper model.

CREDIT CARDS SALES

Credit cards increase sales and increase the size of the sale while cutting down on collection problems. People have become accustomed to telephoning an order and placing the charge on a credit card. VISA and MasterCard are used the most in telephone orders, American Express is third, with Discover and the others used to a much lesser extent. Although the bank wants 3% to 7% of each sale, depending upon the average size of the sale and your monthly volume, it credits your account immediately.

Credit cards increase your cash flow and may decrease your need for expensive short-term loans.

Credit card orders take more time to process because you must process a charge slip. But the sale always comes out even, so there is no additional billing or difference to refund, and there are no accounts receivable collection problems. You have the correct payment in your bank account.

PC Authorize and MAC authorize software is better and less expensive than the mini terminal and printer. For more information and how to purchase it, contact Tellan Software Inc. Through CyberCash, Inc.; 800-4-TELLAN or CyberCash Direct Sales 800-666-5777; info@tellan.com; http://www.tellan.com.

The challenge is in getting the credit card merchant status privilege from the bank. Because of high losses from fly-by-night boiler room telephone operations, banks are reluctant to offer merchant card privileges to mail order and telephone order businesses.

The merchant card packets from most banks list the prohibitions (such as no telephone orders, no mail orders, no working from home), but they also have lists of exceptions. Get merchant card packets from several banks and compare prices and restrictions. Some have higher start-up and monthly fees than others. Ultimately, the bank may send a representative to check out your place of business. Deal only with a bank. Do not contract with an independent service organization (ISO); the costs will be far higher. By the way, Costco offers merchant status to businesses.

ORDER PROCESSING

Get an inexpensive order-entry/accounting program such as *QuickBooks* (http://www.intuit.com) or *PUB123* (http://www.adams-blake.com).

Print out two copies of your (accounts receivable) *invoice* or (cash with order) *sales receipt*. One copy of your invoice is folded in thirds and slipped into a 4.5" x 8.5" clear packing list envelope (Stock #45-3-23, Associated Bag Co., http://www.associatedbag.com). This copy serves as the invoice, a packing list and a shipping label. The second copy is stored in a binder. This is your hard copy backup. A third copy can be generated and sent separately to the customer if requested. Many wholesaler orders (libraries, schools, government. etc.) require that the invoice be sent separately from the actual shipment.

From: **Para Publishing** Post Office Box 8206 Santa Barbara, CA 93118-8206 USA	**Invoice**

	DATE	INVOICE NO.
	5/26/1999	2680

BILL TO	SHIP TO
Borders Inc SPO Dept 100 Phoenix Drive, AP Stores Ann Arbor, MI 48108-2202	Borders Books & Music #23 9108 Metcalf Avenue Overland Park, KS 66210

P.O. NO.	TERMS	SHIP VIA
K-1133C	NET 30	UPS-GRO...

ITEM	DESCRIPTION	QTY	EACH	AMOUNT
PSH7	Parachuting, The Skydiver's Handbook 1-56860-045-3	1	19.95	19.95
40	40% Discount		-40.00%	-7.98
SHIPPING	Shipping charges		4.00	4.00

PLEASE REMIT FROM THIS INVOICE. THANK YOU.

Total $15.97

ISBN: 0-915516- & ISBN 1-56860- ; SAN: 215-8981; DUNS: 09-141-9358; Fed. ID: 95-6532235; Seller's Permit: SR AR 15-633785
Tel: (805) 968-7277; Fax: (805) 968-1379; Street Address: 530 Ellwood Ridge, Santa Barbara, CA 93117-1047 USA

Invoice

Individual orders come from the reader and are usually paid for in advance, cash-with-order (CWO). Enter the sale into your computer and print out a sales receipt. The sales receipt looks like an invoice but shows a zero balance. Set the cheque aside for deposit or process the credit card number.

Save envelopes with their enclosed orders. At the end of each week or month, rubber-band the envelopes and date the pile. Save them for 12 to 18 months, in case a customer contacts you about the order or the package is returned as undeliverable. If a book is returned by the Postal Service as undeliverable, check the postmark to determine when the shipment went out and then go through the envelopes to find the original order. The book may have been sent to the address on the cheque rather than the one on the envelope, numbers may have been transposed, etc.

If a customer complains that the wrong book was shipped, he or she did not order the book or a missing cheque was actually enclosed, looking up the original order will confirm or deny the claim. When replying, enclose a photocopy of the original order so the customer can see what he or she did.

ORDERS NOT RECEIVED: Occasionally, a customer will contact you saying that he or she has not received the book. Check back through the original order envelopes and computer record to make sure you received and processed the order and that the book was sent out and on what date. Then contact the customer, stating the date the book was shipped and how it was sent. Slower, but cheaper, Media Mail can take up to 30 days in the U.S. and 120 days to foreign addresses. Remind the customer that the package had a return address and it was not returned to you. Rarely does the Postal Service lose books. Tell them that if the book does not arrive in a couple of weeks more, they should return the order and you will ship out another book. This is a good way to keep a potentially valuable customer happy.

When you ship the second book, write up the transaction on an invoice, make three copies and mail one to the customer. Note on it that if they receive two books, they should refuse delivery of the second one. If they do that, the Postal Service will return the book to you with only postage due. If the customer accepts delivery, they may never get around to sending the book back and you are out a book. Explain to them that you are sorry for the inconvenience and do not wish to trouble them further by having them rewrap and reship the (second) book. Once they receive a book, the chances are very good they will refuse delivery of the second one because they do not need two copies.

One way to avoid most of these "books not received" challenges is to ship most books via *Priority Mail*. You can use the free cardboard priority mail envelope and the package will arrive in two or three days.

ADDRESS CODES: At the end of each month, total up the orders responding to each address code and record the responses to see if your advertising and promotion is paying off. See the discussion of address codes in Chapter 7.

UNDERPAYMENTS: Short slips can be used to collect small amounts due. Some customers, ordering by mail, will not send enough to cover the book, shipping and sales tax. Sometimes the shortage is too small to bother collecting. Very small improper payments (high or low) are not worth haggling over as it costs more to process a short slip than the amount you might collect. Just ship the book.

Short Slip

Your order was short $_____

We know you will appreciate our sending the books now rather than holding up the shipment pending payment of this small amount.

Please return this slip when you next contact us—now OR with your next order or payment. THANK YOU.

Your name:_____

Cheque number:_____

Send to:

Para Publishing, Accounting Department

PO Box 8206, Santa Barbara,

CA 93118-8206 USA.

orders@ParaPublishing.com; 805-968-7277

Short slip

If you decide to use short slips, set certain limits such as:

0 - .40:	Forget it
.40 - $4.99:	Enclose a short slip
Over $5.00:	Cut an invoice for the balance

Collect these small payments as they come in and bank them once a month. The small amounts add up and are worth collecting. But you must compare the costs of collecting small amounts with the amount that can be collected. Most people are good about short slips and will pay, but it is not worth badgering them for 30 cents if they have to use first class postage to send it to you.

OVERPAYMENTS: If the customer sends a little too much, ship the book a faster way, such as UPS. If he or she sends a lot too much, issue a refund cheque for the balance. Fortunately, credit card orders come out even.

BAD CHEQUES: Cheques to book publishers rarely bounce, and it is not worth the record keeping and loss of customer goodwill to delay shipments until a cheque clears the bank. When a cheque is returned, look at the original order envelope to see if there is more than one address. Send off a photocopy of the returned cheque and the bank notice that came with it. Write across the photocopy "Please send another cheque" and circle the bank charge and the new total amount. Most of these customers will make the bad cheque good. You can always include a short, direct letter, but this photocopy technique is faster and simpler. Since books have a high markup, it probably is not worth your time to expend more effort trying to collect these few small debts from "cheque bouncers."

SHIPPING INSURANCE: Insuring book shipments is a waste of your time and money. The shipper should replace books lost or damaged in the mails. Your only alternative is to insure each parcel. It is far cheaper to *self-insure* by replacing the occasional lost or damaged book. There will not be many lost books, and the cost of replacement is small, compared to the price of insurance and the paperwork and hassle involved to process a claim, to say nothing of the value of a happy customer.

REFUNDS: Refunds should be handled promptly. *The customer is always right.* A cheerful, fast refund will let them know they can trust you, and there is a good chance they will be back.

Unlimited Guarantee

We guarantee your satisfaction. Order any book and look it over. You may return it at any time if not satisfied and your full purchase price will be refunded, no questions asked. There is no 10-day or 30-day limit; you may return it even after a year.

Set up as few barriers to ordering as possible. If your product is good, most customers will keep it. Since there is no limit on the free trial period, most unsatisfied customers will put off the return—forever.

The customer usually pays the shipping on an order and on a return. This means that you will refund or issue a credit (against future purchase) only for the price of the book.

SALES TAX: Sales tax will have to be added onto the invoice on those *retail sales made within your state* to an end user (the reader). Do not collect sales tax on books sold *for resale* to bookstores and other firms in your state because they will in turn resell the book to an end user and collect the tax.

When you sell to another reseller in your state, you must record their state *resale number*. The point is that the ultimate purchaser will pay the tax (either to you or to the reseller). You must either collect the sales tax or get a resale number that indicates who will collect it. In most states, libraries are not exempt from sales taxes; after all, they do not resell the books. Usually, the sales tax is not collected for any sales made out of your state. The sales tax is calculated on the merchandise only, not the shipping charges. Also see the discussion on sales tax in Chapter 3.

The bottom of the invoice can be used for any other pertinent information or even a nice personal note.

SHIPPING LABELS: Labels are not needed for most shipments; you will use a copy of the invoice as this has the "ship to" address at the top. However, you do need labels for sending out review copies and other promotional material.

Labels come in rolls or sheets, and small quantities can be generated on your laser printer. Here is an example of a 3" x 5" label:

Shipping label

Custom-printed labels are available from label manufacturers in various sizes, colors and typestyles. One is Discount Labels at http://www.discountlabel. Com. Do not order labels on slick gloss stock. Addresses will smear and the ink takes much longer to dry.

CREDIT AND INVOICING

Dealer orders come from your distributor, commercial wholesale customers and those individual retail customers (such as libraries and large companies) that must be billed. These customers are usually extended credit and invoiced.

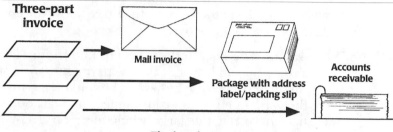

The invoice route

ACCOUNTS RECEIVABLE: When payment arrives, match the cheque with the invoice, and date stamp the invoice to give you a record of the date payment was received. Then move the invoice to a binder of a different color for storage. Update your computer file.

EXTENDING CREDIT: The customer may send a cheque, authorize you to charge his or her credit card, or you may extend credit to them (e.g., net 30 days). Most publishers require a cheque or credit card from individuals and extend credit to bookstores, libraries, their distributor and wholesalers, as long as the orders are not unusually large and the purchase order looks professional.

Individual contracts are rarely required with dealers. The terms of sale (net 30 days, consignment, etc.) are printed on the invoice in the box marked "Terms."

- **Individuals** usually send a check when ordering by mail and authorize a credit card charge to VISA or Master-Card when making a telephone order. Many publishers follow the rule of no credit sales to individuals. Get a cheque or credit card. This rule eliminates many small receivables and occasional uncollectible.

- **Businesses** expect terms (to pay later), but many smaller firms are using credit cards. Though the interest rate is high, cards offer convenience and simple credit to the small business.

For those businesses that insist on sending purchase orders without money, you can extend 30-day credit terms or send a *pro forma invoice*. A pro forma is a regular invoice listing the books, shipping charges, sales tax (if applicable) and the total. Once they pay the invoice in advance, you ship the books.

●◆ **Wholesalers.** The book industry is not known for "fast pay." Sixty-, 90- and even 120-day payments are not uncommon, and since books have to be sold on a return basis, they are, in effect, on consignment anyway. Some publishers have put the large wholesalers on a CWO (cash with order) basis. Even Baker & Taylor will pay up front if requested.

If a bookstore or wholesaler is slow or fails to pay, tighten up or cut them off. Many publishers follow this system: Any dealers over 60 days are put on a CWO basis until their accounts are brought up to date. In other words, they get credit until they abuse it, and then they pay in advance. Some publishers extend credit only to the distributor they have a contract with and college (tax-supported) bookstores. Everyone else pays in advance. Some publishers deal only through their distributor and direct any bookstore, wholesaler and library orders to that distributor.

●◆ **Distributors.** Your relationship with your distributor will be governed by your contract. Many distributors pay 90 to 120 days after they ship the books. Most will send a monthly printout of sales so you will know what size checks to expect. However, most will also hold back a percentage of what is due you to cover anticipated returns, and some may have a laundry list of additional monthly charges.

DELAYED ORDERS

"Back orders" are those that cannot be completely filled when the order is received. Usually, most of the order can be filled and is shipped, and the single "out-of-stock" book order is put aside until that book is received and can be shipped.

Notify your customer immediately via email of the status of the order.

Most publishers use a common code of abbreviations to cover the most frequent back-order problems: OS (out of stock), TOS (temporarily out of stock), OP (out of print), TOP (temporarily out of print), NOP (not our publication) and FP (future publication). If you use these abbreviations, make sure they are explained elsewhere on the invoice, such as on the back. Only librarians and bookstore buyers will already understand the codes.

THE FEDERAL TRADE COMMISSION (FTC) has some strict rules for CWO (cash with order) mail order operations. If you receive money for books:

- You must ship the order within 30 days of receiving it (or charging their credit card), unless your offer clearly stated that shipping would take longer.

- If it appears the order will not be shipped when promised, you must notify the customer before the promised date, giving a definite new date, if known, and offering them the opportunity to cancel the order with a refund or consent to a definite delayed shipping date or an indefinite delay.

- Your notice must contain a self-addressed, stamped card or envelope for the customer to indicate a preference. If there is no response to this notice, you may assume agreement to the delay but must ship the order within 30 days of the original shipping date promised or required, or the order will be automatically canceled. A prompt refund must be made if the order is canceled.

- Even if the customer consents to an indefinite delay, he or she retains the right to cancel the order at any time before the item is shipped.

- If the customer cancels an order that has been paid for by cheque or money order, you must mail a refund within seven business days.

If the customer cancels a credit card order, you must issue a credit within one billing cycle following the receipt of their request. The customer can stop payment pending settlement of the matter if the purchase is over $50 and they are within 100 miles or within the same state.

Credits toward future purchases are not acceptable.

If the book ordered is unavailable, you may not send substitute merchandise without the customer's consent.

This FTC discussion regarding credit card rules may be redundant, because your contract with the credit card company probably says if the customer purchases by mail or telephone (that is, without physically handing you the card) and later contests the bill, you must issue a credit.

Request *A Business Checklist for Direct Marketers* and *A Business Guide to the FTC Mail or Telephone Merchandise Order Rule* from the FTC, Washington, DC 20580; 800-382-4357; or print them off the Web site at http://www.ftc.gov.

As long as you guarantee satisfaction by offering to send a refund for any merchandise returned for any reason, you shouldn't have any run-ins with the FTC. Just treat your customers right and keep in touch with them. Use email.

PROMPT SHIPMENTS: Orders should be shipped as soon as possible after receipt, usually the next day. This involves a trip to the post office once each day to pick up the mail and to deliver the packaged books from orders received the previous day. The sooner the orders are processed, the sooner the money will be deposited; this is the best incentive for speedy fulfillment.

Customers want their books as soon as possible. A few who are not familiar with mail order will even write two days later asking about their package, but this is rare. When business is slow, post office runs can be made every other day, say Monday, Wednesday and Friday. If you must be away from the business, you will find that only one or two inquiries will be received if you fail to ship for up to a month.

UNORDERED BOOKS: Customers receiving unordered merchandise cannot be pressured to pay for it or return it. They may use it or discard it as they see fit. So be careful where you ship books. See the *Postal Service Domestic Mail Manual*.

QUALITY CONTROL

One way to avoid shipping errors is to employ as few people as possible in the order-entry and packaging functions. Fewer people in the loop provides accountability. The second secret is *cross training* so everyone understands the system (and can fill in during absences). If an error is made punching up an order, the packer may spot it if he or she understands the system. Try to limit order handling to the mail opener/telephone operator who receives the orders, the order-entry computer operator who punches up the orders, and the shipper who picks, packs and posts. In very small companies, one person will perform all these functions, but as you hire staff, be sure to cross-train. If the same person handles mail opening or order entry and accounts receivable, he or she will remember the bad debts and other challenges and will flag the questionable new orders.

COMPLAINTS: Complaints must be viewed as an opportunity, not a problem. Complaints can be expensive if not handled quickly, and they mean a lost sale unless you can make a substitute or convince the customer you are worthy of a future order. Complainers can also spread their hostility to others. Some mail order companies, such as Quill, the large office-supply company, enclose a return form with every order to emphasize how easy it is to do business with them.

Complaints should be answered promptly. Even if the book has probably arrived by the time you get the complaint, you should answer. You must maintain credibility.

Written complaints should be handled with a call, unless a lot of photocopied documentation is required. Customers can be cooled down more easily over the telephone.

When someone calls in a complaint, you have an opportunity to wrap up the problem on the telephone at their expense, so do not offer to get back to them. Remind the caller or writer that you guarantee satisfaction. You will try to work out the problem, but if you can't, you will refund the money. Most customers want the book, and the problem works itself out.

Find out what the customer wants before suggesting a solution. Ask, "What do you want?" The answer is usually much easier and less expensive than you would have offered.

A checklist form letter can be used to handle common small problems, but because they are impersonal, they should not be used for major complaints.

INVENTORY AND STORAGE

Book storage cannot be taken lightly, because books are not light. If your floor will not support a waterbed, do not haul in a ton of books. The people downstairs will not like your books any better than the water. The best place to store your new product is in the garage, alongside the shipping table. This way, the books can be off-loaded in the driveway and stacked in the garage, wrapped as needed and placed back in the car for the post office run. All these operations can be done with a minimum of carrying. Hauling books down steep steps into a cellar, only to wrap them and haul them back up, gets very old very soon and makes no sense at all. This is heavy work.

Tell the printer you want the finished books plastic shrink-wrapped in stacks of two books each. The plastic runs about 20 cents per shrink. If you shrink-wrap them individually, stores and potential customers will not remove the plastic, so they will not read the inside of your book, and you will probably lose the sale.

The plastic wrap will keep the books clean, dry and dust free, and the books will not rub on the carton. Small publishers need shrink-wrapping and tightly packed cartons because they often store the books in places without climate control, such as in an unheated garage. If the cartons are not tightly packed (filled to the top), they will crush and tip, rather than stack well.

Do not stack cartons directly on top of each other. Stack them to overlap like bricks (this is the way your boxes are usually stacked on the wooden pallets from the printer). The alternating stack will be solid and will not tip over. Very little shelving is required in your shipping area, because you should store books in their original cartons.

If your state has an inventory tax, you can avoid most of the bite by careful ordering or by having your printing done in another state. Then, keeping an eye on the tax date, have the printer ship you a pallet of books as needed.

As noted above, the books should be shrink-wrapped at the printer, boxed and sealed. Then the cartons will be palletized, banded three ways (with straps or plastic wrap) and trucked to you as a unit. This keeps the books from shifting in the cartons, which can scratch the covers. Palletized and banded cartons are less likely to be broken open en route, but always expect to find at least one torn carton, which a curious trucker has opened to see if the contents are pornographic books (books delivered to home addresses, as opposed to normal places of business, are sometimes pornographic). Of course, if you are publishing pornography, also expect some books to be missing from the shipment.

New titles can be "drop shipped" directly from the printer to your wholesale accounts in various quantities. This cuts down on reshipping. There is no reason to expend the time and money to route them, for example, from Michigan to you in California and then back to your distributor, wholesaler, book clubs and other major accounts.

Books must be kept in a cool, dry, dust-free place. Dampness can ripple or curl the pages, make covers stick together and rust wire stitches (staples) in saddle-stitched books. Depending upon your location, moisture and type of flooring, it is wise to stack the cartons on pallets, so air can circulate under the boxes. Always leave an air space between the stack and a wall. Sunlight will fade and yellow paper. Dust will scratch the covers and dirty the edges of the books.

Fire is always a concern, but insuring the inventory in a noncommercial (hence non-fire rated) area may be impossible. Ask your insurance agent.

If your books become damaged, slowly or quickly, you are out of business. Your inventory must be protected, and this means leaving the books in their protective cartons and bags and opening only one carton at a time as needed. Unbelievably, some publishers unpack their books and place them on shelves, exposed to sun and dust.

If the pages of the books ripple due to high humidity, they may straighten out when the moisture returns to normal. Again, leaving the books stacked in their cartons will hold the pages flatter.

INVENTORY CONTROL is simpler if all the books are stored in a single place. When you have cartons of books scattered around your garage, in the office, at the printer's, with friends, and in a mini-storage warehouse, some will disappear and you will never know how many you have. If you do not have a garage or spare room, try renting warehouse space. Mini warehouses are quite common now; check the *Yellow Pages*. Then try to store books in one place, or no more than two: the bulk in the warehouse and a few cartons in the shipping area.

Physical inspection is the easiest way to get stock information; it is faster than going through the invoices. If you quickly count the books on hand monthly, you will be able to plot a good inventory chart. These figures will be a great help in your planning next year. Reorders must be scheduled so the reprints will arrive just before the previous supply is exhausted. Having to report a delay in filling an order costs money in terms of paperwork, and time is money. The decision to reprint will be determined by rate of sale, stock level, seasonal sales expectations (outdoor books sell better in the spring), the time required to print and, in some states, the date of the inventory tax.

Dun & Bradstreet reports that 9.5% of all business failures are due to excessive inventory. Keep the inventory low and order more often.

PICKING AND PACKING

The Shipping Area is where you do the picking, packing and posting. It should be arranged so as to require as little motion as possible; books, bags, cartons and other materials must all be within easy reach. Position the fast-selling books closer to the shipping table.

Packing involves the placing of the books in a protective wrapper so that your customer receives the clean, non-mutilated goods he or she is paying for. Books must be packaged well enough to arrive in good condition the first time. It costs too much to ship them twice.

Single orders can be prepackaged and stacked to wait for a label. Done in front of the TV set, the time passes quickly.

SADDLE-STITCHED BOOKLETS: Small, wire-stitched (stapled) paperbacks can be safely shipped in Priority Mail envelopes: *regular envelopes* (up to one pound) or *flat rate envelopes* (two pounds or more). Flat Rate envelopes are mailed at the two-pound rate, regardless of the total weight. These envelopes are free from the Postal Service. The Postal Service will even ship quantities of these envelopes to you free. Just call 800-222-1811.

Get the right type and size (EP 14G-regular or EP 14F-flat rate) and fold the envelope to immobilize the book(s). If the envelope is too large, the book(s) will slide around inside and the covers will be scuffed. (See the Postal Service Web site at http://supplies.usps.gov.) Put the book(s) into a plastic bag before inserting them into the cardboard envelope.

HARDCOVER AND PAPERBACKS: For hardbound and perfect-bound (square-back) paperbacks up to 6" x 9", use the #0-1096 large video boxes, free from the Postal Service. Just insert the book and wedge in some dunnage such as newsprint to immobilize the book in the carton.

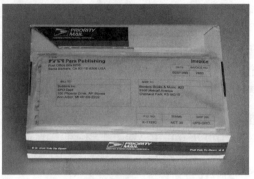

Priority Mail (large) video box

PADDED BAGS: Review copies can be sent in padded bags at the Media Mail rate (formerly Book Rate and Special Standard Mail) which is less expensive than Priority Mail.

Fiber-filled padded bags are heavy, dirty and can only be stapled closed. The plastic-bubble Jiffy-Lite® bag, on the other hand, is clean, light and waterproof when heat-sealed. Compared to other plastic-lined bags, the Jiffy-Lite is not as smooth inside, making it difficult to stuff large books, but it offers the best protection. We have tested every type of plain and padded bag, lightweight and heavyweight, and have found the Jiffy-Lite bag to be the best.

Jiffy-Lite bags cost more than fiber-filled bags, but you will save on postage. A standard 6" x 9" hardcover book measures a half-inch wider and longer and is a quarter-inch thicker than its paperback edition. Both fit the #1 Jiffy-Lite bag when they have less than 200 pages. Contact Sealed Air Corp. for the name of the local paper dealer who handles their Jiffy-Lite bags at 201-791-7600; fax 201-703-4205; http://www.sealedair.com.

Also contact Quill Corp. for a catalog and compare bag prices: 800-789-1331; http://www.quill.com. Remember to add in shipping charges when comparing prices.

Shipping bag

STAPLERS AND HEAT-SEALERS: The shipping bags can be stapled closed (get the heavy, hand grip type of stapler) or heat sealed. Sealing machines come in several sizes and provide a moisture-tight closure. Sealed Air runs heat-sealer promotions from time to time, but if your Sealed Air distributor is not running a promotion when you are ready to buy, contact the manufacturer directly: Heat Seal Equipment, Cleveland, Ohio; 216-341-2022, 800-342-6329; fax 216-341-2163; custserv@ heatsealco.com; http://www.heatsealco.com. Call for the number of the dealer nearest you. Jiffy-Lite bags are also available in self-seal models.

OVERSIZED PAPERBACKS: 8.5" x 11" softcover books can be shipped in Postal Service Priority Mail envelopes. Put the book(s) into a plastic bag before inserting them into the cardboard envelope.

Vari-depth mailer

Some thinner books require more protection for the spine and require a Vari-depth mailer. Vari-depth mailers are die-cut, flat shippers that can be folded around one or more books. The mailers cost more than padded shipping bags but offer excellent protection when the books are first placed in a plastic bag. Amazon.com uses this packaging for individual books.

CARTONS: Three or more books require a carton for protection. Check the yellow pages for nearby paper goods dealers, and purchase standard 5.5" x 8.5" or 6" x 9" cartons (as applicable) of various depths. They ordinarily come 25 to the bundle. Many times large box manufacturers and distributors will give you free samples so that you can select the right size carton for your books.

Bookstores are a good source of shipping cartons. They usually get more than they can recycle and disposal is expensive. Ask the storeowner and check the dumpster.

If you standardize the trim size of all your books, you will minimize the carton and bag sizes required for shipping. The best measurements for books are 5.5" x 8.5" and 8.5" x 11", because they will stack together (two of the smaller size books, side by side, over one of the larger books).

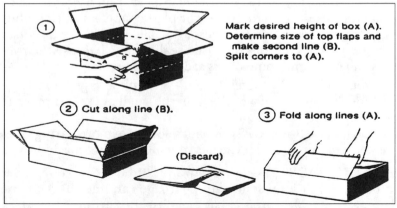

How to cut down a carton

Incidentally, some states, such as California, do not charge sales tax on shipping supplies, such as cartons and tape. This is probably to encourage exports. Check on this with your office supply store or state sales taxing authority.

Sealing a carton with non-reinforced paper tape

PAPER TAPE AND DISPENSERS: The least expensive way to seal cartons is with 3" non-reinforced brown paper tape. Reinforced paper tape is strong, but it is also dirty and hard to cut with inexpensive tape dispensers.

Fancy paper tape machines cost several hundred dollars—quite a shock—so look around for a used one. Check used office equipment stores and swap meets. Compare the prices at Quill at http://www.quill.com. Also contact Arrow Star Discount for a catalog: 800-645-2833.

The water will flow onto the paper tape more easily if you add a little vinegar to the reservoir in the tape machine. You may, alternatively, use a couple of drops of detergent, but detergent can gum up the machine more quickly than vinegar.

PLASTIC TAPE: Plastic sealing tape costs more than paper tape and is harder to use, but the handheld dispensers are much less expensive. The lightest-weight plastic tape is sufficient; buy the cheapest, lowest mil thickness available. But be very careful of the special sales on rolls of plastic sealing tape because the rolls vary in length and some offers are no bargain.

You will need ½" reinforced "strapping tape" for large cartons, so you should also use it on the small ones. Do not waste money buying wider tape.

Do not use twine; UPS does not allow it anymore. String takes too long to put on and it catches in mail-handling machinery.

PLASTIC BAGS: Take a carton and 20 books to your paper goods store. Pick up some large garbage can liner bags to line large cartons. Measure the bags against the carton. Then stack some books in one pile to fit the smaller cartons you are buying, and get some smaller plastic bag can liners to match. You have to run these packaging tests each time you buy, because the bag manufacturers are continually changing the measurements, mil thickness and gussets.

RAZOR KNIFE: Get a common razor knife for opening cartons and keep it sharp. A sharpening stone will prolong the life of the blades. Be very careful when cutting open cartons. It is common to score the covers of the top books by cutting too deeply.

RUBBER STAMPS: The common rubber stamps you will need are pictured on the following page. Order them from your local office supply store. Some are commercially available and others must be made to order.

Rubber stamps

When shipping a package by air, stamp the notice *near the address* on the package so that it will be more noticeable to the mail sorters. A red air mail stamp over in one corner of the carton might be missed, resulting in a high-priced, slow delivery.

Rubber stamps come with a variety of inking mechanisms: non-refillable (not very economical), refillable (with the ink held in a reservoir), and those that use a stamp pad. If using a stamp pad, turn it over every night to make the ink flow to the top of the pad.

LADDER: Get a short, sturdy ladder or step stool so you can stack cartons higher and retrieve them easily.

SCALES fall into two categories (spring and electronic) and two general ranges. Electronic scales are more accurate.

The two ranges are 0-2 lb. or 0-5 lb. *letter scale* and 0-50 lbs. (or more) large *parcel scale*. The larger scale need only read from 0-50 lbs. Packages heavier than 40 lbs. do not protect their contents well (will be dropped) and should not be shipped.

Book publishers do not need fancy zone and rate-computing scales since books shipped by Media Mail, Airmail and up to 6 pound Priority Mail are not zoned. A simple scale and a rate chart are all that are needed.

The scale should be accurate, but do not be obsessed with its being perfect. The Postal Service rarely checks the postage on a stamped package at the loading dock.

THE PACKING PROCESS

There are two important steps in successful book packaging: keep the books clean and immobilized. Start with cartons that are close to the size of your book. If you have 5.5" x 8.5" books and can get 5.5" x 8.5" cartons in several depths, the fit will be perfect and there will not be any sliding and scuffing between books. Slip the books into a plastic bag and slide them into the carton. For the best fit, cut down the top of the carton rather than fill it with dunnage. The books will be kept clean by the plastic bag and immobilized by the perfect-fitting carton.

STUFFING MATERIALS: Styrofoam peanuts and disks are greasy, gritty and will work their way between the pages of a book if not separated by a plastic bag. Reuse any peanuts sent to you, but do not buy them. The best shipping carton is a perfect fit or one that has been cut down to fit. The next best choice is to stuff with newspaper, but remember that newspaper is dirty, another reason to place the books in a plastic bag first. Other stuffing materials include cheap newsprint paper in sheets or in rolls, plastic bubble wrap, and inflatable plastic and rubber balloons. Uline offers a wide range of shipping supplies, phone 800-295 -5510, http://www.uline.com.

LABELING: Once the bag is stuffed or the carton is wrapped, it is time to apply the packing list/shipping label. This copy of the invoice is simply folded and inserted into a large, pressure-sensitive, adhesive-backed clear envelope and placed on the bag or carton. (Stock #45-3-23, Associated Bag Co., http://www. associatedbag.com) Now the person receiving the shipment will have exactly the same information as the person receiving the bill.

Occasionally, the person receiving the separate bill will not want the person receiving the books to know the prices and terms (such as in a drop shipment). In this case, simply use scissors to clip off the pricing information. When the *ship to* address is not the same as the invoiced address, cross out the latter and circle the former with a felt tip pen, or use a common 1 x 3.5 address label to cover the *sold to* address.

TAPING: Using non-reinforced paper or plastic tape, seal the ends of the carton as well as the long flaps. Sealing the ends will make the carton far sturdier. Place the shipping label/packing slip in its self-adhesive, clear envelope on top. Place this envelope over the carton closure, so the recipient will have to remove the envelope to open the carton. Then reinforce the carton by banding in at least two directions with reinforcing tape. Run the tape over the clear packing slip envelope to secure it to the carton. Then if another heavy package is skidded across this one, the label will not be spindled off.

When assembling cartons with paper tape, cut the tape long enough to hang over the carton by 2" to 3" on each end. Since folding down the four flaps and taping is a three-hand job, try this: With all four flaps closed, place the tape on the far long flap. Pull the carton up against you, and seal the tape over the near long flap and the ends of the carton.

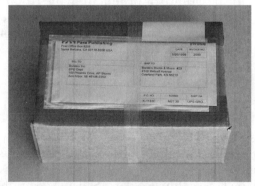

The wrapped and addressed carton

SHIPPING RATES

Obtain both the domestic and international rates from the Postal Service at http://usps.gov and make up postal charts for both the invoicing and wrapping areas. Inflate the figures on the chart for the invoicing area to allow for the price of the shipping bag, invoice, tape, envelope, the first class postage of the invoice and self-insurance (because you will replace any books that are lost or damaged in transit). It is cheaper to replace a lost book than to pay for postal insurance.

Why pay the Postal Service 34 cents to store your mail?

For Postal Service publications and Web sites, see Postal Books, Manuals & Web Sites in Appendix 2. For the most current rates, see http://www.usps.gov.

MEDIA MAIL (BOOK RATE): Books can be shipped via the Postal Service's Media Mail (formerly called Book Rate and Special Standard). To qualify, books must have at least eight pages, contain no advertising and be permanently bound. Media Mail is cheaper than regular parcel post and there are no postal zones to compute. The same low rate applies to any destination with a zip code from Guam to the Virgin Islands, including APOs and FPOs.

If, however, you are shipping a heavy parcel in the nearest postal zones to yours, compare the Postal Service's Media Mail rate with their regular parcel post rate, and with UPS, for the lowest rate available. Get a copy of the Postal Service Domestic Mail Manual from the post office or print it from the Postal Service Web site at http://pe.usps.gov. For a free comparison chart, send a self-addressed, stamped envelope to Upper Access Books, PO Box 457, Hinesburg, VT 05461; 800-310-8320, 802-482-2988; fax 802-482-3125; or print it from their Web site under "Publishers Services" at http://www.upperaccess.com; info@upperaccess.com.

PRIORITY MAIL: Flat rate envelopes (EP-14F) can be shipped for just $3.85, regardless of the weight. And since you save 30 cents because the envelope is free, your cost is really just $3.55. You can get up to four books in the envelope, or just over four pounds. Eighty-four percent of Priority Mail is delivered anywhere in the U.S. within two days. See http://supplies.usps.gov to order free supplies. We ship virtually every single book via Priority Mail. Customers love the quick delivery.

Postal Rates for Book Publishers—July 1, 2002

Media Mail—Books—Surface

Lbs.	U.S.	Canada	Foreign*	Library Rate-USA
1	1.42	1.70	See rate	1.35
2	1.84	Rates in	Group	1.75
3	2.26	2 oz.		2.15
4	2.68	increments		2.55
5	3.10	----------4 lb. Limit--------		2.95
6	3.52			3.35
7	3.94			3.75
8	4.24			4.04
9	4.54			4.33
10	4.84			4.62
11	5.14	11 lbs. and over: Use		
12	5.44	"Direct Sack of Prints."		
13	5.74	Economy (Surface) M-Bags		
14	6.04			
15	6.34	Canada: Other Countries:		
16	6.64	.80/lb. 1.00/lb.		
17	6.94	(8.80 min.) (11.00 min.)		
18	7.24	See Rate Groups		
19	7.54			
20	7.84			
21	8.14			
22	8.44			
23	8.74			
24	9.04			
25	9.34			
26	9.64			
27	9.94	Package over 40 lbs. are		
28	10.24	difficult to handle &		
29	10.54	are subject to damage.		
30	10.84			
31	11.14	41	14.14	
32	11.44	41	14.44	
33	11.74	43	14.74	
34	12.04	44	15.04	
35	12.34	45	15.34	
36	12.64	46	15.64	
37	12.94	47	15.94	
38	13.24	48	16.24	
39	13.54	49	16.54	
40	13.84	50	16.84	
		+.30/lb.		

First Class Mail

Oz.	Rate
1	.37
2	.60
3	.83
4	1.06
5	1.29
6	1.52
7	1.75
8	1.98
9	2.21
10	2.44
11	2.67
12	2.90
13	3.13
14	3.36
15	3.59
16	Use Priority Mail

Priority Mail

Lbs.	Rate
1	3.85

(No weight limit on "Flat Rate" envelopes)

2+   Zoned. See http://postcalc.usps.gov

*Consider Global Priority (air) Mail at $7.00 to North America and the Caribbean and $9.00 to the rest of the world.

To get the latest rates, see http://postcalc.usps.gov & http://www.uspsglobal.com/new/welcome.htm

UNITED PARCEL SERVICE: UPS provides excellent service, including daily pickup, but their prices for single books are not competitive with the Postal Service, and their shipments require more paperwork. Daily pickup service costs only $7 per week. Contact your local UPS office for prices and a UPS Customer Materials Kit or see http://www.ups.com.

By way of comparison, a one-pound parcel shipped coast to coast in the U.S. in 2002 costs the following:

Postal Service		United Parcel Service	
Media Mail (surface):	$ 1.42	Surface:	$ 5.66
Library Mail (surface):	$ 1.35	Second Day Air:	$12.12
Parcel post (surface):	$ 3.75	Next Day Air:	$26.51
Priority Mail (air):	$ 3.85		
Express Mail (air):	$17.85	**Federal Express**	
		Ground:	$ 4.04
		Second Day:	$10.04
		Overnight:	$23.43

OVERNIGHT DELIVERY SERVICE: Some customers want the books right away, and they will pay the extra cost, so it is wise to offer overnight delivery. Federal Express is the largest of the overnight companies, followed by UPS, Airborne, Purolator and Emery. UPS, the U.S. Postal Service and Federal Express are the three largest second-day delivery services. Most offer pickup service, but charges are lower if you drop off the package at their office or drop box. Check the *Yellow Pages* and call all the overnight services listed for supply kits of envelopes, cartons and bills of lading.

Overnight and fast deliveries to foreign countries vary greatly in price. Always call for prices before selecting a carrier. DHL is the oldest and largest international carrier.

See the Web sites of these delivery services in Appendix 2 under Shipping Services.

INTERNATIONAL SHIPMENTS: International parcels of printed matter are limited by the Postal Service to 5 kg. (11 lbs.). Larger shipments must be broken down into 5 kg. increments or wrapped in a larger carton weighing over 15 lbs., inserted into a mail sack and shipped as a *direct sack of prints* in *M bags*. Visit your post office for some No. 2 sacks and PS 158 tags. Also take some time to read section 225.953 of the *International Mail Manual*.

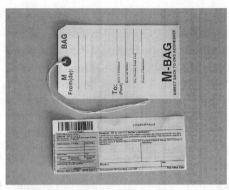

PS tag 158 & PS Form 2976

To ship in *direct sacks of prints*, line a carton with a heavy plastic bag and insert the books. Make sure the books are tightly packed and that they fit the cartons perfectly. Seal and reinforce the carton in all directions to guard against splitting. Then "double-box" by inserting the package into another carton and seal with paper or plastic tape. Xerox copier paper cartons are slightly larger than the cartons holding four stacks of 5.5" x 8.5" books and work very well. Affix the shipping label with the added words "Postage paid—direct sack of prints." Then band with reinforcing tape in all three directions. Weigh the package at this point and affix postage to a PS 158 tag. (Postage is paid on the contents, not the weight of the bag.) Turn the carton on end and slip a No. 2 mail sack down over it. Attach a shipping label to the PS 158 tag and attach the tag to the cinch clip on the mail sack. The Postal Service will pull the package out of the sack at the border, keep the sack and let the package continue by itself.

Most international shipments weighing more than 1 lb. require a "customs sticker." The type (PS2976 or PS2976A) depends on weight and/or shipping method.

POSTING

If your shipment weighs less than 1 lb., you can drop the weighed and stamped package off at the loading dock at the rear of the post office. Just drop it into a wheeled bin; do not wait in line at the counter inside. Most postal employees do not know much about classes and rates (just quiz one about direct sacks), so they aren't much help after a long wait in line. If you have a postage meter, you can drop off heavier packages at the loading dock because the meter imprint has a serial number and is traceable to you. If you don't have a postage meter, you have to hand over packages that weigh more than 1 lb. to an employee inside the post office because of the Unabomber rule.

Mail is usually sent from each post office to a centralized mail-handling facility before it is shipped out of town. If you drop the packages at this central facility, they will move out faster and will be subjected to less handling. For the address of your nearest mail-handling facility, consult the white pages of the telephone directory under the U.S. Government listings.

> Some years ago, I dropped off a load of packaged books at the branch post office where I have my postal box. Six days later, I was dropping off another load at the central mail-handling facility and discovered the previous shipment. It had taken the books six days to travel 10 miles at book rate.

If you like the large 3" rubber bands used by the Postal Service, you can get a box free. Just stop by the bulk mail office and tell them you are planning a large mailing. While there, pick up some mail trays, mail bins and some no. 2 mail bags. The trays are useful when processing and carrying large direct mailings of envelopes. The bins can be used to carry many small parcels to the post office, and the sacks will be used for direct sack shipments. Do not be bashful about asking for bins, sacks and trays. The Postal Service wants to lend them to you, because they make it easier for them to handle the mail.

ALTERNATIVES TO LICKING AND STICKING

POSTAGE METERS AND STAMPERS: Metered mail travels faster and is handled less. Stamped parcels are taken out of the bins at the post office, canceled and thrown back in. Another advantage is that whereas the postal clerks may compare stamps with weight, they rarely return metered mail for more postage.

Once your firm has grown and you are afraid some employees might be walking off with stamps, you might consider a meter. You can never stop employees from running a few personal letters through the machine, but this is better than losing a couple of $1 stamps every day.

A meter imprint makes your publishing company appear more established by eliminating that "postage-stamped, loving hands at home" look. The meter also allows you to print an advertising message on the outgoing mail.

On the other hand, postage meters cost money. There is no discount on postage, and the machine must be rented from a meter company.

Most postage meters come in two parts: the meter and the base unit. The base unit can be purchased outright, but the meter (the part holding the postage) can only be rented. Shop for a base unit that imprints on both envelopes and tapes for packages. Look for bases on the used market: at used business machine stores, swap meets and in the classified ads in local newspapers. Once you have purchased the base, contact the meter dealer for a matching meter. If you contract for your meter first, you will limit yourself in your choice of base units.

Make sure your base is for an electronic meter. Mechanical meters have been phased out.

Pitney Bowes used to have a lock on the market, but now there are some other companies competing with them. Check out Francotype-Postalia, Neopost and Ascom Hasler. Currently, the best deal is the Pitney/Bowes Personal Post™ postage meter. See http://PB.com.

Meters usually rent by the month on a yearly contract. Check prices for each model and make; they vary widely.

First-class mail can also be handled with a stamper machine filled with rolled stamps. Use the 100-stamp rolls; the rolls of 500 are too heavy to feed well. Stamper machines cost less than $25 at most office supply stores.

ONLINE DIGITAL POSTAGE is here. SimplyPostage.com/ USPS, Stamps.com, Neopost and Pitney Bowes let you print your own postage. For example, at Stamps.com, you download their software and send them a check for postage in advance. Their charge for this service ranges from $1.99 to $19.95 per month. They make their money on the monthly fee plus interest on your deposit account. See the Postal Service Web site for approved vendors: http://www.usps.gov.

You must go on line to type in the address of your customer and then print out the postage on your laser printer. Online postage is not yet as fast or as easy as a meter. See the online demonstrations. Compare the monthly service charge with the cost of a meter, and the time each involves.

METER SUPPLIES: If your meter permits, use regular, gummed paper meter tape; the pressure-sensitive labels are more expensive. Some rolls of meter tape have the gum on the outside, and some have it on the inside. Get the right one for your machine. Tape from sources other than the meter company is often less expensive but is sometimes a bit too narrow. Shop around. Newer meters use a thermal print ribbon instead of ink, which has the advantage of a consistent imprint, no smearing and no inking (you just have to replace the ribbon). If your meter uses ink, do not use just any ink. The postal machinery that turns the envelopes face up recognizes the fluorescent red ink supplied by the meter companies.

RETURNED BOOKS

Processing returns is not the best part of the book business. Anytime you are feeling depressed over a returned book, remember that some large publishers get a lot of their books back. The industry considers 20%, or a little more, to be normal. Smaller publishers rarely suffer such a high return rate.

When a book comes back, make out a receiving slip. This does not have to be a fancy form; a note on a scratch pad or your notation on the packing slip will do. But you need some written record. Note the date received, the sender and the condition of the book. Determine whether any damage was caused in mailing, or before shipping, by the condition of the package.

Bookstore shipments almost always arrive damaged, because they just will not pack the books correctly. Bookstores dump the books in a carton without a protective plastic bag or cushioning material, so the books rattle around and become scuffed and bent, or they throw three books in an oversize Jiffy bag, and the books rub against each other as they journey across the country.

On receipt, the good books should be returned to the storage area and the bad ones set aside in their box, pending settling up with the customer. Return the damaged books to the dealer with an invoice for the shipping and an explanation regarding the condition. Be sure to mark the books so they will be easy to spot if returned to you again. One publisher places a small black dot with a fine felt tip marker on the bottom edge of the book near the spine.

One well-known Eastern book wholesaler frequently orders books and returns them from different departments on the same day.

The object is to get your books into the stores. If the store has tried your book on the shelf and it hasn't sold, they should not be penalized for returning it. If, on the other hand, the book is not just shelf-worn but was obviously damaged in return transit due to poor packaging, the store or wholesaler should eat the cost.

Books returned by the customer because they were received damaged should be replaced at once. This is a cost of doing business and keeping happy clients.

Damaged books can be offered to acquaintances as *selected seconds* and donated to institutions. Some publishers offer them to the walk-in traffic at a 50% discount with the explanation that "all books look like this after a week."

When an individual retail order is returned by the Postal Service marked "Undeliverable," check the original order to verify the address. If the address is wrong, type a label with the correct address, then slip the whole book and package into another, larger package so the addressee will see what happened and why the shipment took so long.

If the address is correct, date the package and put the order and book aside and wait for your customer's anxious letter or call.

Some publishers have "order from" addresses that are different from their "return shipping" addresses because it is expensive and disruptive when cartons of books are delivered to the editorial offices. Be specific about your receiving address in your returns policy.

ORDER FULFILLMENT ALTERNATIVES

There are many ways to fulfill your orders besides doing it yourself. The alternatives are listed below.

Remember, however, that you will still need a small shipping facility for review copies, sales samples and other mailings. Keeping your fulfillment in-house will provide better inventory control, faster shipping of orders, fewer shipping errors, fewer damaged books and lower fulfillment costs.

JOINT REPRESENTATION: This is where a large publisher accepts a smaller one with like titles. Commonly, the big firm takes over all the marketing, distribution and billing functions as well. The cost can be high: 25% or more of the net sale. Like the commissioned sales reps, the firm gets credit for all the sales regardless of who generates them. Not only does the arrangement cost more than doing it yourself, but you never learn the ropes. You become more dependent than ever, and the large publisher may push its titles (which are more profitable) before selling yours. Unless you simply do not have the time or the will to do your own marketing and fulfillment, joint representation should not be considered until you have operated long enough to make an educated decision and draft an iron-clad contract.

FULFILLMENT WAREHOUSES: If you are unable to spend the time picking, packing and posting, lack the necessary space, or would rather concentrate on writing and marketing, there are commercial fulfillment firms that will do the job for you. Typically, they have a price list of charges for packaging and many other services, plus postage and packing materials. Some charge a percentage of the order. They may also charge per month per skid of books for storage. Figure roughly one cent per book per month for warehousing. You can send your orders and invoices to these fulfillment warehouses (or they will cut the invoices for you). Most also accept credit card orders from your customers via a toll-free telephone number and offer accounting, invoicing, order tracking, returns and sometimes even collection services. The best have 24-hour order taking via mail, phone, fax, email and their Web site.

Fulfillment firms advertise in the classifieds in *Publishers Weekly,* and a large listing can be found in *Literary Market Place* under "Shipping Services."

Remember, fulfillment houses only store, take orders and ship; they do not *sell*. They will not get your books into bookstores or sell subsidiary rights. Moving books from your garage to someone's warehouse does not mean your books have been turned into cash.

For more information on fulfillment, see *Book Fulfillment* at http://ParaPublishing.com or under Para Publishing Special Reports in Appendix 2. See the list of fullfillment services in Appendix 2.

11
Electronic Book Publishing and Promoting

Electronic Books, Downloadable Books, Automated Printing, Print on Demand and Online Promotion

Nonfiction book writing, production and promotion are changing due to the increasing demand for information and rapid advances in technology. Instead of investing money in long print runs and inventory space, books can now be delivered electronically and/or printed one at a time as needed.

This chapter is a recapitulation of the book writing and publishing process according to the **New Book-Publishing Model.** These pages will repeat some items from previous chapters but will also bring all the elements of writing, production and promotion together.

We have seen the future and it beeps. Welcome to digital smoke and mirrors.

INFORMATION @ THE SPEED OF THOUGHT

The opportunities for authors are expanding so quickly that we are no longer sure what a "book" is. We do know that nonfiction authors are information providers, that the Web is facilitating rapid delivery of text and that there are new economical printing techniques.

To save money on book printing, many of the larger publishers have resorted to smaller type, reduced leading between lines and narrower margins (resulting in a wider text block). These books are more difficult to read. The type size in an "eBook," (electronic book), however, can be adjusted to suit the reader.

The electronic edition of your book will be far more useful to your reader. In addition to being searchable and less expensive, all the referenced URLs (Web addresses) will be hyperlinked for quick access. Online readers can just click on the address and go to the referenced Web site.

The only ink-on-paper ("dead tree") books in the future will be coffee table books—books as an art form. These books will be used to decorate homes and offices. Information will ultimately be disseminated electronically without sacrificing trees.

Publishing ink on paper is going to become a mere service to readers. The real product we're going to sell is the digital product.
—Bruno de Sa Moreira, *Zeroheure* **magazine**

People need more information to make critical decisions, and they want their information fast. As an author, you have the information some of them need, and you can get it to them faster electronically than through traditional hand or Postal delivery.

We are not just in the "information age"; we are in the "electronic information age" or, better yet, the "communication age." Fortunately, authors deal in content that can be communicated. The world of knowledge is going from a paper culture to an electronic culture. It is only a question of how we want to package our information.

If book publishers can't see the writing on the wall, it's because the writing is not on the wall. It's on a computer screen.

ELECTRONIC COSTS: The costs of *electronic* delivery of information are decreasing, while the costs of *physical* storage and delivery are increasing. That is why the fax has become a common office machine. We have learned it does not pay to give someone a letter and 34¢ to hand deliver the message across the country. Fax will do it faster and cheaper.

We used to recommend a budget of $12,000 to produce the pages and cover, print 3,000 copies and initially market a 192-page softcover book. Today, that book can be electronically produced, printed (500 copies) and launched in the marketplace for far less.

Be leery of electronic publishing services that claim they will provide you with a book cover and typesetting for a few hundred dollars. Most likely, you will wind up with a simple, unattractive generic cover that will be rejected by distributors, bookstores and buyers. The typesetting may be done overseas with a pre-set page layout and typestyle rather than a unique page design or type to match the book's content. They will not do proofing or spell-checking because they don't speak English and must grind out as many pages as possible. Ultimately, you get what you pay for.

Books are going electronic. Some bound books will soon be as dead as the trees they are printed on.

DISINTERMEDIATION is a new marketing buzzword. It means cutting out all the intermediaries such as publishers, distributors, wholesalers, bookstores and printers so customers can deal directly with manufacturers. In our case, readers can buy directly from the author.

Customers for many products are dealing directly with manufacturers. Dell does not assemble a computer until after it is sold and they receive the money. In fact, Dell gets paid before they have to pay for the parts going into the computer. Compare that production model with the Detroit style. The automobile manufacturers make cars and put them on lots. They often sit on 60 days of inventory. It would make more sense to allow people to order a car online, pay for it and get it built and delivered in two to three weeks—custom configured like many computers. The new buzzword for this process is "mass customization."

In our case, readers can buy directly from the author. By cutting out the middleperson, we can sell the written product for less and still make more money. With this new technology, authors can spend more time writing and less in production and fulfillment.

The breakthroughs are leading authors to bypass publishers, retailers to become publishers and publishers to become bookstores.
—Don Clark in the *Wall Street Journal*.

BEGIN WITH RELEASE 1.1: Now you do not even have to finish writing the nonfiction book to sell it. You can post an initial chapter or two on your web site and/or at a "content site" and invite feedback. Then as you add to the "book," you can post new material as versions 2.0, 3.0 and so on, and sell to the same customers again.

Traditionally, books are published as one-shot one-season (four-month) projects. If the book sells well, it is reprinted. If it does not, it is pulled from the shelves (and eventually remaindered). This model makes sense for fiction (entertainment) that will not be updated. It does not make sense for nonfiction (information). Savvy publishers have been updating their nonfiction and publishing new editions for years.

Electronic editions can even contain a pop-up message inviting the reader to click on a hyperlink to the author's Web site to see if there is a new edition. Now you can remind the reader over and over again—even if a friend loaned the "book."

NEW BOOK-PUBLISHING MODEL

Electronic production with the new book-publishing model is easier, faster, less expensive and will bring authors a greater return. You *can* do it yourself. You can make more money, get to press sooner and keep control of your work. You can repurpose or multipurpose your content, publish it in several different ways and wring maximum value out of your literary effort.

The new book-publishing model is not strictly self-publishing. It is a trial run of 500 books that allows you, not only to sell them, but also to approach some agents and publishers with a book rather than a manuscript. You can also send out review copies, approach distributors, wholesalers, book clubs and make other sales. The new book-publishing model allows you to cover all your bases. Here are the steps.

> *Soon, eBook sales will be the test market for print books: if it sells well in e-version and POD, the author and/or publisher will feel better about undertaking the design and production costs of a print run, and traditional printing will make economic sense.*
>
> **—Tom Brosnahan,** *InfoExchange*

WRITING FOR ELECTRONIC PUBLISHING

Write your books in "book layout format"; make your manuscript page look like a book page. Do not use traditional Courier typeface and double spacing. The advantages are that the text looks like a book and not a manuscript, you always know approximately how many finished pages you have, and the book is nearly typeset. Use the margin measurements of a similar book you like, or see the recommended margin settings in "Manuscript Pages" in Chapter 4.

On the Web, a journey of a thousand leagues begins with the first keystroke.
—**Scott Gross**, *Positively Outrageous Service*

SPEECH RECOGNITION SOFTWARE converts speech directly to computer text. Now you can bypass the keyboarding and dictate right into your computer. Just speak into the microphone, giving punctuation and formatting commands as you go. While speech recognition software at one time was very expensive, today it doesn't cost much more than a fancy keyboard. For more details, see *Writing Nonfiction: Turning Thoughts into Books* by Dan Poynter at http://ParaPublishing.com.

The speech recognition software programs currently available are Dragon Systems' NaturallySpeaking, IBM's Via Voice and a MicroSoft product. See Speech Recognition Software in Appendix 2 for their locations. Also see *The Dragon Naturally Speaking Guide* by Dan Newman at http://www.SayICan.com.

DON'T JUST WRITE—BUILD: Today, authors "build" their books; writing is just part of the building process. As an author, you know your subject. You can describe it, explain it and teach it. The eBook simply provides you with more visual aids to help you get your point to your reader. Now, in addition to the printed word, you have photos, graphics, animation, color, dimension, motion, sound and hyperlinks to more information. Your pBook (paper) will have static words and b/w photographs but the eBook version will be far more versatile.

USE HYPERLINKS: As you write, research the Web for URLs (web addresses) that will provide more information to your readers. Include these addresses in your text. The downloadable edition of your book will be even more valuable with these hyperlinks. As you visit these Web sites, you will also pick up some late information, facts and figures that will improve your own text.

Another electronic enhancement is hyperlinking words in the glossary to references in the text.

ART can include photographs, line drawings, animated GIFs, backgrounds, borders, bullets, buttons, icons, horizontal lines, charts, graphs and more. Many of these are available to you copyright-free from http://www.ClipArt.com for a very low annual fee. For custom-drawn cartoons, see http://www.cartoonresource.com.

PHOTOGRAPHS involve the use of a digital camera to import the JPG image into your manuscript. Images can be imported into the word processing file or linked. If linked, you will find it easier to extract the photo for making adjustments such as the light/dark level.

For both ink and toner printing, photographs should be converted to black/white 300 dpi TIF files. For Web, computer or CD use, the photographs should be converted to color 72 dpi JPG files.

Once you select a book printer, request scanning instructions so that your photos will reproduce well on their printing equipment.

The book printer will screen each black and white photo file when going to film or plate. Using digital photo files will make the whole process faster, easier and cheaper; you will not have to screen the photos yourself.

DRAWINGS: Use a scanner to scan your line illustrations and import the images into your manuscript. For both ink and toner printing, drawings should be converted to black/white 300 dpi TIF files. For Web, computer or CD use, the drawings should be converted to color 72 dpi GIF files.

INDEXING: Use the indexing feature in Microsoft Word to mark the words you want automatically inserted into the index. To find a professional indexer, see http://www.asindexing.org.

COPYEDITING: Submit your completed manuscript to your copy editor on a Zip disk or rewritable CD and have the editor make changes directly onto the disk and return it to you. If the corrections are made on a hard copy instead of directly onto the disk, you or someone else will have to enter the changes and proof them, creating additional opportunities for errors.

ELECTRONIC PAGE PRODUCTION

Typesetting is nearly finished if you leave your work in the word processing program. Microsoft Word is the most popular word processing software and can be coupled with programs to quickly translate the work into HTML, XML and PDF files.

PAGE DESIGN AND LAYOUT: Books with simple layouts may be produced solely in a word processing program, such as Microsoft Word or WordPerfect. Or they may be given a more professional polish by using page design and layout programs such as Microsoft Publisher, PageMaker, InDesign, QuarkXpress and Ventura Publisher. These programs will aid in page design and will refine the page layout and typesetting look of your book beyond that of standard word processing software.

FILE CONVERSION: Convert the book file to PDF, XML and LIT for electronic book readers. The electronic version of your book will have excellent photos and drawings and can even be in color.

- **PDF.** Convert the word processing or page layout file directly to an Adobe Acrobat 5.0 Portable Document Format file. Acrobat is a page-oriented image file. In effect, it "photographs" the page you see on your screen. Acrobat 5.0 integrates with Microsoft Office (including Microsoft Word). When installed, Acrobat automatically adds a toolbar button in Word, Excel and PowerPoint. A single click brings up the PDF Maker output plug-in. PDF has become easy to use, predictable and it saves time and money.

  Once in PDF format, your manuscript can be used in many ways or multipurposed. The PDF file can be used for downloadable online delivery, put on a CD or sent to a book printer. The PDF file is also much smaller than your word processing file, so it can fit on a floppy or be sent as an email attachment.

  Adobe's PDF Merchant/Web Buy allows you to encrypt your file so that only the purchaser can read it.

  Acrobat lists for $249, but street prices are under $180. Upgrades are $100 or less. Look for manufacturer's part no. 22001201 or see http://www. adobe.com.

•❖ **XML/OEB.** Convert the word processing or page layout file to Open Ebook (OEB) format, which is based on the HTML and XML Internet core languages. The OEB format can be read on notebook computers, Palm Pilots, Handspring's Visor, the Rocket eBook, the Softbook and even on a $30 Nintendo Gameboy. Softbook Press announced a software add-on that will save Microsoft Word files as Open eBook files. See Open Book Publication Structure 1.0 at http://www.openebook.org.

•❖ **LIT.** The "Microsoft Reader" with ClearType™ is based on XML. ClearType sharpens the text on LCD (notebook, palmtop, etc.) screens, making it easier to read.

The Microsoft Reader software also improves the typography with ample margins, justified text, proper leading and kerning. You can highlight text, bookmark a page and annotate the book—just like a paper book. In addition, you can search for words, click to a dictionary and resize the type. The Bookplate technology electronically encodes the purchaser's name on the title page to discourage unlawful distribution. More severe copy protection is also available. See http://www. microsoft. com/reader.

COVER PRODUCTION

To make your "book" look credible, you still need a "book cover" for Web site display and magazine reviews. Packaging attracts consumers to products. Even if you decide to forego the print edition of your book and publish just the electronic version, you will need a cover image to sell it. We recommend that you deal with a recognized cover artist. You can, however, cut out a lot more of the traditional expenses besides printing.

Online bookstores such as Amazon.com want a flat, straight-on image of the cover. They do not want an angled shot that shows the thickness of the book.

A traditional paperbound cover can cost you $1,200 or more for design and production, $300 for color separations (film) and the expense of extra trips through the press. The front cover requires artistic creativity and the back cover needs copy fitting. Both take time and cost money. For example, Robert Howard, who pioneered flashy book covers for the small press, might charge up to $1,800 for the concept, design, production and film for a front/spine/back cover that will be printed in the traditional way. The comparative cost might be $1,000 for the concept, design and production of *only* the front cover on disk (for a Web site, the back cover sales copy can be in straight text). And he might charge $1,900 for both the electronic and print versions. Contact Robert Howard at http://www.Book Graphics.com. Also see http://ParaPublishing.com/supplier and Book Designers & Cover Artists in the Appendix.

On the other hand, if you plan just an electronic edition (no printed version) and require only a cover image for the Web, you may save by doing it yourself. If you are on a tight budget for this project, add the title, subtitle and author's name to a background image. You may choose from a variety of color photos and drawings at http://www.ArtToday.com; http://www.Artville.com; and http://www.eyewire.com.

COVER FOR TRADITIONAL PRINTING: Have your cover artist oversee the color separation and printing stages of the cover. Make the color separations locally and then send the composite film negatives and match print to the printer. If you send the cover file directly to the printer on disk or as an attachment to email, you will not have an example to proof before printing unless you have the printer make a color check print and send it to you for approval.

COVER FOR DIGITAL PRINTING: If you are printing a short run using digital disk-to-image printing machinery, send the printer the disk and a digital color proof such as an Iris or Rainbow print.

PRINTING THE BOOK

DIGITAL PQN (Print Quantity Needed): PQN printing machines produce books from a PDF file on a disk. This short run printing uses a higher speed direct-to-image (disk to drum) electrostatic process with a *toner* blend that reproduces photographs well. There is no film, plate or liquid ink as in traditional printing. The process is cost effective for quantities from 100 to 2,500 copies. It is no longer necessary to print 3,000+ books; 100 or 500 can be produced at a reasonable per-unit cost. Color covers are usually done with the same digital process.

Putting a lot of ink on paper is now just an option; a good one if there is large prepublication demand such as advanced sales to bookstores and/or a sale to a book club. However, there is no longer any reason to print 3,000 or more copies of your book on spec. In the future, most books will not be manufactured until after they are sold.

COMPARING COSTS: Let's compare prices for traditional ink-press printing, digital PQN and digital POD (print-on-demand, one book at a time. We will compare a softcover (perfect bound) 144 page 5.25" x 8.25" book with black text and a four-color cover. Prices will vary with the current cost of paper.

1. **Press (ink on paper):** $1.55 each but you have to print 3,000 to get a price this low. So, your print bill will be $4,650.

2. **Digital PQN (short run):** 500 copies for $3.00 each or a print bill of $1,500, or 100 copies for $5.17 each for a print bill of $517.

3. **Digital POD (single copies):** May run $6 to $10 each as they are often bundled with other services. Print-On-Demand is a good option when a book has run its course, your inventory is exhausted and you still receive orders for a couple of copies a month. Rather than invest in inventory, you can have books made as needed. You may even increase the price slightly to cover the higher unit cost because the book is a "special order" of a limited or out-of-print edition.

HARDCOVER PQN BOOKS: Most PQN books are manufactured with soft covers, called "perfect binding." In traditional printing, hard or "case" binding runs about $1.00 extra per book. For PQN production, the additional cost is $1.65 to $3.25 each, depending on the page count (thickness) of the book due to setup charges. Those prices include the hard covers and the dust jackets.

TECHNICAL ASPECTS: The **quality** of the toner-based PQN and POD printing is actually better. The softcover or hardcover books look just like traditional books. There are no light and dark pages as in ink-on-paper printing. The print density is maintained electronically unlike offset printing where a variation of 5% to 10% from page to page is a regular occurrence.

Delivery time for PQN books is measured in days not weeks (depending on your printers back-up of projects). With your disk on file, reprints can be initiated with a telephone call and the books may be shipped directly to your buyers.

Signatures of PQN short-run printing are just two pages because the print engines print 2 pages (both sides) at a time instead of 32 or 48. Now you do not have to design your book's page count in large signature increments.

CUSTOMIZING AND SPECIAL VERSIONS: Because your books can be printed in short runs and since the new print engines print two pages at a time, you may customize your book for your customer. If you make a premium sale to a company, it will cost just pennies to bind in a letter from the CEO or to add the company logo to the cover. This is called "Mass Customization."

Since the laser printers are driven by computer, books can have several versions of some chapters, each aimed at a particular type of reader. These are called "Module Books," as the book can be assembled for a particular reader. The customer might be asked some basic questions such as "What stage are you in? Are you new to the subject, familiar with it or an expert in it? Where are you located?" The information may be different in some sections if the reader is located outside the U.S. "What language do you want the book to be in?" And so on. Then the program would select various versions of the chapters or modules and assemble them into a "specialized book" to meet the needs of the buyer.

BENEFITS TODAY AND TOMORROW: Economical **color digital printing** is also here. Four-color children's and coffee table books can be manufactured at reasonable prices in quantities as low as 100 copies. Digital technology eliminates the color separations, long print run requirements, and 10-week printing and shipping schedules from overseas color printers.

But if your book is *black and white* inside, you can have just 100 to 500 books electronically produced and used for promotional purposes. Authors can send copies to agents and publishers. Publishers can send copies to major reviewers, distributors, wholesalers, catalogs, specialty stores, associations, book clubs, premium prospects, foreign publishers suggesting translations and various opinion molders.

Digital production offers lower investment costs, reduction in inventory, custom publishing, quicker revisions/reprints and elimination of obsolescent inventory. Now you can get into print cheaper and produce books only after they are sold.

Historically, a book had to be published in hard cover to be taken seriously by the media. In a few years, a book will have to be in paper form, as well as digital, to be considered a commercial success. A printed-paper edition will signify that the book is selling well enough to justify the ink printing.

For more information on PQN and POD book production, see the listing of Digital Printers in the Appendix 2.

ELECTRONIC PUBLISHING

Once your manuscript is written and converted to a PDF file, it may be "repurposed:" put on your Web site for downloading by a buyer, uploaded to eBooksellers such as Amazon.com, BarnesAnd Nobel.com or BookLocker, read on eBook readers, put on a CD or the disk can be sent to any of the three types of book manufacturers discussed. Now you can provide your book in any version your customer wants (called "multi-purposing") and wring maximum value out of your work. Today, we are no longer sure what a "book" is.

CD-ROM VERSION: Make up a few CDs so those who do not have wideband Internet access can play the book on their PCs. Include the Adobe Acrobat Reader on the CD for those who do not have it loaded on their machine. Your CD edition will be searchable, have live hyperlinks, etc. You could even add motion and sound.

For low-quantity CD duplication, see http://www.natlcass. com. Currently, they are quoting 10 copies at $5.75 each and 100 duplicates for $2.28 each.

List the CD with online bookstores that are not set up for the downloadable version.

EBOOK READERS (hardware devices) provide info-to-go; they make the electronic information portable and are usually small enough to be held in one hand. Make your entire book available for eBooks in PDF and LIT formats. Here are the major players. See their Web sites for details.

- **Everybook,** a two-screen, portrait facing-page system, uses the PDF format; http://www.everybook.net.

- **Gemstar eBook by RCA,** a portable device that comes with its own software; http://www.ebook-gemstar.com. Order the Gemstar eBook by RCA from Barnes & Noble stores or http://www.bn.com.

- **Pocket PC,** a powerful multipurpose device. http.//www.Pocketpc.com.

See Document 615, *Electronic Books: Moving from a Print Culture to an Electronic Culture*, at http://ParaPublishing.com.

By 2020, 50% of everything we read will be in electronic form.
**—Dick Brass, Microsoft vice-president
in charge of technology development**

DOWNLOADABLE BOOKS FROM THE WEB: "Downloadable virtual books" allow you to write, store, sell and read your work without printing it out. Put your entire book on your own Web site in PDF and LIT. Customers can then pay for, download and read your book on their computer screens. For example, Para Publishing sells 51 unlockable reports. You can read them or print them out at http://ParaPublishing.com.

If you publish fiction, place the first chapter of your book on your site as a free read. The first chapter is usually full of action and encourages readers to continue. If you publish nonfiction, place the first page of each chapter on your site as a free read or "skim." In nonfiction, you are selling information, not entertainment. You will convert more browsers into buyers if you give them an overview of the material in each chapter throughout the book.

Also put the entire book on other Web sites in PDF or LIT for downloading. Since these sites are proliferating at a great rate and because their offerings are constantly evolving, minimal information is given below. See the sites for more information.

- **Amazon's Zshops.** You can sell almost anything with Amazon's one-click ordering; http://www.amazon.com.

- **BookLocker** sells downloadable books in PDF format; http://www.booklocker.com.

- **Cyclopsmedia.com** sells downloadable books in PDF format; http://www. cyclopsmedia.com.

- **E-reads** delivers eBooks in Microsoft, Adobe or RCA format. They also supply books printed on demand; http://www.e-reads.com.

- **1stBooks Library** will post your book for download and will print POD copies for you; http://www.1stbooks.com.

- **iUniverse.com** http://www.iUniverse.com.

- **NetLibrary,** sells downloadable books to consumers and libraries. Online access to the entire collection is $29.95 per year; http://www.netlibrary.com.

- **Palm Digital Media** provides eBooks for palm and CE computers. Handspring's Visor has a 50-book cartridge; http://www.palmdigitalmedia.com.

For more eBook and POD services see http://www.bookwire. com.

Today there are only two types of publishers: those in danger of missing the electronic boat and those who do not even know there is a boat to catch.

PRICING DOWNLOADABLE BOOKS: No pricing standards have been established yet because there has not been enough experience with various pricing strategies.

Since part of the "sale" does not have to be shared with publishers, distributors, wholesalers or bookstores, the author makes more on each sale than he or she would with royalties from a traditional publisher.

Conventional thinking is that since electronic downloads are cheaper to produce than ink-on-paper (dead tree) printed books, they should sell for less. Also, when products are less expensive, people tend to buy more. On the other hand, this thinking overlooks the "value," real or perceived, of the product, especially if the book is unique and has little competition or a very narrow "specialized" market that needs the information.

All "books" are not the same. We should not even think of them as books. They are either entertainment (fiction) or information products and reports (nonfiction).

Fiction has to compete with all forms of entertainment, from other books to movies to taking the kids to the zoo. People are short of time today and have a wide range of entertainment from which to choose. Thus the price of fiction is an issue: some authors are cutting the eBook price by 75%. For example, a $19.95 softcover book sells for $4.95 as a download. Unless the eBook is priced low, people may rent a couple of videos instead.

Nonfiction can be priced lower for the electronic version with the hope that the lower price will increase the volume of sales. Some authors have cut the price 65%. For example, their $19.95 softcover book sells for $6.95 as a download.

Reports that provide up-to-date specialized information, often sell for the same amount as the paper edition, because the buyer needs the latest information instantly, and will pay your price to get it. In the future, reports will be posted on Web sites in PDF and LIT forms and there won't even be a paper edition. The only price will be for the downloadable edition.

Some larger publishers are testing the electronic waters by pricing their books at or near the printed book price. They seem to be protecting their (outdated) print editions.

PRICING PRINTED BOOKS: While you do not have to cut prices on your downloadable "books," some publishers are tempted to reduce the list price on their "dead tree" editions. They know that potential customers learn about their books on their Web site and then click over to Amazon.com to buy at a discount. They figure they must give away 30% or more to get the sale on their Web site rather than through Amazon. However, by cutting the price, they are cheapening the product and competing with all their dealers. It is better to maintain your list price, support your dealers, not compete with them or worry about those customers who buy from a dealer, online or elsewhere. It is better that someone makes the sale as a portion comes to you anyway.

Do not charge so little for your book that it does not appear to have much value, especially if it is timely, unique and has a narrow market. Fortunately, with downloadable books, it is easy to change the price. Experiment.

AUDIOBOOKS

Once your text is on disk, you have a script for your audio book. Some of your potential clients do not have time to read your book but would like to listen to it while commuting.

Spoken word audio turns your car into a university.

—Judit Sinclair

Spoken-word audiotapes and CDs will soon be replaced by downloadable files. We will listen to these files on MP3-type players. See the following Web sites:

http://www.audible.com
http://www.diamondmm.com
http://www.nomadworld.com

PROMOTING ELECTRONIC BOOKS

Since you are not printing a quantity of books, you can't promote the title the traditional way: sending out 500 review and opinion-molder copies. But the book must still be promoted in order to sell it. Fortunately, you can now promote books electronically and avoid long book print runs, large inventories, brochure printing and postage fees. You can get reviewers and potential buyers to come and see/try/buy your book with broadcast email. Use email to draw people to your Web site. List the URL in your email signature.

EMAIL PROMOTION: When email is sent selectively, it is not "spam" or unwanted junk mail. Book announcements should only be sent to existing customers, potential customers on opt-in lists and targeted members of the press. Match your offer to those who have already expressed an interest in this type of information.

> ➷ **House List.** Start now to gather email addresses from your existing customers. You will use this list to send announcements of new information products ("books"), seminars and appearances at book signings. Enter the names into your email address book or a database program such as Microsoft Access.

•• **Rental Lists.** You can rent email address lists of people who have requested information about certain types of products. Match your book to the listees as closely as possible. If your book is on skydiving, you do not want a list of general book buyers, you want a list of skydivers.

To find email lists, go to Liszt at http://www.liszt.com, for newsgroups, go to Excite at http://www.exite.com or even better, Deja.com at http://www.deja.com. Deja even lets you "subscribe" to certain topics.

•• **Reviewer Lists.** Some periodical editors prefer to receive email, some like faxes and some favor traditional Postal Service delivery. Eventually, everyone will get used to email announcements and news releases. Your mission is to send an email announcement that is perfectly targeted to the interests of the editor (and his or her readers) and is so interesting that he or she will want to print it in their periodical or list it on their Web site.

Make up fax and email lists of appropriate reviewers. For example, if you have a book on skydiving, make up lists of the 72 parachute and 243 aviation magazines worldwide. Review the magazine and newsletter directories at the library and photocopy the email addresses. Enter the names into your email address book or a database program such as Microsoft Access. Check Chapter 7 as well as the following directories:

- *Standard Periodical Directory* (thousands of magazines; http://www.mediafinder.com.

- Ulrich's *International Periodicals Directory* (many U.S. and foreign periodicals); http://www.ulrichsweb.com.

- Hudson's *Subscription Newsletter Directory*, PO Box 311, Rhinebeck, NY 12572; 914-876-2081; mail to: hphudson@aol.com; http://www.Newsletter-clearinghse.com.

- Gale Group's *Newsletters in Print*; http://www.Galegroup.com.

- E-Zine-List. Thousands of electronic magazines by category. Send your news releases to those who match the subject matter of your book; http://www.meer.net/johnl/e-zine-list.

ELECTRONIC MEDIA KITS AND READING COPIES: email a pitch letter to the editors and reviewers and invite them to your Web site to see your book and press kit: bio, testimonials, news releases, etc. Tell them what is in the press/media kit and remind them they will save time because they can download what they want, and do not have to retype the material. Send them to a reviewers' area on your site to read the book free online. Capture the reviewer's address when they log on. Add the reviewer to your list and notify them directly when you are promoting your next book.

Your mission is to design an online press kit that is so useful the reviewers will flock to use it.

Send an email to editors of newsletters, magazines and e-zines and offer them the opportunity to excerpt parts of your book free. Ask them to include source, copyright and ordering information at the end of the excerpt.

Sending out 500 printed review copies uses up a lot of books and postage. Some reviewers do not want the review copies. Some will request a book without intending to review it, because they plan to make it a gift to someone else or sell it. Inviting the reviewer to come to your site for a free read and promotional information is a great qualifier and it saves a lot of your money.

Email promotions can result in slightly fewer responses than traditional mailings and follow-up telephone calls. But the costs in time and money are far less and the responses begin immediately. You can also inexpensively repeat the email pro- motion with a new slant ("hook") every couple of months.

PROMOTION SERVICES: Do not hire the "spammers" who flood your email box with offers to promote your site or product. Doing so will cost you a lot of money as spammers send their mass junk email to broad unqualified lists. Their work also encourages more spam, both out and back to you.

Instead, consider hiring a teenage relative to surf the Web and promote your new book. Give the youngster a small commission on every book sold as an incentive. Ask him or her to send individual announcement messages to those interested in your type of book and to periodicals that might review it.

Direct Contact Media Services will send out your news release to carefully selected media via fax and email. Paul Krupin will rewrite your news release to make it more useful to the media. For 25¢ per faxed page (around $400), he will fax or email the announcement to 1,500 to 2,500 targeted print, radio and TV outlets. Contact him at 800-457-8746 or at his Web site: http://www.book-publicity.com.

For more ideas on promoting books online, see *U-Publish.com* by Dan Poynter and Danny O. Snow at http://www.u-publish.com.

CLIPPING SERVICE: You will be able to trace most of the reviews that appear about your book. But to make sure you are alerted to even more, subscribe to a (free) clipping service. See http://www.excite.com/info/newstracker/quickstart .

RADIO INTERVIEWS: To make yourself available for radio and TV interviews, post your own free listing at:

> http://www.PublicityDepot.com
> http://www.guestfinder.com

For more ways to get on radio and TV, see Document 602, Interviews, at http://ParaPublishing.com.

To find out what subjects Oprah likes to cover on her show, see http://www.oprah.com.

If you build it, they will come.
—Anon

OTHER WEB PROMOTION

Your *Web site* is the center of your promotion program. You want to sell your books there, post all your press kit materials, let visitors register for your mailing list and so on. Make your company "Web-site centric".

Expensive (to print and distribute) four-color brochures are no longer necessary, but you do need ways to get people to visit your site. Use a two-to-four-panel *business card* to explain the benefits of your site and direct people to it. This card can be handed out or enclosed in envelopes and packages. People might toss a brochure, but they usually keep a business card.

Use different cards for each line of your business; they must be subject-specific. For example, Para Publishing has one business card for the book writing/publishing division of our site and another for the parachute/skydiving division. People interested in one subject probably are not interested in the other. When designing your card, think *benefits*.

Your card should have a photograph of the book's cover, your usual contact information and a list of all the resources that can be found on your Web site.

Alternatively, *postcard mailings* can be made to promote and direct people to the site. Postcards are much less expensive to distribute than direct mail letters in envelopes. The postcard should be laden with benefits and be subject-specific. Show what can be found on your site.

Postcards and business cards are available from Jefferson/Keeler, McGrew Color Graphics (800-877-7700) and MWM Dexter Cos. (800-354-9007). Request catalogs.

ONLINE COMMUNITIES: Participate in appropriate email lists (Listservs), chatrooms, newsgroups and other online affinity meetings.

RELATED WEB SITES: Surf the Web for sites related to yours. When you find one that matches your book, contact the owner and suggest a dealership. Get as many opinion molders in your field as possible to sell your book.

POST YOUR PROMOTION SCHEDULE: Autographings, mini seminars, workshops and speaking engagements bring attention to the book and result in some book sales. Post your signing schedule at *Publishers Weekly* Authors on the Highway; http://www.publishersweekly.com. Post your complete promotional schedule on your Web site.

ONLINE BOOKSTORES: Offer both eBook (electronic book) and pBook (printed) editions of your work to the online bookstores. Contact them for their "information for publishers" about how to submit and get listed. Annotate your listings by sending cover art, table of contents, back cover copy, reviews, etc.

http://www.amazon.com
http://www.BarnesAndNoble.com
http://www.borders.com
http://www.booksamillion.com

SELLING ELECTRONIC RIGHTS

Send POD copies of your book to literary agents and publishers and offer to sell the print rights. See their listings in *Literary Market Place* and *Writers Market* to match the subject matter of your book to the specialties of the publishers and/or agents. Do not send to all and do not send to those unqualified. Pitch only those with a good track record for your genre or category of book.

To reach even more agents and publishers, send a POD copy to the Maui Writers Conference Manuscript Marketplace. For registration forms, see http://www.mauiwriters.com.

FOREIGN RIGHTS: Use email to ask foreign publishers if they would like to buy electronic, print or other subsidiary rights and translate your book into their language. Send publishers directly to a Rights section on your Web site. That section will provide a complete book, author bio, testimonials, cover image, news releases, back cover sales copy and other promotional materials. Capture their address when they log on. Then follow up.

For publisher email addresses, see *International Literary Market Place*. It lists publishers outside North America by country. Start with the major language groups: Germany, France, Italy, Spain and Japan. Select publishers that publish in your subject area. If you can't find many, email the national publishing association for that particular country, describe your book and ask for suggested matches.

Send rights information to John Baker at *Publishers Weekly Rights Alert* e-magazine at http://www.publishersweekly.com/rightsalert. Also see the RightsCenter at http://www.rights center.com and PMA's Virtual Book Fair at http://www.pma-online.org.

The time may come when all books are electronic and sold from the author's Web site. Since everyone in the world has access to your site, you will translate your work into other languages and sell it yourself. But, you will still make "dealers" out of the foreign publishers to gain access to their existing customers.

ISBN: Remember that each edition of your book—paper, download, audio, disk, etc.—must have a unique ISBN to differentiate it from the other editions. See the ISBN discussion in Chapter 5.

CONCLUSION

In the future, nonfiction book publishing will see minimized inventories and maximized relationships between authors and customers (readers). Publishing will become customer-centric through electronic targeting and "books" will thrive on uniqueness, customization and variety. Book writing and publishing is changing—for the better.

The New "Book" Model

© Dan Poynter

Creating the Content → PDF → Producing the "Work" → Promoting the Editions

Creating the Content

A. Set up.
Idea for your book
Qualify project according to the Six Musts. WN pg. 40
See *Writing Nonfiction: Turning Thoughts into Books*
Research the subject, title and competition.
Stores, Amazon, Ingram 615-213-6803
Get a Model Book.
Draft back cover sales copy. Doc 116, WN Ch 6.
Select a working title. WN Ch 5.
Set up the binder for the manuscript. WN Ch 7&8
Assemble research materials into chapter piles.

B. Build the content. WN Ch 8.
1st draft. Assemble the elements
Write text in MS-Word in page-layout format.
Import digital photographs
Adobe PhotoDeluxe or PhotoShop or PhotoSuite
Import scanned drawings
Add art from Web: http://www.ClipArt.com
Find quotations on Web:
http//www.geocities.com/~spanoudi/quote.html
Request stories from colleagues with email
Add URL hyperlinks to references

2nd draft. Content edit. Fill in the blanks.

3rd draft. Peer review for feedback. Use email.
Get testimonials for back cover, etc.

4th draft. Copy edit (punctuation, grammar).
Fact check.
Proofread.
http://www.iog.wayne.edu/FR/html/proof.html

C. Convert to: WN pgs 29-30
1. PDF file with Adobe Acrobat
2. LIT file, MS-Reader with ReaderWorks

D. Get cover art
http://ParaPublishing.com/supplier.cfm?

Producing the "Work"

Publish: print & electronic versions. SPM Ch 11.

A. pBooks (Photos & Dwgs: 300 dpi TIF)
1. Press (ink on paper)
2. PQN (short-run, disk to drum)
   Mass Customization
3. POD (one at a time, disk to drum)
   Print 300-500 and test the market.

B. eBooks (72 dpi. Photos: JPG; dwgs: GIF).
Interactive
Downloadable
   From your site
   From other sites
Portable eBook readers. PDF and LIT files.
Also in XML/OEB
CDs & DVDs

Media Asset Management
Multi-purpose your core content
Wring maximum value out of your work.
A. Versions (downloadable) from your Web site
Audio version (Digital-MP3)
Special reports (spin off from book)
Articles (spin off from book)
   Pricing pBooks & eBooks
B. Sell from Web site (not downloadable)
Seminars/Speeches
   Record and sell the audio
Consulting
   Expert witness testimony
Compatible (non-information) products

Help: http://ParaPublishing.com/supplier.cfm?

WN: *Writing Nonfiction*
SPM: *The Self-Publishing Manual*

For more information, contact
DanPoynter@ParaPublishing.com
http://ParaPublishing.com

Promoting the Editions

Make your company "Website-centric."
Set up pressroom.

A. Book industry. Send sample books to:
Agents (if you wish to sell out)
Publishers (if you wish to sell out)
Distributor/bookstores/online bookstores
"Galleys" to pre-pub reviewers-SPM pg 173
   http://ParaPublishing.com
Industry and early review copies.SPM pg 176
Book clubs. See LMP & SPM pg 260
Foreign rights-translations. See ILMP & SPM

B. Nontraditional markets. ID and Locate buyers.
Make Dealers (wholesale)
   Specialty stores (think products not books).
   Associations
   Magazines
   Events
   Catalogs. SPM pg. 287
   Premiums. SPM pg. 253
   Fundraisers. SPM pg. 256
   Military and government. SPM pg. 254

C. Disintermediation: sell directly to individual
reader/buyers (retail).
Promote your book with:
Review copies to magazines. SPM pg. 187
   Lists: http://ParaPublishing.com
News releases to magazines. SPM pg. 201
   Services: http://www.book-publicity.com
eMail announcements (broadcast email)
eZine: Newsletter/List.
Business cards (no brochures)
Postcards (invite to Web site)
Online : Listservs, chat rooms & news groups
Autographings/mini-seminars. See Doc. 639
   Posters & buttons
Radio and TV interviews. See Doc. 602

Dan Poynter's Book Writing, Publishing & Promoting Presentations

Dan Poynter is circling the world to show people how to make a difference and make a living through their books. He shares The New Book Model: how to approach agents, publishers and self-publish all at the same time. He will show you how to use innovative techniques and leading-edge technology to write your books faster, produce your books for less and promote your books more effectively. He makes writing, publishing and promoting books easy, profitable and fun. See The New Book Model and http://parapub lishing.com/getpage.cfm?file=newbook.html.

Dan Poynter's seminars have been featured on CNN, his books have been pictured in *The Wall Street Journal*, and his story has been told in *U.S. News & World Report*. The media comes to Dan because he is the leading authority on book writing, producing, marketing, promoting and distributing. The author of more than 100 books and revisions and more than 500 magazine articles on publishing, he is one of the industry's most energetic, experienced and respected leaders.

Dan is on a mission:

He does not want people to die with a book still inside them.

At some events he provides the entire four-hour writing, publishing & promoting program while at others he gives a shorter presentation. Most presentations are in PowerPoint with motion and sound.

See http://parapub.com/calendar.cfm?

12
Coping with Being Published

Or What Do I Do Now?

Once you become a published author, your life will change. Being in the limelight may not always be as much fun as you used to dream about. This chapter discusses some of the interesting challenges you will face and will provide some suggestions on how to deal with them.

YOUR STATUS WILL CHANGE from that of a private person, the "writer," to a public person, the "expert," possibly even the "celebrity." Your friends will treat you differently once you are published. Some will be very happy for you, and some will be jealous—jealous because they did not write the book. People new in your field will treat you like an idol, while those who have been around for years may feel threatened and be rather unkind.

Many new authors do not foresee their new popularity, their growing celebrity status. There is little you can do about your new treatment except be prepared for it. Be nice, and in a few years your reputation will be so solid that no one will take swipes at you any more.

Gary Glenn spent 27 years working as a fire investigator. When he and his wife, Peggy, wrote *Don't Get Burned! A Family Fire-Safety Guide*, life at work changed. The new firefighters put him on a pedestal—they followed him around the firehouse, hoping he might drop a few pearls of wisdom—while some of his contemporaries in the very status-conscious firefighting community were very cool toward him.

> Bob Johnson wrote the first book on the triathlon. When he was 62, he took off for Hawaii to practice for the IronMan competition. Bob found himself followed by a covey of young groupies. This was quite a challenge, because he had an obligation to his public but he wanted to get away to practice alone.

AUTOGRAPHING BOOKS is something you will be asked to do both in person and by mail. It is surprising how many prolific authors have never given much thought to how they might autograph a book. Confronted with an admiring fan, they are suddenly at a loss for words. Most authors simply sign "To Kathy with best wishes," add their signature and sometimes the date. At times, you want to be more personal, such as thanking a contributor for his or her help and support on the book. If there is something special about the buyer, include it in your autograph. Often there is a question of time. On a mail order book, you can dream up something special, but at a well-attended autograph party with people standing in line, it is difficult to think of a few well-chosen words while trying to give witty answers. And, by the way, especially when rushed, make sure you spell your buyer's name correctly. In all the hustle, it is easy to draw a blank and misspell the simplest name or word, ruining a book.

To autograph your book to a stranger is easy, to autograph for a friend is difficult.
—Rex Alan Smith, *Moon of Popping Trees*

One author takes this sign to books fairs and book events:

> Autographed books are more valuable.
> Have your book autographed by the author.

Some authors autograph a number of books before an event so all they have to do is add the name of the individual.

WRITING ARTICLES: Once your book is published and you become better known, editors will contact you for material. Usually they will ask you to write an article on your subject—something you probably will not have time to do. Additionally, once your book is in print, you will find new, pertinent information and will devise unique ways of explaining your program and methods. Your solution to these two challenges is the "interview article."

Other people are the pioneers and make the history. I just write it down—and sell it back to them.

As you think of a point you want to make, draft it in the form of a question and answer. Let these questions and answers build until you have several pages of them entered into your computer. Then when an editor calls, just say you are too busy to generate a specific piece, but that you have this Q&A article with all the very latest information. Tell them they may select the Q&As most likely to be of interest to their readers, and to call if they need any more. Editors love this system and rarely can think of any more questions. Some editors run the Q&As as is, while some reporters use them to generate an original article. What is important is that you have supplied an interview with written, well-thought-out answers. This system gets editors off your back, saves you a lot of time, fulfills your obligation to the media and generates a lot of publicity for your book.

SPIN-OFF is an important concept. Repackaging the same information for various markets or in various formats (expanded and condensed versions, various sizes and bindings, etc.) will bring in more money while promoting the original book. Magazine articles can be extracted from the book, book chapters can be used as a basis for conference workshops, a series of magazine articles can be combined into a new book, or the book can be rewritten and directed toward a new audience. With a computer, it is easy to pull out part of the book, add an introduction and a conclusion and turn the piece into an article, or add new material and turn it into a special report.

Always end your article with an "Editor's note," where you mention that the article was extracted from your book, and then give ordering information. Do not simply ask the editor to do this for you; place the words at the end of the article yourself.

One-On-One Book Production & Marketing "recycled" a client's extensive business information in the following ways: a $149.95 oversized hardbound edition for libraries and large corporations, a $34.95 trimmed down hardbound for medium-sized businesses, a $19.95 further reduced softbound version for small businesses and individuals, a $24.95 book of forms and contracts, and a $59.95 loose-leaf ringbound version with the forms on computer disk for mail order. It was all the same information, expanded, condensed, updated and reworked in various formats for different markets.

CONSULTING: Many authors consult on their area of expertise. For example, I consult as a technical expert in parachute and skydiving legal cases. If you decide to sell your time, set your fee schedule early, so you will be ready with figures when you receive a call. Be advised that most beginning consultants price themselves too low. For guidance on legal consulting, see *The Expert Witness Handbook* at http://Para Publishing.com.

SPEAKING ENGAGEMENTS: As a published author, you will be asked to address all sorts of groups. Make sure the gathering will be large enough to make the trip worthwhile. Even if they guarantee a large group where you might sell a number of books ("back-of-the-room sales"), you should require an honorarium.

Place photographic blowups of your books at the front of the room when you speak. They will act as *continuous communicators* because your audience will look at them all during the speech.

Make sure your book can be sold in the "back of the room." Do not try to handle the money yourself; you will be too busy fielding questions. Try to get the organization sponsoring the event to sell the books, and give them a 20% commission on each one they sell. That way, you will gain their support and an implied endorsement for your books, possibly even some extensive promotion. If they do not wish to sell the books, draft an assistant to sell them for you. Compensate this helper with a free book.

Another approach is to have the room set up classroom style, with long tables in front of the audience members. Put books at every other place and an order form at each place. Explain that the books are not part of the course but may be purchased and that you put them out for inspection because there is not enough time to look at them during the break. Tell the audience (1) all they have to do is to fill out the form, (2) you take cash, cheque and credit cards, (3) turn in the sheet and (4) keep the book. This procedure is a self-service and honor system. Process the cards when you get home. You will sell a much higher percentage of the room.

The top sheets of your handout should have an outline of the speech, and the back can contain a list of important contact addresses, resources and a listing of your other products. The outline will help the audience follow your presentation and will suppress questions during your speech. Staple this cover sheet to any supplementary materials and your brochures. This system ensures that everyone will keep your promotional materials. For more on speaking, see Chapter 7.

AUTHOR PROMOTION: Once your book is out, you will have to switch gears and put on your promotion hat. Your creativity will be redirected to brochures, sales letters and advertising copy. When sales slow down, you will have time to write another book. Remember that writing the book is just the tip of the publishing iceberg. The real work begins after you send the disk off to the printer, because books will not sell without constant marketing and promotion.

YOUR WILL: Your books are valuable assets. Draw up a living trust or have your current trust amended. You will die, but you want your work to live on. Name an executor who understands publishing so that your books and papers will continue. The cost of a living trust is very little compared to the expenses of taxes and litigation, not to mention the time and the heartache a trust could save your family and friends. By doing this, you insure that your "intellectual property" will continue its life.

STAY IN YOUR FIELD OF EXPERTISE: It is nice to have your eggs in more than one basket, but you might spread your talents too thin. You are primarily an expert in one field—that one in which you are a *participant*. You can stay in that field and become a "super expert", or you can branch out into another field and run the risk of being unable to keep up with both of them adequately. Spin off your message into speeches, articles and more books. Do more of what you do best.

PUBLISH MULTIPLE BOOKS: Distributors will be more interested in your publishing company if you have a line of books. Mailing and brochure printing will be more cost effective as you can gang books on a flyer and spread the costs over multiple titles—there is an economy of scale. With more books, you can pursue repeat business. It is much easier to sell additional product to an existing customer than to find a new one. Spin off your information into multiple products (books, reports, audio and video tapes, CDs, electronic books, etc.).

Your big day arrives when your second book is out, someone calls to order a book and you get to ask, "Which one?"

PRODUCT-LINE PACKAGING: Maintain consistent and appropriate packaging. If your books look similar, you will have a recognizable product line. They will look as though they are members of the same family. Standardize your measurements to facilitate shipping. You want to stock as few shipping cartons and bags as possible.

LOCAL STORES: Place your books in local stores. Then, when traveling fans call up asking where they can purchase your book, you can send them to the store. This approach avoids the awkward situation where fans try to talk you into a free book, and it limits their late-hour visits. A one-hour visit for a one-book sale is not very cost efficient. The store is a more objective sales rep. You don't have to try to talk the customer out of his or her money, and the customer does not have to decide against the purchase with you standing there.

THE HONOR OF BEING COPIED: When you do research to revise your book, you may get a surprise. Other books may have come out on the same subject after yours was published. In reading them, you will find many interesting (though familiar) ideas. Many will be copied directly from your own work. Remember that when you are writing you are *committing history*—you will be quoted, or at least copied (but hopefully not completely plagiarized). See Document 619, *Write It Once—Sell It Forever*, at http://ParaPublishing.com.

Once you have published, you will know what it is like to be an author. Treat yourself to a copy *of Successful Nonfiction: Tips and Inspiration for Getting Published.* See http://ParaPublishing.com.

Afterword

We *learn by doing*, and your first book will be your hardest. *We learn from our mistakes*, and hopefully, through the use of this book, your mistakes will be small ones. Learn the entire business by doing every-thing yourself before you begin to farm out some of the work, because doing it all yourself will provide you with a better understanding of publishing. I hope it introduces and guides you to a richer, more re-warding life.

The first step, the next one, is up to you. I hope you will take it. As you write, publish and market, refer to this manual. As you learn the business, make notes in it. Tell me your experiences. Let me know where this book could be improved. When you do get that first book into print, please send me a copy—autographed, of course.

Good luck,

Dan Poynter

The world is before you, and you need not take it or leave it as it was when you came in.
—James Baldwin (1924-1987)

Book Shepherds are a particular kind of consultant. They specialize in taking a book project through all the necessary steps that may include editing, design, typesetting, locating the right printer, getting a distributor, marketing and promotion (including your Web presence). Shepherds work with the author/publisher to assure that the book is produced and marketed efficiently and economically. These godparents use their experience and contacts to make sure all the publishing bases are covered and that they are covered in the right order. Some of the better-known Book Shepherds are:

Cynthia Frank:	Cynthia@Cypress House.com
Alan Gadney:	OneBookPro@aol.com
Greg Godek:	GregGodek@aol.com
Brian Jud:	iMarketBooks@aol.com
Gail Kearns/Penny Paine:	Gmkea@aol.com
Janice Phelps:	janice@indypub.com
Linda Radke:	info@FiveStarSupport.com
Ellen Reid:	ellen@smarketing.com
Simon Warwick-Smith:	sws@vom.com
Ernie Weckbaugh:	CasaG@wgn.net

The Book Shepherd: A virtual production & marketing director who is your mentor, tutor, coach and friend in the book business. Contact them to see what each one can do for you.

More help. If you want help with your editing, proofreeding, printing, etc., see our Suppliers List at http://parapublishing.com/supplier.cfm?

There are two major reasons the Chicken Soup *books are successful. One is Jack and the other is Mark. They spend every waking moment creatively promoting the books.*

Appendix 1
Your Book's Calendar

WHAT TO DO

Now

While Writing Your Book

When Your Manuscript Is Nearly Complete

When the Manuscript is Ready to Be
Delivered to the Typesetter

While the Book Is Being Typeset

While the Book Is Being Printed

When the Books Arrive

Publication Date

Ongoing Promotion

CALENDAR

One of the biggest pitfalls in small publishing is the lack of sufficient planning, especially the first time around. You don't want to tie up funds by purchasing materials too soon and you don't want to miss some important publicity because you missed a filing date.

This checklist will help to keep you on track. Follow this schedule for your first book. On your second, you will want to move some items up, and skip some others.

Chapter and appendix references below are to *The Self-Publishing Manual*. Refer back to the explanations of each resource for Web addresses. Some forms and applications are available online.

Now (Here are the things you should do right now.)

☐ Join the Publishers Marketing Association. Call 310-372-2732 for a copy of the newsletter and an application. One co-op marketing program will pay for your membership. See Professional Organizations in Appendix 2.

☐ Send for five copyright forms. See Chapters 2 and 5. See Document 112 (free).

☐ Subscribe to *Writer's Digest* and *Publishers Weekly* (or read them at your library). See Magazines for Publishers in Appendix 2.

☐ Review Appendix 2. Send for the books, magazines, brochures and catalogs that interest you. Join those associations that can help you. See our Web site.

☐ Choose a company name. File a fictitious name statement, if required. See Chapter 3.

☐ Order some office supplies, such as business cards and envelopes. See Chapter 3 and Office & Shipping Supplies in Appendix 2.

☐ Contact R.R. Bowker for ABI Information and forms. See Chapter 5 and Document 112 (free).

☐ Apply for a post office box. See Chapter 3.

☐ Read the latest edition of *The Self-Publishing Manual* completely and highlight important areas.

☐ Visit the library and study *Literary Market Place*. Order a copy now or wait until you are finished with your manuscript.

☐ Contact the Small Business Administration about its services. Call your local office.

☐ Apply for any local business licenses. Check your chamber of commerce for advice. Do not call the city licensing offices.

☐ Draft your book cover copy. See Chapter 2. Decide on your audience and what you promise to give them. See Document 116 (free).

☐ Contact Para Publishing for copies of *Writing Nonfiction* and *Successful Nonfiction*. Call 800-PARAPUB or see our Web site: http://ParaPublishing.com.

While writing your book

❑ Review Chapter 2.

❑ Write the CIP Office of the Library of Congress for *Information for Participating Publishers* and some *Publisher Response* forms. See Document 112 (free).

❑ Send to R.R. Bowker for ISBN/SAN information. See Chapter 5 and Document 112 (free).

When your manuscript is nearly complete

❑ Send requests for quotation to the 40+ printers. See Document 603 ($7.95) at http://ParaPublishing.com.

❑ Purchase a set of ISBNs from R.R. Bowker. See Chapter 5 and Document 112 (free).

❑ Design the book covers. Hire a cover designer.

❑ Fill out the ABI form. See Chapter 5.

❑ Write the Library of Congress for your LCCC number. See Chapter 5 and Document 112 (free).

❑ Send a photocopy of your ABI form to Baker & Taylor Co., Academic Library Services Selection Dept., PO Box 6885, Bridgewater, NJ 08807.

❑ Send to R.R. Bowker for your own copy of *Literary Market Place*.

❑ Research your title to make sure it is not being used. See *Books in Print* and *Forthcoming Books* at the reference desk of your public library. Or see an online bookstore such as Amazon. com.

❑ Get any needed permissions from people pictured or quoted in the book. See Document 609 ($4.95) at http://ParaPublishing.com.

❑ Send your manuscript out for peer review and copyedit. See *Writing Nonfiction* by Dan Poynter.

❑ Select a distributor. See Special Report *Book Marketing* for a discussion of distributors and lists of what categories of books they want. Or see Document 605 ($7.95) at http://Para Publishing.com.

❑ Solicit testimonials. See *Blurbs for Your Books*, Document 609 ($6.95) at http://ParaPublishing.com.

When the manuscript is ready to be delivered to the typesetter (or when you are about to typeset it)

❑ Set the publication date. It will be at least four months in the future. See Chapter 7 and Document 608 ($3.95) at http://ParaPublishing.com.

❑ Assign the ISBN(s). See Chapter 5.

❑ Prepare a news release. See Chapter 7 and Document 150 (free).

❑ Contact book clubs. See Chapter 8.

❑ Apply for a resale permit. See Chapter 3.

❑ Prepare a CIP data block. Contact Quality Books at . See Chapter 5 and Document 112 (free) http://www. quality-books.com.

While the book is being typeset

❑ Set up storage and shipping areas. See Chapter 10. Send for Special Report *Book Fulfillment, Order Entry, Picking, Packing and Shipping*.

❑ If you are subcontracting the typesetting, maintain a good proofreading schedule. Don't hold up your typesetter.

❑ Write *Contemporary Authors* for information. See Chapter 5 and Document 112 (free).

❑ Prepare mailing lists. See Chapter 9.

❑ Order shipping supplies and the rest of your office supplies. See Chapter 10 and Office & Shipping Supplies in Appendix 2.

❑ Send galleys to certain review magazines. See prepublication reviews in Chapter 7 and Document 149 (free).

❑ Prepare ads for specialty magazines. See Chapter 9.

❑ Send a book announcement to all wholesalers. See our Special Report *Book Marketing*.

❑ Prepare brochure. See Chapter 9 and Special Report *Brochures for Book Printers*.

❑ Write to the *International Directory of Little Magazines and Small Presses* for an application form. See Chapter 5 and Document 112 (free).

❑ Prepare your prepublication offer. See Chapter 8.

❑ Print book review slips and order rubber stamps. See Chapter 7.

❑ Pursue subsidiary rights. See Chapter 8 and Special Report *Book Marketing*.

❑ Order reply postcards. See Chapter 7.

❑ Write to *Publishers Directory* for an application form. See Chapter 5 and Document 112 (free).

❑ Send for Special Reports *Book Marketing: A New Approach, Book Reviews, News Releases and Book Publicity* and *Direct Mail for Publishers: Export/ Foreign Rights*.

❑ Develop your marketing plan using the *Book Marketing* Special Report. Also see *Best Sellers*, Document 612 ($6.95), at http://ParaPublishing .com.

❑ Order bar code.

❑ Select a book printer. See Special Report *Buying Book Printing* or see Document 603 ($7.95) at http:// ParaPublishing.com.

While the book is being printed

❑ Proof the "bluelines" carefully. See Special Report *Book Production*.

❑ Prepare review copy materials. Stuff and label the bags, then put them aside until books arrive.

❑ Mail your prepublication offer to individuals.

When the books arrive

(Four months before the official publication date). See Document 608 ($3.95) at http://ParaPublishing.com.

❑ Check the quality of the books. Make a count for your inventory. See Special Report *Book Fulfillment*.

❑ Fill orders.

❑ Make promotional mailing. See Chapter 7 and Document 112 (free).

❑ Photograph book and order prints.

❑ Print brochure. See Chapter 9 and Special Report *Brochures for Book Printers*.

❑ Pursue dealer sales. You want the books to be in the stores when all the promotion hits on the publication date.

❑ Draft magazine articles. See Chapter 7.

❏ File copyright form. See Chapter 5.

❏ Pursue book reviews. See in Chapter 7.

❏ Pursue promotional possibilities in Chapter 8 and see *Best Sellers*, Document 612 ($6.95), at http:// ParaPublishing.com.

❏ Send copy of book to CIP Office. See Chapter 7 and Document 112 (free).

❏ Send for Special Report *Brochures for Book Publishers* and see Document 132 (free).

❏ Visit bookstores in your area.

❏ Implement your continuing review program.

❏ Consider more direct mail solicitations.

❏ Look for spin-off ideas. Repackage your information: audiotape, electronic books, etc. Consider consulting in your area of expertise. See Document 615 ($9.95) at http:// ParaPub lishing.com.

❏ Make up a review/testimonial sheet. Paste up good reviews and reproduce them.

Publication date

Ninety percent of your initial promotional effort will be done before your official publication date. Your consumer advertising/promotion should be concentrated in the first few weeks after the publication date. See Document 608 ($3.95) at http://ParaPublishing.com.

❏ Pursue consumer-oriented promotions such as autograph parties, talk shows, author tours, etc. See Chapter 7 and *Interviews: How Authors Get on Radio and TV*, Document 602 ($9.95), at http://ParaPublishing.com.

❏ Outline your continuing promotional program.

Ongoing promotion

Never give up. You have given birth to your book; now you have an obligation to raise it. Review what has worked and do more of it. Review what has not worked and cut your losses.

❏ Send to Para Publishing for the promotion and marketing books that will be most useful to you.

❏ Work on nontraditional or special sales.

You are not an author, a publisher, or a publicist, you are an information provider. You must provide your knowledge in any form your buyer wants: books, reports, audiotapes, videotapes, CDs, seminars, speeches or private consulting.

Appendix 2
Resources for Publishers

Recommended Reading/Bibliography

Publishing Books & Reports
Para Publishing Special Reports
Book Catalogs
Magazines for Publishers
Newsletters
Pamphlets & Reports
Reference Books & Directories
Postal Books, Manuals & Web sites

Book Production & Promotion Resource

Bar Code Suppliers
Book Clubs
Book Designers & Cover Artists
Book Fair Exhibiting Services
Book Reviewers
Bookstores (Chain)
Bookstores (Online)
Consultants
Copywriters—Advertising &
  News Releases
Courses, Conferences &
  Seminars
Discount Stores & Warehouse
  Clubs
Distributors to Bookstores
Distributors to Libraries
eBook Readers
Editorial Services
Fulfillment Warehouses

Office & Shipping Supplies
Order-Entry Software
Printers, Ink
Printers , Digital
Printers, POD
Printers, Brochures
Professional Organizations
Publicists/Marketing
Shipping Services
Speech Recognition Software
U.S. Government Procure-
  ment Offices
Web Site Design
Wholesalers

RECOMMENDED READING/BIBLIOGRAPHY

There are many good references on writing, publishing, printing, marketing, distribution and other aspects of book publishing. The best are listed here. As noted, some are available from Para Publishing. For the rest, ask the reference librarian at your library and visit an online bookstore.

Be advised the R.R. Bowker Co. is a large firm with numerous functions, products and services. Although they have several offices, most of them are at the same New Jersey address, each office should be treated as a separate entity.

We check every address just prior to going to press. Remember that over 20% of our population moves every year, so if you find an address that is no longer valid, make an online search or call directory assistance for the new telephone number.

PUBLISHING BOOKS & REPORTS

Books can be ordered from your favorite bookstore. Books by Dan Poynter are available from Para Publishing. Also see our Special Reports *Book Marketing: A New Approach; News Releases and Book Publicity; Book Reviews; Direct Mail for Book Publishers; Publishing Forms;* and *Exports/Foreign Rights: Selling U.S. Books Abroad.*

Book Promotion & Marketing

101 Ways to Promote Yourself by Raleigh Pinsky is an absolute gold mine of marketing and promoting ideas. She shows you how to promote yourself, your company and your book. Do not be fooled by the low price of the mass-market paperback. An essential reference. ISBN 0-380-78508-0 Softcover, 4.25 x 7 396 pages $5.99

1001 Ways to Promote Your Book by John Kremer is an essential reference for every book publisher. It is chockfull of ideas, tips and references. Kremer writes from detailed research and hard-earned experience. There is very little he does not cover and cover well. ISBN 0-912411-48-1 Soft-cover, 6 x 9, 704 pages $27.95

Book Blitz: Getting Your Book in the News by Barbara Gaughen-Müller and Ernest Weckbaugh provides the 60 steps to making your book a bestseller. A book promotion plan with case studies. Over 40 pages of resources. ISBN 1-881474-02-X Softcover 5.5 X 8.5, 268 pages $12.95

Book Fairs: An Exhibiting Guide for Publishers by Dan Poynter, contains everything you need to successfully select, arrange and operate a booth at a book fair. It contains inside tips on how to work a fair to your maximum advantage whether you are staffing a booth or working the floor. Required reading for first time exhibitors and a valuable reminder/checklist for the seasoned veteran. Don't leave for an exhibit without it. ISBN 0-915516- 43-8 Softcover, 5.5 x 8.5, 96 pages $7.95

📖 *Bulletproof News Releases* by Kay Borden shows you how to get free publicity rather than spend money on advertising. You will learn how to write news releases that get published. You will discover what editors want, how to anticipate "sudden" opportunities, where to send your releases for maximum return plus hundreds of ideas that will work for you. ISBN 0-9637477- 0-3 Softcover, 8.5 x 11, 185 pages $18.95

📖 *Words That Sell* by Richard Bayan is a thesaurus designed to be used to promote products, services and ideas. This unusual *advertising copy stimulator* provides a short course in writing advertisements and lists synonyms for the words you want to use. Useful and unique; worth every penny. Ad copywriters cost a lot more. One of our top sellers. ISBN 0-8092-4799-2 Softcover, 8.5 x 8.75, 128 pages $14.95

Book Publishing

📖 *How to Get Happily Published* by Judith Appelbaum. How to write, find a publisher, locate an agent or publish yourself by an author with years of varied experience in New York publishing. Learn how the book publishing industry works. This is a gold mine of publishing information with a lengthy resource section. This is the book you need if you want to find the right publisher for your book. ISBN 0-06-273509-8 Softcover, 5.25 x 8.25, 317 pages $14.00

📖 *The Joy of Publishing* by Nat Bodian. This is the most interesting, fascinating and fun book about books and publishing. Bodian provides anecdotes, curiosities, fascinating facts, and historic origins about books, authors, editors, publishers, bookmaking and bookselling. This book is not just good reading, it is a valuable

industry reference. ISBN 0-912411-47-3 Hardcover, 6.5 x 9.5, 240 pages $29.95

📖 *The Self-Publishing Manual: How to Write, Print & Sell Your Own Book* by Dan Poynter is a complete course in writing, publishing, marketing, promoting and distributing books. It takes you step by step from idea through manuscript, printing, promotion and sales. Along with an in-depth study of the book publishing industry, the book explains in detail numerous innovative book marketing techniques. The *Manual* is a bible and a constant reference for publishers. Writer's Digest Book Club selection. Revised edition. ISBN 1-56860-073-9 Softcover, 5.5 x 8.5, 432 pages $19.95

📖 *Words on Tape* by Judy Byers is simply a *Self-Publishing Manual* for spoken-word audio. Judy shares her years of experience and shows you how to design, record, duplicate, package and sell your words. Turn your books into profitable audiotapes and CDs. The appendix is loaded with resources. ISBN 0-9655721-4-5 Softcover, 6 x 9, 234 pages $27.95

The Business of Publishing

Also see Special Reports *Book Fulfillment: Order Entry, Picking, Packing and Shipping*; *Publishing Forms: A Collection of Applications and Information for the Beginning Publisher.*

📖 *Small Time Operator: How to Start Your Own Small Business, Keep the Books, Pay Your Taxes & Stay Out of Trouble!* by Bernard Kamoroff, C.P.A. Kamoroff covers licenses, permits, business setup, bookkeeping, accounting, business expansion, taxes, deductions and more. This is *the* book on accounting written and published by a small publisher. 35th printing, over 350,000 in print. ISBN

0-917510-15-1 Softcover, 8.5 x 11, 192 pages $16.95

Contracts/Publishing Law

📖 *Business & Legal Forms for Authors & Self-Publishers* by Tad Crawford provides *actual tear-out forms and contracts*, explains each one and offers negotiation check-off lists. Some of the contracts are author-agent, author-publisher, collaboration, licensing of audio rights, lecture contract, privacy release, permission form, non-disclosure agreement, publisher-book designer, publisher-printer, sales representative, book distributor, copyright transfer, invoice and confirmation of assignment. Essential. ISBN 1-880559-50-1 Softcover, 8.5 x 11, 192 pages $19.95

📖 *Business Guide to Copyright Law* by Woody Young explains the new copyright law. He shows you how much research material you may legally use and how to protect your work from others. Young covers fair use, permissions, licensing, foreign protection, Registration procedures and much more. Examples of forms. Glossary. ISBN 0-939513-71-4 Softcover, 8.5 x 11, 100 pages $14.95

📖 *Handbook of Publishing Law* by Jonathan Kirsch, Esq. You will find the answers to the most often asked legal questions: idea protection, co-authorship and copyright, the role of agents and packagers, copyright infringement, defamation, invasion of privacy, trademarks, subsidiary rights, electronic rights, and a book publishing contract is discussed clause-by-clause. With resources, sample contracts and forms. This book is a valuable reference. ISBN 0-918226- 33-3, Softcover 6 x 9, 277 pages $21.95

📖 *Publishing Agreements* by Charles Clark provides several sample book contracts with explanations of each paragraph. Contracts range from those for general books to academic books, to paperback rights, translator's agreements, a book club contract and much more. Very strong on international publishing contracts. A must if you sell translation rights. ISBN 0-941533-56-5 Hardcover, 6 x 9, 238 pages $29.95

Printing

Also see Special Reports *Buying Book Printing* and *Brochures for Book Publishers*.

📖 *Getting it Printed, How to Work with Printers and Graphic Arts Services to Assure Quality, Stay on Schedule and Control Costs* by Mark Beach. An extraordinary text for anyone who plans, designs or buys printing. Avoid costly mistakes by learning the processes of type, layout, color, design, halftone, printing, binding and much more. Recently updated with details on electronic design and prepress. Good glossary, resources. You will treasure this beautiful and useful book. ISBN 0-89134-858-1 Soft-cover, 8.5 x 11, 200 pages $32.99

📖 *Pocket Pal: A Graphic Arts Production Handbook* from International Paper. This is the best basic reference on prepress and printing. It provides specifications and descriptions for paper (weight, comparisons, etc.), inks, copy preparation, film imposition, the mechanics of printing, binding and much, much more. Invaluable reference; you will always look it up in *Pocket Pal* first. Order #91838 Softcover, 4.25 x 7.5, 234 pages $12.95

Product Development

📖 *How to Make a Whole Lot More Than $1,000,000 Writing, Commis-*

sioning, Publishing and Selling "How-To" Information by Jeffrey Lant is an exhaustive, absolute last word on information creation and selling. This book says it all and is the best there is. Highly recommended to nonfiction book publishers. ISBN 0-940374-26-9 Softcover, 6 x 9, 552 pages $39.95

Is There a Book Inside You?: Writing Alone or With a Collaborator by Dan Poynter and Mindy Bingham. You will learn how to pick your topic, how to break it down into easy-to-attack projects, how and where to do research, a process that makes writing (almost) easy, how to improve your material, how to manage writing partnerships, how to evaluate your publishing options, as well as how to develop an individualized and workable plan. They will show you how to write your book, get the help you need and publish or get it published. With self-paced quizzes and resources. A Writer's Digest Book Club main selection. ISBN 1-56 860-046-1 Softcover, 5.5 x 8.5, 236 pages $14.95

Successful Nonfiction: Tips & Inspiration for Getting Published by Dan Poynter. This gorgeous gift book for writers has over 100 inspirational tips with matching stories and appropriate quotations. It is a gift for the writer within or the writer in your life. ISBN 1-56860- 061-5 Softcover, 5.5 x 8.5, 144 pages $14.95

Write Right! by Jan Venolia. This desk drawer digest of punctuation, grammar and style is an important reference that should be next to your dictionary. Demonstrating proper usage with quotes from literature and politics, *Write Right!* makes editing reports and books easy and fun. This style manual is essential when copy-editing. Over 250,000 copies sold. ISBN 0-89815- 676-9 Softcover, 5.5 x 7, 144 pages $6.95

Writing Nonfiction: Turning Thoughts into Books by Dan Poynter. You will discover how to select your topic, find your niche, gather your materials, make your project portable, a speed-writing process, ways to verify/check your work, where to get help, how to decide whether to sell to a publisher or publish yourself and how to handle the interviews and throngs of fans. There is even a chapter on speech recognition software so you can dictate your book rather than type it. If you are in the thinking, planning or writing stages, start with this book. ISBN 1-56860-064-X Softcover, 5.5 x 8.5, 168 pages $14.95

Radio & TV Interviews

It's Showtime: How to Perform on Television & Radio by Brian Jud. The top talk show producers reveal tips that will help you perform like a pro on talk shows, news shows, call-in shows and interviews from home. You will learn the 3 things you should tell every audience, the 14 words that are guaranteed to make you a hit, the 23 winning ways to answer questions correctly, the 9 tips for using body language and gestures effectively and much more. ISBN 1-880218-26-7 Soft-cover, 5.5 x 8.5 90 pages, $14.95

Perpetual Promotion: How to Contact Producers and Create Media Appearances for Book Promotion by Brian Jud is all about media tours. Here are step-by-step directions for reaching the people who decide who gets on the show—and who doesn't. Jud shows you how to organize the media trip to publicize your book—and turn it into a successful marketing campaign. And there is more to do in each city besides TV and bookstores. Jud describes an assortment of publicity-generating opportunities. ISBN 1-880218-27-5 Softcover, 5.5 x 8.25, 103 pages $14.95

📖 *Publicity for Books and Authors* by Peggy Glenn shows authors and publishers how to get free and effective publicity for their books. You will learn what it is like to handle your book publicity yourself. The author shares her own experiences on television talk shows, radio, with magazines and newspapers—what worked and what did not. Author/publisher Glenn knows the theory of promotion, practices it with success and teaches it well. If you plan to promote your book through radio and TV interviews, you must be well prepared by reading this book. Don't get caught without an answer. Examples and ideas. ISBN 0-936930-91-8 Softcover, 8.5 x 11, 182 pages $12.95

📖 *You're on the Air: Perform Like a Pro on Television & Radio* by Brian Jud is a videotape of interviews with the top producers, hosts and other media professionals. They describe the secrets of performing on the air successfully and demonstrate the nuances of projecting the desired image verbally and visually. You will learn how to draft a pitch letter, where to sit, how to use the microphone properly, how to answer questions flawlessly, how to project your voice to sell your book, how to use voice inflection to reach your audience and how to be an informative and entertaining guest. **Save $20**: order this video and the two Jud books described above for just $99.95. Get the set and be ready. ISBN 1-880218-25-9 90-minute videotape, $89.95

Speaking

📖 *Speak and Grow Rich* by Dottie and Lillet Walters shows you how to break into paid speaking. how to select topics that attract paid bookings, promotion, getting paid, over-coming stage fright and heck-lers, organizing your office, speakers bureaus and much more. This is the complete book on how to get into the speaking game. Resources. ISBN 0-13-490400-1 Softcover, 6 x 9, 288 pages $16.95

Para Publishing Free Documents

Many of our free documents have been referenced in the text of this book. Other documents from Para Publishing are available from our Web site at http://ParaPublishing.com.

📖 **112**: *Poynter's Secret List of Book Promotion Contacts*. Names and numbers for ABI, LC, CIP, ISBN and more; list of prepublication reviewers; list of directories you should be listed in and over 50 places to send your book for review. 8 pages.

📖 **113**: *List of attorneys* who specialize in book publishing. Names and numbers. 1 page.

📖 **116**: *Book Cover Layout*. Paint-by-the-numbers instructions on how to lay out your covers. The wrapper sells the book; your covers must follow this outline to be successful. 2 pages.

📖 **139**: Note to renters of mailing lists. 1 page.

📖 **149**: Layout example for a galley cover (prepublication review copy) 2 pages.

📖 **150**: News release outline. Shows you how to construct a news release. 2 pages.

📖 **155**: *Books That Were Originally Self-Published*. Many bestsellers were published by their authors. A list. 1 page.

PARA PUBLISHING SPECIAL REPORTS

We have developed detailed, step-by-step, in-depth reports to take you through some of the critical steps in book publishing. These reports are ideal for training employees or guiding interns. To order these reports, see the order blank on the last page and our Web site: http://ParaPublishing.com.

Book Fulfillment: Order Entry, Picking, Packing and Shipping explains in detail how to set up and run your shipping department. The report covers order-taking (letter openers, credit cards, card terminals, 800-numbers, fax, order services, order forms, and discount structures); order processing (computer hardware and software, shipping labels, short slips, bad checks, overpayments, invoices, back orders, the Federal Trade Commission rules, complaints, book return policy, statements and collections); inventory and storage (shipping instructions to printer, book receiving, book returns, inventory control, stacking, and shipping room layout) and book packaging (how to wrap, where to get and how to use shipping bags and cartons, machinery such as tape dispensers, scales, postage meters and bag sealers with sources, using UPS, direct sacks and various postal rates, foreign shipping and customs duty). Then the report covers the alternatives to in-house fulfillment: using wholesalers, distributors, joint representation and fulfillment warehouses, with a list of those to contact. Complete with forms and shipping rate charts, an action plan and an appendix full of resources. ISBN 1-56860-037-2 51 pages $19.95

Book Marketing: A New Approach is a low-cost marketing plan for your book. It leads you through the three-step plan for selling direct to the buyer, the five-step plan for selling to bookstores, the seven-step plan for libraries, all the subsidiary rights, and our specialty: the more lucrative nontraditional markets. This step-by-step plan will make sure you have completely covered every possible market. An absolute gold mine of book-promotion references and sources. Start your book promotion with this Special Report. ISBN 1-56860-029-1 67 pages $14.95

Book Reviews shows you in detail how to take advantage of the free publicity available to books from the prepublication galleys to a continuing review program. Book reviews are your least expensive and most effective form of book promotion. Reviews are not hard to get if you follow the unwritten (until now) rules. This report provides paint- by-the-numbers instructions for making galleys and describes in a detailed action plan how to set up a review program so your books will be reviewed again and again. It covers prepublication reviews, early reviews, retail reviews and continuing reviews, with examples of the packages for each. The report even tells you what to do with the reviews after you receive them. Complete with lists of major reviewers and sources for the rest. Examples and resources. ISBN 1-56860-032-1 40 pages $19.95

Brochures for Book Publishers shows you how to draft and print full-color brochures for less than you are currently paying for black and white locally. Imagine full-color brochures for less than 4¢ each! This report covers everything from choosing the right photographer to money-saving tricks and even includes a sample request for quotation letter, a mailing list of specialized brochure printers and examples of color brochures. Complete with an action plan and an appendix full of resources. ISBN 1-56860-036-4 25+ pages $19.95

Business Letters for Publishers: Creative Correspondence Outlines is a collection of 75 letters drafted especially for publishers. They save time for the older firm and enable the newer publisher to establish company policy that conforms to current, sometimes peculiar, publishing industry standards. The PC disk has files for three word processing programs: Word for Windows 6.0, WordPerfect for Windows, and ASCII. The MAC disk has two word processing programs: MS Word and MacWrite. Now you not only do not have to draft the letters, you do not have to type them. ISBN 0-915516-47-0 (disk) $29.95

Buying Book Printing answers the question we hear most: how to find the best and least expensive printer for your particular book. Each printer is set up to manufacture certain kinds of books. Specialties vary depending on type of binding, book measurements, print run, etc. This report shows you how to make up a request for quotation and provides a mailing list of printers who specialize in book manufacture. A section on color printing describes how to contact local representatives of Hong Kong and other foreign printers. This report helps you decide how many books to print, how to select the appropriate binding, what to look for when checking bluelines, whether you should use a printing broker, how to evaluate quotations, what kind of a printing job you can expect, how to inspect the final product, and even how to resolve disputes. This report will save you thousands of dollars in printing, binding and trucking costs. Includes an action plan, forms, sample letters and an appendix full of resources. ISBN 1-56860-055-0 36 pages $19.95

Direct Mail for Book Publishers shows how you can compete with the larger publishers by taking your message directly to the reader. Study the rules of direct mail, such as repetition, timing, response formulas and profit analysis. Learn to find and evaluate lists. Follow the plan for drafting your brochure and cover letter; assemble a direct mail package that brings results. This report also shows you how to assemble your own lists to rent to others, providing you with a new profit center. If you have a nonfiction book with an identifiable audience (and can find or assemble a mailing list for it), you may use direct mail successfully to sell books. ISBN 1-56860-030-5 42 pages $19.95

Exports/Foreign Rights: Selling U.S. Books Abroad shows you how to expand your markets by selling direct to foreign readers, using an exporter in the U.S., contracting with a foreign distributor, and selling subsidiary rights to foreign publishers, with variations such as international book packaging, co-production and format rights. Special sections cover options, taxes, shipping, agents, the Frankfurt Book Fair and more. Exports expand your market, while foreign rights are frosting on your publishing cake; they bring in revenue, while the sale amounts to a significant endorsement of your book. These endorsements help to sell more books at home. Complete with sample contracts, postal rate charts, sample letters and instructions for locating compatible foreign publishers. Glossary and an appendix full of resources. ISBN 1-56860-035-6 34 pages $19.95

Financial Feasibility in Book Publishing by Robert Follett presents a step-by-step method for evaluating the financial future of new book projects. Worksheets, guidelines, projection methods, rules of thumb and estimating methods with explanations help you decide whether your book will make money. Highly recommended. ISBN 1-56860-026-7 Softcover 8.5 x 11, 39 pages $19.95.

News Releases and Book Publicity shows you how to draft news releases and other publicity. After book reviews, news releases are your most effective and least expensive form of book promotion and you can send one out every month. Yet, few publishers use or even know about news releases. Newspaper and magazine editors want to pass on interesting information to their readers. The trick is to draft an interesting news release (tied into your book) that the editor will want to use. Editorial matter is believed; advertising is viewed with skepticism. Do not spend money on advertising when you can use the same effort and less money to send off a news release. If you are not sending out a news release on each book every 30 days, get this report. Step-by-step instructions, paint-by-the-numbers format outlines, many examples and resources are included. ISBN 1-56860-033-X 38 pages $19.95

Publishing Contracts: Sample Agreements for Book Publishers on Disk is a collection of the 22 most needed legal documents covering every facet of the book publishing business, including an author-publisher contract for a trade book, a publisher-illustrator agreement, a foreign rights agreement and 19 more. Just slip the disk into your computer, call the appropriate contract to the screen, fill in the names and check the suggested percentages. Then print out these 12-page contracts. You do not have to draft the agreements, you do not even have to type them. The PC disk has files for three word processing programs: Word for Windows 6.0, WordPerfect for Windows, and ASCII. The Mac disk has two word processing programs: MS Word and MacWrite. ISBN 0-915516-46-2 (disk) $29.95

Publishing Forms: A Collection of Applications and Information for the Beginning Publisher. Get your new book listed in all the right directories easily and registered with appropriate agencies correctly. Included are applications for ABI, LC, copyright, and more. Important reviewer, wholesaler and other contacts are supplied. ISBN 1-56860-031-3 61 pages $14.95

Book Catalogs

R.R. Bowker Company
121 Chanlon Rd.
New Providence, NJ 07974
Tel: 888-269-5372
Fax: 908-665-3502
info@bowker.com
http://www.bowker.com
http://www.bowkerlink.com

Direct Marketing Association
1120 Avenue of the Americas
New York, NY 10036-6700
Tel: 212-768-7277
Fax: 212-302-6714
http://www.the-dma.org

Dustbooks
PO Box 100
Paradise, CA 95967-9999
Tel: 800-477-6110; 530-877-6110
Fax: 530-877-0222
dustbooks@dcsi.net
http://www.dustbooks.com

Gale Group
27500 Drake Rd.
Farmington Hills, MI 48331
Tel: 800-347-GALE
Fax: 800-414-5043
http://www.galegroup.com

Peachpit Press
1249 Eighth Street
Berkeley, CA 94710
Tel: 510-524-2178
Fax: 510-524-2221
http://www.Peachpit.com

Writer's Digest Books
1507 Dana Ave.
Cincinnati, OH 45207
Tel: 800-289-0963, 513-531-2222
Fax: 513-531-4082
http://www.writersdigest.com

The Writer, Inc.
21027 Crossroads Circle
Waukesha, WI 53187
Tel: 262-796-8776
Fax: 262-798-6468
writer@kalmbach.com
http://www.writermag.com

http://www.corporate.kalmbach.com/kal
mbach/magazines/writer.asp.

J. Whitaker & Sons, Ltd.
12 Dyott St.
London WC1A 1DF
Great Britain
Tel: 011-44-171-420-6000

Magazines for Publishers

Write for a sample copy and current subscription rates.

ALA Booklist
American Library Association
50 East Huron St.
Chicago, IL 60611
Tel: 800-545-2433, 312-944-6780
Fax: 312-440-9374
http://www.ala.org

Bookselling This Week
American Booksellers Assn.
828 S. Broadway
Tarrytown, NY 10591
Tel: 800-637-0037, 914-591-2665
Fax: 914-591-2720
info@bookweb.org
http://www.bookweb.org

Canadian Author
Canadian Authors Association
Box 419
Campbellford, ON K0L 1L0
Canada
Tel: 705-653-0323
Fax: 705-653-0593
canauth@redden.on.ca
http://www.canauthors.org

Choice Magazine
100 Riverview Ctr.
Middletown, CT 06457
Tel: 860-347-6933
Fax: 860-704-0465
http://www.ala.org/acrl/choice/home.html

ForeWord Magazine
129½ East Front St.
Traverse City, MI 49684
Tel: 231-933-3699
Fax: 231-933-3899
mlink@ForewordMagazine.com
http://www.Forewordmagazine.com

Horn Book Magazine
(children's books)
56 Roland St., #200
Boston, MA 02129
Tel: 800-325-1170, 617-628-0225
Fax: 617-628-0882
Http://www.hbook.com

Kirkus Reviews
770 Broadway
New York, NY 10003-9597
Tel: 646-654-4602
Fax 646-654-4706
kirkusrev@kirkusreviews.com

Library Journal
360 Park Avenue South
New York, NY 10010-1710
Tel: 888-800-5473, 646-746-6819
Fax: 646-746-6734
http://www.LibraryJournal.com

Publishers Weekly
360 Park Avenue South
New York, NY 10010-1710
Tel: 646-746-6758
Fax: 646-746-6631
http://www.PublishersWeekly.com

School Library Journal
360 Park Avenue South
New York, NY 10010-1710
Tel: 800-456-9409, 646-746-6759
Fax: 646-746-6689
http://www.SchoolLibraryJournal.com
http://www.slj.com

Writer's Digest
1507 Dana Ave.
Cincinnati, OH 45207
Tel: 513-531-2222
Fax: 513-531-4082
http://www.writersdigest.com

Newsletters

Write for a sample copy and
current subscription rates.

Book Marketing Update
Bradley Communications
Bill Harrison
135 East Plumstead Ave.
Lansdowne, PA 19050-8206

Tel: 800-989-1400 x. 119,
  610-259-1070
Fax: 610-284-3704
rtirmag@aol.com
http://www.rtir.com

Book Publishing Report
Cowles Simba Report on Directory Publishing
Electronic Advertising and Marketing Report
Electronic Information Report
  (formerly *IDP Report*)
Information Marketplace (directory)
Information Publishing (report)
Multimedia Entertainment and
  Technology Report
Professional Publishing Market Report
Trade Book Publishing (report)
Simba Information, Inc.
11 Riverbend Dr. South
P.O. Box 4234
Stamford, CT 06907-0234
Tel: 800-307-2529, 203-358-9900
Fax: 203-358-5824
http://www.simbanet.com

Direct Response Specialist
(Free thru e-mail only)
Galen Stilson
4036 Mermoor Ct.
Palm Harbor, FL 34685
Tel: 727-786-1411
Fax: 727-785-7049
tdrs@galenstilson.com

Editorial Eye
Editorial Experts, Inc.
66 Canal Center Plaza, #200
Alexandria, VA 22314-5507
Tel: 703-683-0683
Fax: 703-683-4915
http://www.eeicommunications.com

PMA Newsletter
Publishers Marketing Association
627 Aviation Way
Manhattan Beach, CA 90266
Tel: 310-372-2732
Fax: 310-374-3342
PMAonline@aol.com
http://www.pma-online.org

Publishing Poynters
(Free through email)
Dan Poynter
PO Box 8206-380
Santa Barbara, CA 93118-8206
info@ParaPublishing.com
http://ParaPublishing.com

Pamphlets & Reports

Pamphlets, reports and other help of interest to publishers. Write for latest prices.

Library of Congress
Copyright Office
101 Independence Ave. S.E.
Washington, DC 20559-6000
Tel: 202-707-3000
Forms/Publications: 202-707-9100
Fax: 202-707-2600
http://www.loc.gov/copyright
Circular 1, Copyright Basics
Circular 2, Publications on Copyright

Federal Trade Commission
Washington, DC 20580
Tel: 202-326-2222
http://www.ftc.gov
Best Sellers (free), a complete list of
  FTC publications
A Business Checklist for Direct Marketers
A Business Guide to the FTC's Mail
  or Telephone Merchandise Rule

National Endowment For The Arts
1100 Pennsylvania Ave. NW
Washington, DC 20506-0001
Tel: 202-682-5400
http://www.arts.gov
Assistance, fellowships and residencies
  for writers

Poets & Writers, Inc.
72 Spring St.
New York, NY 10012
Tel: 212-226-3586
Fax: 212-226-3963
http://www.pw.org
Poets' and Writers' Copyright Basics
Directory of American Poets & Fiction Writers
Literary Agents, A Writer's Guide

Reference Books and Directories

Most of these books can be found in the reference section of your public library. Write to the publishers for ordering details.

American Booksellers Association
828 S. Broadway, Tarrytown, NY 10591
Tel: 800-637-0037; 914-591-2665
Fax: 914-591-2720
info@bookweb.org
http://www.bookweb.org
Book Buyers Handbook
Directory of American Publishers. (20,000
  U.S. and Canadian publishers.)

American Library Association
50 East Huron St., Chicago, IL 60611
Tel: 800-545-2433; 312-944-6780
Fax: 312-440-9374
http://www.ala.org
Membership Directory
Marketing to Libraries Through
  Library Associations

Bacon's Information
332 South Michigan Ave. #900
Chicago, IL 60604-4301
Tel: 800-621-0561; 312-922-2400
Fax: 312-922-3127
http://www.bacons.com
Newspaper/Magazine Directory

B. Klein Publications
PO Box 6578
Delray Beach, FL 33482
Tel: 561-496-3316
Fax: 561-496-5546
Directory of Mailing List Companies
Guide to American Directories.
  (8,000 directories.)
Mail Order Business Directory
  (Over 10,000 mail order and
  catalog houses.)

Broadcast Interview Source
2233 Wisconsin Ave. NW
Washington, DC 20007-4132
Tel: 202-333-4904
Fax: 202-342-5411
editor@yearbook.com
http://www.yearbook.com
Talk Show Selects
Yearbook of Experts,
  Authorities & Spokespersons

Columbia Books
P.O. Box 251
Annapolis Junction, MD 20701
Tel: 888-265-0600
Fax: 240-646-7020
http://www/columbiabooks.com
*National Trade & Professional Associations
of the U.S.
State & Regional Associations*

Dustbooks
PO Box 100
Paradise, CA 95967-9999
Tel: 800-477-6110; 530-877-6110
Fax: 530-877-0222
dustbooks@ dcsi.net
http://www.dustbooks.com
*Directory of Editors
Directory of Poetry Publishers
Directory of Small Press/Magazine
Editors and Publishers
International Directory of Magazines
and Small Presses.* (A comprehensive
listing of smaller publishers.)
Small Press Record of Books in Print

Editor and Publisher
770 Broadway, New York, NY 10003-9595
Tel: 888-313-5530
http://www.mediainfo.com
*International Year Book
Market Guide
Syndicate Directory*

Editorial Freelancers Association (EFA)
71 West 23rd St.
Suite 1910
New York, NY 10010
Tel: 212-929-5400
Fax: 212-929-5439
info@the-efa.org
http://www.the-efa.org

EEI Press
66 Canal Center Plaza, #200
Alexandria, VA 22314-5507
Tel: 703-683-0683
Fax: 703-683-4915
press@eeicom.com
http://www.eeicommunications.com/press
EEI Press has many publications
available on the writing, editing
and production aspects of

publishing, including:
*Mark My Words: Instructions and
Practice in Proofreading
My Big Sourcebook: For People
Who Work with Words or Pictures
Stet Again! More Tricks of the
Trade for Publications People*

Gale Group
27500 Drake Rd.
Farmington Hills, MI 48331
Tel: 800-347-GALE
Fax: 800-414-5043
http://www.galegroup.com
*Business, Organizations, Agencies, and
Publications Directory
Contemporary Authors
Directories in Print
Directory of Special Libraries
Encyclopedia of Associations*
(22,000 associations).
*Gale Directory of Publications and
Broadcast Media* (formerly *Ayer Directory
of Publications*)
*International Book Trade Directory
International Organizations.*
(11,000 groups.)
*National Directory of Non-Profit
Organizations*
(273,000 associations.)
*National Fax Directory
Newsletters in Print
Publishers Directory
Publishers Interntional ISBN Directory
Standard Periodical Directory* (Oxbridge)
World Guide to Libraries

Gebbie Press
PO Box 1000
New Paltz, NY 12561
Tel: 845-255-7560
Fax: 845-256-1239
gebbie@pipeline.com
http://www.gebbieinc.com
All-In-One Media Directory

Grey House Publishing
185 Millerton Rd.
Millerton, NY 12546
Tel: 800-562-2139
Fax: 518-789-0545
books@ greyhouse.com
http://www.greyhouse.com

Directory of Business Information Resources
Directory of Business to Business Catalogs
   (5700 entries.)
Directory of Mail Order Catalogs
   (7500 entries.)

Hudson Associates
PO Box 311, Rhinebeck
NY 12572-1403
Tel: 845-876-2081
Fax: 845-876-2561
hphudson@aol.com
http://www.newsletter-clearinghse.com
Hudson's Subscription Newsletter Directory
   (Lists thousands of newsletters
   by category.)

K.G. Saur Publishing, Inc.
121 Chanlon Rd.
New Providence, NJ 07974
Tel: 800-521-8110; 800-877-GALE
International Books in Print

Online Computer Library Center, Inc.
6565 Frantz Rd.
Dublin, OH 43017-3395
Tel: 800-848-5878; 614-764-6000
Fax: 614-764-6096
oclc@oclc.org
http://www.oclc.org/fp
Dewey Decimal Classification
   and Relative Index

Oxbridge Communications, Inc.
150 Fifth Ave., #302
New York, NY 10011
Tel: 800-955-0231; 212-741-0231
Fax 212-633-2938
info@oxbridge.com
http://www.mediafinder.com
College Media Directory
National Directory of Magazines
   (21,000 magazines.)
National Directory of Mailing Lists
Oxbridge Directory of Newsletters

PEN American Center
568 Broadway, New York, NY 10012-3225
Tel: 212-334-1660
Fax 212-334-2181
http://www.pen.org
Grants and Awards Available to
   American Writers

R.R. Bowker
121 Chanlon Rd.
New Providence, NJ 07974
Tel: 888-269-5372
Fax 908-665-3502
info@bowker.com
http://www.bowker.com
American Book Trade Directory (Lists
   29,000 booksellers, wholesalers, etc.)
American Library Directory (Lists 35,000
   U.S. and Canadian libraries.)
Books in Print (Lists all books currently
   available by subject, title and author—
   annual.)
Broadcasting & Cable Yearbook
   (Comprehensive info on radio, TV
   and cable industries.)
Forthcoming Books (Books that will appear
   in the next edition of *Books in Print.*)
International Literary Market Place (Lists
   sources outside the U.S. and Canada.)
Literary Market Place (Very important.)
   (Lists agents, artists, associations, book
   clubs, reviewers, exporters,
   magazines, newspapers, news
   services, radio and TV, and many
   other services—annual.)
   http://www.literarymarketplace.com
Publishers, Distributors & Wholesalers of the
   United States (A directory.)
Publishers' Trade List Annual
   (A compilation of 1,500
   publishers' catalogs.)
Ulrich's International Periodicals Directory
   (Lists 120,000 newsletters and
   magazines.)
Working Press of the Nation (A
   three-volume reference covering
   many aspects of the media.)

SRDS, Inc.
1700 Higgins Rd.
Des Plaines, IL 60018
Tel: 800-851-7737; 847-375-5000
Fax: 847-375-5001
http://www.srds.com
Direct Marketing List Source

Writer's Digest Books
1507 Dana Ave.
Cincinnati, OH 45207
Tel: 800-289-0963; 513-531-2222
Fax: 513-531-4082;
http://www.writersdigest.com

Writer's Digest Books publishes
many specific books on writing well and
getting published.
Children Writer's and Illustrator's Market
How to Write Like an Expert about Anything
Writer's Market
Writers Yearbook

POSTAL WEB SITES, BOOKS & MANUALS

The following Postal Service publications should be consulted for more information. They can be obtained from your local Postal Business Center (call 800-275-8777 for the one nearest you) or downloaded from the general Postal Service Web site at http://www.usps.com.

Postal Service Web Sites

Business Center: http://www.usps.com
Canadian post office general Web site: http://www.canadapost.ca
Domestic Zip code lookup: http://www. usps.gov/ncsc
Postal Explorer: http://www.pe.usps.gov contains the following:
   Domestic Mail Manual (with rate calculator)
   International Mail Manual (with rate calculator)
   Designing Letter Mail (Pub. 25)
   Quick Service Guides
   Designing Flat Mail (Pub. 63)
   Designing Reply Mail (Pub. 353)
   Ratefold (Notice 123)
   Postal Addressing Standards (Pub. 28)
   Packaging for Mailing (Pub. 2)
Shipping supplies online: http://supplies.usps.gov
Universal postal union (links to the Web sites of most countries): http://www.upu.int

Postal Service Booklist & Manuals (Call for prices: 800-238-3150)

Addressing for Automation, Notice 221
Bar Code/FIM Pattern Locator Gauge, Model 005
Basic Addressing, Notice 23A
Computer Programming for Presort First-Class Mail, Notice 244
Courtesy Reply Mail, Publication 12
Designing Business Letter Mail, Publication 25

Express Mail Rate Chart, Poster 189

Directory of Zip+4 Coding Services, Publication 148

Domestic Mail Manual. Complete rules, regulations & postal rate information for all classes of mail sent/received in the U.S. $20 per year (2 issues) or free from Web.

Express Mail Service Guide, Publication 273

Information Guide on Presort First Class Mail, Publication 61

INTELPOST Service Directory and Users Guide, Publication 82A

International Mail Manual. Complete rules, procedures, regulations & postal rate information for all classes of mail sent out of the U.S. $20 per year or free from the Web Site.

International Postage Rates and Fees, Publication 51

International Priority Airmail Mailer Guidelines, Publication 507

International Surface Airlift (ISAL) Service Guide, Publication 31

Mailer's Guide, Publication 19

Metered Better, Treated Better, Notice 125

National Change of Address, Notice 47

National Five-Digit Zip Code and Post Office Directory (2 vols.) (Publication 65).

On-site Meter Setting, Notice 112

Postage Rates, Fees and Information, Notice 59

Postal Addressing Standards, Publication 28

Postal Bulletin. Bi-weekly newsletter providing specific details on procedures, rates regulations. $103 per year or free from Web

   See http://www.usps.gov/cpim/ftp/bulletin/pb.htm

Postal Facts. Interesting folder with postal statistics.

Ratefold (Notice 123). All the rates on a fold out card.

Zip+4: Helping You Help Your Business, Notice 189

Zip+4 Codes...Why They Add Up for Business Mailers, Notice 186

Zip+4 State Directory (Publication 66)

BOOK PRODUCTION & PROMOTION RESOURCES

Bar Code Suppliers

Bar Code Graphics
875 North Michigan Ave., #2640
Chicago, IL 60611
Tel: 312-664-0700
Fax: 312-664-4939
sales@barcode-us.com
http://www.barcode-us.com

Film Masters
Kathy Paugh
11680 Hawke Rd.
Columbia Station, OH 44028
Tel: 800-541-5102; 440-748-8060
Fax 800-826-1410
barcodes@en.com
http://www.filmmasters.com

Fotel
1125 E. St. Charles Rd. #100
Lombard, IL 60148
Tel: 800-834-4920; 630-932-7520
Fax: 630-932-7610
sales@fotel.com
http://www.fotel.com

General Graphics
T, Craig Thickey
PO Box 3192
Arnold, PA 15068
Tel: 800-887-5894; 724-337-1470
Fax: 724-337-6589
sales@ggbarcode.com
http://www.ggbarcode.com

J& D Barcodes
433 W. Fleetwood Place
Glendora, CA 91740-5969
Tel: 626-914-1777
jdbarcodes@earthlink.net

Book Clubs

There are over 200 book clubs and most are very specialized. Only three to six will be appropriate to any particular book. For more, see *Literary Market Place*.

Book-of-the-Month Club
Children's Book-of-the-Month Club
Quality Paperback Book Club
1271 Avenue of the Americas, 3rd Fl.
New York, NY 10020-2686
Tel: 212-522-4200
Fax: 212-522-0303
http://www.bookspan.com

Doubleday Select, Inc.
101 Park Ave., 23rd Fl.
New York, NY 10178
Tel: 212-455-5000
Fax: 212-455-5001
http://www.booksonline.com

The Literary Guild
Bookspan
1540 Broadway, 16th Fl.
New York, NY 10036
Tel: 212-782-7200
Fax: 212-782-7205; 212-782-7201
http://www.literaryguild.com

Writer's Digest Book Club
1507 Dana Ave.
Cincinnati, OH 45207
Tel: 800-289-0963; 631-851-5232
Cust. Svc.: 877-889-6290
Fax: 513-531-4082
http://www.writersdigest.com

Book Designers & Cover Artists

Book producers or book packagers are graphic arts services that specialize in the design, typesetting and layout of book pages and covers. Some will convert files to HTML and PDF. Send for brochures with prices.

Arrow Graphics, Inc.
Alvart Badalian
PO Box 0291
Cambridge, MA 02238
Tel: 617-926-8585
Fax: 617-926-0982
arrow@arrow1.com

Be It Now/Karen Ross Design
Karen Ross
12516 Washington Place
Los Angeles, CA 90066
Tel: 310-915-0920
Fax: 310-390-0419
http://www.beitnow.com/publishingdesign.htm

Casa Graphics
Ernie & Patty Weckbaugh
1718 Rogers Pl., #1-A
Burbank, CA 91504
Tel: 818-842-4278
Fax: 818-842-2960
CasaG@wgn.net

Cypress House
Cynthia Frank
155 Cypress St.
Fort Bragg, CA 95437-5401
Tel: 707-964-9520
Fax: 707-964-7531
qedpress@mcn.org
http://www.cypresshouse.com

Dunn + Associates
Mary Jo Jirik
PO Box 870
Hayward, WI 54843
Tel: 715-634-4857
Fax: 715-634-5617
info@dunn-design.com
http://www.dunn-design.com

Janice Phelps
126 South Maple St.
Lancaster, OH 43130
Tel: 740-689-2950
Fax: 740-689-2951
janice@indypub.com
http://www.indypub.com

Kleine Editorial Service
Walter Kleine
PO Box 8207
Berkeley, CA 94707
Tel: 800-240-0054; 510-654-8406
wkleine@netwiz.net
http://www.kleineedit.com

Knockout Design
Peri Poloni
2584 Greenwood Lane, #11
Cameron Park, CA 95682
Tel: 530-676-2744
Fax: 530-676-2741
peri@knockoutbooks.com
http://www.knockoutbooks.com

Lightbourne
Gaelyn Larrick, Shannon Bodie
2565 Siskiyou Blvd., #1-G

Ashland, OR 97520
Tel: 800-697-9833; 541-488-3060
Fax: 541-482-1730
lightbourne@lightbourne.com
http://www.lightbourne.com

MacGraphics
Karen Saunders
3454 So. Cimarron Way
Aurora, CO 80014
Tel: 303-680-2330
Fax: 303-680-2331
Karen@MacGraphics.net
http://www.MacGraphics.net

1106 Design, LLC
Michele O'Hagan
15414 North 7th Street, #8-173
Phoenix, AZ 85022-3519
Tel: 602-866-3226
Fax: 602-866-8166
ohagan@irisheye.com
http://www.irisheye.com/master

One-On-One Book Production,
   Editing and Marketing
Carolyn Porter & Alan Gadney
7944 Capistrano Ave.
West Hills, CA 91304
Tel: 818-340-6620
Fax: 818-340-6770
onebookpro@aol.com

PageCrafters, Inc.
ReNae Grant
8441 Cove Avenue
Pensacola, FL 32534
Tel: 850-494-1513
Fax: 850-478-5368
rGrant@PageCraftersInc.com
http://www.PageCraftersInc.com

Phillips Design
Kathy Phillips
42 Caray Hill Rd., #A
Sharon, CT 06069
Tel: 860-364-1121
Fax: 860-364-1127
renfrew@ct2.nai.net

Pro-Art Graphic Design
Robert Aulicino
2031 Holly Dr.
Prescott, AZ 86305

Tel: 520-708-9445
Fax: 520-708-9447
aulicino@cableone.net
http://www.aulicinodesign.com

Quest Press
Pamela Terry
1858 So. Crescent Heights Blvd
Los Angeles, CA 90035
Tel: 323-935-6666; 800-590-7778
Fax: 323-934-2881
pam@opus1design.com;
http://www.opus1design.com

Robert Howard Graphic Design
Robert Howard
631 Mansfield Dr.
Fort Collins, CO 80525
Tel: 970-225-0083
Fax: 970-225-0083
RHoward@BookGraphics.com
http://www.BookGraphics.com

Rutledge Books
Art Salzfass
107 Mill Plain Road
Danbury, CT 06811
Tel: 800-278-8533
Fax: 203-798-7272
info@RutledgeBooks.com
http://www.RutledgeBooks.com

Sara Patton Book Production
    Services
160 River Rd.
Wailuku, HI 96793
Tel: 800-433-4804, 808-242-7838
Fax: 808-242-6113
sarapatton@compuserve.com

Synergistic Data Systems
Dale Schroeder
3579 E. Foothill Blvd., #A-329
Pasadena, CA 91107
Tel: 800-944-8973; 626-351-8622
Fax: 626-351-7717
sds.design@gte.net

Book Fair Exhibiting Services

If you cannot attend the fair yourself, you
might contract with an exhibiting service
to show your books. See the discussion in
Chapter 9 and read *Book Fairs*.

Association Book Exhibit
Mark Trocchi
8727-A Cooper Road
Alexandria, VA 22309
Tel: 703-619-5030
Fax: 703-619-5035
info@bookexhibit.com
http://www.bookexhibit.com

Combined Book Exhibit
Jon Malinowski
277 White St.
Buchanan, NY 10511
Tel: 800-462-7687; 914-739-7500
Fax: 914-739-7575
info@combinedbook.com
http://www.combinedbook.com

PMA Book Exhibits
627 Aviation Way
Manhattan Beach, CA 90266
Tel: 310-372-2732
Fax: 310-374-3342
PMAonline@aol.com
http://www.pma-online.org

Scholar's Choice Exhibits
1260 Sibley Tower
Rochester, NY 14604
Tel: 716-262-2048
Fax: 716- 262-2228
Information@scholarschoice.com
http://www.scholarschoice.com

Book Reviewers

Here is a short list of reviewers. For a
longer one, see earlier chapters of this
book and *Literary Market Place*. For a
complete list on labels, contact ParaLists at
800-PARAPUB or info@ParaPublishing.
com.

Bloomsbury Reviews
Tom Auer
1553 Platte St., #206
Denver, CO 80202-1167
Tel: 303-455-3123
Fax: 303-455-7039
bloomsb@aol.com

Book Talk
Carol Myers
8632 Horacio Place NE
Albuquerque, NM 87111
Tel: 505-299-8940
Fax: 505-299-8940
(books of Southwest interest,
fiction or non-fiction)

Curtis Casewit
PO Box 19039
Denver, CO 80219
Tel: 303-935-0277

King Features Syndicate
Submissions Editor
235 East 45th St.
New York, NY 10017
Tel: 212-455-4000
http://www.kingfeatures.com

Jerry Mack
PO Box 5200
San Angelo, TX 76902
Tel: 915-653-1795

Midwest Book Review
Jim Cox
278 Orchard Dr.
Oregon, WI 53575
Tel: 608-835-7937
mbr@execpc.com
http://www.execpc.com/~mbr/bookwatch/

New York Review of Books
Barbara Epstein, Robert Silvers
1755 Broadway, 5th Fl.
New York, NY 10019
Tel: 212-757-8070
Fax: 212-333-5374
nyrev@nybooks.com

New York Times Book Review
Charles McGrath
229 West 43rd St.
New York, NY 10036
Tel: 212-556-1234
Fax : 212-556-1320; 646-698-8344
http://www.nytimes.com/books

Rainbo Electronic Reviews
Maggie Ramirez
8 Duran Court
Pacifica, CA 94044

Tel: 650-359-0221
http://www.rainboreviews.com

Reference and Research Book News
Jane Erskine
5739 NE Sumner St.
Portland, OR 97218
Tel: 503-281-9230
Fax: 503-287-4485
booknews@booknews.com

Rouse Reviews
John Culleton
2401 Haight Ave.
Eldersburg, MD 21784
john@wexfordpress.com

United Media
Sidney Goldberg
200 Madison Ave., 4th Fl.
New York, NY 10016
Tel: 800-221-4816; 212-293-8500
Fax: 212-293-8600
sgoldberg@unitedmedia.com
http://www.unitedmedia.com

Washington Post Book World
Marie Arana
1150 15th St. NW
Washington, DC 20071
Tel: 202-334-6000
Fax: 202-334-5059
aranam@washpost.com
http://www.washingtonpost.com

Bookstores (Chain)

Here are the major chains. For smaller ones, see *The American Book Trade Directory*, available at your public library. Address the fiction or nonfiction, hardcover or paperback buyer. Also see Special Report *Book Marketing*.

Barnes & Noble, Inc.
122 Fifth Ave., 4th Fl.
New York, NY 10011-5605
Tel: 212-633-3300
Fax: 212-675-0413
http://www.bn.com

Borders Group, Inc.
100 Phoenix Dr.
Ann Arbor, MI 48108-2202

Tel: 800-770-7811, 734-913-1100
Tel: 734- 477-1100
http://www.borders.com

Books-A-Million, Inc.
402 Industrial Lane
Birmingham, AL 35211-4655
Tel: 800-201-3550, 205-942-3737
http://www.booksamillion.com

Chapters, Inc.
90 Ronson Dr.
Toronto, ON M9W 1C1
Canada
Tel: 416-243-3138
Fax: 416-243-8964
http://www.chapters.ca.com

Little Professor Book Centers LLC
405 Little Lake Dr.
Ann Arbor, MI 48103
Tel: 800-899-6232; 734-994-1212
Fax: 734 994-9009
littleprofessor.net
http://www.lpbchome@net.com

Bookstores (Online)

Contact the online bookstore's Web site
for publisher's information.

http://www.amazon.com
http://www.bn.com
http://www.booksamillion.com
http://www.borders.com

Consultants

Some consultants specialize. Contact
each one for a list of services and fees.

Cypress House
Cynthia Frank
155 Cypress St.
Fort Bragg, CA 95437-5401
Tel: 707-964-9520
Fax: 707-964-7531
qedpress@mcn.org
http://www.cypresshouse.com

Five Star Publications, Inc.
Linda Radke
Publishers Support Services
PO Box 6698
Chandler, AZ 85246-6698

Tel: 480-940-8182
Fax: 480-940-8787
info@fivestarsupport.com
http://www.fivestarsupport.com
http://www.authorsandexperts.com
http://www.publicitydepot.com

Penelope C. Paine
817 Vincente Way
Santa Barbara, CA 93105
Tel: 805-569-2398
Fax: 805-563-0166
pennypaine@aol.com
http://www.equitybooksforgirls.com
http://www.topressandbeyond.com
(children's picture books,
educational materials)

Para Publishing
Dan Poynter
PO Box 8206-380
Santa Barbara, CA 93118-8206
Tel: 805-968-7277
Fax: 805-968-1379
DanPoynter@ParaPublishing.com
http://ParaPublishing.com

Copywriters—Advertising News Releases

AWM Books
Shel Horowitz
PO Box 1164
Northamton, MA 01061
Tel: 800-683-WORD
shel@frugalfun.com
http://www.frugalfun.com

Joe "Mr. Fire" Vitale
Vitale Estate
121 Canyon Gap Rd.
Wimberley, TX 78676
Tel: 512-847-3414
jgvitale@ix.netcom.com
http://www.mrfire.com

Quinn's Word for Word
Robin Quinn
PMB 345
10573 W. Pico Blvd.
Los Angeles, CA 90064
Tel/fax: 310-838-7098
quinnrobin@aol.com

Courses, Conferences & Seminars

There are many educational programs of interest to publishers. Some of the most important are listed here. For more, see *Literary Market Place*.

Publishing Institute
University of Denver
2075 South University, PMB D-114
Denver, CO 80210
Tel: 303-871-2570
Fax: 303-871-2501
pzelarne@du.edu
http://www.du.edu/pi

Santa Barbara Publishing
  Workshops
Dan Poynter
PO Box 8206-380
Santa Barbara, CA 93118-8206
Tel: 805-968-7277
info@ParaPublishing.com
http://ParaPublishing.com

Simba Information, Inc.
11 Riverbend Dr. South
P.O. Box 4234
Stamford, CT 06907
Tel: 800-307-2529; 203-358-9900
Fax (orders): 203-358-5824
  (editorials): 203-358-5825
  (marketing): 203-358-5826
http://www.simbanet.com

Stanford Publishing Courses
Holly Brady, Director
Green Library
557 Escondido Mall
Stanford, CA 94305-6004
Tel: 650-725-4301
Fax: 650-726-1904
publishing.courses@stanford.edu
http://www.stanfordproed.org

UC Berkeley Extension
1995 University Avenue, #7020
Berkeley, CA 94720
Tel: 510-642-4111
Fax: 510-642-0374
http://www.unex.berkeley.edu/enroll

University of Chicago
Publishing Program
Graham School of General Studies
5835 Kimbark Ave.
Chicago, IL 60637
Tel: 773-702-1722
Fax: 773-702-6814
gargoyle@uchicago.edu
http://www.grahamschool.uchicago.edu

Discount Stores & Warehouse Clubs

Blockbuster Entertainment Corp.
1201 Elm St.
Dallas, TX 75270
Tel: 214-854-3000
Fax: 214-854-4324
http://www.blockbuster.com

Costco Wholesale
999 Lake Dr.
Issaquah, WA 98027
Tel: 425-313-8100
http://www.costco.com

Sam's Wholesale Club
608 SW 8th St.
Bentonville, AR 72716
Tel: 501-277-7160
http://www.walmart.com

Target Stores
33 South 6th St.
Minneapolis, MN 55402
Tel: 800-440-0680; 612-304-8637
  612-3047500 (vendor relations)
Fax: 612-304-2323; 612-304-3788
http://www.target.com

Tower Records and Books
2500 Del Monte St.
West Sacramento, CA 95691
Tel: 916-373-2500
Fax: 916-373-2583
http://www.towerrecords.com

Distributors to Bookstores

For descriptions of the distributors with lists of the categories of books they want, see the Special Report *Book Marketing* or our Document 605, *Locating the Right Distributor*, at http://ParaPublishing.com.

Advanced Marketing Services (AMS)
Advanced Global Distribution
5880 Oberlin Dr. #400
San Diego, CA 92121
Tel: 858-457-2500
Fax: 858-452-2237
http://www.advmkt.com

American Software & Hardware
Distributors
406 East Anthony Dr.
Urbana, IL 61802
Tel: 800-998-2743, 217-384-2050
Fax: 217-384-2055
http://www.ashd.com

Antique Collectors Club
91 Market Street, Industrial Park
Wappingers Falls, NY 12590
Tel: 914-297-0003
Fax: 914-297-0068
infor@antiquecc.com
http://www.antiquecc.com

Austin & Company, Inc.
Rebecca Austin
104 So. Union Street, #202
Traverse City, MI 49684
Tel: 231-933-4649
Fax: 231-933-4659
aandn@aol.com
http://www.AustinandCompanyInc.com

Biblio Distribution (NBN)
4720 Boston Way
Lanham, MD 20706
Tel: 301-459-3366
Fax: 301-459-1705

Booklines Hawaii
94-527 Puahi St.
Waipahu, HI 96797
Tel: 808-676-0116
Fax: 808-676-0634
booklines@lava.net (graphics dept.)
http://www.booklineshawaii.com

Book Tech Distributing
5961 E. 39th Ave.
Denver, CO 80207
Tel: 800-758-5492, 303-329-0300
Fax: 303-329-3117

Canbook Distribution Services
1220 Nicholson Road
New Market, ON L3Y 7V1
Canada
Tel: 905-836-5807
Fax: 905-363-2665
inquiry@canbook.com
http://www.canbook.com

Charles E. Tuttle Company
1 Box 231-5
North Clarendon, VT 05759
Tel: 802-773-8930
Fax: 800-329-8885
info@tuttlepublishing.com
http://www.tuttlepublishing.com

Client Distribution Services
425 Madison Avenue, Suite 1500
New York, NY 10017
Tel: 212-223-2969
Fax: 212-223-1504
sblack@cdsbooks.com
http://www.cdsbooks.com

Combined Books
1024 Fayette Street
Conshohocken, PA 19428-0307
Tel: 610-828-2595
Fax: 610-828-2603
combined@combinedpublishing.com
http://www.combinedpublishing.com
(military books)

Consortium Book Sales & Distribution
1045 Westgate Dr.
St. Paul, MN 55114
Tel: 800-283-3572; 651-221-9035
Fax: 651-221-0124
consortium@cbsd.com
http://www.cbsd.com

Cromland, Inc.
1995 Highland Ave., #200
Bethleham, PA 18020
Tel: 800-944-5554; 610-997-3000
Fax: 610-997-8880
info@cromland.com
http://www.cromland.com
(computer books)

Distributed Art Publishers (DAP)
155 Sixth Ave., 2nd Floor
New York, NY 10013-1507
Tel: 212-627-1999
Fax: 212-627-9484

Educational Book Distributors
PO Box 551
San Mateo, CA 94401
Tel: 650-344-8458
Fax: 650-344-7840
orders@publishersservices.net
(educational books to schools)

Faithworks
9247 Hunterboro Drive
Brentwood, TN 37027
Tel: 615-221-6442
Fax: 615-221-6442
1carpenter@faithworksonline.com
http://www.faithworksonline.com
(Christian books)

Greenleaf Book Group
660 Elmwood Point
Aurora, OH 44202
Tel: 800-932-5420
Fax: 330-995-9704
client@greenleafbookgroup.com
http://www.greenleafbookgroup.com

Independent Publishers Group (IPG)
814 North Franklin St.
Chicago, IL 60610
Tel: 312-337-0747
Fax: 312-337-5985
frontdesk@ipgbook.com
http://www.ipgbook.com

Independent Publishers Marketing
6824 Oaklawn Ave.
Edina, MN 55435
Tel: 952-920-9044
Fax: 952-920-7662
stjohns.ipm@blackhole.com
(gift trade distributor)

International Publishers Marketing
22841 Quicksilver Drive
Sterling, VA 20166
Tel: 703-661-1586
Fax: 703-661-1501
ipmcomments@booksintl.com
http://www.internationalpubmarket.com

International Specialized
   Book Services
5824 NE Hassalo St.
Portland, OR 97213
Tel: 800-944-6190; 503-287-3093
Fax: 503-280-8832
orders@isbs.com
http://www.isbs.com

Librera de Habla Hispaña
4441 N. Broadway
Chicago, IL 60640
Tel: 800-883-2126; 773-878-2117
Fax: 773-878-0647
tomas@anet.com

MBI Publishing Company
PO Box 1
Osceola, WI 54020
Tel: 715-294-3345
Fax: 715-294-4448
mbibks@motorbooks.com
http://www.motorbooks.com

Midpoint Trade Books
27 West 20th St., #1102
New York, NY 10011
Tel: 212-727-0190
Fax: 212-727-0195
midpointny@aol.com
http://www.midpointtrade.com

National Book Network (NBN)
4720 Boston Way
Lanham, MD 20706
Tel: 301-459-3366
Fax 301-429-5748
info@nbn.com
http://www.nbnbooks.com

Origin Books
415 N. Neil Armstrong Rd.
Salt Lake City, UT 84116
Tel: 888-467-4446; 801-972-6338
Fax: 801-972-6570; 888-467-4442
jasay@qwest.net
http://www.originbooks.com

Parnassus Book Distributors
200 Academy Way
Columbia, SC 29206
Tel: 800-782-7760; 803-782-7748
Fax: 803-782-7748
mloism@email.msn.com

Penton Overseas
2470 Impala Drive
Carlsbad, CA 92008-7226
Tel: 760-431-0060
Fax: 760-431-8110
info@pentonoverseas.com
http://www.pentonoverseas.com

Prologue, Inc.
1650 Lionel-Bertrand Blvd.
Boisbriand, QC J7H 1N7
Canada
Tel: 800-363-2864; 450-434-0306
Fax: 450-434-2627
http://www.prologue.ca

Publishers Group West (PGW)
1700 Fourth St.
Berkeley, CA 94710
Tel: 800-788-3123; 510-528-1444
Fax: 510-528-3444
info@pgw.com
http://www.pgw.com

Publisher Resources, Inc. (PRI)
(affiliate of Ingram)
1706 Heil Quaker Blvd.
LaVergne, TN 37086
Tel: 800-937-5557; 615-793-5090
Fax: 615-213-4761

Raincoast Book Distribution
9050 Shaughnessy St.
Vancouver, BC V6P 6E5
Canada
Tel: 800-511-6024; 604-323-7100
Fax: 604-323-2600
info@raincoast.com
http://www.raincoast.com

Red Wheel/Weiser
Samuel Weiser, Inc.
PO Box 612
York Beach, ME 03910
Tel: 800-423-7087; 207-363-4393
Fax: 207-363-5799
email@weiserbooks.com
http://www.weiserbooks.com

Rights & Distribution, Inc.
2131 Hollywood Blvd., Suite 305
Hollywood, FL 33020-6750
Tel: 800-771-3355; 954-925-0555
Fax: 954-925-5244

rightsinc@aol.com
http://www.fellpub.com

Samuel French
7623 Sunset Blvd.
Hollywood, CA 90046
Tel: 323-876-0570
Fax: 323-876-6822
samuelfrench@earthlink.net
http://www.samuelfrench.com

Sandhill Book Marketing, Ltd.
99-1270 Ellis St.
Kelowna, BC V1Y 1Z4
Canada
Tel: 250-763-1406
Fax: 250-763-4051
sandhill@direct.ca
(does not import from U.S.)

SCB Distributors
15608 S. New Century Dr.
Gardena, CA 90248
Tel: 800-729-6423; 310-532-9400
Fax: 310-532-7001
info@scbdistributors.com
http://www.scbdistributors.com

Small Press Distribution (SPD)
1341 Seventh St.
Berkeley, CA 94710-1403
Tel: 800-869-7553; 510-524-1668
Fax: 510-524-0852
orders@spdbooks.org
http://www.spdbooks.org

Spring Arbor Distributors
One Ingram Blvd.
LaVergne, TN 37086
Tel: 800-395-5599
Fax: 734-483-3675
orders@springarbor.com
(Christian books)

Wimmer Cookbook, R.R.
4210 BF Goodrich Blvd.
Memphis, TN 38118
Tel: 901-362-8900
Fax: 901-346- 9918

Words Distributing Co.
(distribution div. of Bookpeople)
7900 Edgewater Dr.
Oakland, CA 94621

Tel: 800-593-9673
Fax: 510-553-0729; 510-632-1281
words@wordsdistributing.com
http://www.wordsdistributing.com

Distributors to Libraries

Quality Books
1003 West Pines Rd.
Oregon, IL 61061-9680
Tel: 815-732-4450
Fax: 815-732-4499
http://www.quality-books.com

Unique Books
5010 Kemper Ave.
St. Louis, MO 63139
Tel: 800-533-5446
Fax: 800-916-2455
uniquebks@aol.com

Editorial Services

Includes proofreading, copy and content editing and ghostwriting.

Cross-t.i
Barbara Coster
753 Avenida Pequena
Santa Barbara, CA 93111
Tel: 805 967-4936
Fax: 805-964-6398
bcoster@silcom.com

GMK Editorial & Writing Services
Gail Kearns
825 E. Pedregosa St., #2
Santa Barbara, CA 93103
Tel: 805-898-9941
Fax: 805-898-9460
gmkea@aol.com
http://www.topressandbeyond.com

Kleine Editorial Service
Walter Kleine
PO Box 8207
Berkeley, CA 94707
Tel: 800-240-0054, 510-654-8406
wkleine@netwiz.net
http://www.kleineedit.com

One-On-One Book Production,
    Editing & Marketing
Carolyn Porter
7944 Capistrano Ave.

West Hills, CA 91304
Tel: 818-340-6620
Fax: 818-340-6770
onebookpro@aol.com

Penmark
Karen Stedman
21555 Burbank Blvd., #67
Woodland Hills, CA 91367
Tel: 818-702-9114
Fax: 818-884-5721
Penmarkg@aol.com

PeopleSpeak
Sharon Goldinger
25381-G Alicia Parkway #1
Laguna Hills, CA 92653
Tel: 949-581-6190
Fax: 949-581-4958
http://www.detailsplease.com/peoplespeak

Quinn's Word for Word
Robin Quinn
PMB 345
10573 W. Pico Blvd.
Los Angeles, CA 90064
Tel/fax: 310-838-7098
quinnrobin@aol.com

Fulfillment Warehouses

Send for prices. Also see Special Report *Book Fulfillment*.

Book Clearing House
Nancy Smoller
46 Purdy Street
Harrison, NY 10528
Tel: 800-431-1579
Fax: 914-853-0398
bookch@aol.com
http://www.bookch.com

BookMasters
2541 Ashland Rd.
Mansfield, OH 44905
Tel: 419-589-5100
Tel: 800-537-6727
Fax: 419-589-4040
info@bookmaster.com
http://www.bookmasters.com

Genco Fulfillment West
545 Coney Island Dr.

Sparks NV 89431
Tel: 775-359-9811
Fax: 775-359-9042
http://www.genco.com

PSI Fulfillment
Ben Sorrell
8803 Tara Lane
Austin, TX 78737
Tel: 800-460-0500
Fax: 512-288-5055
ben@PSIfulfillment.com
http://www.PSIfulfillment.com

Publisher Resources, Inc. (PRI)
1706 Heil Quaker Blvd.
LaVergne, TN 37086
Tel: 800-937-5557, 615-793-5090
Fax: 615-213-4761

Tech Mailing Service
1401 Lakeland Ave.
Bohemia, NY 11716
Tel: 631-567-7000
Fax: 631-567-7801

Office & Shipping Supplies

Send for catalogs.

Chiswick Inc.
33 Union Ave.
Sudbury, MA 01776-2267
Tel: 800-225-8708
Fax: 800-638-9899
http://www.chiswick.com

Drawing Board
PO Box 2995
Hartford, CT 06104-2995
Tel: 800-527-9530
Fax: 800-253-1838
http://www.thedrawing-board.com

Grayarc
PO Box 2944
Hartford, CT 06104
Tel: 800-243-5250
Fax: 800-292-4729

Paper Mart
5361 Alexander St.
City of Commerce, CA 90040
Tel: 800-745-8800, 323-726-8200

Fax: 800-651-0008
orders@papermart.com
http://www.papermart.com

Quill Corporation
100 Schelter Rd.
Lincolnshire, IL 60069
Tel: 800-789-1331
Fax: 800-789-8955
(for orders) e-order@quill.com
(for inquiries) info@quill.com
http://www.quill.com

Reliable Office Supplies
PO Box 1501
Ottawa, IL 61350
Tel: 800-328-3034
Fax: 800-326-3233
http://www.reliable.com

Robbins Container Corp.
222 Conover St.
Brooklyn, NY 11231
Tel: 888-251-1297; 718-875-3204
Fax: 718-254-0812

Order-entry Software

PUB123
Adams-Blake Company
Alan Canton
8041 Sierra St.
Fair Oaks, CA 95628
Tel: 916-962-9296
info@adams-blake.com
http://www.adams-blake.com

Publishers Assistant
Book Clearing House
46 Purdy St.
Harrison, NY 10528
Tel: 800-356-9315; 800-431-1579
Fax: 800-242-0036; 914-835-0398
bookch@aol.com
http://www.bookch.com

Quicken & QuickBooks
Intuit, Inc.
2800 E. Commerce Center Pl.
Tucson, AZ 85706
Tel: 800-446-8848
Fax: 800-756-1040
920-901-3201 (sales & svc. fax)
http://www.intuit.com

Printers, Ink

These ink-on-paper printers specialize in manufacturing books. For more, see our Special Report *Buying Book Printing* or our Document 603, *Book Printing at the Best Price*, at http://ParaPublishing. com.

Bang Printing
PO Box 587
Brainerd, MN 56401
Tel: 800-328-0450; 218-829-2877
Fax: 218-829-7145
banginfo@BangPrinting.com
http://www.bangprinting.com

Banta Book Group
David Mead
PO Box 60
Menasha, WI 54952
Tel: 800-933-9612; 920-751-7771
Fax: 920-751-7362
dmead@banta.com
http://www.banta.com

Banta Information Services
Chip Fuhrmann, Dawn Binkley
7000 Washington Ave. South
Eden Prairie, MN 55344
Tel: 800-765-7327; 612-941-8780
Fax: 612-941-2154
cfuhrmann@banta.com
http://www.banta.com

Bertelsmann Industry Services, Inc.
Penny Callmeyer
28210 North Ave. Stanford
Valencia, CA 91355-1111
Tel: 661-257-0584; 800-223-1478 (CA)
Fax: 661-257-3867
Penny.Callmeyer@bisus.com
http://www.bisus.com

Book-Mart Press
Michelle S. Gluckow
2001 42nd St.
North Bergen, NJ 07047
Tel: 201-864-1887; 212-594-3344
Fax: 201-864-7559

BookMasters
Shelley Sapyta
PO Box 2139
Mansfield, OH 44905

Tel: 800-537-6727, 419-589-5100
Fax: 419-589-4040
info@bookmasters.com
http://www.bookmasters.com

Central Plains Book Manufacturing
Becky Pate
22234 C St., Strother Field
Winfield, KS 67156
Tel: 877-278-2726
Fax: 316-221-4762
http://www.centralplainsbook.com

C.J. Krehbiel Co.
Rick Hastings
3962 Virginia Ave.
Cincinnati, OH 45227
Tel: 800-598-7808; 513-271-6035
Fax: 513-271-6082
http://www.cjkrehbiel.com

Color House Graphics, Inc.
Phil Knight
3505 Eastern Avenue
Grand Rapids, MI 49508
Tel: 800-454-1916
Fax: 616-245-5494
PSKNI@aol.com
http://www.ColorHouseGraphics.com

Cushing-Malloy
Thomas Dorow
PO Box 8632
Ann Arbor, MI 48107-8632
Tel: 734-663-8554; 888-295-7244
Fax: 734-663-5731
tdorow@cushing-malloy.com
http://www.cushing-malloy.com

Data Reproductions Corporation
Kimberly Kavanagh
4545 Glenmeade Lane
Auburn Hills, MI 48326
Tel: 800-242-3114; 248-371-3700
Fax: 248-371-3710
Kcolton@DataRepro.com
http://www.datarepro.com

Dickinson Press
Bob Worcester
5100 33rd St. SE
Grand Rapids, MI 49512
Tel: 616-957-5100
Fax: 616-957-1261

sales@dickinsonpress.com
http://www.dickinsonpress.com
Specializes in lightweight papers (Bibles, etc.)

Edwards Brothers
Joe Thomson
2500 South State St.
Ann Arbor, MI 48106-1007
Tel: 734-769-1000
Fax: 734-769-0350
jthomson@edwardsbrothers.com
http://www.edwardsbrothers.com

Eerdmans Printing Co.
Matt Baerwalde
231 Jefferson Ave. SE
Grand Rapids, MI 49503-4569
Tel: 616-451-0763
Fax: 616-459-4356
mbaerwal@eerdmansprinting.com
http://www.eerdmansprinting.com

Friesens Printers
Jim Beckel
415 Queensland Rd. SE
Calgary, AB T2J 3S5
Canada
Tel: 403-250-3486
Fax: 403-250-8648
jimb@friesens.com
http://www.friesens.com

Gagne Printing
Denis Audet
80, Ave. Saint-Martin
Louisville, PQ J5V 1B4
Canada
Tel: 819-228-2766
Fax: 819-228-8390

Hignell Book Printing Ltd.
Chris Young
488 Burnell St.
Winnipeg, MB R3G 2B4
Canada
Tel: 800-304-5553, 204-784-1030
Fax: 204-774-4053
books@hignell.mb.ca
http://www.hignell.mb.ca

Jostens
Ed Bohannon
2400 Crown Point Executive Drive

Charlotte, NC 28227
Tel: 800-458-0319, 704-847-5707
Fax: 704-844-0713
Booksrus@perigee.net

Malloy Lithographing
Bill Upton
PO Box 1124
Ann Arbor, MI 48106-1124
Tel: 800-722-3231,734-665-6113
Fax: 734-665-2326
http://www.malloy.com

McNaughton & Gunn
Ron Mazzola
960 Woodland Dr.
Saline, MI 48176
Tel: 734-429-5411
Fax: 800-677-BOOK
http://www.bookprinters.com

Morgan Printing
Mark Hillis
900 Old Koenig Lane #135
Austin, TX 78756
Tel: 800-421-5593, 512-459-5194
Fax: 512-451-0755
mPrinting@austin.rr.com
http://www.morganprinting.org
(run lengths: 250 - 2000)

Omnipress
Robert G. Hamm
PO Box 7214
Madison, WI 53707
(or 2600 Anderson St.
Madison, WI 53704)
Tel: 608-246-2600
Tel: 800-828-0305 outside WI
Fax: 608-246-4237
sales@omnipress.com
http://www.omnipress.com

Pacific Rim Int'l Printing
Lori Davis
11726 San Vicente Blvd., #280
Los Angeles, CA 90049
Tel: 310-207-6336
LoriD@PacRim-Intl.com
http://www.PacRim-Intl.com
(Color printing in Hong Kong)

Patterson Printing
Linda J. Seaman
1550 Territorial Rd.
Benton Harbor, MI 49022-1937
Tel: 800-848-8826; 616-925-2177
Fax: 616-925-6057
lseaman@patterson-printing.com
http://www.patterson-printing.com

Phoenix Color Corp.
John Sabella
540 Western Maryland Parkway
Hagerstown, MD 21740
Tel: 800-632-4111, 301-733-0018
Fax: 301-791-9560
jruggeri@phoenixcolor.com
http://www.phoenixcolor.com

Professional Press
PO Box 4371
Chapel Hill, NC 27515-4371
Tel: 800-277-8960; 919-942-8020
Fax: 919-942-3094
http://www.profpress.com

Rose Printing Company
2503 Jackson Bluff Rd.
Tallahassee, FL 32304
Tel: 800-227-3725; 850-576-4151
Fax: 850-576-4153
http://www.roseprinting.com
(also specialize in minibooks)

R.R. Donnelley & Sons
Chuck Harpel
1009 Sloane St.
Crawfordsville, IN 47933
Tel: 800-428-0832; 765-364-3693
Fax: 765-364-2559
chuck.harpel@RRD.com

Sheridan Books
Mary Heim
100 Staebler Rd.
Ann Arbor, MI 48103
Tel: 734-662-3291, ext. 243
Fax: 734-475-7337
Mheim@SheridanBooks.com
http://www.sheridanbooks.com

Technical Communication Services
Ray Kiely
110 West 12th Ave.
North Kansas City, MO 64116

Tel: 816-842-9770
Fax: 816-842-0628
http://www.tcsbook.com

Thomson-Shore, Inc.
Mark Livesay
7300 West Joy Rd.
Dexter, MI 48130-9701
Tel: 734-426-3939
Fax: 800-706-4545; 734-426-6216
http://www.tshore.com

United Graphics
Louis Segovia
2916 Marshall Ave.
Mattoon, IL 61938
Tel: 217-235-7161
Fax: 217-234-6274
Lsegovia@att.net
http://www.unitedgraphicinc.com

Van Volumes Ltd.
Russell Tate
PO Box 314
Three Rivers, MA 01080
Tel: 413-283-8556
Fax: 413-283-7884
vanvol@VanVolumes.com
http://www.VanVolumes.com

Vaughan Printing Company
David Prentice
411 Cowan St.
Nashville, TN 37207
Tel: 615-256-2244
Fax: 615-259-4576
bookprint@aol.com
http://www.vaughanprinting.com

Von Hoffmann Graphics
Mark Bawden
400 South 14th Ave.
Eldridge, IA 52748
Tel: 800-422-9336; 319-285-4800
Fax: 319-285-4828
mbawden@vonhoffmann.com
http://www.vonhoffmann.com

Walsworth Publishing Co.
Joe Cupp
306 North Kansas Ave.
Marceline, MO 64658
Tel: 800-369-2646
Fax: 660-258-7798

commercial@walswort.com
http://www.walsworthprinting.com

Whitehall Printing Company
John Gilbertson
4244 Corporate Square
Naples, FL 34104-4753
Tel: 800-321-9290; 941-643-6464
Fax: 941-643-6439
johng@whitehallprinting.com
http://www.whitehallprinting.com

Printers, Digital

These printers produce books through digital printing in small quantities.

Alexander's Digital Printing
Barry Merrell
245 South 1060 West
Lindon, UT 84042-1606
Tel: 800-574-8666
Fax: 801-224-0446
BarryM@Alexanders.com
http://www.Alexanders.com

BooksJustBooks.com
Ron Pramschufer
51 East 42nd Street
New York, NY 10017
Tel: 800-621-2556
Fax: 212-681-8002
(West Coast Tel: 800-754-7089)
Ron@RJC-LLC.com
http://BooksJustBooks.com

C&M Press
Beth Chapmon
4825 Nome St.
Denver, CO 80239
Tel: 303-375-9922
Fax: 303-375-8699
beth@cmpress.com
http://www.cmpress.com

DeHART's Printing Services
Tatiana Promessi, Don DeHart
3265 Scott Blvd.
Santa Clara, CA 95054
Tel: 888-982-4763; 408-982-9118
Fax: 408-982-9912
solutions@deharts.com
http://www.deharts.com

DigiNet Printing
Guillermo "William" Perego
5723 NW 159th Street
Miami Lakes, FL 33014
Tel: 305-825-9260
Fax: 305-825-9294
gPerego@DigiNetPrinting.com
http://DigiNetPrpinting.com

Fidlar Doubleday
Steve Rozewicz, Mgr.
6255 Technology Avenue
Kalamazoo, MI 49001
Tel: 800-632-2259
Fax: 888-999-0655
http://www.FidlarDoubleday.com

Sir Speedy-Scottsdale
Sheri Statt Bercaw
7373 East Camelback Road
Scottsdale, AZ 85251
Tel: 480-947-7277, Ext. 111
Fax: 480-946-3957
sstatt@SirSpeedy21120.com

Sir Speedy-Whittier
Tim McCarthy
7240 Greenleaf Avenue
Whittier, CA 90602
Tel: 562-698-7513
tim@ssWhittier.com

Tri-State Litho
Kumar Persad
71-81 TenBroeck Avenue
Kingston, NY 12401
Tel: 845-331-7581
Fax: 845-331-1571
tristate@ulster.net
http://www.TriStateLitho.com

Printers, POD

These printers produce books one-at-a-time (on-demand).

Infinity Publishing
John Harnish
519 W. Lancaster Ave.
Haverford, PA 19041-1413
Tel: 610-520-2500
Fax: 610-519-0261
jHarnish@BuyBooksOnTheWeb.com

LightningSource/Ingram Book Group
1246 Heil Quaker Boulevard
La Vergne, TN 37086
Tel: 615-213-5815; 800-937-8200
inquiry@lightningprint.com
http://www.lightningprint.com

Replica Books/ Baker & Taylor
1200 US Hwy 22 East
Bridgewater, NJ 08007
Tel: 908-541-7391
http://www.baker-taylor.com

Printers, Brochures

These printers print color brochures, catalog sheets/flyers, postcards, posters, bookmarks, business cards and other promotional materials.

Carl Sebastian Printing
436 E. Bannister Road
Kansas City, MO 64131
Tel: 800-825-0381; 816-444-0044
Fax: 816-361-0003
prepress@trabon-paris.com
http://www.carlsebastian.com

MWM Dexter, Inc.
P.O. Box 261
Aurora, MO 65605
Tel: 800-354-9007
sales@MWMDexter.com
http://www.MWMDexter.com

Simply Brochures/Postcards
700 Silver Spur Road, Suite 206
Rolling Hills, Estates, CA 90274
Tel: 800-770-4102; 310-541-3770
Fax: 310-541-6610
sales@separcolor.com
http://www.simplybrochures.com

Sir Speedy-Whittier
Tim McCarthy
7240 Greenleaf Avenue
Whittier, CA 90602
Tel: 562-698-7513
tim@ssWhittier.com

Tu-Vets Printing
5635 E. Beverly Blvd.
Los Angeles, CA 90022
Tel: 800-894-8977; 323-723-4569

Fax: 323-724-1896
tuvets@aol.com
http://www.tu-vets.com

United Micro Printing
19355 Business Center Drive, Unit 3
Northridge, CA 91324
Tel: 888-774-6889
Fax: 818-993-9009
http://www.UnitedMicroPrinting.com

Professional Organizations

Write for an application and inquire about benefits and dues. Many associations publish a magazine or newsletter. For a list of writers' associations, see *Writer's Market*.

American Book Producers Association
156 Fifth Ave. #302
New York, NY 10010
Tel: 212-645-2368
Fax: 212-989-7542
office@abpaonline.org

American Booksellers Association (ABA)
828 S. Broadway
Tarrytown, NY 10591
Tel: 800-637-0037; 914-591-2665
Fax: 914-591-2720
http://www.bookweb.org

American Library Association (ALA)
50 East Huron St.
Chicago, IL 60611
Tel: 800-545-2433; 312-944-6780
Fax: 312-440-9374
http://www.ala.org

Association of American Publishers, Inc. (AAP)
71 Fifth Ave., 2nd Fl.
New York, NY 10003-3004
Tel: 212-255-0200
Fax: 212-255-7007
http://www.publishers.org

Association of Canadian Publishers
110 Eglington Ave. W, #401
Toronto, ON M4R 1A3
Canada
Tel: 416-487-6116
Fax: 416-487-8815

info@canbook.org
http://www.publishers.ca

Authors Guild, Inc.
31 E. 28th St., 10th Fl.
New York, NY 10016
Tel: 212-563-5904
Fax: 212-564-8363
staff@authorsguild.org
http://www.authorsguild.org

Bay Area Independent Publishers
   Association
PO Box E
Corte Madera, CA 94976
Tel: 415-430-2196, ext. 1175
baipa@onebox.com
http://www.baipa.org

Book Industry Study Group
160 Fifth Ave.
New York, NY 10010-7000
Tel: 212-929-1393
Fax: 212-989-7542
bisg@bookwire.com
http://www.bisg.org

Book Publicists of Southern California
6464 Sunset Blvd. #755
Hollywood, CA 90028
Tel.: 323-461-3921
Fax: 323-461-0917

Catholic Press Association
3555 Veterans Highway, Unit O
Ronkonkoma, NY 11779
Tel: 631-471-4730
Fax: 631-471-4804
CathJourn@aol.com
http://www.catholicpress.org/index.htm

Christian Booksellers Association
PO Box 62000
Colorado Springs, CO 80962-2000
(or 9240 Explorer Dr., zip code 80920)
Tel: 800-252-1950; 719-265-9895
Fax: 719-272-3510
http://www.cbaonline.org

Colorado Independent Publishers
   Association
PO Box 101975
Denver, CO 80275
Tel: 303-722-7200

info@cipabooks.com
http://www.cipabooks.com

Direct Marketing Association
1120 Avenue of the Americas
New York, NY 10036-6700
Tel: 212-768-7277
Fax: 212-302-6714
http://www.the-dma.org

Florida Publishers Association, Inc.
P.O. Box 430
Highland City, FL 33846-0430
Tel.: 863-647-5951
Fax: 863-647-5951
FPAbooks@aol.com
http://www.Flbookpub.org

Independent Publishers Guild
147-149 Gloucester Terrace
London W2 6DX Great Britain

Midwest Independent Publishers
   Association
PO Box 581432
Minneapolis, MN 55458-1432
Tel: 651-917-0021
http://www.pma-online.org
http://www.mipa.org

National Association of Independent
   Publishers
PO Box 430
Highland City, FL 33846-0430
Tel: 863-648-4420
Fax: 863-647-5951
naip@aol.com
http://www.publishersreport.com

Networking Alternatives for Publishers,
   Retailers and Artists, Inc. (NAPRA)
109 N. Beach Rd.
PO Box 9
Eastsound, WA 98245-0009
Tel: 360-376-2702
Fax: 360-376-2704
napraexec@rockisland.com
http://www.napra.com

North American Bookdealers Exchange
Box 606-PT
Cottage Grove, OR 97424
Tel.: 541-942-7455
Fax: 561-258-2625

nabe@bookmarketingprofits.com
http://www.bookmarketingprofits.com

Publishers Association of the South
4412 Fletcher St.
Panama City, FL 32405-1017
Tel: 850-914-0766
Fax: 850-769-4348
executive@pubsouth.org
http://www.pubsouth.org
(Trade organization of book publishers
for southeastern United States)

Publishers Marketing Association (PMA)
Jan Nathan
627 Aviation Way
Manhattan Beach, CA 90266
Tel: 310-372-2732
Fax: 310-374-3342
PMAOnline@aol.com
http://www.pma-online.org

Society for Scholarly Publishing
10200 W. 44th Ave., #304
Wheat Ridge, CO 80033
Tel: 303-422-3914
Fax: 303-422-8894
ssp@resourcenter.com
http://www.sspnet.org

Publicists/Marketing

These professionals will schedule you for
radio-TV appearances, write your news
releases, introduce you to review and
sales sources, secure distributors and
wholesalers, create sales brochures and
perform other marketing/publicity functions. Contact them for prices and
services. For an expanded listing, see
Literary Market Place.

BookMarketing Works
Brian Jud
50 Lovely St.
Avon, CT 06001
Tel: 203-267-2452, 800-562-4357
brianjud@msn.com
sales@strongbooks.com (sales)
help@strongbooks.com (cust. svc.)
http://www.bookmarketingworks.com

Booknote LLC
Lisa Guida

PO Box 2142
Branford, CT 06405
Tel: 203-483-7035
Lisa@BookNote.com
http://www.BookNote.com

The Caruba Organization
Alan Caruba
PO Box 40
9 Brookside Rd.
Maplewood, NJ 07040
Tel: 973-763-6392
acaruba@aol.com
(for reviews) www.bookviews.com
(for publicity) www.caruba.com

Direct Contact Media Services
Paul J. Krupin
PO Box 6726
Kennewick, WA 99336
Tel: 800-457-8746; 509-545-2707
Fax: 509-582-9865
http://www.imediafax.com
http://www.book-publicity.com
http://www.dcnewswire.com
http://www.publicityforum.com
http://www.uscongressfax.com
(email and fax services to print and
broadcast media)

Free Radio Airtime
Alex Carroll
924 Chapala Street #D
Santa Barbara, CA 93101
Tel: 805-564-6868
RadioAirtime@mail.com
http://www.FreeRadioAirtime.com
(Radio publicity)

Great Interviews Media Coaching
  & Consulting Service
Matthew Gray
2043 Makiki Street
Honolulu, HI 96822
Tel: 808-949-TALK (8255)
GreatInterviews@LoveLife.com
http://www.LoveLife.com/GreatInterviews

Integrated Book Marketing
Sharon Castlen
PO Box 321
Kings Park, NY 11754
Tel: 631-979-5990
Fax: 631-979-5989
ibmarket@optonline.net

KSB Promotions
Kate Bandos
55 Honey Creek Ave.
Ada, MI 49301
Tel: 616-676-0758
Fax: 616-676-0759
pr@ksbpromotions.com
http://www.ksbpromotions.com

One-On-One Book Marketing &
   Promotion
Alan Gadney
7944 Capistrano Ave.
West Hills, CA 91304
Tel: 818-340-6620
Fax: 818-340-6770
onebookpro@aol.com

Phenix & Phenix
Marika Flatt
2525 W. Anderson Lake #540
Austin, TX 78757
Tel: 512-478-2028
Fax: 512-478-2117
Marika@BookPros.com
http://www.BookPros.com

Planned Television Arts
Rick Frishman
1110 Second Ave., 3rd Fl.
New York, NY 10022
Tel: 212-593-5845; 212-593-5820
Fax: 212-715-1667
frishmanr@ruderfinn.com
http://www.plannedtvarts.com
(Radio, TV, print media)

Promotion in Motion
Irwin Zucker
6464 Sunset Blvd. #755
Hollywood, CA 90028
Tel: 323-461-3921
Fax: 323-461-0917

Radio-TV Interview Report (RTIR)
Bradley Communications Corp.
Steve Harrison
PO Box 1206
Lansdowne, PA 19050
http://www.FreePublicity.com/info227.htm

Readers Radio Virtual Book Tours
Errol Smith

1010 No. Central Avenue
Glendale, CA 91202
Tel: 818-547-0222
Fax: 818-245-1159

Sherri Rosen Publicity
80 South Main Street, #2A
Milltown, NJ 08850
Tel: 732-448-9441
Fax: 732-448-9441
Sherrirose@mindspring.com
Sherri@SherriRosen.com
http://www.SherriRosen.com

Smarketing Agency
Ellen Reid
269 S. Beverly Drive, Suite #1065
Beverly Hills, CA 90212
Tel: 866-234-0626 or 310-234-0626
ellen@smarketing.com
http://www.smarketing.com

To Press and Beyond
Gail Kearns, Penelope Paine
825 East Pedregosa Street, Suite #2
Santa Barbara, CA 93103
805-898-9941; 866-528-9901(toll free)
info@topressandbeyond.com
http://www.topressandbeyond.com

Shipping Services

Airborne: http://www.airborne.com
DHL: http://www.dhl.com
FedEx: http://www.FedEx.com
        or call 800-GoFedEx.
Purolator: http://www.purolator.com
UPS: http://www.ups.com
USPS: http://www.usps.gov

Speech Recognition Software

Dragon Systems, Inc.
9 Centennial Drive
Peabody, MA 01960
Tel: 978-977-2000
info@dragonsys.com
http://www.naturalspeech.com
http://www.dragonsys.com

IBM (PC & Mac)
Tel: 800-825-5263, code S001
talk2me@vnet.ibm.com
ibmdirect@vnet.ibm.com

http://www.ibm.com/viavoice
http://www.software.ibm.com/is/voicetype

U.S. Government Procurement Offices

For the addresses of other government procurement offices, call your congressional representative's local office. See your telephone directory under U.S. Government. See the "Selling to the Government" discussion in Chapter 8. Also see Instant Report Document 637, *Selling Books to the Military Market*, by Michael H. Sedge.

Air Force Office of Small and
    Disadvantaged Business Utilization
Attn: Anthony J. DeLuca, Director
1060 Air Force Pentagon
Washington, DC 20330-1060
Tel: 703-696-1103
http://selltoairforce.org

Dept. of the Army Small and
    Disadvantaged Business Utilization
Attn: Tracey Pinson, Director
106 Army Defense Pentagon,
Room 2A712
Washington, DC 20310-0106
Tel: 703-697-2868
http://www.sellingtoarmy.org

Education Supplies Procurement Office
101 Buford Rd.
Richmond, VA 23235
Tel: 804-327-0500
http://www.odedodea.edu

Headquarters (193A)
Dept. of Veterans Affairs
Library
810 Vermont Ave. NW
Washington, DC 20402
Tel: 202-273-8523
Fax: 202-273-9125

Web Site Design

BookZone, Inc.
Mary Westheimer
PO Box 9642
Scottsdale, AZ 85252-3642
Tel: 800-536-6162; 480-481-9737

Fax: 480-481-0103
bookzone@bookzone.com
http://www.bookzone.com

Wholesalers

The most important are listed here. For more, see the *American Book Trade Directory* and *Literary Market Place*, available at your public library. You will also want a single national distributor on an exclusive basis. (See distributor list previous)

Academic Book Center
5600 NE Hassalo St.
Portland, OR 97213
Tel: 800-547-7704; 503-287-6657
Fax: 503-284-8859

Airlift Books
26 Eden Grove
London N7 8EF
Great Britain
011-44-181-804-0400

Ambassador Book Service
42 Chasner St.
Hempstead, NY 11550
Tel: 800-431-8913; 516-489-4011
Fax: 516-489-5661
ambassador@absbook.com
http://www.absbook.com

Baker & Taylor
Sue Tomae
Publisher Services Dept.
PO Box 6885
Bridgewater, NJ 08807
Tel: 908-541-7000, 800-775-1500
Fax: 908-704-9315
tomaes@btol.com
http://www.btol.com

Blackwell's Book Services
100 University Court
Blackwood, NJ 08012
Tel: 800-257-7341; 856-228-8900
Fax: 856-228-7262
http://www.blackwell.com

Blackwell's Book Services
6024 SW Jean Rd., Bldg. G

Lake Oswego, OR 97035
Tel: 800-547-6426, 503-684-1140
Fax: 503-639-2481
http://www.blackwell.com

Bookazine Corp., Inc.
75 Hook Rd.
Bayonne, NJ 07002
Tel: 800-221-8112; 201-339-7777
Fax: 201-339-7778
http://www.bookazine.com

Book House, Inc.
208 West Chicago St.
Jonesville, MI 49250
Tel: 800-248-1146; 517-849-2117
Fax: 517-849-9716
bhinfo@thebookhouse.com
http://www.thebookhouse.com

Bookpeople
7900 Edgewater Dr.
Oakland, CA 94621
Tel: 510-632-4700
Fax: 510-632-1281
bpeople@bponline.com
http://www.bponline.com

Brodart Company
500 Arch St.
Williamsport, PA 17701
Tel: 800-233-8467; 570-326-2461
Fax: 800-999-6799
http://www.brodart.com

Coutts Library Service
PO Box 1000
Niagara Falls, NY 14302-1000
Tel: 800-772-4304; 716-282-8627
Fax: 716-282-3831
http://www.coutts-ls.com

DeVorss and Company
PO Box 550
Marina del Rey, CA 90294
Tel: 310-822-8940
Fax: 310-821-6290
gpeattie@devorss.com
http://www.devorss.com

The distributors
702 South Michigan
South Bend, IN 46601
Tel: 800-348-5200, 219-232-8500
Fax: 312-577-0440

info@thedistributors.com
http://www.thedistributors.com

Eastern Book Company
131 Middle St.
Portland, ME 04101
Tel: 800-937-0331; 207-774-0331
Fax: 207-774-4678
info@ebc.com
http://www.ebc.com

Emery-Pratt Co.
1966 West Main St.
Owosso, MI 48867
Tel: 517-723-5291
Fax: 517-723-4677
office@emery-pratt.com
http://www.emery-pratt.com

Ingram Book Company
One Ingram Blvd.
LaVergne, TN 37086-1986
Tel: 800-937-8100; 615-793-5000
http://www.ingrambook.com

International Service Company
333 Fourth Ave.
Indialantic, FL 32903
Tel: 321-724-1443
Fax: 321-724-1443

Koen Book Distributors, Inc.
10 Twosome Dr., Box 600
Moorestown, NJ 08057
Tel: 800-257-8481
Fax: 800-225-3840
kbd@koen.com
http://www.koenbooks.com

Midwest Library Service
11443 St. Charles Rock Rd.
Bridgeton, MO 63044
Tel: 314-739-3100
Fax: 314-739-1326
all@midwestls.com
http://www.midwestls.com

National Association of College
  Stores (NACSCORP)
528 East Lorain St.
Oberlin, OH 44074
Tel: 800-321-3883; 440-775-7777
Fax: 440-775-4769, 800-344-5059
http://www.nacscorp.com

New England Mobile Book Fair
82-84 Needham St.
Newton Highlands, MA 02461
Tel: 617-527-5817
Fax: 617-527-0113

New Leaf Distributing
401 Thornton Rd.
Lithia Springs, GA 30122-1557
Tel: 770-948-7845
Fax: 770-944-2313
http://www.newleaf.dist.com

The News Group
3900-A Industrial Drive E.
Fife, WA 98424
Tel: 253-922-8011
Fax: 253-896-5027

Nutri-Books/Royal Publications
PO Box 5793
Denver, CO 80217
Tel: 303-778-8383
Fax: 303-744-9383

Sunbelt Publications
1250 Fayette St.
El Cajon, CA 92020
Tel: 800-626-6579, 619-258-4911
Fax: 619-258-4916
sunbeltpub@prodigy.net
http://www.sunbeltpub.com

YBP Library Services
(Formally Yankee Book Peddler)
999 Maple St.
Contoocook, NH 03229
Tel: 800-258-3774; 603-746-3102
Fax: 603-746-5628
service@ybp.com
http://www.ybp.com

Glossary

AAP—Association of American Publishers.

AAUP—Association of American University Presses.

ABA—American Booksellers Association.

ABI—Advanced Book Information. Publishers supply information on their book to Bowker for inclusion in *Forthcoming Books* and *Books in Print*. This information is also referenced in other databases.

accounts receivable—Money owed a company by credit customers.

acquisitions editor—The person in a publishing firm who acquires new manuscripts.

advance—An amount paid to the author on signing the contract. An advance is normally applied against (deducted from) royalties.

advance reading copy—A preliminary bound version of the book and cover for review and sales purposes, many times without final correction.

ALA—American Library Association.

American Booksellers Association—The trade association of nonchain retail bookstores in the U.S.

American Library Association—Largest library association in the U.S.

American National Standards (Z39 Standard) Committee—The committee responsible for standards for libraries, information science and publishing.

anthology—A collection of one or more authors published as a single work.

antiquarian bookseller—One who specializes in selling old or rare books.

artwork—Any illustrative matter other than straight text.

Association of American Publishers—The trade association of the largest book publishers in the U.S.

Association of American University Presses—The trade association of university presses.

author's alterations—Changes made by an author after type has been set.

back flap—The back inner flap of a dust jacket that often contains a biography of the author.

back list—Previously published books that are still in print and available from a publisher. Not frontlist books that are recently published.

back order—An order for books which are unavailable, that is held until the books become available.

bar code—The identification and price marking in bar format on books. The bar code for books is called Bookland EAN.

bastard title—Half title. Found on the page in front of the title page.

belt press—A large printing press that prints many pages in one pass.

Benday—Various density screens printed on an adhesive-backed plastic sheet that may be pasted to artwork. The screening provides tonal qualities to artwork.

best seller—A top-selling book. There are several best seller lists that draw sales figures from different markets.

bibliography—That part of the back matter listing books and materials consulted by the author in preparing the book, or which the author wishes to bring to the reader's attention.

binding—The processes following printing: folding, gathering, stitching, gluing, trimming and/or casing a book.

BISAC—Book Industry Systems Advisory Committee. A committee of the Book Industry Study Group (BISG).

bleed—Ink printed over the edge of the paper. The edge is trimmed off. Most magazines have covers with bleed.

blueline—A proof sheet made by exposing a negative to a photosensitive paper. A blueprint.

blurb—A promotional announcement, phrase or advertisement.

boards—The camera-ready, pasted-up copy ready for the printer.

body type—The majority of the type used in a book. Not a headline.

boldface—Type that is heavier than the text type with which it is used.

bond—A hard finish rag or sulphite paper used for stationery and forms.

book—A publication of 49 or more pages that is not a serial or periodical.

book fair—An event where publishers display their books.

booklet—A small book, usually with less than 48 pages.

book packager—A person or company who contracts with publishers to deliver contracted books.

book post—The Postal Service's book rate.

book rate—See Media Mail and Special Standard Rate.

bullets—Large black dots or other icons — used to set off items in a list.

C1S—Coated One Side. Usually refers to a book cover stock that is smooth on one side.

camera-ready copy—A completely prepared paste-up that is ready for the camera or xerographic reproduction. No further graphic arts work is required.

caption—The line of text accompanying an illustration.

cash basis—Accounting system. Not accrual.

case binding—Hardcover.

case-bound—Hardcover or edition binding.

cataloging-in-publication data—Bibliographic information supplied by the Library of Congress that is printed on the copyright page. The CIP data helps libraries to shelve the book properly.

chapbook—A small book or pamphlet of popular tales, ballads or poems.

character—A letter, number, punctuation mark or space in printed matter.

check digit—A number used to validate other numbers in the preceding numerical field. The last number in ISBN is a check digit.

checking copy—Finished book sent to prepublication (galley) reviewer.

clip art—Line drawings, screened pictures and illustrations designed to be cut out and pasted up.

clipping service— A firm that collects articles of interest to the client from periodicals.

coated stock—Paper manufactured with a variety of surfaces, that may be smooth, glossy or matte.

COD—Cash On Delivery. Where merchandise is paid for when delivered.

cold type—Strike-on type, such as that produced by a typewriter, IBM Composer, or photocomposition type. Not hot-metal type.

collating—Gathering of printed sheets into proper order for binding.

colophon—A listing of production details in the back matter.

color separation—A camera technique using different-color lenses to draw out the three primary colors and black from a color illustration or photograph. The resulting negatives (also called film separations or sep negs) are used to make the printing plates.

composition—Typeset material. Typeset text ready to be pasted up.

content editing—Evaluating a manuscript for organization and style.

continuity program—A standing order for succeeding volumes in a related program.

contrast—The degree of difference between the lightest and darkest parts of a picture.

co-op publishing—Where more than one person or company join to produce a book. Co-publishing.

co-op advertising—Where the publisher and the bookstore share the cost of local book advertising. The publisher pays the larger share.

copyediting—Technical editing of a manuscript for spelling, grammar and punctuation.

copyright—The right to retain or sell copies of artistic works that you have produced.

copyright notice—The words placed on the copyright page, such as "Copyright © 2001, Dan Poynter."

Crane—Prepublication galley.

credit memo—A statement showing money due a customer for returned merchandise.

crop marks—The lines used to define the desired limits of the area of a photograph or illustration to be reproduced. See trim marks.

dba— Doing business as. A sole proprietorship operated in another name.

defamation—Libel (written) or slander (spoken) that injures a person.

density—The relative darkness of an image area. In photography, the blackening or light-stopping ability of a photographic image, as numerically measured by a densiometer.

direct mail advertising—Advertising matter mailed directly to a potential customer.

disintermediation—Cutting out intermediaries, such as publishers, distributors, wholesalers and bookstores

display ad—A print advertisement using graphics.

display type—Type that is larger than the text, as in a chapter headline.

distributor—A company that acts as your marketing (usually to one market such as bookstores), warehousing and shipping department. Not a jobber or wholesaler. Distributors are normally exclusive to a particular market, have traveling sales representatives and sell individual titles to wholesalers, jobbers, retail outlets and libraries.

dummy—A preliminary mock-up of a book folded to the exact size of the finished job.

dummy folio—"Working" page numbers added for identification purposes but changed before the book is printed.

dump—A display for books, usually made of cardboard. Also called a counter stand or floor stand (standee).

dust jacket—The thin paper wrap on a hardcover book.

ebook—Downloadable electronic (not printed) book.

editing—Changing, correcting, altering typed text into required form.

edition—All printings of a book from the same unaltered boards. Once changes are made, the book becomes a second edition.

el-hi—The elementary school/high school market.

email—Electronic messages over a computer network

em dash—A dash (–) the width of a capital M.

en dash—A dash (-) the width of a capital N.

endpapers—The heavy sheets that fasten the pages of a hardcover book to the cover.

epilogue—The last part of the text that brings the reader up to date.

errata—A loose sheet listing errors found in the printed book.

exclusive—1. A news or feature story printed by one media source substantially ahead of its competitors. 2. Sole distribution rights to specific markets given to a distributor.

ezine—Electronic magazine available on the Internet

fair use—The allowable and legal use of a limited amount of copyrighted material without getting permission.

first edition—The entire original printing from the same (unchanged) plates.

first serial rights—The exclusive right to serialize a book in a periodical.

flat—A printing term describing the assembling of negatives on a heavy paper sheet for platemaking. See stripping.

flop—To flip over a photographic negative so image will be reversed.

flush—To be even with, such as in "flush right," or "flush left."

flyer—A printed announcement. A flyer becomes a brochure when folded.

FOB—Free On Board. "FOB origin" means the addressee pays the shipping. "FOB destination" means the shipper pays the shipping costs. "FOB Santa Barbara" means the goods are delivered free as far as Santa Barbara; the addressee pays for transportation, if any, from there.

f&g's—Folded and gathered pages. The unbound signatures of a book sometimes sent to reviewers.

folio—The number on the page of a book.

font—The complete set of type in a single typeface, including characters, numbers and punctuation marks.

foreign rights—Subsidiary rights allowing the book to be published in other countries.

foreword—Introductory remarks about the book and its author found in the front matter. Not "forward."

front matter—All the pages in a book before the main text.

frontispiece—An illustration facing the title page.

FTC—Federal Trade Commission.

fulfillment—The process of order processing, picking, packing and shipping.

galleys—1.Originally, a proof sheet run on the press to check the typesetting. 2. Later, the typeset pages prior to paste-up. 3. The prepublication copies of the book sent to some reviewers.

gang run (ganging)—Putting numerous unrelated jobs together for printing. Provides lower costs by economizing on setup charges.

ghostwriter—A professional writer who produces work for others. Work for hire.

glossary—A list of definitions found in the back matter.

glossy—A photograph with a shiny surface. Not matte (not dull).

gripper margin—The unprintable edge of the sheet of paper where the printing press or photocopier clamps the sheet to pull it through the printing machine. Often on top of the sheet and usually .25".

gutter—The space between columns of type, such as the inner margins in two facing pages of a book.

hairline—A very finely ruled line.

half title—Bastard title.

halftone—A screened photograph. A tone pattern composed of dots of uniform density but varying in size. A reproduction of a photograph whereby the various tones (highlights and shadows) are translated into numerous tiny dots for printing.

halftone screen—A screen placed in front of the negative material in the process camera to break up a continuous tone image into dots of black and white to produce a halftone. There are two types: ruled glass screens and contact screens.

hardcover—A book bound in boards. Case-bound.

headband—Reinforcing cloth at each end of the spine of a hardcover book.

headline—A large bold caption at the top of an article or advertisement.

hickey—A speck or blotch on a printed page.

highlights—The lightest (or whitest) portions of a photograph or art-work.

hot type—An older typesetting process using cast hot metal.

HTML—Hypertext Markup Language used for documents on the Web

hyperbole or hype—Exaggerated sales claims for a product or person.

IDs—Independent Distributor wholesalers (jobbers) who buy books and magazines in large quantities for resale to non-bookstore retail outlets such as newsstands, grocery stores, drug stores, hotels and airport shops.

illustration—Photographs and drawings. Artwork.

image area—The printable area of a page surrounded by margins.

imprint—The imprimata the publisher uses for a book. A publisher may have several imprints.

in print—Books that are currently available from publishers.

index—An A to Z listing in the back matter giving the location of specific material.

insertion order—A form used by advertising agencies to place advertising in various media.

International Standard Book Number—A unique number that identifies the binding, edition and publisher of a book. ISBNs are assigned by their publisher.

International Standard Serial Number—A number like an ISBN for serials/books published in a series. ISSNs are assigned by the Library of Congress.

inventory—Books on hand available for sale.

invoice—A bill.

ISBN—See International Standard Book Number.

ISSN—See International Standard Serial Number.

italics—Type with a right-hand slant. Used for quotations, titles and emphasis.

jobber—One who buys books in large quantities for resale to retailers and libraries. A rack-jobber supplies books and magazines to racks in retail outlets.

job printer—One who does not specialize in specific types of printing.

justification—Composing lines of running text so that the left and right margins are even. Automatically performed by computerized typesetting machines.

kerning—Removing space between letters.

layout—1. A sketch or preliminary drawing of what is to be printed. A mockup. 2. A paste-up or mechanical.

leading—The amount of vertical spacing, measured in points, between lines of typeset text. Rhymes with "heading."

leaflet—Printed paper sheet folded in the center to produce four pages.

letterpress—Printing from raised type rather than from photographic plates.

libel—Written defamation.

library edition—A book with a reinforced binding.

Library of Congress—The national library serving the U.S. Congress.

Library of Congress Control Number—A unique title control number assigned by the Library of Congress to a given work.

library rate—The special postal rate available for shipping books to or from libraries and educational institutions.

line art (line drawing)—A black-and-white illustration with no gray tones that does not require screening.

line shot—Any negative, print, copy or printing plate that is composed of solid image areas without halftone patterns.

list price—The suggested retail selling price of merchandise.

listserv—An electronic mailing list that sends messages to all the addresses on the list

LIT—A Microsoft reader file.

Literary Market Place **(LMP)**—The directory of the book publishing industry.

logo—A symbol or illustration used as an identifying mark by a business. Like a trademark.

lowercase—Small letters, not capitals.

mail order—Fulfilling orders via the mail.

make-ready—All the printing press setup in preparation for a print run.

manuscript—The book (typed or handwritten) before it is typeset, pasted up and printed.

margin—The white space around the copy on a page.

marketing plan—A publisher's total promotional plan for a book, including reviews, subsidiary rights, advertising and other customer contact.

mass customization—Using digital printing to place different names, text or images in each book.

mass-market paperback—The smaller, 4" x 7", cheaper editions usually sold next to magazines.

matte—A nonshiny, dull surface.

mechanical—See paste-up.

media—Print, broadcast, recording and other methods for delivering your message to the market.

media flyer—A brochure designed to be sent to talk shows.

Media Mail—The special postal rate available for shipping books.

microfiche cards—A flat-surface film in card size. Many wholesalers periodically send their inventory listings on microfiche to bookstores.

monograph—A short report on a single subject.

multipurpose—Spinning off additional editions of the manuscript—hardcover, softcover, audio, eBook, etc.

negative—The image obtained from the original in the conventional photographic process. The tones are the reverse of those in the original subject. Positive prints are made from negatives.

news release—An announcement sent to a periodical.

nonphoto blue—A light blue pencil or ink that will not be picked up by a plate-making camera. Light blue pens and pencils are used to mark pasted-up sheets. Also called nonrepro blue.

nth name—Incrementally selected names from a mailing list, such as every 10th name. Used in testing lists.

OCR—Optical Character Recognition. A device or computer software that can recognize (read) typewritten characters and convert them to electronic impulses for translation to output media language. An OCR reader can read a printed page into a computer for editing.

OEB—A file format for eBooks, "Open E Book."

offset lithography—Where the image is transferred from the printing plate to a rubber blanket and then to, or "offset" on, the paper. Practically all lithography is done by the offset method.

opaque—Not admitting light. Painting out parts of negatives so they will not reproduce.

opinion molders—People who lead thought, such as authors, editors, celebrities and other high-profile people.

out of print—A book is no longer available.

overrun—The books over the ordered amount. Because there are so many parts to a book, printers are allowed overruns and under-runs of up to 10%.

packing slip—A document sent with a shipment of books itemizing the contents of the shipment.

page proof—A layout of the pages as they will appear in the book.

pagination—The numbering or order of pages in a book.

paperback—A softcover book.

paste-up—An array of reproduction-quality copy arranged in proper position on a paper prepared as line copy ready for the camera. Same as a mechanical.

PDF—Portable Document Format produced by Adobe Acrobat. PDF is the file extension of the document.

peer review—Manuscript editing by an expert in the subject field.

pen name—A pseudonym.

perfect binding—The standard glued-on cover seen on most softcover books. It has a squared-off spine on which the title and name of the author may be printed.

periodical—A periodically issued publication such as a magazine.

photocomposition—Setting type photographically by exposing a photo-sensitive paper or film to images of typed characters, in such a sequence as to create the desired text or copy.

photodirect—Exposing an image directly to a light-sensitive offset plate material.

photomechanical transfer, PMT, diffusion transfer—A process in which the paste-up is exposed to a sheet of sensitized paper, the paper is processed in contact with a receiver sheet, and the sheets are peeled apart to produce a usable image on the receiver.

photostat or stat—A photographic reproduction–that can be negative or positive—made from film, artwork, other stats, etc., and used as line art for many art applications.

PI—Per inquiry advertising, where the media provide the space or time free and get a piece of each sale.

pica—A printing industry unit of measure equal to approximately 1/6 of an inch. There are 12 points to the pica. Usually used to measure width.

plagiarism—Copying the work of another and passing it off as one's own.

plate, printing—Usually the master device bearing the image to be printed. May be paper, plastic or metal.

plugging—A press condition whereby photographs appear muddy or characters fill in. Caused by poor plate burning, over-application of ink or incorrect ink/water balance.

PMS color—The Pantone Matching System for specifying specific shades of color.

POD—See Print On Demand.

point—A vertical measurement used in typesetting. One point equals 1/72 of an inch.

point of purchase display (POP)—A dump or rack of books.

positive—A photographic image in which the tones correspond to the original subject. A positive on paper is usually called a "print."

ppi—Pages per inch. Used to measure the thickness of paper.

PQN—See Print Quality Needed

preface—Introductory remarks by the author in the front matter. The preface gives the reason for the book and defines its aims and scope.

pre-galley—An early comb-bound version of the book and cover assembled during typesetting, used to solicit additional testimonials and distributor/wholesaler interest.

premium—A book given away as part of a promotion.

press kit—A collection of publicity materials used to promote a book, usually presented in a cardboard folder with pockets.

press release—See news release.

print on demand—Producing books one at a time, as needed.

Print Quality Needed—digital (toner) printing. Not one-at-a-time like POD.

printer's error—Mistakes made by the printer in preparing for the press. Not author's alterations.

proforma invoice—A full invoice that must be paid before the product is shipped.

proof—A direct impression of type or plate showing what the printed page will look like.

pseudonym—An assumed name used to conceal an author's identity. A pen name.

public domain—Material not protected by copyright.
publication date—The date on which a book's promotion is slated to peak and books are available for purchase. A launch date usually set three to four months after the book is printed.
publicist—One who prepares promotional materials and/or schedules media appearances.
Publishers Marketing Association (PMA)—A trade association that sponsors co-op promotions to help members sell books.
purchase order—A request for the purchase of merchandise, describing the merchandise, shipping instructions and other conditions of sale. A PO generally represents a promise to pay. Acceptance by the supplier constitutes a contract to supply the merchandise under specified terms.

quality paperback—A softcover or trade paper book.
quick printing—Producing a printing plate or master directly from the original boards (paste-ups) to reproduce multiple copies.
quote—1. An endorsement for a book. 2. A price quotation for printing.

ragged right—An uneven right-hand margin. Not justified.
reduction—A photographic process creating a small image.
register—The correct positioning of print on a page.
remaindering—The selling off of the remaining stock of books after sales fall off.
remnant space—Random advertising space in a periodical, that has not been sold and is available at a reduced rate. Occurs usually in regional editions of national magazines.
reprint—1. To go back to press on the same book. 2. Printing the book in another version, such as paperback version of hardcover book.
returns—Unsold books that are returned to a publisher for credit.
reverse—To print an image white on black, rather than black on white.
review—An evaluation of a book, sometimes critical.
review copy—A complimentary copy of a book sent to reviewers and potential quality purchasers.
revised edition—The printing of a book after substantial changes to the contents. The ISBN should be different.
rights—An agreement to allow someone else to use the book, usually in another form. Examples are foreign rights, first serial rights and film rights.
royalties—Money paid to authors by publishers for the right to publish their work.
RQF—Request for quotation
runaround—Where text is typeset around an illustration.
run-on printing—Continuing to print past the number ordered or quoted.
running heads—The book title or chapter title found at the top of the page in many books. See the top of this page.

saddle stitch—See stitch.
sales rep—An individual who presents books to stores and takes orders. A book traveler.
SASE—Self-addressed stamped envelope.
scaling—Using a proportion wheel to size an illustration for printing. Scaling determines how much to enlarge or reduce a photograph.
scoring—Creasing or pressing a line into paper so that it will fold more readily and more accurately.
screen—See halftone screen.
serial—A publication issued in successive parts, usually at regular intervals.
serif—The "tails" on a character that make it easier to read. The text in this book is set in a serif type.
sheet—Two printed pages, one on each side of a leaf of paper. If the sheet is folded to create four printed pages, it is called a leaflet.
sheet-fed press—A printing press that prints on sheets of paper, not rolls.
short discount—Less than 40%. Textbooks are often sold on a short discount.
signature—A part of a book obtained by folding a large single sheet of paper into sections. A book signature may contain increments of 32 or 48 pages.
Smyth sewn—Where signatures are sewn together with thread prior to installing the cover on a book. Common with hardbound books.
spam—An unsolicited email message
Special Standard Rate—Successor to book rate—now called Media Mail.
spine—The part of the book that connects the front to the back.
spine out—Displaying books on a shelf so that the spine shows. Not "face out."
spiral binding—Continuous wire binding.
Standard Address Number (SAN)—A number assigned to all organizations involved in buying, selling and lending books. The numbers are assigned by the ISBN agency at Bowker.
statement—A periodic (usually monthly) listing of invoices, credit memos and payments. Bookstores expect a monthly statement of account.
stet—A proofreading term to disregard editing notes and leave as is. From the Latin "to stand."
stitch—A staple. The staples seen in magazines and brochures are "saddle stitches."
STOP orders—A cash with order (Single Title Order Plan) used by bookstores.
strike-on type—Cold type created with a typewriter, composer or computer character printer where the typeface makes an impression on paper through a carbon ribbon.
stripping—The assembling of photographic negatives or positives and attaching them to the flat (a large sheet of heavy paper) for plate making.
subsidiary rights—Additional rights to publish the book in other forms. Examples are book club rights, foreign rights and serial rights.

subsidy press—A publisher who charges the author to publish a book. Subsidy presses have a bad reputation for editing, production and promotion. A "vanity press."

tear sheets—Ads, stories, etc., torn from the magazine they appeared in.

terms—Time, in days, allowed a customer for payment of an invoice. For example: Net 30 days.

testimonial—Book endorsement or blurb.

text—The main body of the page. Not the headlines.

tipping-in—The pasting into a book of extra sheets such as foldout maps.

title—1. A book or stock of the same book. 2. The name of the book.

trade paperback—A quality paperback or softcover book.

trade publisher—One who publishes books primarily for the book trade: bookstores and libraries.

transfer type—Sheets of characters, numerals, borders or symbols that may be burnished onto paper and added to the paste-up.

traveler, book—A sales rep.

trim marks—Lines made on the edges of a camera-ready board to indicate where the page will be cut (trimmed) after it is printed.

trim size—The size of the page once trimmed to its final dimension.

uncorrected page proofs—A galley. A crane.

underrun—When a printer manufactures fewer copies than were ordered. See overrun.

unit cost—The cost to print each book.

vanity press—A subsidy press

vendor—The supplier of goods or services.

web press—A fast printing press, using paper on rolls as opposed to sheets.

wholesaler—A company that buys books in quantities for resale to stores and libraries. Wholesalers handle all or most books, do not usually have sales reps and are not exclusive to special markets. Not a distributor.

window—A sheet of red, orange or black paper or acetate on a paste-up, to indicate where a photograph will be positioned. These colors photograph as black, creating a clear "window" in the black negative.

work for hire—Writing in which the writer does not retain ownership. See "ghostwriter."

working title—A preliminary title used during manuscript preparation before the book is named.

XML—Extensible Markup Language lets Web developers create customized tags for presenting electronic information

Index

Colophon

This book was completely produced using the New Model production system described within.

Research and gathering

Web: MS Explorer 5.5

Encyclopedia Britannica at http://ParaPublishing.com

Quotations: AApex BookMaster Software 3.05

Art: http://www.ArtToday.com

Photos: Olympus D-400 digital camera.

Scanning: HP-ScanJet 4100-C.

Writing and manuscript building

Manuscript preparation: MS-Word 2000

Typesetting: CoralVentura Publisher:

    Body text: NewBskvll BT, 10.5 pt.

    Headers: Myriad Roman, 12 pt.

    Chapter titles: Myriad Roman, 25 pt.

    Quotations: Newbskvll Italic, 10.5 pt.

    Stories: Arial, 10.5 pt.

Prepress

Copyediting and fact checking: Carolyn Porter & Nancy Gadney of One-On-One Book Production & Marketing. onebookpro@aol.com

Book design and typography: Carolyn Porter of One-On-One Book Production using Corel Ventura Publisher. onebookpro@aol.com

Cover design by Robert Howard of RH Graphic Design. rhoward@frii.com

Conversion

MS-Word to Ventura Publisher to PDF: Adobe Acrobat 5.0

Printing

Printing by McNaughton & Gunn, Ann Arbor, Michigan FGaynor707@aol.com

From PDF file on disk.

Paper: 50# white offset book

Cover: 10 pt C1S, four color, layflat film lamination, matte.

Binding: Perfect bound (adhesive, softcover)

Trucking

California Western Freight. owwnedson@aol.com

Book trade distribution

Publishers Group West. lance@pgw.com

Have you ever heard anyone say "Simon & Schuster, I love their books, I buy everything they publish"? Of course not. People want to know what this book is about. Is this something I need to know? Who is the author? Is she a credible person? No one ever asks, "who is the publisher"?

ParaPublishing.com
Where authors and publishers go for answers

Quick Order Form

📠 **Fax orders:** 805-968-1379. Send this form.

☎ **Telephone orders:** Call 800-PARAPUB (727-2782) toll free. Have your credit card ready.

💻 **email orders:** orders@ParaPublishing.com

🖥 **Postal Orders:** Para Publishing, Dan Poynter, PO Box 8206-380, Santa Barbara, CA 93118-8206, USA .Telephone: 805-968-7277

Please send the following books, disks or reports. I understand that I may return any of them for a full refund—for any reason, no questions asked.

_____

_____

_____

Please send more FREE information on:
☐ Other Books   ☐ Speaking/Seminars   ☐ Mailing Lists   ☐ Consulting

Name:_____

Address:_____

City:_____State:___Zip:_____

Telephone: _____

email address: _____

Sales tax: Please add 7.75% for products shipped to California addresses.

Shipping by air
U.S.: $4.00 for first book or disk and $2.00 for each additional product.
International: $9.00 for first book or disk; $5.00 for each additional product (estimate).

Payment: ☐ Cheque   ☐ Credit card:
☐ Visa   ☐ MasterCard   ☐ Optima   ☐ AMEX   ☐ Discover

Card number: _____

Name on card: _____Exp. date:_____